REBUTTAL

REBUTTAL

The CIA Responds
to the
Senate Intelligence Committee's
Study of Its Detention
and Interrogation Program

Includes new essays by former CIA officials,
the formal CIA response, and the minority
views of the Senate Select Committee on
Intelligence Study of the Central Intelligence Agency's
Detention and Interrogation Program

Edited by Bill Harlow

Naval Institute Press
Annapolis, Maryland

Proceeds from this work are being donated to the CIA Officers Memorial Foundation.

Naval Institute Press
291 Wood Road
Annapolis, MD 21402

ISBN: 978-1-59114-587-5 (paperback)
ISBN: 978-1-59114-588-2 (eBook)

Library of Congress Cataloging-in-Publication Data is available.

♾ Print editions meet the requirements of ANSI/NISO z39.48-1992
(Permanence of Paper).
Printed in the United States of America.

23 22 21 20 19 18 17 16 15   9 8 7 6 5 4 3 2 1
First printing

CONTENTS

INTRODUCTION

CIA Interrogation of al Qa'ida Terrorists—
The Rest of the Story

George J. Tenet

There is a biblical quotation engraved on the marble walls of the lobby of the Central Intelligence Agency's headquarters. It says: "And ye shall know the truth and the truth shall set you free."

Those who work within the walls of the CIA know better than most people, however, the difficulty of actually learning the truth. It is not a matter of simply amassing mountains of data. Finding it does not rely on stitching together allegations to create a mosaic of what you want to see. And you cannot scrutinize the past with eyeglasses ground with tomorrow's prescription.

Unfortunately, the Senate Intelligence Committee's majority report regarding CIA's Rendition, Detention and Interrogation (RDI) program failed to seek the truth or honestly portray events in the months and years following 9/11 in a manner that bears any resemblance to what my colleagues and I at CIA experienced. Their report was far from the truth and certainly set no one free.

Critical, yet totally absent from the Senate majority's deliberations, are the testimony and recollections of officials at CIA, the White House, the National Security Council, the Department of Justice, and even Members of Congress themselves. They certainly would have provided a totally different perspective. Yet the Senate majority conducted no hearings and interviewed no one with direct knowledge, preferring to issue a report that validated what its members wanted to find.

The history of the post-9/11 period and actions taken by the United States deserved much better. It deserved the kind of tough and critical nonpartisan analysis done by the 9/11 Commission, which made serious recommendations after interviewing all the principals and giving them opportunities to make statements for the record.

What would the majority have learned if they had taken the time to speak with those in positions of responsibility during the months and years after 9/11? Context. They would have learned that on the basis of credible intelligence the country's top officials had a genuine, palpable fear of second-wave attacks on the United States, including the possible use of weapons of mass destruction. It was in many ways a living hell—a race against time in which we often wondered whether today was the day the country would be attacked again.

Nightly meetings in the CIA Director's conference room presented threat reporting of a quantity and quality that led us to believe that the world was in great danger.

To make matters worse, our homeland was unprotected. Borders and visa policies were porous, key transportation and infrastructure nodes vulnerable. There was little or no information on what was happening inside the United States, who might be crossing our border, or whether sleeper cells were poised to conduct another devastating set of attacks—that we simply could not allow to occur. We were at the very low end of our knowledge about al Qa'ida

Decisive action against al Qa'ida's Afghan sanctuary would allow us to learn more about attack plans. Our intelligence partners around the world—some of whom, prior to 9/11, had been dismissive of our warnings about al Qa'ida—took decisive actions to break up cells and to collect data. These actions were critical to getting us to an inflection point, years later, when we could breathe again and, with the benefit of deep knowledge, protect the country against further attack. But in those early days we did not have the luxury of time. This period of sustained vulnerability and threat reporting did not go on for days or weeks, it went on for years.

But that was not all. Just prior to 9/11, as I have noted in my memoir, we learned that Umma Tameer-e-Nau (UTN), a Pakistani nongovernmental organization led by former Palestinian nuclear scientists, hoped to lend the expertise of the Pakistani scientific establishment to help build chemical, biological, and nuclear programs for al Qa'ida. We learned after 9/11 that, just prior to the attacks, officials of UTN had met with Usama Bin Ladin and Ayman al-Zawahiri.

There, around a campfire, they assessed how al Qa'ida should go about building a nuclear device. After President George W. Bush sent me to Pakistan to secure President Pervez Musharraf's cooperation to learn more about UTN's activities with al Qa'ida, we learned a great deal more about the UTN leadership's meeting with Bin Ladin and al-Zawahiri in Afghanistan just a month before 9/11. Upon debriefing in Pakistan, a UTN leader told Pakistani authorities that they had discussed the practicalities of building a nuclear weapon. "The most difficult part of the process," he told Bin Ladin, "is obtaining the necessary fissile material." Bin Ladin asked, "What if we already have the material?"

Around the time of this trip to Pakistan we briefed the President of reporting that indicated a nuclear weapon had been smuggled into the United States destined for New York City.

Our fears of imminent attack did not fade as we slid into 2002 and 2003. In 2003, Ayman al-Zawahiri called off an attack on the New York City subways in favor of "something better." For the rest of my time as Director I often wondered, as I have over the years that followed, whether "something better" would in fact have been the detonation of a weapon of mass destruction on American soil.

This represents a small glimpse into our context during those years. Yet, you will find none of it in the Senate majority report. This context was our reality when we first captured top al Qa'ida operatives and had to decide how best to learn what they might know of plans to attack our homeland.

And yet this terribly flawed report issued by the Senate majority staff of the Senate Intelligence Committee failed to provide any context of either the times or their own acquiescence in a program of detention and interrogation. "Back in the day" they had clearly understood the danger. They exhorted us to avoid being risk averse. They asked us whether we had enough authorities to get the job done.

An honest report, one worthy of history, teaching, and reflection, would have sought out senior intelligence and policy officials directly to capture their frames of mind, the actions they took, and the trade-offs they made. This did not happen.

An honest report would have detailed the yearly deliberations, done at the insistence of the CIA to ensure that the program was being implemented in a manner consistent with the U.S. laws, the Constitution, and international treaty obligations.

An honest report would have asked why I suspended every aspect of the program in the spring of 2004. I did so during a period of heightened threat. I suspended the program because the law was more important than interrogations. It was never about the means justifying the ends. It was about ensuring that we were obeying the law, protecting our officers, and protecting our nation. Yet it remained suspended for a period of months, until after my retirement, when the Attorney General provided the CIA with the necessary legal assurances.

An honest report would have learned that CIA officials, despite the legal approvals of the Department of Justice, on numerous occasions seriously debated the moral and ethical dilemmas posed by the program and how it might be viewed long after the attacks of 9/11 faded from memory. In the end we concluded that we had an equally important moral obligation to protect a just society in order to save thousands of Americans or our allies from another mass-casualty attack.

An honest report would have evaluated what the congressional leadership had been told about the program and it had posed no objection and in fact lent its approval. There was never a single letter or phone call to the President or the Director of Central Intelligence to express opposition. Monies were authorized without conditions. Nevertheless, the Senate majority, years later, portrayed CIA officers as having misled them. It would have been easy enough to hold a hearing with CIA briefers and match their accounts with the contemporaneous notes of briefings that the congressional committees must have kept regarding those briefings. But there were no hearings. None.

An honest effort would have cited a study conducted by the CIA Center for the Study of Intelligence on the CIA's interactions with the congressional oversight committees regarding the rendition, detention, and interrogation program. That study, based on interviews and documents of individuals who briefed the Congress, noted that CIA officials repeatedly briefed the details of the enhanced interrogation program to the leadership over a period of years. But evaluating its contents would have required a self-examination that, to say the least, would have been inconvenient. The study and many other critical documents ignored by the Senate majority staff can be found at the website *CIA Saved Lives,* www.ciasavedlives.com.

Rather than seek to interview officials from the White House, National Security Council (NSC), CIA, Department of Justice, or even reflect on their own actions at the time, the Senate committee's majority staff issued a report that has left the American people with an outrageously false impression that a rogue organization lied to the President, the Attorney General, and the NSC and that the United States derived no value from its program of detention and interrogation. Those assertions are belied by the record and refuted by documents presented in this volume.

There were indeed things that went wrong in the early days of this program, failures of leadership and management that left a stain on our record. To be sure, during these early tumultuous days our own oversight did not meet our professional standards. Yet those errors were immediately corrected and were simultaneously referred to the Department of Justice, the CIA's own statutory inspector general, and to the congressional oversight committees themselves. We were fully transparent and deceived no one. You will read none of this in the Senate committee's majority's report.

I spent seven years as a professional staff member and four of them as staff director on the Senate Select Committee on Intelligence. Respect for the law and for the Congress were deeply embedded in me. In those years, the Committee was truly bipartisan. We never had a party-line vote. Serious inquiries, investigations, and confirmation hearings were conducted. The testimony of intelligence and policy officials was taken; transcripts were kept and often reviewed by witnesses to ensure that the facts would never be in dispute. The Committee was tough, fair, thorough, and widely viewed in the executive branch as the standard of professionalism in congressional oversight. But that is not how the Senate majority conducted itself in this instance.

The Senate majority and its staff violated these standards in fundamental ways and thereby threatened the very fabric of oversight. They undermined and politicized the oversight process in a way that is inimical to the Congress, the Intelligence Community, and the country.

Imagine intelligence officers today being asked to conduct difficult, sensitive activities and being told the same thing that our officers were told regarding the RDI program—that the President authorized the program; that the Attorney General deemed it legal, on numerous occasions; that the program would be overseen by the NSC; and that full transparency would be provided on all aspects to congressional oversight leaders. Their answer might well be, "No thanks, let someone else do it."

Why? CIA officers operated in the most dangerous time in fifty years at enormous risk, with policy, legal, and congressional approval, and then found themselves castigated as criminals without the ability to testify or face their accusers.

On a personal note, I would hope that no President, CIA Director, or NSC team ever is confronted with a 9/11 or its aftermath again. I hope nobody ever has to face the kind of choices we did in an effort to avert the further loss of life, in a threat environment that looked like it might well overwhelm us. We understood what harsh and difficult interrogations would look like in later years. Those moral and ethical choices in preventing the loss of American and allied lives were enormously difficult. They were not then taken lightly, nor should they ever be.

Yet, here is what my colleagues and I know to be true. The program we implemented produced enormous value that was directly responsible for saving hundreds, and more likely thousands, of American and allied lives. It did so at a time when everything we held dear was at risk, when our knowledge was limited and the threat palpable. The notion that no intelligence value came from this program is belied by our analysts, the Senate minority report, and the CIA rebuttal. An honest effort by the Senate majority staff could never have come to such a conclusion.

Fortunately, most Americans are smart enough to figure out that al Qa'ida's present inability to bring more devastation to our homeland is not a coincidence.

It is our hope that in publishing this volume, with essays from those of us who served, along with additional documents sharply at odds with what the Senate majority produced, the American people, as well as students and historians, will have an opportunity to dig deeper into a set of issues that deserves a much more thorough and thoughtful airing than the highly politicized Senate majority report provided.

In early 2015, a number of small publishing houses took the Senate majority report and republished it in book form, under the title *The Report*. No mention was made of the strong rebuttals from the Senate minority, the current CIA leadership, or former senior intelligence and policy officials. It should not be allowed to stand unchallenged.

We were especially pleased when the Naval Institute Press offered to help ensure a balanced discussion of this important issue by publishing "the rest of the story."

In addition to publishing the minority and CIA rebuttals, the Naval Institute Press has agreed to include in this volume a series of essays from a number of prominent former CIA officials who were well positioned to know, among other things, how the interrogation program came about, how it was administered, what was obtained from it, how Congress and the White House were consulted and kept informed. These are precisely the people the Senate should have interviewed—and did not. These former colleagues of mine will offer in these pages insights like those of:

- Former CIA Director and House Permanent Select Committee on Intelligence chairman Porter Goss on the failure of congressional oversight in this matter
- Former CIA Director Mike Hayden on the politicization of intelligence oversight
- Former CIA Deputy Director John McLaughlin writing about the efficacy of CIA's interrogation efforts
- Former CIA Deputy Director Michael Morell about the shortcomings of media coverage of the interrogation issue
- Former CIA Counterterrorism Deputy Director and former senior FBI official Phil Mudd on the enormous value that can be learned from detainee interrogation— even when they lie to you
- Former CIA Acting General Counsel John Rizzo on the legal underpinning of the program
- Former CIA Counterterrorism Center Director Jose Rodriguez on how and why the program was created and how the handling of the Senate Select Committee on Intelligence (SSCI) investigation sends a chilling signal to future generations of CIA officers.

Each of these individuals has unique insights into what really happened during a critical period of U.S. history; how CIA's efforts were judged legal, effective, and necessary; and how, as our website suggests, CIA saved lives.

I recommend that those who truly want to understand a critical period in American history read these documents, essays, and reports to gain perspective that the SSCI majority did not want to hear.

George J. Tenet was the second-longest-serving Director of Central Intelligence in U.S. history, leading the CIA and Intelligence Community from 1997 to 2004. He was Deputy Director of Central Intelligence from 1995 to 1997 and prior to that Special Assistant to the President and Senior Director for Intelligence Programs at the National Security Council and Staff Director of the Senate Select Committee on Intelligence. He is the author of the 2007 number-one *New York Times* bestseller *At the Center of the Storm*.

WHAT MUST NEVER HAPPEN AGAIN?

Porter Goss

Our country urgently needs a robust discussion about what rules of engagement it uses to confront a brutal enemy that has vowed to destroy us by any means possible. And our Intelligence Community deserves and needs a thoughtful decision on those rules.

Unfortunately, Chairman Dianne Feinstein and her Democratic allies on the Senate Select Committee on Intelligence not only missed an opportunity to energize meaningful debate through their "Rendition, Detention and Interrogation (RDI) Study" but actually impeded the way forward by releasing a product that I and others believe to be polarizing and corrupted. They drove the issue from the highway of discourse to the gutter of sniping.

Chairman Feinstein publicly admitted that she began with a predrawn conclusion—that the RDI program "must never happen again." To that end, SSCI Democratic staff selected supporting materials and connected disjointed dots, willfully omitting and avoiding any information that might contradict her preconceptions. Perhaps this is why they chose not to interview a single person with knowledge of, or involvement in, the RDI program.

The world we live in is an ever more dangerous place, and good intelligence is vital to our safety and well-being. The Unites States must continue to have preeminent collection and action resources—which would certainly include a highly proficient clandestine service and customized covert action capabilities. Renditions, detentions, and interrogations inevitably are going to be involved, however labeled. Successfully fighting an unconventional, asymmetric war being waged on us by brutal radicals will require capturing, holding, and questioning the enemy. If Chairman Feinstein has a better plan, she has not revealed it.

I had the opportunity and privilege to serve our country on both sides of the oversight "fence," first as longtime Member and then as Chairman of the House Permanent Select Committee on Intelligence (HPSCI) and later as Director of Central Intelligence (DCI) and Director of the CIA (D/CIA). Yes, there is—and must be—a natural tension between the overseers and the overseen. That tension should always arise from interpretations by professionals on both sides of what are at times intentionally ambiguous directives. When contaminated by the partisan political process, those professional disagreements devolve into distractions that keep the Intelligence Community from doing the real work that keeps our country and our allies safe.

The SSCI "study" is such a distraction. I believe I could have added substantial value to both substance and process as an eyewitness to, if not direct participant in, some of the matters involved. No one from the SSCI reached out to me, suggesting perhaps that the SSCI was more interested in its preconceived narrative than in a full factual exposition.

So, what are some useful facts we could have explored with the SSCI's expenditure of over forty million taxpayer dollars and countless hours of highly paid staff time?

First, the United States does not have clear rules of engagement for describing, let alone dealing with, radical terrorists and terrorism. In recent years we have seen that the work of enemy combatants, detainees, and criminals can be reduced to something as benign as a "man-caused disaster" or as common as "workplace violence." Given the semantic gymnastics energized by political correctness, is it any wonder that members of the Intelligence Community—those on the dangerous front lines in our global war on terror—are fodder for after-the-fact indictments designed to placate political bases? We know the radical Islamic terrorists are not restrained by the Marquis of Queensbury rules or any protocols of the Geneva Convention. Are they are placated by the fact that we conduct "overseas contingency operations" with "no boots on the ground"? Not a chance.

A second fact worth noting is the members of "select" oversight committees are not always selected for their understanding of the Intelligence Community or the vital need to stay ahead of the curve in global intelligence capability. In the official reports after 9/11 of "what went wrong," many recommendations were made to overhaul the Intelligence Community, and several recommendations were made to improve oversight-committee performance. The only recommendations that seem almost entirely ignored were those applying to Congress. What followed were years of failed intelligence authorization bills, continuing leaks, deeply divisive partisanship, and incredible allegations of mistrust between the legislative and executive branches of our government. Maybe the SSCI should have spent some of that time and money trying to figure out how it could make a more positive contribution rather than continuing its own dysfunction.

A third fact, inconvenient as it might be to Chairman Feinstein's narrative, is that there was in fact congressional oversight of the RDI program.

I know. I was briefed by CIA as chairman of HPSCI 2002 and 2003, and I briefed both the HPSCI and SSCI as DCI and D/CIA in 2004 and 2005. Had Chairman Feinstein bothered to ask me, I would have so informed her—under oath. Defenders of the SSCI Democrats might argue that the briefings were not in sufficient detail or that not every Committee Member was included. It is true that specific sources and methods were not generally spelled out in most CIA briefings on the Hill and that extra-sensitive intelligence was limited to the "Gang of Eight," the senior leadership. But in the case of the RDI program, the existence of renditions and detentions was certainly known to all Committee Members, and the specific enhanced interrogation techniques were briefed to and discussed with top Committee leadership. I recall no objections being made. As to the SSCI allegation that the briefings were somehow intentionally "misleading," no one would have been madder about that, had it been true, than I—who went directly from leading the organization that was being briefed to leading the one doing the briefing. I can say nothing that I learned when I left Congress to become CIA Director would substantiate the allegation.

Many in our country have a low opinion of Congress—very low, according to recent polling. Placing partisan agendas ahead of national security is disturbing for the Americans who desire and deserve our government to function effectively for our well-being and safety. This is especially true at times of real danger and of unanswered, pressing questions.

What "Must Never Happen Again" is another 9/11 or anything like it.

What "Must Never Happen Again" is betrayal of those who took the risks to keep us safe while following clear, lawful guidelines under programs properly vetted and approved by lawyers, the Department of Justice, policy makers, and politicians.

What "Must Never Happen Again" is that we fail to understand that weakness—real or perceived—is a magnet that attracts "evildoers."

What "Must Never Happen Again" is for the United States of America to relinquish its leadership as the greatest force for good in the world, as we have seen in the consequences of our abrogations from Syria to Iraq to Africa.

Porter J. Goss was a Member of Congress from 1989 until 2004, at which time he became the Director of Central Intelligence. He served as a member of the CIA's clandestine service from 1962 to 1972.

ANALYSIS

Flawed, Politicized . . . and Rejected

Gen. Michael V. Hayden, USAF, Ret.

The Feinstein report on the CIA's program of detentions and interrogations may be the most flawed analytical document that I have seen in forty years of government service.

The text contains fundamental inaccuracies, along with misrepresentations and the intentional omission of key data. The report's lineage is best described as a series of conclusions that generated a six-plus-year search for supporting data among millions of pages of CIA documents. As one observer has pointed out, with enough people, that much available data, and that much time, he could build what on the surface appears to be a convincing case that I killed Jesus.

Senator Feinstein has long had very firm beliefs about the CIA detention and interrogation program. She has never made any effort to hide those views. In 2008, for example, the Senator used her position on the Senate Judiciary Committee (in addition to her position on the Intelligence Committee) to chair a subcommittee hearing on what she definitively described as torture. The hearings included testimony on what were clear abuses at places like Abu Ghraib, as well as extensive commentary on what the Senator described as torture at Guantanamo and in CIA black sites.

It was taken as a given in the hearing that what had gone on at all these locations was torture and that the predicate for torture was set by the policies of the Bush administration, specifically, the approval of CIA enhanced interrogation techniques.

In another incident that same year, the Senator said publicly that the CIA had slammed prisoners' heads into walls. I quickly got on her calendar to explain the interrogation technique called "walling," pushing a detainee's shoulders into a false plywood wall, all the while protecting their necks with braces or at a minimum towels wrapped around them. I am sure that I also added that walling was no longer an interrogation technique used by the Agency. The Senator took the briefing but a few days later was again publicly claiming that the Agency had been slamming prisoners' heads into walls. In other words, the Senator had reached a conclusion by 2008 (well before the recent study) and showed no indication that contrary evidence would ever dissuade her from her position.

Years later, when the CIA spoke with her staff director as the report was being finalized, the Agency asked him why the report was being done. He answered, "To make sure this never happens again." David Ignatius, the *Washington Post* columnist who frequently writes about intelligence matters, asked Senator Feinstein the same question and received the same answer. In other words, the Senator and some of her Democratic colleagues on the Intelligence Committee had their answers before the research had even begun. The document was designed to buttress their arguments so strongly that alternative views would have little or no hearing, thus ensuring that this would "never happen again."

In intelligence, that is called "politicization" and it's about the worst charge that can be made against any analytic effort. It appears that the Democratic staff quickly picked up on the cues being sent by their leadership and set out to create a document to "prove" their case. Through selective reading, omission, and outright misunderstanding of the intelligence analytic process, the staff prepared a report that condemned the CIA in at least three areas.

First, they claimed that all this was a rogue operation and that the White House was intentionally kept in the dark about important aspects of it. That conclusion was reached without a single conversation with anyone from the Agency involved in the program (or from the Bush White House, for that matter). It gave no credit to President Bush's public commentary that he was briefed on and approved techniques like waterboarding, and it obscured the fact that the staff's research was made woefully incomplete by the Obama administration's refusal to share Bush White House documents on the program, in order to protect executive privilege.

The second major conclusion was that the techniques used were worse than briefed and had been used on more individuals than reported. To get to this conclusion, the staff had to conflate a variety of CIA activities. They also took care not to mention that most of the alleged abuse had already been identified and reported by the Agency to appropriate officials, including to the Department of Justice. The Agency freely admitted that there had been abuses early on, when untrained folks had been sent into the field in emergency circumstances. In fact, I briefed the Committee that the high-value detainee program with an approved suite of interrogation techniques had been developed in response to the Agency's early failures. No matter. The report conflated all these activities and then alleged that the Agency had been misleading Congress, the White House, and the general public in describing the mature program that had been developed.

Some of these accusations struck home for me personally. The Committee took great pains to construct a "he said/she said" comparison of my 2007 testimony, pointing out all the areas in which I was allegedly misleading it. A lot of my supposed inaccuracies remain issues in contention between the Agency and SSCI Democrats. For example, what information we got, when, and under what circumstances from Abu Zubaydah remain in dispute. Other inconsistencies comprise my description of the then-current, mature program, as opposed to the Committee's elaboration of mistakes made early on in the program. In one sense I was briefing the norm, and they were countering with the exceptions.

Not well noted in the report was that I was accompanied by the CIA general counsel, who had been with the program since its inception, and also, to make sure that I had specific operational details correct, one of Khalid Sheikh Mohamed's actual interrogators. I frequently turned to them for confirmation or additional details during the hearing.

There is also the distinct possibility that a Director briefing events that happened five years previously and well before he came on board may simply get a few things wrong. But there was no effort to mislead. In any case, the purpose of the hearing was not to give a history of the detention and interrogation program. Rather, we had the hope that we could engage the Committee in a dialogue about an acceptable way forward for the program. That dialogue never took place.

I was also singled out in a dispute over the actual number of detainees that the CIA had held. The number I briefed the Committee (and that the Agency had been briefing the White House) was a total of ninety-eight. That was the Agency's number for high-value detainees it held under the headquarters-controlled program. We always knew, and made no attempt to hide, that there had been other early battlefield captives who had also been in CIA custody. The dispute, if there ever was one, was simply which detainees should or should not be booked in the program we were describing the Hill.

I encountered this bookkeeping challenge a few weeks before I left the Agency in January 2009, in an incident that the report attempts to document as an instance of my directing the Agency to mislead everyone. When one young CIA officer raised the possibility that a higher number might be more accurate, I simply replied that the number we have been using was ninety-eight and that I was not prepared to change that based on one conversation. I then added that if there were a potential discrepancy, the young officer should carefully check the record, confirm his figures, and then make sure that the new Director was aware of it so that he could inform Congress and the White House.

Multiple participants in the meeting confirmed that, some through contemporaneous notes. That was never mentioned in the report, however. It was inconsistent with the preferred narrative, and the Committee staff never made an effort to confirm their observations by talking with actual participants. This conclusion was based on one e-mail the young officer had sent to himself after the meeting and which the Democratic staffers hungrily pounced on.

The final accusation was that the CIA got no information from enhanced interrogation techniques that was not otherwise available. To bolster this case the Committee staff cited twenty case studies and "proved" that nothing unique had been derived from any of them. Here the Agency's rebuttal is very powerful. Freely admitting occasional hyperbole when justifying the program, the CIA nonetheless shot back with carefully documented information as to how this information proved vital. The Agency even went so far as to show the important role that detainee-derived information played in tracking Usama Bin Ladin to Abbottabad. When you boil the Feinstein report's accusation in this regard down to its essence, it is a claim that the people who tracked Bin Ladin to Abbottabad simply didn't know or understand how they had done it.

The CIA detention and interrogation program was launched out of a sense of duty, not enthusiasm. It will forever remain controversial. The Republic needs a careful historical accounting of what happened, to guide it in the future. This report is not that accounting.

When I was a military attaché in Bulgaria during the Cold War, I once got into a heated discussion with a Bulgarian political officer. Frustrated by some of the things that he had been telling me, I simply asked him what "truth" meant to him. He quickly responded, "Truth is what serves the party." That's a pretty good description of what we have here . . . and why.

Michael Hayden is a retired Air Force general and former Director of the Central Intelligence Agency and the National Security Agency. He is currently a principal at the Chertoff Group and a Distinguished Visiting Professor at George Mason University. He is the author of the upcoming *Playing to the Edge: American Intelligence in the Age of Terror*, a memoir of his time on the national intelligence scene.

THE SENATE MAJORITY REPORT ON INTERROGATION

An Opportunity Lost

John McLaughlin

Of all the charges in the report authored by the Senate Intelligence Committee's then-majority Democrats, the one most pivotal to their argument is that the CIA's detention and interrogation program produced little useful intelligence. It's pivotal because so many of their other charges—that the CIA lied, misled, and embellished— rest on proving that the Agency had run an ineffective program that it portrayed as effective.

The problem the authors are up against is a simple one: everyone at the CIA who worked with the information knows the allegation is false. If you are one of those CIA officers, here's how the report hits you: it's trying to convince you that what you experienced, you did not really experience; that what information you used, you did not really use; that your memory of sitting in the CIA's legendary daily five o'clock meetings and using this information to capture terrorists and disrupt plots was just a dream—this didn't really happen. As one colleague said to me after the report was released, "What they are describing is a twisted parallel universe bearing no relationship to the world I lived in."

CIA officers realized that the program, if revealed, would be controversial and that fair-minded people could differ about the methods it employed. But frankly, the last thing anyone expected was serious questioning of the *effectiveness* of a program that resulted in the capture of more high-level terrorists than before or since. Agency officers wondered if serious people could really think, Was this some kind of dumb luck? Surely not, they thought.

The Agency did expect that someone would charge that it had not adequately considered the moral and ethical implications of a program that involved a degree of coercion—and that charge has been leveled. In fact, though, the Agency did consider that dimension. It was *not* an "ends justifies the means" calculus; it was the belief that no one could really claim to be following a moral path if they were complicit in the death of hundreds or thousands more Americans through failure to get information that these detainees had.

So why not just get this information by "rapport building," as recommended by many CIA critics? Agency officers tried, and sometimes it worked. But with the most hardened of these criminals it did not. Many today forget two things:

- First, that we were dealing with the toughest and most committed top leaders of al Qa'ida, who had been trained to resist interrogation—people like 9/11 architect Khalid Sheik Mohammed, who had coldly beheaded a *Wall Street Journal* reporter long before there was a CIA detention program and long before this tactic became an Islamic State trademark.
- Second, time was of the essence, given the post-9/11 threat context—something not discussed in the Senate Democrats' report.

That context is assessed elsewhere in these essays, but it worth stressing here a few relevant facts from that period, now forgotten or perhaps never known by people who did not wake up to them every day. We knew Bin Ladin had met with Pakistani nuclear scientists, to whom he hinted that he had acquired nuclear explosive material; we knew that al Qa'ida had been working on an anthrax biological weapons program in Afghanistan; we had credible reporting, later confirmed, that a "second wave" attack was planned on the United States; we were virtually blind as to whether there were other terrorist cells still inside the United States; and finally, we were being urged by Congress and the administration to do whatever had to be done to stop another attack—a mission that in the early post-9/11 years no one else was yet prepared to take on. It was the only time in a thirty-year career that I recall feeling like we were in the classic "ticking time bomb" scenario—every single day.

But all this said, reasonable people can still differ on the advisability of the CIA's program, because in the end it involved very personal decisions, complicated trade-offs that everyone has to calculate personally—and that those who were at the Agency at the time truly hope no one will ever face again.

However, when it comes to the issue of the program's effectiveness—whether it produced useful information that helped capture terrorists and disrupt plots—there are *facts* that must be taken into account, not brushed aside, left out, or distorted, as is so frequently the case in the majority report. In nearly all cases the facts say the program was essential and effective.

Problems of methodology and logic run through the majority report's contention that the program was ineffective, a point becoming apparent to scholars who are now comparing the majority report with the minority's and the CIA rebuttal (see below). For example, the majority's conclusions frequently rest on claims that information from CIA detainees was not needed if some version of it—or even a hint of it—could be found elsewhere or if a detainee outside the program or held by another country had provided something similar. This shows no awareness of how analysis works—of the role that corroboration, additional detail, and puzzle solving play in building confident analyses that can serve as the basis for action.

Let's look at a few cases.

Finding Bin Ladin. The al Qa'ida leader was located in a years-long process that involved painstaking integration of information from multiple sources—human and technical. But the pivotal breakthrough was the identification of the courier who carried messages to and from Bin Ladin. The majority report asserts that the Agency acquired the critical knowledge about the courier independent of its detainee program and before detainees in its interrogation program provided the information.

This is incorrect. It is true that the Agency had previously heard of the individual—Abu Ahmed al-Kuwaiti—but only as one of many Bin Ladin associates in Afghanistan. But detainees in the CIA interrogation program threw a spotlight on Abu Ahmed and pushed him to the top of the list of candidates, causing the Agency to focus its research tightly on him.

The most specific information about the courier came from an interrogated detainee, Hasan Gul, who strengthened the case by telling of a particular message the courier had delivered from Bin Ladin to his then operations chief, Abu Faraj al-Libi. Finally, interrogated senior operatives—such as al-Libi and 9/11 architect Khalid Sheikh Mohammed, who by then were compliant and functioning almost as "consultants"—lied when confronted with what we had learned about the courier, denying that they knew of him. That was a dramatic tip-off that they were trying to protect Bin Ladin, and in many ways it was the convincer.

None of this would have been possible without having these individuals in detention and being able to go to them repeatedly for clarification of various points and to see how they reacted to information. The authors who prepared the majority report have not done this kind of work and seem not to understand how accumulating detail and corroboration establish confidence sufficient to make momentous decisions like the Abbottabad operation.

Learning from Abu Zubaydah. Abu Zubaydah was the first major terrorist figure captured after 9/11, captured in an operation that took weeks of painstaking intelligence work.

His interrogation provided highly valuable information that led to important break-throughs, such as the apprehension of Jose Padilla, an al Qa'ida collaborator who had been planning attacks on apartment buildings. His information also led to the capture of Ramzi Bin al-Shibh, a facilitator of the 9/11 attacks who at the time of his capture had recruited four operatives in Saudi Arabia for an attack on London's Heathrow Airport.

The majority report stretches vague "suspicious traveler" reports to assert wrongly that the CIA had known Jose Padilla as a terrorist before questioning Abu Zubaydah. In fact, it was only after Abu Zubaydah provided information on a specific terrorist plot by individuals matching the description of Padilla and an accomplice that the full picture emerged that led to U.S. Government action.

As for the claim that Abu Zubaydah had not been part of the CIA interrogation program when he provided information to the FBI, the majority study leaves out that he could not have been part of a program that had not yet begun. But, he was during this time subjected to significant sleep deprivation; this was then regarded as a standard interrogation technique but was later designated as one of the "enhanced techniques" authorized by the Justice Department for the CIA program.

It was only after Abu Zubaydah was fully integrated into the CIA program that he provided the information that led to Ramzi bin Al-Shibh's capture during Karachi safe-house raids and the disruption of the Heathrow plot.

Capturing 9/11 Mastermind Khalid Sheikh Mohammed. Capturing Khalid Sheikh Mohammed (KSM) led to the disruption of the countless plots on which he was still working. But the Committee says interrogation of detainees did not play a role in getting KSM, because a CIA asset who was not a terrorist detainee helped us find him. This is astounding to those of us involved in capture operations. The operational details are still classified to protect sources, but the majority report simply leaves out that it was information provided by interrogated detainees that connected the key non-terrorist source to KSM.

This is another one of those incredible instances in which the authors of the report are essentially telling CIA officers, "You didn't capture KSM the way you think you did." It's borderline Orwellian.

Capturing Southeast Asian Terrorist Leader Riduan Issamudin ("Hambali"). The Committee says interrogation played no role in bringing down this architect of the Bali bombing. This is incorrect. After interrogation, KSM told us he transferred money to Hambali via an individual named Majid Khan to finance attacks in Asia. This triggered a string of captures across two continents, involving Khan and two accomplices, that led us to capture Hambali in Southeast Asia.

Disrupting a "Second Wave" Plot on the U.S. West Coast. The Committee says a source run by another country mentioned this plot. Here's another case where the majority report fails to understand the role of corroboration and source reliability. The report it cites is *all* we knew; it contained none of the details needed to stop the plot.

The information we needed came from detainees, starting with KSM, who told us after interrogation that Southeast Asian terrorist Hambali would replace him in this plot. This drove our effort to find Hambali. After that capture, KSM, not knowing Hambali had been captured, said Hambali's brother would take over should Hambali ever be gone. We located his brother and found he had recruited seventeen Southeast Asians and was apparently trying to arrange flight training for them to attack the U.S. West Coast.

Disrupting Plots to Bomb Karachi Hotels. The Committee says interrogation played no role in heading off attacks on the hotels where American and other Western visitors stayed. But they leave out the fact that detainee Abu Zubaydah provided information on how to locate al Qa'ida safe houses in Karachi, in one of which we found the "perfume" letter (KSM told us that "perfume" was a code word associated with the plot) that tipped us to the plots.

That is how those famous "dots" really got connected.

Knowledge that the Agency connected them skillfully, particularly in the run-up to the Bin Ladin operation, is presumably why former CIA Director Leon Panetta said, even though he does not support the interrogation program, "At bottom, we know we got important, even critical intelligence" from individuals in the interrogation program.

Panetta is not alone. Scholars are beginning to do what most in the news media have yet to do—compare carefully the majority report with the minority report and the CIA rebuttal—and they are coming to the same conclusion. Georgetown law professor David Cole, no supporter of the interrogation program and a frequent CIA critic, published on February 22, 2015, an assessment in the *New York Times* titled, "Did the Torture Report Give the CIA a Bum Rap?"

After comparing the data in the three reports, Professor Cole concludes that in each instance cited in the majority report "the CIA makes a credible case that the information it obtained using coercive tactics played a critical role." He goes further, to say that this "casts doubt on the Committee's other main finding—namely that the CIA repeatedly lied about the program's efficacy." (http://www.nytimes.com/2015/02/22/opinion/sunday/did-the-torture-report-give-the-cia-a-bum-rap.html?_r=0.)

Legal scholar Benjamin Wittes came to a similar conclusion in the authoritative *Lawfare* blog. (http://www.lawfareblog.com/2014/12/thoughts-on-the-ssci-report-part-iii-the-programs-effectiveness/.) Columbia University professor Robert Jervis has done the same in a *Foreign Affairs* review of the three reports. (https://www.foreignaffairs.com/reviews/review-essay/2015-04-20/torture-blame-game.) To be sure, none of them is prepared to endorse the interrogation program and all clearly have major reservations about it, but they are quick to spot the gaping holes in the majority's argument that the program produced no critical information.

This means that the Senate Intelligence Committee missed an opportunity to produce a balanced study comparable in impact and acceptance to, say, the *9/11 Commission*

Report or that of the Silberman-Robb Commission on weapons of mass destruction. Both of these wrestled with controversial issues, leveled serious but constructive criticism at intelligence agencies, and brought the CIA into a consensus on what needed to be done.

By contrast, the majority report is an unrelievedly prosecutorial brief, *lacking any recommendations* and refusing to wrestle with the tough trade-offs often involved in national security decisions. As such, it should provoke skepticism among even the most committed opponents of the CIA program.

A key reason for the report's one-dimensional quality is the Committee's failure to interview any of the key participants. Its claim that people were unavailable because they were the subjects of legal proceedings is just plain wrong. Three CIA Directors who managed the program and three deputies were not involved in legal proceedings, and the CIA officers who were subjects had completed their involvement in 2012, two years before the report was released.

This contrasts again with successful investigatory efforts such as that of the 9/11 Commission, which not only did extensive interviews but also sought comments on its draft chapters. At the end of the process, the CIA did not agree with everything the Commission said but it accepted the recommendations and acted on them.

Had the Senate majority staff done interviews with participants, it would have had to react to many inconvenient facts that are for the most part left out or "spun" in a way that CIA officers would have disputed:

- The CIA's refusal to proceed with its program without unqualified and repeated Justice Department and White House approval
- The Agency's halting of the program any time either DOJ or the White House blinked
- The Agency's self-policing of the program when infractions occurred—accountability proceedings for thirty individuals with sixteen sanctioned, along with approximately twenty referrals to the Justice Department, resulting in one person imprisoned and a contractor fired
- The approximately sixty instances in which the Senate-confirmed inspector general examined interrogation-related issues
- The years-long review of the program, at the Obama administration's request, by Justice Department special prosecutor John Durham (examining the interactions between CIA personnel and approximately a hundred detainees) and his finding of no prosecutable offenses
- Finally, the sixty-plus occasions between 2002 and 2008 when the CIA briefed the Intelligence Committee leadership (or the full Committee after 2006) on the interrogation program.

Had such a process occurred, the CIA and the Committee would not have agreed on all of this or on how to describe it. But the report would have been a more effective and more responsible one. It would have been an example of "good government," something seen only rarely these days. As Robert Jervis says in his *Foreign Affairs* review of the report, it was "an opportunity lost."

John McLaughlin capped a thirty-two-year career at CIA by serving as its Deputy Director from 2000 to 2004 and as Acting Director in the latter part of 2004. During his career he worked on nearly every part of the world, briefed four American Presidents, and frequently represented the Intelligence Community on diplomatic delegations abroad. He teaches at the Johns Hopkins School of Advanced International Studies, publishes frequent assessments of foreign affairs, and is Chairman of the CIA Officers Memorial Foundation, an organization dedicated to supporting the families of CIA officers who die in the line of duty.

FIRST AMENDMENT
WRONGS

Michael Morell

There were many things to dislike about the Senate Select Committee on Intelligence's release in December 2014 of a redacted version of a report on CIA's post-9/11 detention and interrogation programs. One of those was the national media's coverage of the issue, coverage that fell far short of the standards that Americans should demand of such a critical component of our democracy.

The media failed in three ways. First, led by national security print journalists, the media inaccurately characterized just whose report this was. The *Washington Post* headline read (my emphasis): "*Senate Report* on CIA Program Details Brutality, Dishonesty." The *Wall Street Journal* headline said, "*Senate Report* Calls CIA Interrogation Tactics Ineffective." The first sentence of the *New York Times* piece read, "*The Senate Intelligence Committee* on Tuesday issued a sweeping indictment of the Central Intelligence Agency's program to detain and interrogate terrorism suspects. . . ."

"Senate report?" Senate Intelligence Committee report? Just not true. The report was not a report of the entire Senate Select Committee on Intelligence; it was a report of the Democrats on the Committee, led by the then Chair, Dianne Feinstein. Democratic staff of the Committee prepared the report; not a single Republican staff member participated in the study. The Committee approved the report along largely partisan lines. Only a lone Republican, Olympia Snowe, voted in favor of the report.

The media had a responsibility to make clear that this was a report by only one side of the aisle. By failing to characterize the report as such, the media gave the report more credibility in the eyes of the public than it deserved. A more accurate headline would have been, "Democrats on Senate Intelligence Say . . ." Not a single major media outlet took this approach in its reporting.

Second, and relatedly, the media failed to *highlight* that two other reports were released that same day—one outlining the views of Republicans on the Committee and another outlining the views of CIA. While most news outlets mentioned the Republican and CIA responses, these references were brief and placed far down in the articles (the *New York Times* piece did not even notice the Republican response). No media outlet focused on the multiplicity of reports *as a story*. I kept looking for a media story titled, "Intelligence Committee Members at Odds on CIA Program," but I never found it. During the report's rollout, the media reported the views of one political party without reporting the views of the other.

Third, the media accepted the findings of the Democratic study as the truth. This was perhaps the media's most egregious failure, particularly given the dissenting opinions from the Republicans on the Committee and from CIA.

The acceptance of the report as the truth played out in multiple ways. Certainly the media had a responsibility to outline what the report said, but it went beyond that and used the report's findings as the basis for its account of what actually occurred in the course of the detention of interrogation program. Indeed, the tone of much of the media coverage was, "We now know what happened in the CIA program, and here it is." Many editorials written in the days following the release began with the premise that the report was an accurate and complete rendering of the program.

Moreover, not a single media analyst or commentator rigorously examined the report's assertions. Not a single analyst or commentator took an in-depth look at all three documents and tried to make some judgments as to how to think about the differing views between CIA and the Republicans, on the one hand, and the Democrats, on the other. As of this writing, in the spring of 2015, I am still waiting for such a piece to be written.

In regard to the accuracy of the report, following its release not a single print reporter reached out to me to ask what I thought of it. I found this odd, because reporters knew that I had overseen the CIA's response to the report when I was Acting Director and Deputy Director and because I had stated in interviews on *CBS News* (for whom I consult) after the release of the report that it was a seriously flawed document. In contrast, five reporters reached out to me to ask for my thoughts on Director John O. Brennan's announcement in early spring 2015 that he was reorganizing the Agency.

My only interaction with the media on the report post-release was that I sent to several media outlets a study, conducted by CIA historians at my request when I was Acting Director, of the detention and interrogation program. A redacted version of this historical study was released to the public in early December. I sent it to media outlets because I wanted them to know that this study, produced by trained historians, contradicted the Democratic report on many points. None of the news outlets with which I shared the historical study even mentioned it in their reporting.

If any reporter had asked me, "Michael, why do you say the report is flawed?," I would have said, "Not only is the report deeply flawed, it is the most deeply flawed study I saw during my thirty-three years in government." Then I would have pointed out that there are three types of flaws in the report—errors of fact, errors of context, and errors of logic.

I would have told reporters that the definition of an error of fact is obvious, as are the implications for the quality of any resulting judgments. Errors of context occur when the facts are correct but additional facts are missing that would provide a more accurate understanding of the issue at hand. Errors of logic arise when the facts are correct but those facts simply do not add up to the stated conclusion. Then I would have provided reporters with examples of each type of error from just the report's first several pages.

First, an error of fact. On page 6, a sentence reads, "The CIA restricted access to information about the program from members of the committee beyond the chairman and vice chairman until September 6, 2006. . . ." Wrong. The CIA did not restrict access to the Committee leadership; the White House did, as was its prerogative—a big difference. Also, it was not just the Chairman and Vice Chairman who were briefed; it was also members of their senior staff.

How about an error of context? On page 5, the report states, "The CIA did not brief the leadership of the Senate Select Committee on Intelligence on the CIA's enhanced interrogation techniques until September 2002, after the techniques had been approved and used." Absolutely true, and it sounds bad. It sounds like a great example of the report's conclusion that CIA worked to undermine the Committee's oversight of the program. But not quite—not if you know some additional facts, not if you have the context. Abu Zubaydah was the first detainee subjected to enhanced interrogation techniques (EITs). The first use of EITs on Abu Zubaydah occurred in August 2002—*while Congress was on recess.* The leadership of the House intelligence committee was briefed on September 4, *the very first day Congress returned from recess,* and the leadership of the Senate intelligence committee was briefed on 27 September (the CIA had offered to do the briefing much earlier). So, once you have the context—the additional facts—to make this an example of CIA keeping the Congress in the dark looks all of sudden like a stretch.

What about an error of logic? On page 2, we read the first main finding of the report: "The CIA's use of its enhanced interrogation techniques was not an effective means of acquiring intelligence or gaining cooperation from detainees." Let's take the report's first three pieces of "evidence" for this conclusion.

- Number One: "According to CIA records, seven of the 39 CIA detainees known to have been subjected to the CIA's enhanced interrogation techniques produced no intelligence while in CIA custody." Wait a minute. That is not an argument that EITs were not effective but that they *were,* as presumably thirty-two of thirty-nine detainees subjected to EITs did produce intelligence!
- Number Two: "CIA detainees who were subjected to the CIA's enhanced interrogation techniques were usually subjected to the techniques immediately after being rendered to CIA custody." This might be an argument that CIA moved

too quickly to use EITs—which is not correct by the way—but it is certainly not an argument that those techniques were not effective. No logical linkage there.

- Number Three: "Other detainees provided significant accurate intelligence prior to, or without having been subjected to these techniques." Yes, many detainees did not need to be subjected to the enhanced techniques, because for them traditional interrogation methods worked just fine. Yes, even those subjected to harsh techniques provided some information before enhanced techniques were employed but had been judged not to be providing everything they knew. But again, the fact as presented is simply not a basis on which to judge that the techniques were not effective.

I would have ended my discussion with journalists by saying that these examples are just the tip of the iceberg (the entire six-thousand-page report is riddled with such errors), and I would have told reporters that I pointed out examples just like these to Senator Feinstein and her staff in a meeting in June 2013. I would have summed up the discussion with journalists by saying, "You know, I managed the production of intelligence analysis for almost two decades and, if an analyst had ever handed a report as poor as the Democrats' study, I would have seriously questioned whether that analyst had the skills to succeed in the profession."

A functioning democracy requires a free press. I believe that deeply. But a functioning democracy also requires a press whose reporting is accurate, balanced, and objective. The media's coverage of the report on CIA detentions and interrogations were none of these. This was not the fourth estate's finest hour. And the American people's understanding of an important issue suffered as a result.

Michael Morell served as Deputy Director of the Central Intelligence Agency from May 2010 to August 2013. He served as Acting Director twice during this period. He is the author of *The Great War of Our Time: The CIA's Fight against Terrorism From al Qaida to ISIS*, in which he devotes an entire chapter to the issue of the Agency's detention and interrogation program. He is nonpartisan, having served six administrations—three Democratic and three Republican—during his thirty-three-year career at CIA.

THE CRAFT OF INTELLIGENCE AND THE VALUE OF DETAINEE INFORMATION

Lessons from the CIA's al Qa'ida Prisoners

J. Philip Mudd

In the spring of 2002, the tension in the CIA Director's conference room during Director Tenet's nightly counterterrorism meetings was rising. As the days and weeks passed, the intelligence that allowed us to locate al Qa'ida member Abu Zubaydah grew more and more precise. We had had no direct access to any senior al Qa'ida member at that time, and "AZ," as we sometimes called him, was looking like he might become the first al Qa'ida Bin Ladin operative we would have a chance to speak with face to face. That kind of firsthand access to a senior leader in the adversary's hierarchy is almost unheard of. Intelligence usually involves what one FBI executive once called "sources and wires": human informants and intercepted communications. What if we could add another dimension to this intelligence collage? What if we could actually talk to one of the terrorists at the center of al Qa'ida?

During those post-9/11 years, before and after the hunt for Abu Zubaydah, the demand for information that could enhance our understanding of al Qa'ida was insatiable, from all the traditional consumers of CIA intelligence, ranging from the President to officials in the Departments of State and Defense to the U.S. Congress. I was among those responsible for putting together the nightly compilation of intelligence about al Qa'ida for those high-level decision makers, particularly the President and his closest advisers. The daily distillation of key intelligence we gave him—then, as today, called the President's Daily Brief, or PDB—was heavily weighted toward terrorism after 9/11. There were intelligence articles about other global issues, from Russia to China to fast-breaking global hotspots in Africa and Asia, but everyone in a leadership position had a laser focus on al Qa'ida. In the midst of that appetite for intelligence about the terror group that had just murdered nearly three thousand Americans, though, we were often flying blind. When it came to al Qa'ida, what we didn't know often loomed larger than what we did.

Our picture of the al Qa'ida adversary was fuzzy. Some of the questions we faced were tactical. What are al Qa'ida members talking about in some seemingly disturbing intercepted communication? Where is Bin Ladin? Are there other terrorists in the United States who knew about or supported the 9/11 attacks, and did they associate with the 9/11 plotters? Beyond these day-to-day questions and the daily mix of reports detailing various threats to America, though, we had to work through bigger questions that we could not answer, questions that centered on the basic intelligence requirement: How well do we understand our enemy? How do al Qa'ida leaders think? How are they organized? Who are the key players in the group, and how do they operate? These strategic questions were part of the responsibility that any intelligence officer shares in wartime. We all asked the same question that intelligence professionals have faced since the beginning of history: How can I help those who are making decisions about this battle, including the President, better understand the adversary they face?

The Senate report's single-minded narrative of how much detainee information led to other al Qa'ida members is far too limited in its definition of how we should assess the value of those detainees, and far too narrow in its understanding of what defines intelligence. Intelligence isn't only secrets that lead to arrests, it's a far broader universe of knowledge that helps bring a shadowy adversary into focus. By that definition, what detainees gave us was invaluable.

This basic question of how to understand the detainees' intelligence value leads us back to Abu Zubaydah and the hundred-plus detainees who went through CIA "black sites" in the years after his capture. In my world, in helping to put together the highest-level intelligence the U.S. Government had to offer to the President during those years, the impact of these prisoners on answering such fundamental questions was profound. There was a pre-AZ world, in which we had had to assess this adversary from a distance, without ever being in the same room with a senior al Qa'ida member. Then there was the post-AZ world, where we could talk to the architects of the group face to face, over weeks, and months, and then years. Our assessments would never look the same after those first captures. We could finally talk to the enemy we had only heard about at second hand from informants or listened to on telephones from ten thousand miles away.

The reason for this fundamental shift in our understanding of al Qa'ida after Abu Zubaydah rests at the core of how intelligence works and how intelligence officers measure success. "Decision advantage" is a phrase I learned in measuring how useful our intelligence was—in other words, how well it helped a consumer of intelligence in Washington make better decisions. You can look at the performance of a stock to assess a company's performance, and you can study press releases. If you're considering an investment, though, speaking directly to the company's key executives will give you a window on the company that's irreplaceable. You can learn by talking to that company's players, even if you walk away thinking that those executives obscured key information or even lied.

At the CIA after 9/11, our experience face to face with a generation of al Qa'ida leaders reinforced those same lessons for us. Those detainees never told us everything they knew, and have not even to this day. They lied. They obfuscated. They tried to avoid giving us information that might lead to the detention of other terrorists. As the Senate report correctly concludes, they often succeeded. But that wasn't the sole measure by which we measured the value of these detainees. The measure was much broader, much closer to the heart of the mission of all intelligence services: Did the detainees help us provide decision advantage to the White House and elsewhere? Did those detainees help us understand the adversary, the terror group they had recently helped manage?

The takedown of 9/11 mastermind Khalid Sheikh Mohammed in 2003 highlights the subtle ways in which these detainees helped us, and it helps explain why the metric of whether detainees led us directly to other al Qa'ida members is too narrow. "KSM," the acronym we used for him (or "Mukhtar," the Brain, as we often called him), had characteristics that are rare in terrorists: he knew the United States (he had studied here); he was smart; he was experienced; and he had the trust of and access to the inner circle of al Qa'ida leaders. After KSM was captured in 2003, detainees referred often to the significance of the loss of a leader with those irreplaceable qualities. Meanwhile, in parallel with our capture of senior al Qa'ida leaders, drone strikes resulted in the deaths of others, and al Qa'ida members routinely lamented the devastating effectiveness of missiles from the sky.

I will never forget how detainees characterized the loss of KSM. Their descriptions of KSM and the importance of his capture did not give us a tactical advantage in the war. Nonetheless, coupled with other intelligence information, the words of detainees helped me begin to understand both the importance of experienced, visionary leadership in terror organizations and the inability of terror groups to replace leaders. Despite debates in the world outside the Intelligence Community about the long-term effectiveness of drone strikes in decapitating terror groups, all these bits of intelligence, including detainee comments, led me to judge then, and it does now, that taking terror leadership off the battlefield would inevitably lead to a decline in the threat to America. The captures of al Qa'ida terrorists, along with drone strikes, were among the most effective counterterror tools we had ever developed and deployed. Detainee comments about the loss of al Qa'ida's leadership didn't lead directly to KSM's capture, but they were a crucial thread, for me, to the clear awareness that drones should remain not only a core piece of the campaign against al Qa'ida in South Asia but a tool against other groups, from al-Shabaab in Somalia to al Qa'ida's affiliate in Yemen.

Similarly, during many conversations with analysts and interrogation specialists who spoke with the CIA's al Qa'ida detainees, I came to understand the adversary's mind-set with a clarity that would not be possible on the basis of human sources or intercepted communications alone. Time and again, CIA analysts and interrogators who worked with the detainees spoke of the commitment of these terrorists to the al Qa'ida mission, and the detainees repeatedly talked about their view that al Qa'ida's fight might endure for generations. This lesson about al Qa'ida's long-term commitment, potentially over decades, came to shape my view that we were not at war against a group; instead, we were witnessing the rise of a deeply committed cadre of revolutionaries who would never go home again, who would never be reformed. Despite the initial success expelling al Qa'ida from Afghanistan, we couldn't expect a short battle, with short-term budgets and a workforce that might be return to other jobs. We had to plan to develop a bureaucracy to wage this war for decades.

As al Qa'ida affiliates emerged in countries from Asia to Africa, the deep-seated commitment of the group's terror leaders to a long, grueling battle became even clearer, with implications for us that went well beyond locating the next al Qa'ida leader. We would have to grow analysts who might spend their entire careers on this war; we couldn't just borrow talent for short-term assignments from other areas of the CIA. We would have to build a budget for this long campaign and explain to our congressional overseers that they couldn't measure progress by months, or even years. Decades would be a better measurement for assessing progress against al Qa'ida. I reached all of these judgments partly as a result of personal conversations with the CIA's detainee debriefers, all of whom brought back to CIA Headquarters (in Langley, Virginia) similar observations—these al Qa'ida guys are serious, and they're smart. They will try to stay at this forever. They will return to the cause they so profoundly believe in if we ever release them. This seems self-evident, in retrospect. It wasn't then.

Even tiny pieces of intelligence from detainees, information that seems not only useless but contradictory or deceitful, can play a role in piecing together a hazy picture of the adversary. Take this scenario: an interrogator knows that a detainee has interacted with a courier who carries messages to a senior al Qa'ida figure. The detainee does not know that the interrogators are aware of this fact. So the interrogator begins to investigate, without revealing what he knows, whether the detainee will be truthful about the detainee's relationship with the courier. First, the interrogator might open a line of questioning about al Qa'ida individuals or associates in the detainee's network. The detainee fails to mention the courier. Much later in the interview process, the interrogator might ask the detainee to detail information about al Qa'ida courier networks. Again, the detainee fails to mention this one courier. Even later the interrogator again raises the courier's name; the detainee feigns incomprehension or claims only vague knowledge of the individual.

Let's evaluate this seemingly useless detainee information. Do the detainee's lies lead directly to a capture operation? Surely not. Do the lies suggest that the detainee is compliant or that he is prepared to tell all? Obviously not. Do these lies offer a critical clue to the analyst understanding al Qa'ida? Surely yes. A tiny clue, to be sure, but tiny clues are part of the lifeblood of intelligence analysis. In this case, the detainee may be doing everything he can to protect the courier, and in the mind of the detainee, the best protection he can offer is pretending that he doesn't know him. Why is this lie valuable to us? Possibly, just possibly, the detainee doesn't want to reveal what he knows about the courier because that revelation would help us uncover a key link in al Qa'ida's courier networks. By feigning ignorance, though, that detainee has just signaled that the courier might be a key player, one who should move up the CIA's list of key targets and merits more intelligence resources. The detainee has also unwittingly confirmed that al Qa'ida doesn't know how deeply its network has been penetrated. Both are tiny clues; neither has anything to do with a detainee providing information that links directly to the capture of an al Qa'ida member. If the courier were of no interest, why wouldn't the detainee offer as much detail as he could, hoping that we would spend time on one of al Qa'ida's bit players?

The Feinstein report on the CIA's detention and interrogation program doesn't focus on these questions, and this bedrock concept of decision advantage doesn't come into play in it. Instead, the report centers on a sliver of the detainee business: whether detainee information resulted in the capture of other al Qa'ida members. Whether a detainee has fingered other al-Qaida members is a good litmus test for judging the value of that detainee. But it's not the only litmus test, not by a long shot. Why did the Senate drafters use this narrow metric? Why isn't it important that these detainees helped us understand al Qa'ida in other ways? Why, above all, didn't Senate investigators ask those of us who evaluated this intelligence what we thought, and why? The report claims that investigators didn't want to interfere with Department of Justice investigations. That's a red herring—I was never investigated by the Department of Justice, though I was questioned in the department's investigations of others.

Using the simple metric of whether a detainee has provided such locational information reflects a profound misunderstanding of the business of counterterrorism analysis: it would make the business of intelligence a lot easier if detainees simply offered up information that led directly to al Qa'ida members, but that's closer to a Hollywood spy fantasy than to real life. Detainees, intercepted communications, human sources—they all provide tiny bits and pieces of what an analyst needs to understand the adversary. Those bits and pieces grow over time; the analyst's understanding of the adversary increases at a painstakingly slow pace. The standard for measuring detainee information, then, isn't whether a detainee provided a silver bullet; the standard is, instead, whether the analyst's understanding of the enemy grows as a result of what the detainee says. There, the answer is a resounding yes—even when the detainee starts with a seemingly mundane lie. Even lies, in the world of intelligence, can lead to truth.

The world I discovered after I left the CIA in 2010, a quarter-century after I had joined as a naive twenty-four-year-old with a graduate degree in English literature, led me to understand that our tiny intelligence universe at CIA remained opaque to outsiders, even with all the post-9/11 revelations about the spy business. A world that I had grown to understand after I joined the service in 1985 seemed impenetrable from the outside in 2010; the craft of intelligence seemed foreign, if unsurprisingly, to the widening world I encountered in public life after Langley. During the past few years, the range of Americans I began to encounter outside that clandestine world asked basic questions: How concerned should we be about al Qa'ida? How does the government track these guys? Why do Americans join this group? Also, inevitably, how and when might this war end? Finally, especially after the Senate report about CIA's interrogation program, many ask a reasonable question: Was it worth it? Did you learn anything? Did those detainees help in the war?

These broader questions cut to the heart of the profession of intelligence. How can we understand a national security problem—in this case, the problem of al Qa'ida—and how can we help government officials understand this adversary? When our first al Qa'ida detainee was captured in a bloody raid in the spring of 2002, the answer was emerging: security services around the world were contributing the tiny bits of data that were helping to grow our picture of the enemy. We looked at al Qa'ida only from a distance, though. Later, with Abu Zubaydah's detainee reporting and the mass of additional information other detainees provided, we could draw a picture based on firsthand experience with the al Qa'ida members who had built and run the terror group. Without their words, we had only a limited ability to explain the adversary, so as to give senior officials in government what all intelligence officers strive to give: the advantage of good information that will help make decisions better informed.

I often ask my former colleagues what surprises them today when they look back at the post-9/11 world we lived in at CIA. For almost all of us, the surprises are few. If you had told us during those years, for example, that later critics would question the appropriateness of the CIA's interrogation techniques, all of us would have agreed. Sure, we'd say. We will be vilified, at some point. That's often part of the cost of the dirty business of intelligence. But there is one curious debate that none of us—not one of us—would have anticipated when Abu Zubaydah started talking in 2002: the value of detainee information. We all thought then, as we do today, that our understanding of al Qa'ida, limited before we captured detainees, changed dramatically after we talked to them. Consider the alternative: even if you knew a detainee was lying, would you still judge that detainee to be useless? I wouldn't.

The debate over the CIA's detention and interrogation program can only continue if the question about detainee information limits our evaluation to a criterion we never used then, that of whether detainees led us directly to other al Qa'ida members. Read the CIA's response to the Senate report for an understanding of why the Agency differs from the report's drafters on this narrow issue. But as you're reading, and as this debate filters down through the years, never forget that the debate is colored by one of the most fundamental errors that analysts make: not starting with the right question. Because imperfect questions yield imperfect answers. If your evaluation of detainee reporting centers on how much individual detainees directed us to other al Qa'ida players and plotters, you will get one narrow answer. If the question goes to the heart of the age-old profession of intelligence—Did detainee-derived intelligence give us a decision advantage?—you'll get another answer, and one that explains why those of us who were there then are so surprised by today's debates. And remember one of the lessons of intelligence, where some aspects of the adversary always remain secret: even lies and deceit have value.

Philip Mudd served as Deputy Director of the CIA's Counterterrorist Center and then Senior Intelligence Adviser at the FBI. He joined the CIA in 1985 and spent his career analyzing the Middle East and South Asia, with a particular focus on terrorism. He comments frequently on national security matters and is the author of *The HEAD Game* (Liveright Press, 2015).

THE LEGAL CASE
FOR EITs

John Rizzo

As the CIA's chief legal adviser for seven of the first eight years following 9/11, I was indisputably one of the key legal architects of the enhanced interrogation program, which I monitored and oversaw from its beginning to end. Like every other one of the hundreds of CIA employees who participated in the EIT program during its six-year existence, I was never interviewed by the staff assembled by Senate Intelligence Committee chair Dianne Feinstein, without any Republican staff participation, during the course of its four-year investigation that ultimately culminated in the public release of its 550-page executive summary on December 9, 2014. Indeed, although I am cited by name over two hundred times in the summary, I was rebuffed by Senator Feinstein in the summer of 2014 when I asked, as a matter of simple courtesy and fairness, to be allowed to read the summary before its release. In short, I saw what it said about me at the same time the rest of the world did—and, I should add, twenty-four hours after the Feinstein staff provided it to the media, on an embargoed basis, to give it a head start.

Given the way the Feinstein staff had conducted its inquiry, its outcome was clearly preordained, and so I was not surprised at its final product—a one-sided, unremitting, wholesale assault on the EIT program and on the competence and integrity on virtually everyone at the CIA associated with it, including—and in particular—me.

Since my retirement from the Agency in late 2009, I have made numerous public statements describing my central role in the creation and implementation of the EIT program, including a lengthy portion I devoted to it in *Company Man*, my memoir of my CIA career published in 2014. In all of these statements, I have tried to be as complete, honest, and candid as I could. Yes, I have defended the program—its necessary birth in the immediate aftermath of an unprecedented national catastrophe, the overall care with which it was implemented and calibrated over the years, the resoluteness of CIA career professionals who were convinced of its value and thus steadfastly, stoically carried it on for years in the face of shifting political winds and increasingly toxic public controversy. But I have also fully acknowledged and detailed publicly that the long-running program was not conducted without flaws, without mistakes, some made by me personally.

Nevertheless, I cannot let stand one of the Feinstein summary's central themes—that the CIA made repeated "inaccurate claims" over the years about the EIT program to the White House, the National Security Council, the Department of Justice (DOJ), the Congress, and the public. As the lead CIA interlocutor with Justice during the entire course of the program, I consider that accusation especially unfair and galling.

Basically, the Feinstein summary seems to label as "inaccurate claims" anything the CIA said over the years about the necessity and demonstrated results of the program, statements that the Feinstein staff, years after the events in question and with the luxury of time and hindsight, summarily dismisses as not aligning with the staff's preordained conclusion: that the EIT program was totally unnecessary and totally useless. I won't get into the merits of that conclusion here; for that, read the detailed CIA rebuttal to the Feinstein staff report contained in this volume; it meticulously catalogues the concrete, critical intelligence the program produced over the years. When you do, keep in mind that the senior CIA analysts who wrote the rebuttal, several years after the program ended, had never been involved in it and thus had no axes to grind. Also, keep in mind that Leon Panetta, President Obama's first CIA Director, acknowledged in his 2014 memoir that the EIT program yielded "important . . . even critical intelligence." This from a man who was no cheerleader for the program; like his boss, Panetta was a Democrat long on record as describing the program as "torture."

Instead, I will address the issue of my years-long interactions with Justice regarding the EIT program. My approach was certainly not to "repeatedly" make "inaccurate claims." To do so would have been not only wrong but stupid and counterproductive. I was the CIA lawyer responsible for ensuring that the EIT program complied with U.S. law. I was also focused on providing my clients—the CIA workforce, from top to bottom—the most unassailable protection possible from future investigation for what I knew from the outset would be a highly risky and controversial activity.

The record is clear, even in the Feinstein summary's skewed narrative, that from the outset, and then as the EIT program proceeded, the Agency again and again proactively sought authoritative written guidance from DOJ's Office of Legal Counsel (OLC), the ultimate legal authority in the executive branch for the interpretation of U.S. law and treaty obligations. I approached OLC days after being first told by our counterterrorism experts about the unavoidable need to apply unprecedented interrogation measures—the EITs—on the CIA's first captured significant al Qa'ida figure, Abu Zubaydah. In all of my previous quarter-century of service as an Agency lawyer, I had never encountered anything remotely similar to these proposed measures. Right off the bat, I knew that some of the EITs—like the waterboard—sounded harsh, if not outright brutal. What I didn't know was whether they crossed the legal line into torture, forbidden under a U.S. law with which I had absolutely no prior experience. So that's why I went to OLC in early April 2002, just a few months removed from 9/11 and a time when the country was still gripped with horror and dread about a possibly imminent second major terrorist attack on the homeland. Four months later, the first so-called OLC torture memo addressed to me arrived, filled with graphic detail describing how the techniques would be administered and laying out our best analysis about Zubaydah's place in the al Qa'ida hierarchy and what he might know—and was holding back—about future attacks. We provided OLC with everything we knew at the time, holding nothing back, because that's what we in the Agency insisted upon ourselves. As the world now knows, the OLC concluded that the proposed EITs did not violate the torture statute. If it had concluded otherwise, the Agency would have accepted that conclusion, and the program never would have begun. Period.

Yet even as the program proceeded and was refined over the years, we returned to the OLC three more times—in mid-2004, late 2005, and late 2006—seeking updated written guidance in light of intervening U.S. Supreme Court decisions and congressional restrictions. The Agency provided our career analysts' best and most honest assessment, in real time, about the important benefits and results the EIT program was producing. The fact was, DOJ and some in the White House were not happy about the CIA's persistence; the OLC would have much preferred that we simply rely on its original 2002 memo to me approving the program—from which DOJ never backed away—and leave it at that. But we pushed and ultimately prevailed; ten OLC memos and letters, from three different leaders of that office, were issued to me between 2002 through the end of the program in 2008.

Years later, the Feinstein staff has deemed that the information we provided to OLC over all that time was "repeatedly . . . inaccurate." Leave aside that over the five years of its existence the staff never once provided me the opportunity to confront and defend myself from this accusation (nor, for that matter, from its one-sentence assertion elsewhere in the summary that in 2007 congressional testimony I "provided inaccurate information on the legal reasons for CIA detention facilities overseas"). As best I can tell, the staff's conclusion is based on its fundamental, preordained narrative that the program was unnecessary and useless. Put another way, any information we gave the OLC—demonstrating, say, why in 2002 we assessed Abu Zubaydah to be a plugged-in guy who was holding out on more al Qa'ida plots—was perforce "inaccurate," as was presumably every intelligence benefit derived from the program we cited to the OLC over the years.

With everything that is known now about al Qa'ida that wasn't known in those frantic, pressure-filled early post-9/11 years, I am not in a position to guarantee that every statement we ever made to DOJ all that time ago remains empirically unchallengeable today. Very little does in the intelligence world. But I can guarantee that we did our utmost to give everything in as straight and forthright and complete a way as we could. The CIA was so persistent in banging on OLC's door because we were so focused—obsessed, really—with constantly checking to make sure that the program continued to retain firm legal underpinnings. We were also focused, at the same time, on affording legal protection to the Agency counterterrorist workforce whose dedicated people were protecting the country.

To sabotage those objectives by "repeatedly" feeding DOJ/OLC false information would not only have been wrong but self-defeating. We doggedly sought and obtained those ten OLC memos over the years because we considered it essential to have authoritative, reliable, and credible guidance. To undermine that objective by consistently providing bad data to succeeding OLC lawyers would have made the memos not worth the paper in the hundred or so pages they were collectively written on. And that outcome would not have served anyone, least of all the CIA.

John Rizzo was a CIA lawyer for thirty-four years and served as its chief legal adviser from 2001 through 2002 and from 2004 until he retired at the end of 2009. He is author of *Company Man*, a 2014 memoir of his CIA career.

BROKEN COVENANT

Jose A. Rodriguez Jr.

I n the summer of 2002, I was the chief of the CIA's Counterterrorism Center. A small group of our targeting analysts came to my office to urge me to restart the interrogation of Abu Zubaydah, a key al Qa'ida operative we had captured a few months before. Abu Zubaydah, whom we referred to as "AZ," had been put in isolation at the black site where he was being held since he had stopped talking. The CIA leadership had decided we were dead in the water and needed to do something different to get him to cooperate.

The targeting analysts were concerned that the threat level of a second wave of attacks was at an all-time high and that we risked another catastrophic and devastating attack against the homeland. Intelligence reporting pointed to al Qa'ida's having developed anthrax at its lab near Kandahar, Afghanistan. We had also recently learned of discussions Bin Ladin had held with Pakistani scientists about developing a nuclear or radiological bomb to use against us. "The United States is in grave danger and AZ is the key to helping us disrupt the plots we are facing," the analysts said to me.

AZ was a senior planner and logistician, up to that point the highest-level al Qa'ida (AQ) terrorist ever in our custody. Among the materials we had found at the site where he was captured were some videotapes that he had prerecorded to celebrate a successful second wave of attacks on the United States. Clearly, AZ expected new devastating attacks, and we believed he held the keys to stopping them. We felt we were in a ticking-time-bomb situation; we could not see the bomb, but we could hear it ticking.

In the past we had transferred terrorists like AZ to friendly countries to hold and interrogate for us. But I had become convinced that we could not rely on others to interrogate high-value detainees for us effectively. There was simply too much at stake for us to contract out to foreign countries the interrogation of high-level AQ operatives. We knew nobody was going to look after our national security as we would ourselves. Also, frankly, no foreign government, no matter how friendly, was going to care about protecting our homeland and safeguarding American lives as we would. We knew CIA had to get back into the interrogation business.

AZ had been badly wounded during his capture, and at first he had provided some useful information to a joint CIA/FBI team questioning him. But as he regained his strength he also gained resolve to provide no further information of value. We were getting nowhere, we needed a new approach. We had in our custody an AQ detainee who could have information about the next wave of attacks. If a second wave of attacks devastated other U.S. cities and we had failed to do all we could to stop it, we would have felt we had blood on our hands.

So, we put AZ in isolation at the black site where he was being held while a set of interrogation techniques based on a U.S. military course called "Survival, Evasion, Resistance, and Escape" (SERE) was developed. Over the years tens of thousands of U.S. Army, Navy, and Air Force personnel have endured the enhanced interrogation techniques of SERE, which include waterboarding. I am convinced that when years later President Obama and his Attorney General said that waterboarding is torture they were referring to the waterboarding method used by the Spanish Inquisition, or by the Japanese during World War II, or the Khmer Rouge in Cambodia—not the waterboarding technique used in SERE. Otherwise hundreds, if not thousands, of U.S. military trainers would be guilty of torture.

Even though our program was based on a U.S. military training program, we were well aware of the legal risks involved for CIA personnel using techniques that went beyond traditional interrogation techniques. Over the summer months of 2002 our lawyers coordinated with the White House and the Office of Legal Counsel twelve interrogation techniques (later trimmed down to ten). We wanted to be sure that we were on firm legal ground and that the CIA personnel involved in the interrogation program were protected. We wanted to make sure that the President and his national security team, the Attorney General and his Office of Legal Counsel, and the leadership of both houses of Congress were on board.

When the targeting analysts came to my office in the summer of 2002 to urge me to restart the interrogation of AZ, we had not yet completed the coordination of the enhanced interrogation techniques with the White House, the Justice Department, and the Congress. The CIA had been left to hold the bag many times in the past when it had been directed to undertake covert action that was later questioned and second-guessed. I was determined not to let that happen again. As I said in a *60 Minutes* interview in 2012, I wanted the senior leadership of our government in the executive and legislative branches to "put their big-boy pants on" and give us the authorities and the protections we needed to use enhanced interrogation techniques on AQ terrorists.

On August 1, 2002, the Office of Legal Counsel at the Justice Department gave us in writing a binding opinion that waterboarding and other techniques were legal. We then went to the White House and got final policy approval from the President and his national security team to proceed with the implementation of the interrogation program. When the Congress got back from recess in September we briefed the leadership of the House and the Senate; they had no objection. I felt then that we had all the legal opinions and approvals necessary to protect the CIA officers involved in the program. I felt that we were bullet proof. Boy, was I wrong!

Contrary to the baffling conclusions of the majority Select Senate Committee on Intelligence report a dozen years later on the CIA's interrogation program, the enhanced interrogation program was very successful. The program added enormously to our base knowledge of AQ and helped us disrupt plots and capture or kill the generation of AQ terrorists that had attacked us on 9/11, to include Usama Bin Ladin ten years later.

Notwithstanding our successes in the war on terror against AQ in faraway lands, however, at home in the months and weeks before the 2004 national elections we felt a gradual shift in the strong political support we had received from our elected representatives. Leaks and speculation in the press regarding our black sites questioned and second-guessed the effectiveness and legality of our programs. Some politicians running for office used misinformation about our programs to score political points. Some Congressmen and Senators who had been briefed and had been supportive of our programs at the outset began to criticize and distance themselves from them. Unable to defend ourselves publicly because of a traditional and long-standing code of silence that CIA practices, as well as the attitude of not talking back, we allowed politicians, the media, human rights organizations, and some in academia to define our narrative.

Worse yet, by 2004–2005 we felt that the legal foundation of our program was eroding and that the protections that we had sought for our officers were slowly going away. Unwilling to put its officers in legal jeopardy, the CIA went to the Attorney General for legal rulings four times during this period. We stopped the program twice to ensure that the Department of Justice still saw it consistent with U.S. policy, law, and treaty obligations. The CIA sought guidance and reaffirmation of the program from senior administration policy makers at least four times. We were reassured that we were following the law and that our people were protected.

In any human endeavor that involves hundreds of people and a lot of moving parts, you are always going to find people who break the rules and do stupid things. This is especially true in complicated and risky covert-action programs involving secret sites, airplanes picking up detainees in the middle of the night from faraway places and transporting them to black sites, operations coordinated with foreign intelligence services, and al Qa'ida terrorist interrogations that require strict adherence to legal and procedural guidelines provided by CIA Headquarters. As we have acknowledged publicly, some CIA officers did not follow the rules, and a few abuses were committed. Upon learning of alleged abuses and other problems, however, we immediately self-reported to the CIA's statutory inspector general and the Department of Justice. About twenty cases of alleged abuses were forwarded to the Department of Justice; career prosecutors decided that only one of these cases, unrelated to the formal interrogation program, merited prosecution. Some officers received administrative sanctions, while others were cleared of any wrongdoing.

In the run-up to the 2008 national elections, once again we found ourselves in the middle of political football between politicians of the two parties. Most disturbing of all was the allegation by candidate Obama that waterboarding was torture and that our interrogation program was against our values. Writing in *Foreign Affairs* in 2007, Obama called for building a "better, freer, world by ending the practice of shipping away prisoners in the dead of night to be tortured in far-away countries, of detaining thousands without charge or trial, or maintaining a network of secret prisons to jail people beyond the reach of the law." Later, as President, he repeated his charge that "we tortured some folks," most recently after the SSCI report was released in December 2014.

I cannot tell you how disgusted my former colleagues and I felt to be labeled "torturers" by the President of the United States. To hear that we had acted contrary to American ideals was infuriating. But by far the worst day for us was when in August 2009 Attorney General Eric Holder announced his intention to reopen criminal investigations of CIA officers who had been involved in incidents involving the interrogation of detainees. Holder made the decision despite the fact that career Department of Justice lawyers had closed the investigations during the previous administration, finding that no prosecutions were warranted. For three years (2009–2012) special prosecutor John Durham conducted a criminal investigation of these cases. In the end, he concluded that no prosecutable offenses had occurred.

Having been the subject of a criminal investigation myself, I can tell you of the terrible effects such investigations have on the morale and well-being of individuals being investigated and their families. You get the feeling that your own government has abandoned you; you worry that some overly zealous prosecutor will indict you and that justice will fail you. You worry about the financial burden, the legal costs of defending yourself. You worry about the psychological effects on your spouse and children and on your other family members and close friends. To make people go through this agony twice over several years, as some CIA officers had to as a result of Holder's reopening of the investigations, was unconscionable.

Following the 9/11 attacks the CIA was the only entity in government ready to respond to the crisis. The President directed the Agency to take the lead, and hundreds of CIA officers responded to the call of duty. We all felt honored and fortunate to be part of the team delivering the American response to the attacks. We succeeded in avenging the death of three thousand innocents and delivering a knockout blow to AQ. We protected the homeland, we saved American lives.

We did not expect to be hounded by our own government once the political winds changed. We did not expect the authorities that had been given to us by our President with the blessing of our Congress at a time of a national emergency to be questioned and second-guessed by a new administration. We did not expect our President to call us torturers and to tell us that our actions were against American values. We did not expect cases that had been closed by professional prosecutors to be reopened by our Attorney General in a politically and ideologically based investigation.

CIA officers responded to the call of duty after 9/11 in good faith, thinking that their government had their backs. By calling them torturers and hounding them in the courts, President Obama has broken the covenant that exists between the government and the CIA officers hanging way out at "the pointy end of the spear," where the government had directed and authorized them to go.

As bad as the impact might be of ill-considered statements made by the President or the revisionist history peddled by some Members of the Senate Select Committee on Intelligence on those who served in the past, the biggest negative effect may well be for the future. Today, CIA officers are conducting highly sensitive classified operations at the behest of the current President. They are being assured that they have the full legal backing of the Department of Justice and the consent of the congressional oversight committees. Yet in the back of their minds must be the question of whether assurances of support are real. I worry whether current and future generations of CIA leaders will question whether the authorities they receive from their President will last longer than one election cycle. It would be easy for Agency officers to assume that pledges of support are written in quicksand. If they do, they will be tempted to avoid taking risks. I worry about what this means for the safety of our nation.

Jose A. Rodriguez Jr. is a thirty-one-year veteran of the CIA. He served as Chief of CIA's Counterterrorism Center and Director of the National Clandestine Service. His book *Hard Measures: How Aggressive CIA Actions after 9/11 Saved American Lives* was published in 2012.

THE CIA
REBUTTAL

THE DIRECTOR
CENTRAL INTELLIGENCE AGENCY
WASHINGTON, D.C. 20505

27 June 2013

MEMORANDUM FOR: The Honorable Dianne Feinstein
                 The Honorable Saxby Chambliss

SUBJECT: (S) CIA Comments on the Senate Select
                 Committee on Intelligence Report on the
                 Rendition, Detention, and Interrogation Program

1.   (S) I appreciate the opportunity for the Central
Intelligence Agency to comment on the Senate Select Committee on
Intelligence's Study of the Agency's long-terminated Rendition,
Detention, and Interrogation Program (hereafter referred to as
the "Study"). As I noted during my confirmation hearing and in
subsequent discussions with you and with Committee members, the
lengthy Study deserved careful review by the Agency in light of
the significance and sensitivity of the subject matter and, of
particular concern, the serious charges made in the Study about
the Agency's performance and record.

2.   (S) As you know, one of the President's first acts in
office more than four years ago was to sign Executive Order
13491, which brought to an end the program that is the subject
of the Committee's work. In particular, the President directed
that the CIA no longer operate detention facilities and banned
the use of all interrogation techniques not in the Army Field
Manual. Thus, before getting into the substance of the CIA's
review of the Study, I want to reaffirm what I said during my
confirmation hearing: I agree with the President's decision,
and, while I am the Director of the CIA, this program will not
under any circumstances be reinitiated. I personally remain
firm in my belief that enhanced interrogation techniques are not
an appropriate method to obtain intelligence and that their use
impairs our ability to continue to play a leadership role in the
world.

SUBJECT: (S) CIA Comments on the Senate Select Committee on
              Intelligence Report on the Rendition, Detention,
              and Interrogation Program

3.   (S) Nevertheless, as Director of the CIA, it is not my
role to engage in a debate about the appropriateness of the
decisions that were made in a previous Administration to conduct
a detention and enhanced interrogation program of suspected
terrorists following the attacks on 11 September 2001. Rather,
it is my responsibility to review the performance of the CIA
with regard to the program and to take whatever steps necessary
to strengthen the conduct as well as the institutional oversight
of CIA covert action programs. This is the perspective I took
when reviewing CIA's comments on the Study.

4.   (S) The CIA's comments on the Study were the result of
a comprehensive and thorough review of the Study's 20
conclusions and 20 case studies. In fulfilling my pledge to
you, I want you to have the full benefit of the overall findings
and recommendations of the Agency review team (TAB A) as well as
the team's analysis of each of the Study's 20 conclusions and 20
case studies (TABS B and C, respectively). I strongly encourage
you as well as all Committee Members and Staff to read the
entirety of the Agency's comments.

5.   (S) I have carefully reviewed and concur with the
Agency's comments, which I would like to summarize briefly.
First of all, we agree with a number of the Study's conclusions.
In particular, we agree that the Agency:

   • Was unprepared and lacked core competencies to respond
     effectively to the decision made in the aftermath of the
     9/11 attacks that the Agency undertake what would be an
     unprecedented program of detaining and interrogating
     suspected Al Qa'ida and affiliated terrorists. This lack
     of preparation and competencies resulted in significant
     lapses in the Agency's ability to develop and monitor its
     initial detention and interrogation activities. These
     initial lapses, most of which were corrected by 2003 and
     have been the subject of multiple internal and external
     investigations, were the result of a failure of management
     at multiple levels, albeit at a time when CIA management
     was stretched to the limit as the CIA led the U.S.

SUBJECT: (S) CIA Comments on the Senate Select Committee on
             Intelligence Report on the Rendition, Detention,
             and Interrogation Program

Government's counterterrorism response to the 9/11 attacks
against the Homeland;

• Struggled to formulate and gain policy approval for a
viable plan to move detainees out of Agency-run detention
facilities;

• Failed to perform a comprehensive and independent
analysis on the effectiveness of enhanced interrogation
techniques;

• Allowed a conflict of interest to exist wherein the
contractors who helped design and employ the enhanced
interrogation techniques also were involved in assessing
the fitness of detainees to be subjected to such techniques
and the effectiveness of those same techniques;

• Detained some individuals under a flawed interpretation
of the authorities granted to CIA, and;

• Fell short when it came to holding individuals
accountable for poor performance and management failures.

6. (S) Notwithstanding the above areas of agreement,
there are several areas of disagreement as well. In particular,
the Agency disagrees with the Study's unqualified assertions
that the overall detention and interrogation program did not
produce unique intelligence that led terrorist plots to be
disrupted, terrorists to be captured, or lives to be saved. The
Study's claims on this score are inconsistent with the factual
record, and we provide detailed comments in TAB C on where and
why the Study's assertions and representations are wrong.

• The Agency takes no position on whether intelligence
obtained from detainees who were subjected to enhanced
interrogation techniques could have been obtained through
other means or from other individuals. The answer to this
question is and will forever remain unknowable.

SUBJECT: (S) CIA Comments on the Senate Select Committee on
            Intelligence Report on the Rendition, Detention,
            and Interrogation Program

   • After reviewing the Committee Study and the comments of
the Agency review team, and as I indicated at the outset of
this memorandum, I personally remain firm in my belief that
enhanced interrogation techniques are an inappropriate
method for obtaining intelligence. Moreover, it is my
resolute intention never to allow any Agency officer to
participate in any interrogation activity in which enhanced
interrogation techniques would be employed.

   7. (S) Regarding the Study's claim that the Agency
resisted internal and external oversight and deliberately
misrepresented the program to Congress, the Executive Branch,
the media, and the American people, the factual record
maintained by the Agency does not support such conclusions. In
addition, the Study's conclusion regarding CIA's
misrepresentations of the program rely heavily on its flawed
conclusion regarding the lack of any intelligence that flowed
from the program. Nevertheless, we do agree with the Study that
there were instances where representations about the program
that were used or approved by Agency officers were inaccurate,
imprecise, or fell short of Agency tradecraft standards. Those
limited number of misrepresentations and instances of
imprecision never should have happened.

   8. (S) As a result of the Committee's Study and our
review, I have approved and the CIA has started to implement
eight recommendations made by the Agency review team, which are
included in TAB A. It is critically important that the Agency
leadership team take immediate steps to prevent any shortcomings
in Agency covert action programs, as flawed performance--on the
part of the Agency as an institution or by individual Agency
officers--can have devastating consequences. In addition, our
review team is ready to brief Committee members as well as meet
with Committee staff at any time to walk through our comments.

   9. (U) I sincerely hope that, as a result of the
Committee's work and our subsequent review and comments, we can
take steps to enhance the Agency's ability to meet successfully
the ever-growing array of intelligence and national security

4

SUBJECT: ~~(S)~~   CIA Comments on the Senate Select Committee on
Intelligence Report on the Rendition, Detention,
and Interrogation Program

challenges that face our Nation. By learning from the past
while focusing on the future, we will be able to best meet our
mutual responsibility to protect and advance the national
security interests of the American people. As always, I look
forward to working with you and the entire Committee on these
important matters.

John O. Brennan

SUBJECT: ~~(S)~~   CIA Comments on the Senate Select Committee on
             Intelligence Report on the Rendition, Detention,
             and Interrogation Program

Attachment

cc: Denis McDonough, Assistant to the President and Chief of
         Staff
      Kathy Ruemmler, Assistant to the President and Counsel to
         the President
      The Honorable Mike Rogers
      The Honorable Dutch Ruppersberger
      Thomas Donilon, Assistant to the President for National
         Security Affairs
      James R. Clapper, Director of National Intelligence

Comments on the *Senate Select Committee on Intelligence's Study of the Central Intelligence Agency's Former Detention and Interrogation Program*

1. (U//FOUO) The comments presented in this paper on *The Senate Select Committee on Intelligence's Study of the Central Intelligence Agency's Detention and Interrogation Program* (hereinafter referred to as the *Study*), along with the more detailed discussion accompanying this paper, are the product of a review of the *Study* originally commissioned in December, after the Committee adopted the report, by then Acting Director Morell. The purpose of the review was to focus, as the *Study* does, on the Agency's conduct of the RDI program, in the interest of promoting historical accuracy and identifying lessons learned for the future, with the ultimate goal of improving the Agency's execution of other covert action programs. Indeed, as the former detention and interrogation program was ended as of 22 January 2009, and has been completely dismantled, forward focus on ongoing covert action activity is critically important. Accordingly, in this submission, we do not address the policy decision made to utilize coercive interrogation techniques as part of the RDI program, nor do we advocate or otherwise express any judgments concerning the wisdom or propriety of using those techniques.

2. (U//FOUO) We would like to note at the outset the limits on what we were able to accomplish, even with the additional time we took beyond the Committee's initial 15 February 2013 deadline. Recognizing the impossibility of poring over each of the *Study's* almost 6,000 pages in the time allotted, ADCIA Morell asked a select group of CIA analysts and managers, none of whom had decision-making responsibility for the former rendition, detention, and interrogation (RDI) program, to concentrate on the *Study's* 20 conclusions and to dive deep on a discrete portion of the main text. Specifically, he asked the group to focus on the portion of the *Study* that assesses the value of the information derived from CIA's RDI's activities. That portion of the *Study* is important because it serves as the basis for a number of assertions in the *Study's* conclusions as to the veracity of CIA's representations regarding the program.

3. (U//FOUO) ADCIA Morell then asked three senior officers to carefully review the group's work, to develop recommendations with regard to remedial measures that flowed from their review of the *Study,* and to provide their main findings and recommendations in this paper.

4. (U//FOUO) To be clear, although we did mount a serious effort to respond, we were not able to perform a comprehensive fact check or provide the "technical corrections" requested by the Committee. That proved impossible for two reasons. First, it was simply impractical to provide line-by-line comments on a document of such great length in such a short period of time. Second, and just as important, for those portions we were able to review in detail, we found that accuracy was encumbered as much by the

authors' interpretation, selection, and contextualization of the facts as it was by errors in their recitation of the facts, making it difficult to address its flaws with specific technical corrections.

5. (U/~~FOUO~~) The *Study* has all the appearances of an authoritative history of CIA's RDI effort. As Chairman Feinstein announced to the press the day it was approved by the Committee, its authors had access to 6 million pages of records—most provided by CIA—and they cite more than 35,000 footnotes. However, although the *Study* contains an impressive amount of detail, it fails in significant and consequential ways to correctly portray and analyze that detail. Simply put, the *Study* tells part of the story of CIA's experience with RDI, but there are too many flaws for it to stand as the official record of the program. Those flaws stem from two basic limitations on the authors:

- (U/~~FOUO~~) A methodology that relied exclusively on a review of documents with no opportunity to interview participants, owing to the Department of Justice investigation of the program; and

- (U/~~FOUO~~) An apparent lack of familiarity with some of the ways the Agency analyzes and uses intelligence.

6. (U/~~FOUO~~) Accompanying this paper are responses to each of the 20 examples in the *Study* of the value of the intelligence acquired during CIA interrogations of detainees and the Agency's representations of that intelligence. In addition, we provide responses to each of the *Study's* 20 conclusions. In each response we have identified those points in the relevant conclusion or supporting text with which we agree, and those we think are in error. These responses offer the fullest sense of our views on the *Study's* accuracy.

Key Themes

7. (U/~~FOUO~~) For the purposes of this paper, the *Study's* findings have been consolidated into four key themes that emerged from our reading of the *Study's* conclusions. Those themes are:

a) *(U) CIA was unprepared to conduct an RDI effort and inadequately developed and monitored its initial activities.*

b) *(U) The program was poorly managed and executed. Unqualified officers and contractors imposed brutal conditions, often used unapproved interrogation techniques, used approved techniques excessively, and were rarely held accountable.*

c) *(U) Contrary to CIA representations, the program failed to produce intelligence that was otherwise unavailable and that enabled CIA to disrupt plots, capture terrorists, or save lives.*

    d) (U) CIA resisted internal and external oversight, and it misrepresented the program to Congress, the Executive Branch, and the media.

A. (U) CIA was unprepared to conduct an RDI effort and inadequately developed and monitored its initial activities.

8. (U/~~FOUO~~) We fully agree that CIA was unprepared to initiate an RDI effort. CIA did not have a cadre of trained interrogators, particularly with adequate foreign language skills. CIA had little experience handling, moving, and interrogating detainees and no core competency in detention facility management. Moreover, the Agency faced this challenge at a time when it was overwhelmed by the other aspects of its worldwide response to the threat of more mass casualty attacks.

- (~~S//OC/NF~~) At the same time that CIA encountered the need to hold and interrogate terrorists, it also was focused on redirecting substantial resources to the Counterterrorism Center (CTC), undertaking high-risk operations in ███████████ trying to find Usama Bin Ladin, and enlisting the aid of liaison partners across the globe in the fight against al-Qa'ida.

9. (U/~~FOUO~~) We also agree with the *Study* that "CIA did not adequately develop and monitor its initial detention and interrogation activities." In agreeing with this statement, however, we draw particular attention to the word "initial." One of the main flaws of the *Study* is that, especially in its Summary and Conclusions, it tars CIA's entire RDI effort with the mistakes of the first few months, before that effort was consolidated and regulated under a single program management office.

10. (U/~~FOUO~~) While we take issue with the way the *Study* conflates distinct chapters in the history of the program, we acknowledge that there were serious shortcomings in the first such chapter. Perhaps the single biggest mistake in carrying out the RDI effort was CIA's failure to immediately respond to the extraordinary and high-risk requirements of conducting RDI activities by establishing a dedicated, centrally managed office tasked with quickly promulgating operational guidelines for RDI activities. Such an office should have been properly resourced and empowered to take control of those activities worldwide and monitor them on a day-to-day basis. This happened, but not fast enough.

- (~~TS/~~██████████████~~NF~~) As a result, although the confinement conditions and treatment of high profile detainees like Abu Zubaydah were closely scrutinized at all levels of management from the outset, the same cannot be said for the first few of months of CIA's handling of lower-profile detainees in ██████████

11. (~~S//OC/NF~~) It was during those months that grim conditions and inadequate monitoring of detainees were allowed to exist at ██████████ culminating in the death of Gul Rahman in November 2002, two months after the first detainee arrived there. During

this time there were several instances of unauthorized, improvised techniques, including mock executions and "hard takedowns" at █████████

12. (TS/█████████████████████████NF) Contrary to the *Study*'s assertion that the confinement conditions during the early days of ██████████ were not "previously known," they were exhaustively reviewed by the Office of the Inspector General (OIG) and described in detail in its 2004 *Special Review,* as well as in its separate April 2005 *Report of Investigation: Death of a Detainee* ████████████ These reports were shared with the Chairman and Vice Chairman of the oversight committees.

13. (S//OC/NF) We believe this period represents a failure at all levels of management. CIA simply did not devote the kind of attention to managing the risk of this new challenge that it should have at the outset. However, in contrast to the impression left by the *Study*, the confusion over responsibility, lack of guidance, and excessively harsh conditions that detainees experienced in the early days of ██████████ did not characterize more than a few months of our RDI effort. Unfortunately, it took Rahman's death in CIA custody to focus management's attention.

- (S//OC/NF) In response to the problems on which Rahman's death shone a light, CIA centralized the management of and accountability for all detention facilities in a single program office, which endeavored to address the shortcomings at ██████████ as well as isolated problems elsewhere.

- (S//OC/NF) That office also developed standards and guidelines for operating all CIA-controlled detention and interrogation facilities and monitored adherence to those guidelines. The *Study* makes much of the fact that CIA did not issue such guidance until January 2003. It fails to note that this was only four months after ██████████ accepted its first detainee.

14. (TS/█████████████████████NF) We are not suggesting CIA solved all its problems in early 2003. Resource constraints dogged the RDI program throughout its existence, especially in ██████████ and especially after the invasion of Iraq increased the competition for language-capable personnel. Although conditions at ██████████ improved after early 2003, CIA never did—as we believe it should have—put the facility under ████████████████ the dedicated full-time management of a more senior CIA officer, as was standard practice at other Agency detention sites. CIA also was unable to fully bring the facility up to the standard of our other detention facilities by the time it was closed in ██████████

- (TS/██████████████████NF) There were substantial practical and cover constraints on the Agency's ability to accomplish this in ██████████ that it eventually overcame by replacing ████████████████ with a much better facility. We believe, however, CIA could have done more in the interim between Rahman's death and the closure of ██████████

15. (S//OC/NF) Looking ahead, the lesson we draw from the Agency's initial handling of the RDI effort is that senior leadership must ensure that appropriate structures, lines of authority, and resources are available for major new initiatives, especially risky ones, from the outset. Responsible risk management must be a core competency for Agency leaders. In recent years, CIA has instituted carefully structured and detailed annual reviews ▓▓▓▓▓▓▓▓▓▓▓▓ Our experience with RDI indicates that there may well be programs ▓▓▓▓▓▓▓▓▓▓ that carry with them sufficient risk to merit similar reviews.

B. (U) The program was poorly managed and executed. Unqualified officers and contractors imposed brutal conditions, often used unapproved interrogation techniques, used approved techniques excessively, and were rarely held accountable.

16. (U//FOUO) Reviews by the OIG clearly show that, in contrast to the impression left by the conclusions of the *Study*, once responsibility for the program was consolidated, the oversight and management of CIA's RDI activities improved substantially. This was not a panacea—other mistakes were made, investigated, and corrected along the way—but the program was much better developed and managed after the initial months.

17. (U) Let us address briefly the most important management and execution issues raised in the *Study*, highlighting those of greatest concern:

18. (TS/▓▓▓▓▓▓▓▓▓▓▓▓▓▓▓▓NF) **Legal Interpretation.** CIA clearly fell short when it detained some people under a flawed legal rationale, as discussed in the *Study*. Looking back on it now with the benefit of a dozen years of institutional experience interpreting and conducting operations under authorities granted in the 2001 Memorandum of Notification (MoN), it is hard to imagine how Agency lawyers could have developed and applied differing interpretations of the MoN's capture and detain authorities.

- (TS/▓▓▓▓▓▓▓▓▓▓▓▓NF) Although it is a good thing that this seems inconceivable under the legal structures and lines of authority currently in place, we are concerned that it took the accountability exercise mounted after the improper detention of Khalid al-Masri to shed light on and correct this situation.

- (TS/▓▓▓▓▓▓▓▓▓▓▓▓NF) A review that resulted from the accountability board considering the improper detention of al-Masri showed that others detained under the incorrect MoN standard would have met the correct standard, had it been applied correctly. Nevertheless, these incidents remain a blemish on CIA's record of interpreting and working within its counterterrorism authorities.

19. (TS/▓▓▓▓▓▓▓▓▓▓▓▓NF) **Devising an Exit Strategy.** One aspect of the program that Agency managers recognized and struggled with was the inability to formulate

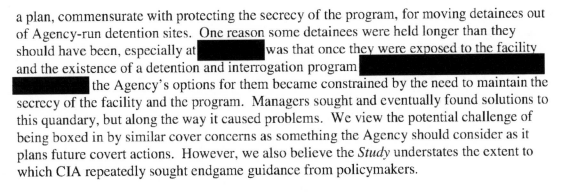

a plan, commensurate with protecting the secrecy of the program, for moving detainees out of Agency-run detention sites. One reason some detainees were held longer than they should have been, especially at ████████ was that once they were exposed to the facility and the existence of a detention and interrogation program ████████████████ ████████ the Agency's options for them became constrained by the need to maintain the secrecy of the facility and the program. Managers sought and eventually found solutions to this quandary, but along the way it caused problems. We view the potential challenge of being boxed in by similar cover concerns as something the Agency should consider as it plans future covert actions. However, we also believe the *Study* understates the extent to which CIA repeatedly sought endgame guidance from policymakers.

- (S//OC/NF) Throughout this period, CIA repeatedly sought guidance on the disposition of detainees. The White House and Attorney General had determined that CIA detainees would not be handed over to the US criminal justice system; the Department of Defense refused to accept custody of CIA detainees; and liaison partners were nervous about hosting detention facilities indefinitely.

20. (S//OC/NF) **Interrogation Techniques**. The *Study* is correct that some officers used unauthorized techniques. In contrast to the impression created by the *Study's* conclusions, however, after the initial period at ████████ and the promulgation of DCI Guidelines, significant improvisation in interrogations occurred only in isolated cases that were reported to and investigated by the OIG and, in some cases, the Department of Justice. Moreover, the *Study* exaggerates how often unauthorized techniques were used because some of the techniques counted as such by the authors— such as cold water dousing and sleep deprivation—were categorized as standard techniques at the time and did not require Headquarters permission for each use.

21. (S//OC/NF) With regard to the waterboard, which was used on three detainees, we acknowledge, as was pointed out in the IG's 2004 *Special Review* and reiterated in the *Study*, that this technique was used with a frequency that exceeded CIA's representations to the Department of Justice's Office of Legal Counsel (OLC), and that this intensity raised serious concerns on the part of the Agency's own medical staff about the lack of available data upon which to draw conclusions about its safety.

- (S//OC/NF) The Attorney General later reaffirmed the legality of the technique despite the intensity of use, but the medical concerns, combined with CIA's increasing knowledge base, its improving skill using less coercive techniques, and the move of al-Qa'ida's senior leaders beyond its reach, ended the use of this technique.

- (U//FOUO) As a result, the waterboard was last used in March 2003—just over a decade ago.

22. (U//FOUO) In considering the manner in which enhanced techniques were used more broadly, we would fault the *Study* for discounting the discretion that officers

applied when the detainees were cooperative or were judged not to have valuable information. The *Study* portrays an Agency zealously seeking to apply enhanced techniques, a judgment that inaccurately characterizes CIA's own internal deliberations about the conduct of interrogations.

- (S//OC/NF) Contrary to the representation outlined in the *Study's* second conclusion, the Agency did not advocate "a novel application of the necessity defense" to justify interrogations. Rather, the draft internal memorandum the *Study* cites warned that invoking the "necessity defense" would be "novel," meaning tenuous or untested, because US courts had previously neither considered nor accepted such an argument.

- (U//FOUO) CIA leadership twice suspended the use of enhanced techniques pending reaffirmation of legal clearance and policy approval from OLC and the White House.

- (S//OC/NF) In some cases where the *Study* criticizes CIA for immediately applying enhanced techniques too quickly, ▮▮▮

- (S//OC/NF) In some instances the only technique used was sleep deprivation, and there were multiple occasions—ignored by the *Study*—in which the Agency applied no enhanced techniques because officers judged detainees were cooperating as a result of standard interrogation and debriefing techniques, or opted to forego specific techniques because officers judged they would most likely only stiffen the resolve of the detainee.

- (S//OC/NF) The *Study's* conclusions also fail to note the general trend that, beginning in April 2003, as interrogators became more knowledgeable, as it became easier to use information from one detainee to get more from another, and as our understanding of the effectiveness of various techniques grew, CIA's interrogations gradually relied less on coercion.

23. (TS//▮▮▮▮▮▮▮▮▮▮▮▮▮▮▮//NF) **Study of Effectiveness.** Although CIA gradually became more knowledgeable about and selective in its use of enhanced interrogations techniques, we agree fully with the *Study's* critique of the Agency's failure to perform a comprehensive analysis of the effectiveness of those techniques. As we discuss in the next section, CIA did, for the most part, accurately assess the value of <u>what</u> it derived in its interrogations; but that does not equate to a robust assessment of the efficacy of <u>how</u> it derived that information relative to other possible approaches. The internal and external studies commissioned in response to an OIG recommendation offered some useful insights, but they fell well short of the kind of systematic, comprehensive, independent assessment of program effectiveness that the Agency should be looking for while assessing its covert actions in the future.

24. (S//OC/NF) **Personnel.** There is no doubt that the shortage of personnel able and willing to participate in the program was a huge challenge. Language-capable officers were in particularly short supply, even more so after the US invasion of Iraq. We agree with the *Study* that some officers with ████████ issues were among the over ████ officers (managers, interrogators, debriefers, linguists, security officers, support and medical personnel), not including contractors, who carried out the program. In some cases, these individuals possessed unique, hard-to-find skills, such as regional languages or debriefing/paramilitary skills. We do not agree, however, with the *Study's* implication that Agency managers made a routine practice of knowingly sending ████ individuals to the field.

25. (U//FOUO) **Accountability.** We gave very careful consideration to the *Study's* assertion that CIA officers who violated policy were only rarely held accountable. Our review of this Conclusion did indeed indicate significant shortcomings in CIA's handling of accountability for problems in the conduct and management of CIA's RDI activities. As we note in our response to Conclusion 16, however, the *Study* lays out two supporting arguments that are best assessed separately, because we agree with—and have expanded on—the first, but the second appears unfounded.

- (S//OC/NF) The first argument is that in some important cases involving clearly evident misconduct, CIA did not in the end sufficiently hold officers accountable even after full investigation and adjudication. We largely concur, although we would take the *Study's* argument one step further. The *Study* focuses on the inadequate consequences meted out for line officers who acted improperly when conducting interrogations in the field or by providing insufficient rationales necessary to justify detentions. To us, an even more compelling concern is that the Agency did not sufficiently broaden and elevate the focus of its accountability efforts to include more senior officers who were responsible for organizing, guiding, staffing, and supervising RDI activities, especially in the beginning.

- (S//OC/NF) The Conclusion's second supporting argument is that there were many more instances of improper actions for which some form of accountability exercise should have been conducted but was not. We found problems with the factual basis for this argument, which we lay out in our response to Conclusion 16.

26. (S//OC/NF) With regard to the first argument, although considerable attention was paid to cases of wrongdoing, we acknowledge that, particularly in the cases cited in the *Study*, the narrow scope of the Agency's accountability efforts yielded outcomes that are, in retrospect, unsatisfying in view of the serious nature of the events. Most notably, we believe that CIA leaders erred in not holding anyone formally accountable for the actions and failure of management related to the death of Gul Rahman at ▮▮▮▮▮▮▮ in 2002.

27. (S//OC/NF) In that case, we can appreciate the reasoning underlying CIA management's decision to overturn an accountability board recommendation that would have imposed sanctions on the least experienced officer involved. The most junior in the chain of command should not have to bear the full weight of accountability when larger, systemic problems exist and when they are thrust into difficult warzone situations by their supervisors and given a risky and difficult task with little preparation or guidance. Still, it is hard to accept that a CIA officer does not bear at least some responsibility for his or her actions, even under trying circumstances.

- (S//OC/NF) Moreover, deciding to minimize the punishment for a junior officer should not have been the end of the matter. CIA had an affirmative obligation to look more deeply into the leadership decisions that helped shape the environment in which the junior officer was required to operate, to examine what could have been done better, and to determine what responsibility, if any, should be fixed at a more senior level.

28. (TS/▮▮▮▮▮▮▮▮▮▮▮▮▮▮NF) The Agency did better in that regard in the case of the improper capture and rendition of Khalid al-Masri, when it went on to hold those who offered flawed legal advice accountable. But in neither the ▮▮▮▮▮▮ nor the al-Masri case—nor in the other cases for which the Agency conducted accountability exercises—were those with broader responsibility for the program held accountable for any management shortcomings that contributed to the outcome.

29. (U//FOUO) Although we do not believe it would be practical or productive to revisit any RDI-related case so long after the events unfolded, we do believe that, looking forward, the Agency should ensure that leaders who run accountability exercises do not limit their sights to the perpetrators of the specific failure or misconduct, but look more broadly at management responsibility and more consistently at any systemic issues. At a minimum, no board should cite a broader issue as a mitigating factor in its accountability decision on an individual without addressing that issue head on, provided it remains practical to do so.

30. (U//FOUO) Having said that, we believe the *Study* is too dismissive in general of the accountability measures taken when officers deviated from policy, regulations, or the law in their conduct of the program. As detailed in our responses to Conclusions 4 and 16, misconduct was reported to the IG, investigated, and if the allegations were substantiated, subjected to accountability review.

- (S//OC/NF) In addition to OIG investigations and criminal prosecutions—including an extensive, multi-year investigation of RDI activity by a Department of Justice special prosecutor, which involved the review of more than 100 detainee cases—CIA convened six accountability proceedings, either at the directorate or higher level, from 2003 to 2012.

- (S//OC/NF) In total, these reviews assessed the performance of 30 individuals (staff officers and contractors), and 16 were deemed accountable and sanctioned. This included administrative actions against CIA officers who engaged in unauthorized interrogation techniques as well as against officers involved in the detention of detainees who did not meet the required standard for Agency detention.

- (S//OC/NF) The OIG conducted two separate major reviews and at least 29 separate investigations of allegations of misconduct. Some of these reviews were self-initiated by Agency components responsible for managing the program. CIA made numerous referrals to the OIG relating to the conduct of Agency officers and their treatment of detainees, during the life of the program as well as after.

- (U//FOUO) CIA took corrective action both in response to OIG recommendations and on its own initiative. And when actions appeared to violate criminal prohibitions, referrals were made to the Department of Justice.

31. (S//OC/NF) All this oversight did, in fact, lead to tensions between CIA leaders and the OIG, owing to the sheer number of investigations underway and some concerns within the workforce about the impact on mission achievement and about the OIG's objectivity. But the dialogue that ensued did not inhibit the OIG from conducting its mission and resulted in recommended changes to the OIG's own practices that Inspector General Helgerson embraced in 2008.

32. **Contractors.** The *Study* correctly points out that the propriety of the multiple roles performed by contracted psychologists—particularly their involvement in performing interrogations as well as assessing the detainees' fitness and the effectiveness of the very techniques they had devised—raised concerns and prompted deliberation within CIA, but it fails to note that at least some of these concerns were addressed. Early in 2003, Headquarters promulgated guidance on the scope of the contractor psychologists' involvement in individual interrogations. It affirmed that no contractor could issue the psychological assessment of record.

- (TS/███████████NF) We acknowledge that the contract for the company that the two psychologists formed, ███████████ ███ called on them to evaluate the effectiveness of the techniques they had devised, thereby creating a conflict. CIA has since taken steps to ensure that our contracts do not have similar clauses with the contractors grading their own work.

- (TS/ ████████████████ NF) The *Study's* citation of the cost of ████████ contract requires clarification. Although the *potential* "value" of the contract was in excess of $180 million if all options had been exercised, in fact the firm was actually paid less than half of that by the time the contract was terminated in 2009.

- (TS/ ████████████ NF) The Study's assertion that the two psychologists had "no relevant experience" is incorrect. ████████████ ██████ had the closest proximate expertise available to CIA at the time the program was authorized. They had ████████ years of experience, respectively, with the US Air Force's Survival Evasion Resistance and Escape training program, where each of them had served as ████████████████ ████████ In addition, ████████████ had conducted academic research and written a number of research papers on such topics as resistance training, captivity familiarization, and learned helplessness.

33. (TS/ ████████████████ NF) **Monetary Costs.** The *Study* suggests that CIA acted improperly when it made lump-sum payments to foreign government officials to encourage governments to clandestinely host detention sites, in some cases without requiring ████████████████████████ Inducement payments ████████ ████████████████████████████ are neither unusual nor improper.

- (S//OC/NF) CIA has statutory authority to make subsidy payments to foreign officials without requiring the receiving governments to provide ████████████ ████████████████████████ CIA accounted for funds in the RDI program internally according to required procedures.

34. (S//OC/NF) **Relations with Partners.** In its assessment of the costs of the program, the *Study* cites "tensions with US partners and allies" and "damage to bilateral intelligence relationships with nations unwilling to provide intelligence that might contribute to CIA detention and interrogation operations." It is certainly true that CIA, as did the US Government as a whole, called on allies and friends after 9/11 to assist in a variety of ways in the fight against international terrorism. It is also true that leaks resulted in varying amounts of domestic fallout in these countries. However, the assessment of our own political analysts who had no connection to the program, as well as contemporaneous diplomatic reporting, do not support the conclusion that the leaks "strained relations" between the US and its partners. ████████████████████████ ████████████████████████████████

35. (S ████ NF) The *Study* also incorrectly characterizes the impact on our relationship with liaison partners who could not help in this area. CIA is occasionally

faced with situations in which we have authorities to undertake activities that our partners cannot or in which our partners are permitted to undertake activities that we cannot. The *Study* correctly notes, for example, that ███████████████████████████ decided not to provide "information that could lead to the rendition or detention of al-Qa'ida or other terrorists to the US Government." This decision did inhibit some potential sharing of operational information. However, the *Study* exaggerates the overall negative impact on the Agency's intelligence relationship.

- (S████████NF) The constraint on sharing lead information that might result in a rendition or detention did not prevent a substantial growth in overall sharing on counterterrorism after 9/11. ████████████████████
██

36. (U//FOUO) Looking forward, we drew the following lessons from our review of the management and execution of the RDI program. We must:

- (TS/███████████████NF) More robustly, objectively, and systematically evaluate the effectiveness of the various tools, techniques, and operations used in our covert actions.

- (TS/███████████████NF) Design all covert actions under the assumption the action may eventually leak. Include an exit strategy in our planning and resist proceeding without careful policy consideration and approval of that strategy.

- (S//OC/NF) Try to better factor information ██████████████ ████████████████ into the selection process for particularly sensitive assignments.

- (U//FOUO) Further institutionalize the significant improvements made in recent years to our close relationship with OLC by establishing a formal mechanism for regularly reviewing OLC guidance to ensure that it reflects any material change in circumstance.

- (U//FOUO) Ensure that accountability adequately extends to those responsible for any broader, systemic or management failures, and that corrective actions are taken to address those failures.

C. (U) Contrary to CIA representations, the program failed to produce intelligence that was otherwise unavailable and that enabled CIA to disrupt plots, capture terrorists, or save lives.

37. (U//FOUO) Our group conducted a careful review of the *Study's* 20 examples of the value of the information CIA obtained as a result of the RDI effort, and

12

we have provided detailed responses to each in Tab C. We summarize below the results of our review, which are in fairly stark contrast to the *Study's* conclusions. In commenting on the value of the information derived from detainees, we are not arguing in favor of the decision to use the enhanced techniques to which these detainees were subjected. We are not endorsing those techniques, we are not making an "ends-justify-the-means" case for them, nor are we implying that those techniques were the only way to obtain the information from detainees. We only are assessing the accuracy of CIA's representations in response to the *Study's* allegations that those representations were false.

38. (U/~~FOUO~~) We concluded that all of the examples fit within and support CIA's overall representations that information obtained from its interrogations produced unique intelligence that helped the US disrupt plots, capture terrorists, better understand the enemy, prevent another mass casualty attack, and save lives. We must add, however, that in some of the Agency's representations it failed to meet its own standards for precision and accuracy of detail. An Agency whose reputation and value to the policymaker rests on the precision of the language it uses in intelligence reporting and analysis must ensure that such representations are as accurate as possible.

- (U/~~FOUO~~) Nonetheless, even in those cases, we found that the actual impact of the information acquired from interrogations was significant and still supported CIA's overall judgments about the value of the information acquired from detainees.

39. (U/~~FOUO~~) In one of the 20 examples, we found that CIA mischaracterized on several occasions, including in prominent representations such as President Bush's 2006 speech, the impact on specific terrorist plotting of information acquired from a set of CIA interrogations.

- (U/~~FOUO~~) CIA said the information "helped stop a planned attack on the US Consulate in Karachi," when it should have said it "revealed ongoing attack plotting against the US official presence in Karachi that prompted the Consulate to take further steps to protect its officers."

40. (U/~~FOUO~~) There were four instances in which CIA used imprecise language or made errors in some of its representations that, although regrettable, did not significantly affect the thrust of those representations.

41. (U/~~FOUO~~) In another four examples, we found single, isolated representations in which CIA was imprecise in describing the relative impact of the information or the manner in which it was acquired. These were not "frequently cited" or "repeatedly represented" as the *Study* asserts, and they did not appear in the President's speech.

42. (U//FOUO) In the other 11 examples, we determined that CIA's representations were consistently accurate, contrary to the *Study's* assertion that the Agency misrepresented them all.

43. (S//OC/NF) One such example—the information that helped identify the courier who ultimately led CIA to Bin Ladin's compound in Abbottabad—is worth separate comment due to the Congressional and media attention it has garnered. The *Study* claims that "much of the critical intelligence on Abu Ahmed [sic] al-Kuwaiti was acquired prior to—and independently of—the CIA detention and interrogation program." We found that the intelligence the Agency had on Abu Ahmad before acquiring information on him from detainees in CIA custody was insufficient to distinguish him from many other Bin Ladin associates until additional information from detainees put it into context and allowed CIA to better understand his true role and potential in the hunt for Bin Ladin. As such, the information CIA obtained from these detainees did play a role—in combination with other streams of intelligence—in finding the al-Qa'ida leader.

- (U//FOUO) As DCIA Panetta and ADCIA Morell have stated to Congress and publicly, it is impossible to know in hindsight whether CIA could have obtained from detainees without using enhanced techniques the same information that helped it find Bin Ladin. It is also unknowable whether the Agency eventually would have acquired other intelligence that would have allowed it to successfully pursue the Abu Ahmad lead or perhaps some other successful lead without the information acquired from detainees in CIA custody.

44. (U//FOUO) Finally, we should note that our review showed that the *Study* failed to include instances of important information acquired from detainees that CIA cited more frequently and prominently in its representations than several of the examples the authors chose to include.

- (U//FOUO) In the same set of documents from which the authors of the *Study* selected some representations we made only once, there are other examples we cited in those same documents seven times.

45. (U//FOUO) In the *Study's* treatment of the 20 examples, we note a number of errors of fact, interpretation, and contextualization that appear to have led the authors to conclude that the information CIA derived in each instance had little-to-no unique value. It is just as important to note that the *Study* also discounts the <u>aggregate</u> impact of the intelligence derived from detainees in CIA custody.

- (S//OC/NF) Perhaps the most important context that the *Study* ignores in its assessment of the information obtained from detainees is how little CIA knew, despite considerable effort, about al-Qa'ida and its allies on 9/11 to inform efforts to prevent another terrorist attack. The sum total of information provided from detainees in CIA custody substantially advanced the Agency's strategic and tactical understanding of the enemy in ways that continue to allow it to disrupt al-Qa'ida's leadership and its terrorist planning to this day.

46. (U/~~FOUO~~) We do want to add, however, that in hindsight, we believe that assertions the Agency made to the effect that the information it acquired could not have been obtained some other way were sincerely believed but were also inherently speculative. Although it is indeed impossible for us to imagine how the same counterterrorism results could have been achieved without <u>any</u> information from detainees, we also believe—as we note above—that it is unknowable whether, without enhanced techniques, CIA or non-CIA interrogators could have acquired the same information from those detainees.

- (~~S//OC/NF~~) CIA officers who witnessed detainees' initial demeanor believed they would not have succumbed to less coercive approaches, at least not in time for their information to be operationally useful.

- (~~S//OC/NF~~) But CIA is a resourceful organization, and we believe it is unwise for its officers to make categorical and ultimately hypothetical assertions about what might or might not be accomplished using alternate means.

47. (~~TS/████████████████NF~~) Looking forward, the lesson to be drawn under this theme is obvious: We must ensure that our representations of the effectiveness of covert action are drawn from assessments that are made at arm's length from the component running the program and that they adhere to the highest standards of analytic tradecraft, especially precision of language.

D. (U) CIA resisted internal and external oversight, and misrepresented the program to Congress, the Executive Branch, and the media.

48. (U/~~FOUO~~) While we were able to find points in the preceding themes with which to both agree and disagree, the *Study* seems to most seriously diverge from the facts and, indeed, from simple plausibility in its characterizations of the manner in which CIA dealt with others with regard to the RDI program. The *Study* would have the reader believe that CIA "actively" avoided and interfered with oversight by the Executive Branch and Congress, impeded other agencies, withheld information from the President, and misled the American people.

- (U/~~FOUO~~) We would observe that, to accomplish this, there would have had to have been a years-long conspiracy among CIA leaders at all levels, supported by a large number of analysts and other line officers. This conspiracy would have had to include three former CIA Directors, including one who led the Agency after the program had largely wound down.

49. (U/~~FOUO~~) We cannot vouch for every individual statement that was made over the years of the program, and we acknowledge that some of those statements were

wrong. But the image portrayed in the *Study* of an organization that—on an institutional scale—intentionally misled and routinely resisted oversight from the White House, the Congress, the Department of Justice, and its own OIG simply does not comport with the record.

- (U//~~FOUO~~) Many of the *Study's* charges that CIA misrepresented are based on the authors' flawed analysis of the value of the intelligence obtained from detainees. But whether the Committee accepts their assessment or ours, we still must question a report that impugns the integrity of so many CIA officers when it implies—as it does clearly throughout the conclusions—that the Agency's assessments were willfully misrepresented in a calculated effort to manipulate.

50. ~~(TS/~~   ~~NF)~~ With regard to how widely CIA briefed among other agencies and the Congress, there is no question that, for sound operational and liaison equity reasons, the RDI program was extremely sensitive. As a result, the White House, which has responsibility for determining need to know for covert action, placed significant restrictions on who could be read in, limiting the oversight committees to the Chair and Vice Chair only. We do not want to suggest that CIA chafed under these restrictions; on the contrary, it undoubtedly was comfortable with them. But as we have detailed in our responses to Conclusions 3, 5, 8, and 13, briefings did occur for those the White House determined had a need to know; and in the case of briefings for the leaders of the oversight committees, those briefings occurred regularly, to include briefings from the IG about problems in the program.

51. ~~(C//OC/NF)~~ Looking forward, having engaged in an effort to piece together the record of our interactions with others on this sensitive program, a key lesson we took away is that recordkeeping in the Office of Congressional Affairs and in the Office of Public Affairs on CIA's interactions with Congress and the media, respectively, should be improved. We would note, however, that Agency records were sufficient to show that CIA did not, as the *Study* alleges, intentionally misrepresent to anyone the overall value of the intelligence acquired, the number of detainees, the propensity of detainees to withhold and fabricate, or other aspects of the program.

Recommendations

52. (U) In the foregoing discussion, we have identified a number of broad lessons learned that we believe still apply to CIA today, even though the Agency has made substantial progress in a number of areas since—and in part because of—its

experience with RDI. From these lessons learned, we developed recommendations for specific, concrete actions going forward.

(S//OC/NF) **Recommendation 1:** **Improve management's ability to manage risk by submitting more covert action programs to the special review process** ███████ Direct the Executive Director, ████████ to expand the current process of conducting special annual reviews of the execution of CIA ████████████ to include the execution of authorities that cover other particularly sensitive activities, ████████████████████ At the inception of a new covert action program, ████████ would consider and recommend to DCIA whether a special review is warranted. Such operations would include, but not be limited to, those that:

- (S//OC/NF) Have unusually high potential, if they are disclosed or fail, to damage important US Government foreign policy interests or entail other high costs;

- ████████████████████████████████

- ████████████████████████████████

- (S//OC/NF) Involve unusually large expenditures of resources;

- ████████████████████████████████

(S//OC/NF) **Recommendation 2:** **Better plan covert actions by explicitly addressing at the outset the implications of leaks, an exit strategy, lines of authority, and resources.** Direct the Executive Director, ████████████████ to ensure that the Agency submits for inclusion in all future covert action findings a section that fully addresses the implications of unauthorized public disclosure for the program and US foreign policy, as well as a section that lays out an exit strategy and the challenges that entering into the program will pose for ending that program. Also, direct that all findings are to be accompanied by an internal use memorandum that addresses program implementation, to include lines of authority, specific organizational responsibilities for key elements of the program, and how resource requirements will be met.

(S//OC/NF) **Recommendation 3:** **Revamp the way in which CIA assesses the effectiveness of covert actions.** Direct the Executive Director, ████████████████ to develop within 90 days concrete options and a recommendation for a structure and/or process that would be capable of producing regular, systematic, and analytically rigorous assessments of the effectiveness of CIA covert action programs, and ensuring the accuracy and consistency of CIA representations of the same.

(U/~~FOUO~~) **Recommendation 4:** **Ensure that all necessary information is factored into the selection process for officers being considered for the most sensitive assignments.** Direct the Executive Director, working with the General Counsel and Chief of Human Resources, to develop options within 90 days for better factoring into the selection process for sensitive covert action positions relevant information ███████ ███████████████████████ and to make a recommendation as to whether or how to amend current procedures.

(U/~~FOUO~~) **Recommendation 5:** **Create a mechanism for periodically revalidating OLC guidance on which the Agency continues to rely.** Recognizing that CIA maintains frequent communication with the Office of Legal Counsel (OLC) concerning counterterrorism and other covert action activities and the legal authorities and prohibitions governing them, direct the General Counsel to continue such communication and, working with the Executive Director, to develop a formal mechanism for triggering systematic reviews of OLC opinions regarding ongoing covert action programs with the goal of ensuring that OLC's legal analysis is confirmed or updated as warranted by material changes in facts and circumstances.

(U/~~FOUO~~) **Recommendation 6:** **Broaden the scope of accountability reviews.** Direct that the Executive Director ensure that all memoranda establishing and laying out the scope of an accountability review board, including directorate level boards, explicitly call on the board to assess and make recommendations to address any systemic issues revealed by the case, and to expand the scope of the review as warranted to include officers responsible for those systemic problems.

(~~C/OC/NF~~) **Recommendation 7:** **Improve recordkeeping for interactions with the media.** Direct the Director of the Office of Public Affairs (OPA) and the Chief Information Officer to develop a concrete plan to improve recordkeeping on CIA's interactions with the media. OPA's records going forward should reflect each interaction with the media and the content of that interaction. This plan should be completed within 90 days of the arrival of a new Director of OPA.

(U/~~FOUO~~) **Recommendation 8:** **Improve recordkeeping for interactions with Congress.** Direct the Director of the Office of Congressional Affairs (OCA) and the Chief Information Officer to develop a concrete plan to improve recordkeeping on CIA's interactions with Congress. OCA's records going forward should reflect each interaction with Congress and the content of that interaction. OCA should work with the oversight committees to develop better access to transcripts of CIA testimony and briefings. This plan should be completed within 90 days of the arrival of a new Director of OCA.

> **(U) Conclusion 1: The CIA was unprepared as it initiated a program of indefinite, clandestine detention using coercive interrogation techniques. The CIA did not adequately develop and monitor its initial detention and interrogation activities.**

(U) We fully agree with Conclusion 1 of *The Senate Select Committee on Intelligence's Study of the Central Intelligence Agency's Detention and Interrogation Program* (hereafter referred to as the *Study*), as the conclusion is broadly summarized above. We have a different perspective, however, on some of the points made in the *Study's* supporting discussion for Conclusion 1.

(S//OC/NF) CIA was indeed unprepared to initiate a rendition, detention, and interrogation (RDI) program. In response to 9/11, with the expectation that more mass casualty attacks were in the offing, CIA quickly redirected substantial resources to counterterrorism, undertook high risk operations ▮▮▮▮▮▮▮▮▮▮▮▮▮▮▮▮▮▮▮▮▮▮▮▮▮ and enlisted the aid of liaison partners across the globe in the fight against al-Qa'ida.

(TS/▮▮▮▮▮▮▮NF) Prior to 2001, CIA had only limited experience rendering detainees ▮▮▮▮▮▮▮ and a 1998 Memorandum of Notification (MoN) limited the Agency's authorities to detain individuals, ▮▮▮▮▮▮▮▮▮▮▮▮▮▮▮▮▮▮▮ ▮▮▮ Following the 9/11 attacks and the President's subsequent approval of the 2001 MoN, CIA was granted unprecedented, broad authority to render individuals who "pose continuing or serious threats of violence or death to U.S. persons or interests or who are planning terrorist attacks"

- (TS/▮▮▮▮▮▮▮NF) Almost immediately, discussions with the National Security Council (NSC) began that covered the legal and policy parameters for how al-Qa'ida and Taliban prisoners would be managed and treated by DoD and CIA. Abu Zubaydah's 28 March 2002 capture provided the impetus to draw upon those discussions and formally structure a program to render, unilaterally detain and interrogate al-Qa'ida leaders.

- (TS/▮▮▮▮▮▮▮NF) Simultaneously, in 2001 and 2002, CIA engaged in a variety of planning efforts to develop locations and guidelines for how it would execute detention authorities and explored options with contract psychologists for interrogating al-Qa'ida members.

- (U//FOUO) CIA faced the need to stand up a program to house and interrogate al-Qa'ida leaders and operatives ▮▮▮▮▮▮▮▮▮▮▮▮ with no cadre of trained and experienced interrogators, little experience handling and moving prisoners, and no core competency in prison management. The Agency had too few analysts and linguists with the expertise required to support an RDI program.

(S//OC/NF) We also agree with the broad conclusion that "The CIA did not adequately develop and monitor its initial detention and interrogation activities." In agreeing with this statement, however, we draw particular attention to the word "initial." As we discuss further in response to other conclusions, one of the main flaws of the *Study* is that it tars the Agency's entire RDI effort with the mistakes of the first few months. We are not minimizing the early consequences of CIA's failure to adequately manage its *initial* RDI activities, consequences that include the initial conditions and treatment of detainees at ▮▮▮▮ that culminated in the death of Gul Rahman in November 2002, two months after the first detainee arrived there. But the *Study* as

1

a whole leads the reader to believe that the management shortcomings that marked those initial months persisted throughout the program, which is historically inaccurate.

(S//OC/NF) As noted in the *Study*, CIA sought to fill the vacuum in its RDI capabilities in part by turning to others inside and outside the government for expertise and manpower, and in part by leveraging liaison assistance. As we discuss in our response to Conclusion 15, what CIA failed to do at the outset was to <u>immediately</u> respond to the extraordinary and high-risk requirements of conducting RDI activities by establishing and giving adequate management attention and resources to a dedicated, centrally managed program office tasked with quickly promulgating operational guidelines for RDI activities, taking control of those activities worldwide, and monitoring those activities on a day-to-day basis.

- (S//OC/NF) As a result, although the confinement conditions and treatment of high profile detainees like Abu Zubaydah were closely scrutinized at all levels of management from the outset, the same cannot be said for the first couple of months of CIA's handling of lower-profile detainees in ▮▮▮▮▮▮ It was during those months that grim confinement conditions and inadequate monitoring of detainees were allowed to exist at ▮▮▮▮

- While we do not minimize the gravity of the mistakes made early in the program, none of the Study's key observations relating to this period are new, but rather have been chronicled by multiple internal and external investigations

(TS/▮▮▮▮▮▮▮▮NF) Following the death of Gul Rahman, CIA centralized the management of and accountability for all detention facilities in a single program office, which endeavored to address the shortcomings at ▮▮▮▮ as well as isolated problems elsewhere. That office also developed standards and guidelines for operating all CIA-controlled detention and interrogation facilities and monitored adherence to those guidelines.

- (TS/▮▮▮▮▮▮▮▮NF) As discussed in our responses to Conclusions 15 and 19, we acknowledge that resource constraints dogged the program throughout its existence, especially in ▮▮▮▮▮▮ and especially after the invasion of Iraq increased the competition for language-capable personnel. We also acknowledge that, although conditions at ▮▮▮▮ improved, the Agency did not—as we believe it should have—put the facility under ▮▮▮▮▮▮▮▮ the full-time management of a more senior CIA officer, as was standard practice elsewhere. The Agency was also unable to fully bring the facility up to the standard of our other detention facilities by the time it was closed in ▮▮▮▮

- (S//OC/NF) Nonetheless, IG reviews show that the program office substantially improved the oversight and management of the RDI program as a whole, including in ▮▮▮▮▮▮ from early 2003 onward. This was not a panacea—other mistakes were made, investigated, and corrected along the way—but the program was much better developed and managed after the initial months of RDI activities.

(U//FOUO) With regard to some of the other claims in the *Study's* discussion of Conclusion 1:

- (TS/▮▮▮▮▮▮▮▮NF) The *Study* implies that CIA's transfer of Abu Zubaydah to Country ▮ was conducted without adequately consulting appropriate officials in the US

2

Government. After Abu Zubaydah was captured, CIA was forced to move quickly to identify and prepare a suitable location, and to do so with great secrecy. The Agency does not have records indicating exactly which US officials were consulted before the decision was made, but the *Study* cites documentation of Presidential approval for the plan to render Abu Zubaydah on 29 March. The *Study* also quotes from the paper CIA prepared for the Principals highlighting a range of options for his disposition. Once the plan was approved, but *before* Abu Zubaydah was transferred on █ March 2002, CIA notified the Assistant Secretary of State ██████████████ who pledged to brief the Secretary and Deputy Secretary, as well as ████████████ host country leaders in Country █ As cited in the *Study*, no one who was briefed on the transfer objected, and several US officials were described as supportive.

- (TS/ ████████████████ NF) While we have acknowledged that CIA Headquarters in the initial months inadequately organized and monitored our RDI activities, the delegation of some select detention authorities from the DCI to Headquarters subordinates was a practical step necessitated by the pace of operations in 2002 and consistent with current practice. The Deputy Director of Operations (DDO) further delegated these authorities to CIA officers on the ground ████████████████ because of the concern that situations would arise where officers could not delay action for Headquarters to deliberate and communicate capture and detention approval. That delegation was largely rescinded in June 2003, although it was recognized that unusual, exigent circumstances could still apply in isolated cases.

- (TS/ ████████████ NF) We believe that the *Study* errs by implying that 60 individuals were detained without any review through 10 June 2003 . In fact, the vast majority of these 60 detainees were captured and initially detained ██████ ████████ they were rendered for detention in ████████████ with Headquarters approvals. The case of Ibrahim Haqqani is also instructive. The U.S. Military captured him in Afghanistan on 4 May 2003 and brought him to ████████ Following review at Headquarters and subsequent direction, ████████ Station transferred him to ██████ custody after eight days while working out approvals and logistics for subsequent transfer to U.S. Military custody, as the *Study* acknowledges, because Headquarters judged that he did not merit detention by the CIA.

(S//OC/NF) **Conclusion 2: Prior to the detention of the first CIA detainee, CIA officers began examining the legal implications of using interrogation techniques considered to be torture by foreign governments and non-governmental organizations. The CIA Office of General Counsel assessed that "a novel application of the necessity defense" could be used "to avoid prosecution of US officials who tortured to obtain information that saved many lives." After these determinations—beginning in July 2002 and continuing to the present day—the CIA has represented that the CIA's enhanced interrogation techniques were necessary to acquire "otherwise unavailable" intelligence that "saved lives."**

(S//OC/NF) We disagree with this conclusion. The draft research memorandum prepared by CIA Office of General Counsel (OGC) attorneys in 2001 (the "Draft Memo") outlined, among other things, the possibility of asserting necessity as a defense to potential criminal torture charges arising from RDI Program activities. But nothing in record indicates either that CIA relied upon the Draft Memo in implementing the RDI program or that the Draft Memo was the motivating force behind CIA's subsequent representations regarding the program.

(S//OC/NF) First, the Draft Memo did not advise CIA to rely upon elements of the necessity defense either as a means to exonerate officers of potential criminal torture charges or as a legal basis for applying enhanced interrogation techniques to detainees. Instead, the Draft Memo pointedly stated: "In sum: US courts have not yet considered the necessity defense in the context of torture/murder/assault cases. . . . It would, therefore, be a novel application of the necessity defense to avoid prosecution of US officials who torture to obtain information that saved many lives; however, if we follow the Israeli example, CIA could argue that the torture was necessary to prevent imminent, significant, physical harm to persons, where there is no other available means to prevent the harm."

- (S//OC/NF) Rather than advocating reliance upon a necessity defense to exonerate officers charged with torture, the Draft Memo instead warned that no US court has ever considered—let alone accepted—such a "novel"[1] argument. Although the Draft Memo further stated that CIA "could argue" such a defense under certain circumstances, the Draft Memo cannot be read to advocate reliance on the necessity defense.

- (S//OC/NF) In addition, the Draft Memo made clear that with reference to the experience of Israel, legal authorities there "specifically note[] that although necessity can be used as a *post factum* defense, it cannot serve as a source of positive, *ab initio* authority for the systemic (even if rare) use of torture as a valid interrogation tool." This contradicts the implication of Conclusion 2 that the Draft Memo invited reliance upon availability of a necessity defense in designing or implementing the program.

---

[1] (U) In the legal context, "novel" is generally not a laudatory characterization of an argument. To the contrary, lawyers and courts typically apply the term to connote skepticism of an argument that is tenuous or untested. *See, e.g., Kingsland v. Dorsey*, 338 U.S. 318, 325 (1949) (Jackson, J., dissenting) ("If, however, a lawyer is to be called upon to be the first example of condemnation for an offense so tenuous, vague and *novel*, the least courts should require is that the case against him be clearly proved.") (emphasis added); *Mathur v. Board of Trustees of Southern Illinois University*, 317 F.3d 738, 744 (7th Cir. 2003) ("A client's case could present *novel* or untested legal theories which an attorney may not believe will be successful.") (emphasis added).

4

- The legal basis for the program was not a speculative "necessity defense," but rather paragraph 4 of the 17 September 2001 MoN. Enhanced techniques were one tool used to implement these authorities, and were reviewed by DoJ's Office of Legal Counsel (OLC) explicitly for the purpose of determining that they did not constitute torture or otherwise violate the law; the only conditions under which a "necessity defense" would ever, even theoretically, arise.

(S//OC/NF) The *Study* also suggests that burnishing CIA's defense against potential criminal charges served as a motive to disseminate inaccurate information about the effectiveness of the program. In fact, the Draft Memo and CIA's research on potential criminal defenses had no bearing at all on CIA's disclosures or factual representations regarding the program, and the *Study* provides no factual support for this claim.

- (S//OC/NF) To support the contention that the Draft Memo motivated or colored CIA's subsequent disclosures, the *Study* quotes a 2004 email in which ███████████CTC/LGL requested that personnel compile specific examples in which use of enhanced techniques directly led to information that saved lives. However, there is no causal link between the rather obscure 2001 Draft Memo, which set out a speculative, "novel" legal theory, and CIA's independent operational assessment that the program was effective and produced intelligence that enabled disruption of terror plots, thereby saving lives. Also absent from the *Study* is the further admonition contained in █████ CTC/LGL's email that any such examples provided must be "iron clad," "demonstrably supported by cable citations" or other sources, and "absolutely verifiable."

- (S//OC/NF) In addition, the *Study* critiques CIA—and the Draft Memo in particular—for failing to provide a "factual basis for the belief that the use of torture might be necessary to save 'thousands of lives.'" In fact, the Draft Memo professed no such belief, nor did it attempt to address the efficacy of torture as an interrogation tactic in any of its six pages. In context, the Draft Memo addressed torture "saving thousands of lives" only as a hypothetical scenario under which foreign states might be unlikely to condemn the act.

(TS/███████████████NF) In sum, the *Study* overstates the Draft Memo's significance. The Draft Memo and the associated MON draft legal appendix documents represented an effort by CIA to conduct initial legal research regarding the body of laws that could be applicable to the program. The Draft Memo served as an exercise to evaluate the prospect of asserting a necessity defense in the event criminal torture charges were ever asserted against CIA officers; it provided no analysis regarding the likelihood of such charges arising, the potential effectiveness of torture in obtaining intelligence, or whether particular enhanced interrogation techniques should be implemented as part of the RDI program. Moreover, it did not advocate reliance on the elements of the necessity defense to exonerate officers of potential criminal charges arising out of the RDI program or to justify the application of enhanced interrogation techniques. The Draft Memo is simply an example of Agency lawyers doing their jobs; examining all contingencies and producing legal analysis of issues of potential relevance to CIA programs.

> **(U) Conclusion 3: The CIA avoided Executive Branch oversight of its detention and interrogation activities by the White House and the National Security Council Principals and staff by withholding information related to the CIA detention and interrogation program and providing inaccurate information about the effectiveness and operation of the program.**

(U) We disagree with the *Study's* conclusion that the Agency avoided Executive branch oversight or that it withheld or provided inaccurate information about the effectiveness and operation of the Program.

(S//OC/NF) The record and the *Study* are replete with documentation of CIA's consultation and coordination with elements of the Executive branch, beginning as early as November 2001 with policy discussions among the various agencies on detention facilities, including multiple instances of Executive branch engagement on the detention and interrogation program. This coordination directly involved the Vice President; Counsel to the President and Vice President; the National Security Advisor and Deputy National Security Advisor; the National Security Legal Advisor; elements of the Department of Justice's Office of Legal Counsel and Criminal Division; and the Attorney General and Deputy Attorney General.

- (S//OC/NF) The *Study* asserts that the President was not briefed in a timely way on program details. While Agency records on the subject are admittedly incomplete, former President Bush has stated in his autobiography that he discussed the program, including the use of enhanced techniques, with then-DCIA Tenet in 2002, prior to application of the techniques on Abu Zubaydah, and personally approved the techniques.

- (S//OC/NF) The decision to delay briefing the Secretaries of State and Defense, referenced in the *Study*, was made by the White House, not CIA, which stood ready to brief them as directed. This was a Presidential program, authorized, coordinated, and administered through the President's National Security Advisor and staff. CIA did not have the unilateral authority to brief individuals or groups independent of Presidential direction as conveyed by the National Security Advisor.

(U) The Study also asserts that the CIA withheld and provided inaccurate information about the effectiveness and operation of the program. CIA's response to Conclusion 9 and Appendix A provides a detailed discussion of matters relating to the effectiveness of the program and Agency assertions regarding that issue.

> **(U) Conclusion 4: The CIA avoided effective oversight of its detention and interrogation activities by the CIA's Office of Inspector General. The CIA resisted efforts by the Inspector General to examine aspects of the CIA detention and interrogation program, and provided significant inaccurate information to the Office of Inspector General during the drafting of the Inspector General's Special Review of the program. The inaccurate information was included in the final May 2004 Special Review. In 2005, CIA Director Porter Goss directed the Inspector General not to initiate any new reviews of the program until it had completed the reviews already underway. In 2007, CIA Director Michael Hayden conducted an unprecedented review of the CIA's Office of Inspector General, largely in response to its inquiries into the CIA detention and interrogation program.**

(U) We do not agree with the *Study's* assessment that it avoided effective oversight of its detention and interrogation activities by its Office of Inspector General (OIG). CIA engagement's with the OIG over the years was robust and the Agency did not block institutional or individual cooperation. Throughout the period, the OIG affirmed in its Semiannual Reports that it found full and direct access to all Agency information relevant to the performance of its duties. Had circumstances been otherwise, the IG would have been obligated to make that fact known to Congress. As further evidence of this access, the OIG produced a wealth of assessments, which were made available not only to CIA senior leadership but also to Congressional overseers from 2003, when the first OIG RDI-related review began, to 2012 when the last OIG RDI-related investigation was concluded. We acknowledge that two DCIA's did engage with the OIG with respect to its efforts on the RDI program, but, in both cases, this reflected an effort to find an appropriate balance between OIG's mission and those of other CIA components.

(S//OC/NF) OIG oversight included counterterrorism audit, inspection, and numerous investigations that resulted in both positive and negative findings on the conduct of the RDI program.

- (U/FOUO)The comprehensive Special Review, *"Counterterrorism Detention and Interrogation Activities (September 2001-October 2003),"* was published in May 2004.

- (S//OC/NF) The OIG conducted nearly 60 investigations on RDI-related matters. In over 50, OIG found the initial allegations to be unsubstantiated or otherwise did not make findings calling for accountability review. Of the remaining cases, one resulted in a felony conviction, one resulted in termination of a contractor and revocation of his security clearances, and six led to Agency accountability reviews.

(U/FOUO) The *Study* is correct in noting that the OIG's work resulted in some tension within CIA. However, on balance we concluded that, although CIA officers may not have been comfortable engaging with the IG on RDI-related matters, when they did so they nevertheless generally provided accurate information on the operation and effectiveness of the program.

- (S//OC/NF) Some CIA officers clearly did perceive a lack of objectivity on the part of some OIG officers who were evaluating the program. In a memorandum for the record dated 25 August 2005, a CTC officer stated that an OIG officer opined that Gul Rahman had been "killed" and that the OIG officer "appeared to have presumed ill intent" with regard to the role of CIA officers. ████████████████████████

- (U/FOUO) This is only a small part of the story, however. Many OIG investigations associated with the RDI program were initiated as a result of concerns expressed by Agency employees working in the program, evidence that employees believed they could reach out to OIG and have their views taken seriously. Many allegations were found to be unsubstantiated, and did not lead to OIG Reports of Investigation.

- (S//OC/NF) We assess that CIA officers, with rare exceptions, provided accurate assessments to the OIG. The *Study's* assertion to the contrary is simply reflective of its more general conclusion that CIA repeatedly misrepresented the effectiveness of the program. There were two factual errors conveyed to OIG by CIA officers for the 2004 Report that we did not rectify at the time. We address both of these issues in detail in our response to the *Study's* Conclusion 9 and in our comments on the Case Studies. As discussed there, we disagree with the *Study's* overall appraisal of our representations.

- (S//OC/NF) Finally, it is worth highlighting that OIG reviews included instances in which the OIG recommended that individuals be reviewed for lack of candor during the course of the investigations. In four of those instances, the review process confirmed there had been a lack of full cooperation and candor, and the individuals involved were given disciplinary sanctions. Accountability is further discussed in our response to Conclusion 16.

(S//OC/NF) The *Study's* contention that actions by two DCIAs were intended to impede OIG's activities is also flawed. DCIA Goss did send a memo on 21 July 2005 with a request that the OIG not begin new reviews of the Counterterrorism Center and instead address the backlog of uncompleted OIG RDI work. He noted that he was "increasingly concerned about the cumulative impact of the OIG's work on CTC's performance." His request came at a time when OIG claims on CTC attention and resources were growing as a result of an increasing number of reviews, some of which were taking months or longer, even as intelligence indicated, and events on the ground demonstrated, that al Qa'ida was reconstituting itself. The DCIA's request thus sought to strike a balance between the critical missions both OIG and CTC had to perform.

- (S//OC/NF) It is worth underscoring that DCIA Goss's request ultimately had no impact on the OIG's role. A 25 July 2005 response memo from the Inspector General (IG), in which the IG resolutely held his ground, ended the matter. Our records indicate the OIG did not halt or reduce its efforts.

(S//OC/NF) DCIA Hayden's engagement sought to address and clarify competing missions. OIG's active posture sparked debate regarding its role vis-a-vis other CIA components. As a result, Director Hayden in 2007 initially tasked Special Counselor Robert Dietz to assess how OIG and OGC interacted on legal issues. This was intended to address the issue of whether the CIA was being caught between OIG and OGC as differing sources of "final" legal guidance. Also at the time, an Accountability Board, convened in response to an OIG report of investigation on the death of detainee Manadal al-Jamaidi, received complaints of alleged OIG bias and unfair treatment of CIA officers. Dietz was subsequently asked to include those complaints as part of his review.

- (S//OC/NF) Dietz's review included a number of recommendations intended to strengthen the methodology and conduct of OIG investigations, and the results of the review were reported in writing to the HPSCI and SSCI Chairmen and Vice Chairmen in January 2008.

(U//FOUO) The IG accepted over a dozen recommendations from the review, and implemented actions intended to clarify, document, strengthen and increase transparency, primarily related to the conduct of OIG investigations. These included:

- (U//FOUO) Establishing the position of a Quality Control Officer in the Investigations Staff and the creation of an OIG Ombudsman position separate from the Quality Control Officer.

- (U//FOUO) Establishing procedures allowing individuals or components to provide rebuttals for the purpose of establishing factual accuracy, and establishing a uniform procedure allowing the subjects of reports the opportunity to review their interview reports and subsequent draft investigation reports.

- (U//FOUO) Acquisition of audio/video equipment allowing for the taping of investigations interviews, to ensure accuracy and clarity, and protect both interviewees and investigators in the event of disagreements about interview content.

> **(U) Conclusion 5: The CIA detention and interrogation program impeded and undermined the national security missions of other Executive Branch Agencies— including the Federal Bureau of Investigation, the State Department, and the office of the Director of National Intelligence—by withholding information relevant to their missions and responsibilities, denying access to detainees, and by providing inaccurate information.**

(U) We disagree with the assertion that CIA impeded or undermined the mission of other Executive Branch Agencies. In fact, intelligence derived from the detention and interrogation program greatly facilitated the work of other agencies in carrying out their national security missions. While we take no position on the decision to use enhanced techniques or on their necessity in acquiring information from detainees, we believe Conclusion 5 fails to sufficiently acknowledge the cumulative impact of intelligence obtained from those detainees on al-Qa'ida's capabilities, tradecraft, targeting priorities, and recruiting had in enabling other Executive branch agencies to develop countermeasures and disruption strategies that directly contributed to the security of the US and its interests abroad. CIA provided the interagency, including the FBI, with a wealth of information derived from detainee interrogations that was critical in shaping the whole of government response to the al-Qa'ida threat after the 9/11 attacks.

(S//OC/NF) Prior to the capture of Abu Zubaydah in March 2002, the Intelligence Community had significant gaps in knowledge concerning al-Qa'ida's organizational structure, key members and associates, intentions and capabilities, recruitment practices and strategies, and potential targets for future attacks. To fill these gaps, CIA over the years serviced hundreds of requirements directed at detainee interrogations from the FBI, the Department of Homeland Security, the National Counterterrorism Center (NCTC), the Department of Defense, the Department of State, and the Department of Treasury, among others.

- (S//OC/NF) CIA shared thousands of intelligence reports obtained from detainees with the Intelligence Community, covering strategic and tactical matters related to al-Qa'ida and its militant allies and facilitators. Other agencies—including the FBI, whose cables indicate it used that information to support investigations—repeatedly made clear that it highly prized this detainee-derived intelligence.

- (S//OC/NF) For instance, over three quarters of the intelligence reports that the FBI cited in a paper assessing the activities of US-based al-Qa'ida sleeper operative Salih al-Marri and explaining the reach of al-Qa'ida's network in the US were sourced to Khalid Shaykh Muhammad (KSM), our first and most important source of information on al-Marri's role. Prior to KSM's information, CIA and the FBI were aware of al-Marri's links to al-Qa'ida but lacked the detail to more fully understand al-Qa'ida's plans for him.

- (S//OC/NF) ██████████████████████████████████████
  ██
  ██ A separate
  ██████ forwarded a CTC finished intelligence product on al-Qa'ida's evolving

efforts to defeat US security measures—written based on detainee reporting—and requested all consular and DHS officers at overseas posts review the report.

(S//OC/NF) The *Study's* allegations regarding CIA's relationship with the FBI in the context of the program require clarification. In the first instance, it was the FBI's decision to exclude its personnel from participation in the RDI program, based on a leadership decision that the FBI did not want to be involved with the use of coercive techniques at secret facilities. That said, we acknowledge CIA had significant concerns regarding the possibility that any FBI participation in an interrogation might unintentionally result in later disclosures in a legal forum regarding the program and the detention site locations.

(TS/███████████NF) We disagree with the characterization that the FBI received "the most significant intelligence" information from Abu Zubaydah using only rapport building techniques. The FBI officers were part of an around-the-clock effort, in conjunction with CIA, to interrogate Abu Zubaydah in order to weaken his resolve to resist. This effort involved sleep deprivation for Abu Zubaydah, which was later characterized as an enhanced technique. The FBI learned about Jose Padilla during this period of sleep deprivation, which required interrogators to alternate (so they could rest). Even after the admission concerning Padilla, both FBI and CIA interrogators assessed that Abu Zubaydah was continuing to withhold important information; an assessment that served as the impetus for seeking a DOJ opinion on additional techniques which might further weaken Abu Zubaydah's resolve.

- (S//OC/NF) The *Study's* allegation that CIA was directed not to share intelligence from Khalid Shaykh Muhammad's interrogations unless it was "actionable" is simply wrong. Of course, all intelligence collected from KSM was shared with the FBI via disseminated reports and ███ from Headquarters. The cable cited by the report is not to the contrary. It's focus is on preserving the "status quo"—in which CIA had custody of physical materials captured with KSM and information he initially provided—pending interagency discussions on how to manage those materials and information. The intent was to avoid complicating criminal trials involving other terrorist detainees, who might seek access to the materials and information through the discovery process if they were provided to the FBI. Notwithstanding this, the cable explicitly states that CIA must "continue to provide [the FBI or other law enforcement agencies] immediate access to any information" or physical materials "that relates to imminent threats or is otherwise actionable."

- (S//OC/NF) Finally, with regard to the *Study's* claims that the State Department was "cut out" of information relating to the program, the record shows that the Secretary of State, Deputy Secretary of State and Ambassadors in detention site host countries were aware of the sites at the time they were operational. In addition, Station Chiefs in the respective countries informed their Ambassadors of developing media, legal, or policy issues as they emerged, and provided a secure communication channel for discussion of these matters with Washington.

- (TS/███████████NF) As detailed in our response to Conclusion 3, and as is the case with all covert action programs, the National Security Council established the parameters for when and how CIA could engage on the Program with other Executive branch agencies. The 2001 MoN compartmented the rendition, detention, and interrogation program, while it permitted CIA to enlist the assistance of other relevant

US Government agencies. The NSC, not CIA, controlled access to the ███████████ ███████████ within the Executive branch.

(T̶S̶/̶ ███████████████ N̶F̶) Overall, although we disagree with the premise that the RDI program impeded or undermined the national security missions of other Executive Branch agencies, we agree with the 9/11 Commission and others who have observed that, before 9/11, we could have been more closely linked with the FBI. Improving information sharing and operational ties in the wake of the attacks became not just a CIA priority, but a focus of the entire intelligence community. We have made great strides since then; to cite just one example, we have moved to embed significantly more FBI detailees within CIA's Counterterrorism Center (CTC)—moving from ██ detailees in 2003 to ██ today.

> (S//OC/NF) **Conclusion 6: The CIA's detention and interrogation program required secrecy and cooperation from other nations in order to operate, and both had eroded significantly before the President publicly disclosed the CIA detention and interrogation program in September 2006. It was difficult for the CIA to find nations willing to host CIA clandestine detention sites, as well as to address emergency medical care for its detainees. By 2006, the CIA detention and interrogation program had largely ceased to operate due to press disclosures, reduced cooperation from nations hosting detention facilities, the inability to find new nations to host detention sites, as well as oversight and legal concerns. After detaining at least 113 individuals, the CIA brought on six additional detainees into its custody after 2004: four in 2005, one in 2006, and one in 2007.**

(S//OC/NF) We agree that secrecy had eroded significantly prior to the President's disclosure of the CIA detention and interrogation program in September 2006. We also share the view that identifying nations willing to host new facilities and provide emergency medical care for detainees in CIA custody grew more challenging after information about the program and other nations' participation in it leaked to the press. As information about the program became public, both CIA and our foreign partners faced worsening challenges to operational security. Further, we agree with the *Study* that by 2006 the interrogation program had largely ceased to operate, and that legal and oversight concerns were significant reasons for this.

(S//OC/NF) We believe, however, that the *Study* omitted an additional important factor responsible for this situation: al-Qa'ida's relocation to the FATA, which was largely inaccessible to ▮▮▮▮▮▮▮▮ Government of Pakistan, made it significantly more challenging to mount capture operations resulting in renditions and detentions by the RDI program.

- (S//OC/NF) By 2004 and especially by 2006, al-Qaida in the Afghanistan-Pakistan theater was under constant pressure from both military and intelligence operations, important leaders had been captured, cells had been neutralized, and almost all Afghan territory as well as the settled areas of Pakistan had been denied to the group. Consequently, by mid-decade the remaining senior al-Qa'ida leaders had already begun relocating to the tribal areas of Pakistan ▮▮▮▮▮▮▮▮▮▮▮▮▮▮▮▮▮▮▮▮▮▮▮▮▮▮

(S//OC/NF) We agree with the *Study* that unauthorized disclosures about the program made it difficult for foreign governments to host detention sites, even when they were willing. However, foreign governments, including those that had hosted sites, continued to support CIA's overall counterterrorism efforts. By September 2006, CIA's program had also significantly changed from one focused on interrogation to one focused on long-term detention, due to the relative dearth of newly captured al-Qa'ida operatives. The Agency took seriously its responsibility to provide for the welfare of CIA's detainee population, including being able to address emergency and longer term medical and psychological needs. As such, when RDI managers were not confident that these needs could be met in a changing political environment in the countries where the detainees were interned, detainees were moved and facilities were closed or kept empty. (The impact of disclosures on both intelligence and foreign relations is reviewed in CIA's response to Conclusion 7).

(S//OC/NF) Finally, the *Study* observes that CIA Directors on two occasions suspended the use of enhanced techniques, implying that these actions illustrated the tenuous nature of the legal foundation supporting the program. In fact, we believe these suspensions are further evidence of the care taken throughout the life of the program to ensure that all aspects of Agency activities remained in sync with an evolving legal and political landscape.

- (S//OC/NF) The first suspension occurred in May 2004 in response to the Inspector General's Special Review, as well as an internal review of the program. That internal review recommended continued use of 13 techniques, and in May 2005 DOJ provided an opinion that those 13 techniques were legal under US statutes and treaty obligations.[3]

- (S//OC/NF) The second suspension was in December 2005, when enactment of the Detainee Treatment Act of 2005 (DTA) was imminent. The DTA signaled Congress's declining support for this kind of program, so following an updated internal review the CIA limited to seven the types of techniques its officers could utilize. However, because of continued uncertainty over legal interpretations, use of those techniques did not immediately resume.

(U//FOUO) As the *Study* notes, in the wake of the *Hamdan v. Rumsfeld* Supreme Court decision in 2006 and Executive Order 13440 on Common Article 3 in July 2007, DOJ issued a legal opinion finding six of the seven enhanced techniques that CIA had proposed in late 2005 were lawful. The DCIA then issued new guidelines on interrogations and allowed resumption of the permitted techniques.

(S//OC/NF) Overall, we assess that the Agency acted prudently to voluntarily cease program operations at critical times, such as when legislation like the DTA indicated that Congress no longer supported the program, as well as when the IG identified important program shortcomings and recommended that CIA reaffirm its legal guidance.

---

[3] (S//OC/NF) Notwithstanding this general suspension, enhanced techniques were approved on a case-by-case basis for use in the interrogation of five detainees during this period through December 2005, with Department of Justice concurrence and NSC concurrence or—beginning in September 2004—notification after DOJ approval.

(S//OC/NF) **Conclusion 7: The CIA's detention and interrogation program had significant monetary costs to the United States. Those costs included funding for the CIA to build detention facilities, including two facilities for a stated cost of nearly $▓ million that were never used due to political or medical care concerns. To encourage governments to clandestinely host CIA detention sites, the CIA provided cash payments, in some cases with no** ▓▓▓▓▓▓▓▓▓▓▓▓▓▓▓▓▓ **At least one lump sum payment amounted to $▓ million. The CIA detention and interrogation program also had non-monetary costs, such as tensions with US partners and allies, formal** *demarches* **to the United States, and damaged bilateral intelligence relationships with nations unwilling to provide intelligence that might contribute to CIA detention and interrogation operations.**

(S//OC/NF) We largely agree with the *Study's* conclusion that the program had significant monetary costs. Lump sum payments to several countries did facilitate their willingness to host detention sites, although there was nothing improper about such payments. While the RDI program also had non-monetary costs, we believe that the *Study* overstates the damage to US relations.

(TS/▓▓▓▓▓▓▓▓/NF) The *Study* correctly lays out some of the significant, monetary costs associated with the detention and interrogation program over its lifespan. Between FY2001 and FY2006 – the years the program was most active–CIA's RDI program cost approximately $246.4 million, excluding personal services. To put that into context, during this same period, ▓▓▓▓ ▓▓▓

(S//OC/NF) To encourage governments to clandestinely host detention sites, CIA provided cash payments to foreign government officials, in some cases with no ▓▓▓▓▓▓▓▓▓▓▓▓▓ The *Study* suggests we did not properly ▓▓▓▓▓▓▓▓▓▓▓▓▓ or that they were made in violation of government ▓▓▓▓▓▓▓ Through legislation, however, CIA has independent authority to make subsidy payments ▓▓▓▓▓▓▓▓▓▓▓▓▓▓▓▓▓▓▓▓▓▓▓▓▓▓▓

Such non-standard ▓▓▓▓▓▓▓▓▓▓▓▓▓▓▓▓▓▓▓▓▓ are governed by Agency regulations that detail special approval requirements before such payments are made. In the case of the RDI program, CIA accounted for disbursed funds internally according to these required procedures, and did so in a timely manner. The Agency has no responsibility to determine or assist in overseeing our partner services' adherence to ▓▓▓▓▓▓▓▓▓ Such payments contributed greatly to CIA's ability to influence these countries to support the RDI program as well as other ▓▓▓▓▓▓▓▓ operations.

(U//FOUO) The *Study* also notes that there were non-monetary costs to the detention and interrogation program, citing tensions with partners and allies as well as damage to bilateral intelligence relationships. The leaks related to the detention and interrogation program at first presented challenges of varying degrees to the Agency's bilateral relationships with a number of partners, but this represents only a small part of the story.

(S//OC/NF) As the *Study* accurately conveys, in the first years after 9/11, many foreign governments were enthusiastic about assisting CIA in prosecuting its counterterrorism mission, and most of those approached were willing to host detention facilities on the understanding that CIA would keep their cooperation secret. It was only as leaks detailing the program began to emerge that foreign partners felt compelled to alter the scope of their involvement.

(TS// ██████████ NF) Nevertheless, ██████████████ in the countries that hosted detention facilities remained supportive partners of our overall counterterrorism efforts and ████████ assisted CIA in numerous ways. Country █ maintained its close operational collaboration with CIA across a range of intelligence objectives, including counterterrorism as well as unrelated ████████████████ We found no evidence that the RDI program in any way negatively affected US relations overall with Country █ Country █ continued to provide high-risk support to ████████ collection operations ████████████████ ███████████████ Country █ increased its work with CIA on other ████████ and deepened its support to ████ operations even after the exposure of its role ████████ ████████████ These relationships endure and prosper today.

(S/ ████ /NF) The *Study* also cites costs to relationships with other US partners and allies. The *Study* singles out ████ countries as examples of relationships damaged by the detention and interrogation program, overstating the impact in each instance:

> (U) Conclusion 8: The CIA marginalized or ignored internal criticism from interrogators, analysts, the Office of Medical Services, the Office of Inspector General, and others regarding the CIA's representations on the effectiveness and operation of the CIA's detention and interrogation program. Contrary views provided to CIA leadership were excluded from representations to the CIA's Inspector General, the White House, and others; in other instances, CIA officers recognized inaccuracies, but failed to take action to report them.

(U) We do not agree that CIA "marginalized or ignored" internal criticism of the program or otherwise sought to stifle internal debate relating to its operation or effectiveness. The *Study* attempts to support the broad finding of Conclusion 8 by citing to a compilation of isolated e-mails and informal electronic "chat" sessions between officers, but virtually all of the cited evidence is out of context, anecdotal, or simply inaccurate.

(S//OC/NF) First, the *Study* claims that in the course of reviewing a draft Presidential speech on the Program in 2006, some CTC officers questioned the accuracy of statements in the speech indicating that Abu Zubaydah had been "defiant" in response to initial interrogation, and had declared America "weak." The *Study* alleges that these officers failed to raise the concerns with their seniors. There is no evidence, however, that officers quoted in the *Study* restrained themselves from providing feedback on these or other speech-related issues. To the contrary, their concerns were evidently clearly heard, and on September 4, 2006, CTC specifically objected to the language in the speech that the officers questioned, and provided Agency seniors, including the Director, with nine pages of other comments and corrections.

- (S//OC/NF) With regard to the "defiant" and "weak" references, one officer the *Study* claims failed to raise concerns sent the following to her leadership : "CIA has no documentation to substantiate page 4, lines 9-11. Abu Zubaydah employed a number of counter-interrogation techniques—including feigning ignorance, feigning neurological problems, stalling, diversions, digressions and non-specific answers—but none of the documentation describes him as `defiant' nor can we find the quote from him cited above." Upon further review of the record, this officer appears to have later changed her mind and agreed that use of the word "defiant" would in fact be appropriate.

(S//OC/NF) Second, the fact that one officer, speaking to another in a "chat" session, felt "ostracized" for expressing his belief that Zubaydah and KSM "did not tell us everything" falls well short of establishing that the Agency "marginalized" those who criticized the Program. We do not know why the officer felt "ostracized" at that moment, but the officer's view was neither unique nor controversial; CIA never represented that detainees told us all they knew. Indeed, numerous CIA officers, including the Director of CTC, have acknowledged that detainees often withheld information they considered the most valuable. Moreover, the comment is removed from its illuminating context. A complete review of the dialogue from which the quote is taken shows that the two officers are primarily focused on expressing their dismay over the decision to cease applying enhanced techniques and the loss of important intelligence they believe will result.[4]

(S//OC/NF) Third, we disagree with the *Study's* implication that statements made by Director Hayden to the effect that CIA held 98 detainees reflected an attempt to misrepresent the scope of the program to the incoming administration. Director Hayden did meet with CTC and other officers in January, 2009, to discuss his upcoming briefing to incoming officials. At that meeting, a CTC officer briefed the research he had performed on the number of total detainees through the life of the Program. Although this research, which indicates the total number of detainees could have been as high as 112, is heavily cited by the SSCI *Study*, SSCI neglects to point out that the findings were not final. As the briefing stated, "these numbers will continue to be refined as methodical reviews of operational records are completed and disparately compartmented information is researched and consolidated."

- (TS/███████████NF) At the time, uncertainty existed within CIA about whether a group of additional detainees were actually part of the program, partially because some of them had passed through ███████ prior to the formal establishment of the program under CTC auspices on 3 December 2002. ████████ was the only CIA detainee facility that housed transient ██████████████ and the only one that ████████████ where complete recordkeeping was sometimes neglected. CTC's research was ultimately intended to provide a definitive answer as to how many additional detainees who passed through ██████ in its early days, if any, should be considered to be part of the Program.

(S//OC/NF) Officers we spoke to who were present at the 2009 meeting, including Director Hayden, recall that CTC's conclusions seemed somewhat speculative and incomplete, and that more work was required before a final number could be determined. Moreover, Hayden did not view the potential discrepancy, if it existed, as particularly significant given that, if true, it would increase the total number by just over 10 percent. The participants we spoke with who recalled the meeting agreed that there was an institutional need to bring the research into better focus and make a principled evaluation of which detainees should be considered formally part of the program, not to ignore the discrepancy or fix the number at 98 for all time.

- While it would have been more accurate to conclude at the time that the number of detainees was approximately 100, rather than falling unambiguously below that number, there was plainly no intent on the part of the Director to turn a blind eye to evidence or misrepresent the total.

---

[4] (S//OC/NF) Immediately prior to the "ostracized" statement, one officer remarked that "if we actually capture someone important we think they are just going to tell us what they know because they like us, we are nice to them, or what? Just another example that people who make these decisions do not know what we are up against with these guys. They haven't told us all the important stuff with [EITs], they will definitely not tell us anything important without them." The other officer replied, "there are new 'influence and persuade' techniques. Essentially you're right—we're going to make them like us, and they'll tell us everything. How sophomoric!"

(S//OC/NF) Fourth, the request by the Director of CTC (D/CTC) for officers in the field to refrain from speculating on the "legal limit" of authorized enhanced interrogation techniques was made in the context of keeping individual officers focused on their assigned tasks and areas of expertise. D/CTC relied on CIA lawyers to provide legal guidance and on CIA officers in the field and at Headquarters to implement the program within the approved guidelines set out by DOJ's OLC.

- (S//OC/NF) We know that some officers expressed concern about the "legal limit" of enhanced techniques, and we suspect that many more had similar reservations. CIA expects its professional cadre to be alert to potential concerns, to broadly construe their responsibilities, and to take ownership of problems. But as in any large organization, ultimately individuals must perform their assigned roles. D/CTC was simply reminding officers to permit those responsible for making legal judgments to do so.

(S//OC/NF) Finally, the *Study* claims that CIA personnel objected to CIA's representation that the program produced intelligence leading to the thwarting of the "Dirty Bomb" plot, but Agency seniors failed to correct the record. As detailed in our Response to the Case Studies of Effectiveness, we regret that it took the Agency until 2007 to refer to Padilla without reference to the "Dirty Bomb" plot, but rather as a legitimate threat who had been directed to put together a plan to attack tall residential buildings. There was insufficient attention paid to clarifying this issue across the Agency. It does not follow, however, that there was a deliberate attempt to ignore the record or propagate misleading information.

- (S//OC/NF) For example, the *Study* ignores the fact that, in responding to the draft Presidential speech discussed above, the Agency proposed language that deleted the reference to Padilla as a program success story.

- (S//OC/NF) In addition, the evidence cited by the *Study*—including an email from the former Chief of the AZ Task Force that Zubaydah didn't provide "this is the plot" type of information—is taken out of context. The same officer also stated that Padilla's "identification would not have been made without the lead from Abu Zubaydah." Moreover, in the cited email the officer went on to describe Zubaydah as a strategically significant source of intelligence, stating that after Zubaydah received enhanced techniques, "he became one of our most valuable sources on information on al-Qa'ida players." The officer backs up that assertion with a detailed recitation of concrete ways in which Zubaydah facilitated interrogations of other detainees by providing specific information concerning their identities and plans.

(S//OC/NF) CIA officers, who feel passionately about their mission, are not known to mince words or "keep silent," as the *Study* alleges. There is no evidence they did so here; to the contrary, some of the very emails and "chats" cited by the *Study* point to the existence of an atmosphere in which officers are unafraid to give voice to their dissenting views. Throughout the life of the program, a vibrant internal debate allowed senior CIA officers to consider and, as appropriate, accept the perspectives of field and Headquarters officers directly involved in the interrogations.

> (U) **Conclusion 9: The evidence the CIA provided for the effectiveness of the CIA's enhanced interrogation techniques was found to be inaccurate. From 2002 through at least 2011, the information the CIA provided to the White House, National Security Council, the Department of Justice , the Congress, the CIA Office of Inspector General, and the public on the operation and effectiveness of CIA's detention and interrogation program was consistently inaccurate. The CIA informed policymakers that the only measure of the effectiveness of the CIA's enhanced interrogation techniques was the 'otherwise unavailable' intelligence produced that 'saved lives' and enabled the CIA to 'disrupt specific terrorist plots' and 'capture' specific terrorists. A review of the 20 most frequent CIA examples provided to policymakers and others as evidence for the effectiveness of the CIA's interrogation program found all 20 representations to be inaccurate.**

(U//FOUO) We conducted a careful review of the *Study's* 20 examples of the value of the information obtained as a result of CIA's RDI effort, and we have provided detailed responses to each in separate section. We have summarized our conclusions here. In commenting on the value of the information derived from detainees, we are not arguing in favor of the decision to use the enhanced techniques to which these detainees were subjected. We are not endorsing those techniques, we are not making an "ends-justify-the-means" case for them, nor are we implying that those techniques were the only way to obtain the information from detainees. We only are assessing the accuracy of CIA's representations in response to the *Study's* allegations that those representations were false.

(U//FOUO) We concluded that all the cases fit within and support the Agency's overall representations that information obtained from CIA interrogations produced unique intelligence that helped the US disrupt plots, capture terrorists, better understand the enemy, prevent another mass casualty attack, and save lives. We were dismayed to see that, in some of the Agency's representations, CIA failed to meet its own standards for precision of language and we acknowledge that this was unacceptable. However, even in those cases, we found that the actual impact of the information acquired from interrogations was significant and still supported CIA's judgments about the overall value of the information acquired from detainees, including detainees on whom the Agency used enhanced interrogation techniques.

(U//FOUO) **Summary of the 20 Examples.** In one of the 20 examples, we found that CIA mischaracterized on several occasions, including in prominent representations such as President Bush's 2006 speech, the impact of information on specific terrorist plotting acquired from a set of CIA interrogations.

- (U//FOUO) CIA said the information "helped stop a planned attack on the US Consulate in Karachi," when the Agency should have said it "revealed ongoing attack plotting against the US official presence in Karachi that prompted the Consulate to take further steps to protect its officers."

(U//FOUO) There were four cases in which CIA used imprecise language or made errors in some of its representations that, although deeply regrettable, did not significantly affect the thrust of those representations. Those cases were the arrest of Jose Padilla, the "Second Wave" plot, the arrest of laman Faris, and intelligence on Ja'far al-Tayyar.

(U//FOUO) In another four examples, we found single, isolated representations in which CIA was imprecise in describing the relative impact of the information or the manner in which it was acquired.

- (U//FOUO) In two of these examples, CIA made mistakes that caused the IG to incorrectly describe in its 2004 *Special Review* the precise role that information acquired from KSM played in the detention of two terrorists involved in plots against targets in the US. These were not "frequently cited" or "repeatedly represented" as *The Study* claims. Numerous other representations of one of these cases were accurate; we found no other representations for the other.

- (U//FOUO) In two cases, we found a one-time error not noted in the *Study*. In a set of talking points prepared for DCIA, CIA incorrectly said enhanced interrogation techniques played a role in acquiring two important pieces of information about KSM. In the Agency's other representations, including our most prominent, we stated correctly that this information was acquired during initial interviews of Abu Zubaydah.

(U//FOUO) In the other 11 examples, we determined that CIA's representations were consistently accurate, in contrast to the *Study*, which claims the Agency misrepresented them all.

(U//FOUO) Finally, we note that our review showed that the *Study* failed to include examples of important information acquired from detainees that CIA cited more frequently and prominently in its representations than several of the cases the authors chose to include.

- (S//OC/NF) In the same set of documents from which the authors of the *Study* selected their examples, some of which CIA only represented once, the Agency cited the disruption of the Gulf shipping plot seven times; learning important information about al-Qa'ida's anthrax plotting and the role of Yazid Sufaat seven times; and the detention of Abu Talha al-Pakistani seven times.

(S//OC/NF) **Overall Value of Detainee Reporting.** Our judgment about the worth of the intelligence acquired from the RDI Program is based on the counterterrorism value that CIA, other US government agencies, and our foreign partners derived from it. Across the life of the program, detainee-derived intelligence was responsible for:

- (S//OC/NF) *Uncovering or discovering important new information.* While a ▮▮▮▮▮ detainee had told us of an al-Qa'ida plot to attack the US West Coast, CIA first learned about Hambali's involvement in that plotting from KSM.

- (S//OC/NF) *Making vague information actionable.* Prior to debriefings from Abu Zubaydah, the CIA had a few vague reports on a US passport holder with links to al-Qa'ida external plotting, as well as a seemingly unrelated report on a potential illegal traveler in Pakistan. Abu Zubaydah's description of Jose Padilla allowed the Agency to link him to the other reporting on the al-Qa'ida external operative, ▮▮▮▮▮▮▮▮▮

▮▮▮▮▮▮▮▮▮▮▮▮▮▮▮▮▮▮▮▮▮▮▮▮▮▮▮ Similarly, inconclusive HUMINT and SIGINT had alerted CIA to the existence of an al-Qa'ida external operative by the name of Ja'far al-Tayyar who spoke American-accented English and had lived in the

22

United States, but it was not until KSM provided biographic information on him that CIA was able to work with the FBI to specifically identify the Ja'far al-Tayyar upon whom the Agency needed to focus.

- (TS/ ██████████████████ NF) *Providing strategic, contextual information.* Even detainees who did not have perishable threat intelligence often provided intelligence that advanced CIA's understanding of terrorist networks. For example, Hassan Gul's information on al-Qa'ida presence and operations in Shkai, Pakistan, was the most definitive first-hand account of the identities, precise locations, and activities of senior al-Qa'ida members in Shkai at that time. Likewise, Abu Zubaydah, KSM, Zubair, and Hambali deepened the Agency's understanding of the structure, reach and capability of al-Qa'ida and its Southeast-Asian network.

-

(S//OC/NF) In our review of the Study's 20 examples, we note a number of errors of fact, interpretation, and contextualization that appear to have led the authors' to conclude that the information CIA derived in each case had little to no unique value. It is just as important to note that the *Study* also discounts the aggregate impact of the information derived from detainees in CIA custody. Perhaps the most important context that the *Study* ignores is how little CIA knew, despite considerable effort, about al-Qa'ida and its allies on 9/11. The sum total of information provided from detainees in CIA custody substantially advanced the Agency's strategic and tactical understanding of the enemy in ways that continue to inform counterterrorism efforts to this day.

(S//OC/NF) **Otherwise Unobtainable.** In hindsight, we believe that assertions that the information CIA acquired, including the critical intelligence obtained from detainees on whom the Agency used enhanced interrogation techniques, could not have been obtained some other way were sincerely believed but inherently speculative. It is impossible to imagine how CIA could have achieved the same results in terms of disrupting plots, capturing other terrorists, and degrading al-Qa'ida without <u>any</u> information from detainees, but it is unknowable whether, without enhanced interrogation techniques, CIA or non-CIA interrogators could have acquired the same information from those detainees. Since 2011, when then-Director Panetta publicly outlined this view, it has stood as the official Agency position, and it remains so today.

(S//OC/NF) **Conclusion 10: The CIA never conducted its own comprehensive analysis of the effectiveness of the CIA's enhanced interrogation techniques, despite a recommendation from the Inspector General and requests to do so by the National Security Advisor and the Senate Select Committee on Intelligence. The sole external analysis of the CIA interrogation program relied on two reviewers; one admitted to lacking the requisite expertise to review the program, and the other noted that he did not have the requisite information to accurately assess the program. Informal internal assessments of the effectiveness of the CIA's enhanced interrogation techniques were provided to CIA leadership by CIA personnel who participated in the development or management of the interrogation program, as well as by CIA contractors who had a financial interest in the continuation and expansion of the CIA detention and interrogation program.**

(TS/ NF) We agree with Conclusion 10 in full. It underpins the most important lesson that we have drawn from *The Study*: CIA needs to develop the structure, expertise, and methodologies required to more objectively and systematically evaluate the effectiveness of our covert actions.

(U//FOUO) We draw this lesson going forward fully aware of how difficult it can be to measure the impact of a particular action or set of actions on an outcome in a real world setting. This was very much true for enhanced techniques. A systematic study over time of the effectiveness of the techniques would have been encumbered by a number of factors:

- (U//FOUO) The variability of each detainee's personality, state of mind at capture, ideological commitment, and the importance of the information he was attempting to conceal.

- (U//FOUO) Federal policy on the protection of human subjects and the impracticality of establishing an effective control group.

- (U//FOUO) The difficulty in isolating the impact of any given technique or set of techniques from the cumulative impact of the overall experience, which from the moment of capture was structured to induce compliance and resignation.

- (U//FOUO) Variations in the manner in which enhanced techniques were administered, the types of techniques favored over time, the skill with which they were used, the substantive expertise and interpersonal skills of the debriefers, as well as the baseline of intelligence pertinent to any given detainee.

- (U//FOUO) The need to devote to mission execution the analytic resources that might have been used in an evaluation program, especially during the years just after 9/11 when CIA was recovering from a depletion of its personnel resources during the 1990s.

- (U//FOUO) The need for secrecy and the consequent requirement for strict compartmentation of the information required to evaluate it.

(S//OC/NF) These hindrances notwithstanding, we believe that CIA should have attempted to develop a more sustained, systematic, and independent means by which to evaluate the effectiveness of the approaches used with detainees.

24

- (S//OC/NF) CIA remains grateful to ██████████ and ██████████████ who applied their considerable experience in program oversight as effectively as they could to the task of providing overviews of the effectiveness of enhanced techniques. Their reports offered important insights. We agree with the *Study*, however, that they were heavily reliant on the views of the practitioners, and that this short-term effort was no substitute for a more sustained and systematic evaluation of the program.

- (S//OC/NF) As discussed in our response to Conclusion 17, we agree that CIA should have done more from the beginning of the program to ensure there was no conflict of interest—real or potential—with regard to the contractor psychologists who designed and executed the techniques while also playing a role in evaluating their effectiveness, as well as other closely-related tasks.

(S//OC/NF) Although no systematic, comprehensive assessment of the effectiveness of various techniques was performed, as it should have been, officers involved in the program did regularly make such assessments on an ad hoc basis in an effort to achieve the best results with the least coercion. Officers concluded that various enhanced techniques were effective based on their own "before and after" observations.[56] A number of officers, having witnessed detainees' initial demeanor, believed that they would not have succumbed to less coercive approaches, at least not in time for their information to be operationally useful.[78]

- (S//OC/NF) Corporately, however, CIA has concluded that is impossible in hindsight to know whether intelligence as valuable as that summarized in our response to Conclusion 9 and in our responses to the case studies could have derived by using less coercive techniques.

[5] [CIA | ██████ 41373 | | ██████████ | | | | (TS/██████NF) |]
[6] [CIA | ██████ 41484 | | ██████████ | | | | (TS/██████NF) |]
[7] [CIA | ██████ 10496 | | 16 February 2003 | | | | | (TS/██████NF) |]
[8] [CIA | HEADQUARTERS ██████████ | | | | (TS/██████NF) |]

> (U) **Conclusion 11: In its representations about its interrogation program the CIA did not inform policymakers and others that CIA detainees fabricated information during and after the use of the CIA's enhanced interrogation techniques. CIA detainees also withheld information, notwithstanding the use of such interrogation techniques. Multiple CIA personnel directly engaged in the CIA interrogation program stated that the CIA's enhanced interrogation techniques were ineffective in eliciting increased cooperation or obtaining accurate information from CIA detainees.**

(S//OC/NF) We believe the *Study* is wrong in asserting that CIA failed to inform policymakers and consumers of detainee-related intelligence about fabricated information. The CIA took pains to ensure that all involved were fully aware from the outset that detainees might fabricate and withhold information, and CIA reporting carried clear warnings of this possibility. Senior CIA officers also shared this assessment in meetings with Congressional overseers. Unsurprisingly, throughout the course of their detention, detainees frequently both lied and told the truth, and CIA worked diligently to discern the difference, engaging in detailed analysis of the data available from all streams of reporting.

(S//OC/NF) CIA detainee reports clearly specified that the source was a detainee and that the information was gained during custodial debriefings. Reports included warnings that the detainees may have intended to influence as well as inform, intentionally withhold information, and employ counter-interrogation techniques. CIA included additional information as circumstances warranted—for example, when a detainee changed his claims over time. These caveats are attached at the bottom of our response to Conclusion 11.

(S//OC/NF) Evaluating the truthfulness of sources is an integral part of HUMINT collection and analysis tradecraft. The reality that detainees lied or changed their accounts, with or without being subjected to enhanced techniques, did not come as a shock to anyone involved in the program or to consumers of detainee-derived intelligence. The *Study* generally appears to accept at face value detainees' accounts that they lied under enhanced techniques and told the truth afterwards. However, in some cases comparing information provided by a detainee to intelligence from other sources indicates that detainees told the truth after undergoing enhanced techniques and then, perhaps regretting what they had revealed, tried to rescind it later.

- (S//OC/NF) For example, after being subject to enhanced techniques, Hambali admitted that the 16 Malaysian students whom he had hand selected for participation in a cell in Karachi, Pakistan were being groomed as pilots—probably as part of a plot to attack the west coast of the United States, in response to KSM's request. Months later, Hambali claimed he lied about the pilots because he was "constantly asked about it and under stress" and stated that KSM never asked his assistance in identifying a pilot. CIA assesses that Hambali's recantation was a lie, because his claim directly contradicts information provided by KSM, Hambali verified his original admission in multiple instances, and because of independently-obtained intelligence confirming the cell members' interest in aircraft and aviation.

(S//OC/NF) When detainees fabricated or retracted information, CIA issued new or revised reports with that information. However, the Agency's general practice was not to recall the original reports. IC terrorism analysts preferred that the original reports remain available, because they gained important insights from understanding the choices detainees made in formulating their fabrications. In one case—Abu Faraj's false statement that he did not recognize a courier—analysis of the fabrication contributed to the hunt for Usama bin Laden.

(S//OC/NF) As we have stated elsewhere and publicly, CIA will never know whether use of enhanced techniques resulted in more actionable or truthful information than otherwise would have been available. But the fact that some detainees successfully withheld information does not, by itself, invalidate the program. As we noted in a 2004 monograph, "[t]he interrogation techniques. . . in and of themselves provide no silver bullet." The purpose of the program was to minimize what was withheld with the understanding that obtaining complete disclosures from detainees in every case was not possible.

Caveats and Corrections in Detainee Reporting

(S//NF) All disseminated reports from detainees clearly specified that the source was a detainee and carried a warning notice indicating specific caveats regarding potential unreliability. The report text always specified that the information was gained during a custodial debriefing. The bullets in the *Study* under Conclusion 11 also cite several cases where a detainee changed his information in the course of interrogation. We highlight a number of specific examples below:

- (S//NF) **General Caveat**. The following caveat was the basic version and was used on most reporting from detainees. This example is drawn from a report from Khalid Shaykh Muhammad:

  > THE FOLLOWING COMMENTS FROM SENIOR AL-QA'IDA OPERATIONAL PLANNER KHALID SHAYKH ((MUHAMMAD)) AKA ((MUKHTAR)) MAY HAVE BEEN MEANT TO INFLUENCE AS WELL AS INFORM. MUKHTAR HAS ALSO BEEN KNOWN TO INTENTIONALLY WITHHOLD INFORMATION AND EMPLOY COUNTERINTERROGATION TECHNIQUES.

- (S//NF) **Samir Hilmi 'Abd al-Latif al-Barq.** The following caveat appeared even in the earliest reporting from Samir Hilmi 'Abd al-Latif al-Barq, who during his interviews frequently changed his account of his involvement with anthrax:

  > THE FOLLOWING COMMENTS FROM A MID-LEVEL AL-QA'IDA ASSOCIATE MAY HAVE BEEN MEANT TO INFLUENCE AS WELL AS INFORM. THE DETAINEE ALSO MAY HAVE BEEN INTENTIONALLY WITHHOLDING INFORMATION. AS DEBRIEFINGS WITH THIS DETAINEE CONTINUE, HIS ACCOUNT OF EVENTS ARE AND MAY CONTINUE TO EVOLVE AND CHANGE.

- (S//NF) **'Abd al-Rahim al-Nashiri.** The *Study* notes, based on █████ 10216 ████ that 'Abd al-Rahim al-Nashiri recanted information on terrorist operations targeting Jeddah, Saudi Arabia. (NOTE: The footnote on p. 1404, Vol. 3, of the study incorrectly cites █████ 10220 as the source of the quotation.) The following language was added to a caveat in a revised report ████████ alerting the IC to 'abd al-Rahim al-Nashiri's retraction of information on terrorist operations in Jeddah, Saudi Arabia.

  > (S/█████/NF) UPON FURTHER CUSTODIAL INTERVIEWS, THE SENIOR OPERATIVE RETRACTED HIS STATEMENTS REGARDING THE INVOLVEMENT OF TWO SAUDI AL-QA'IDA MEMBERS IN POSSIBLE ATTACKS AGAINST US VEHICLES IN JEDDAH.

- (S/███/NF) **Majid Khan.** The *Study* says that Majid Khan retracted "a lot of his earlier reporting." ████████████ provides an example of such a retraction.

  > (CONTEXT STATEMENT: THE FOLLOWING COMMENTS ARE FROM DETAINED AL-QA'IDA OPERATIVE ((MAJID KHAN)), AKA ADNAN, WHO WAS CAPTURED IN MARCH 2003 AND WAS AWARE HIS STATEMENTS WOULD REACH US GOVERNMENT OFFICIALS AND MAY HAVE INTENDED HIS REMARKS TO INFLUENCE RATHER THAN INFORM. MAJID KHAN HAS BEEN UNCOOPERATIVE DURING DEBRIEFINGS AND ADMITTED TO WITHHOLDING INFORMATION. WHEN ASKED FOR FURTHER DETAILS REGARDING THIS PARTICULAR THREAT, MAJID STATED HIS IMPLICIT INTENTION TO LIE TO DEBRIEFERS. AS SUCH, WE ASSESS THAT THE FOLLOWING THREAT INFORMATION PROVIDED BY MAJID MAY LIKELY HAVE BEEN FABRICATED, HOWEVER BECAUSE WE CANNOT DISPROVE THIS INFORMATION WITH COMPLETE CERTAINTY, WE ARE REPORTING IT FOR THE RECORD. DUE TO MAJID'S LACK OF CREDIBILITY, WE DO NOT INTEND TO FURTHER DISSEMINATE THIS INFORMATION IN AN FOUO TEARLINE.)

- (S//NF) **Ramzi bin al-Shibh.** The *Study* notes, based on ███████ 10633 (1 Mar 03), that Ramzi bin al-Shibh recanted information on al-Qa'ida nuclear projects. This information was disseminated on 18 October 2002 in ███████████ and was formally recalled on 7 May 2003 with the following notice:

  > TEXT: NOTICE: AN INFORMATION REPORT WITH THE ABOVE HEADING AND SERIAL NUMBER ████████████ WAS ISSUED ON 18 OCTOBER 2002 AS ███ 529921, ████████████ BECAUSE THE SENIOR AL-QA'IDA OPERATIVE SUBSEQUENTLY SAID HE HAD LIED, THIS REPORT IS BEING RECALLED. RECIPIENTS SHOULD DESTROY ALL HARD COPIES OF THE REPORT AND REMOVE IT FROM ALL COMPUTER HOLDINGS. RECIPIENTS SHOULD ALSO PURGE ANY FINISHED INTELLIGENCE PUBLICATIONS WHICH DREW ON THIS REPORT.

  - (S//NF) The following information was disseminated in ████████████

    > DURING AN EARLY OCTOBER 2004 CUSTODIAL INTERVIEW, BIN AL-SHIBH CLAIMED THAT HE HAD NO KNOWLEDGE OF ANY SPECIFIC AL-QA'IDA EFFORT TO ACQUIRE NUCLEAR MATERIAL OR WHETHER ANY INDIVIDUALS ASSOCIATED WITH AL-QA'IDA HAD EVER ACQUIRED NUCLEAR MATERIAL. BIN AL-SHIBH SAID HE HEARD OF ABU HAFS AL-MASRI'S DEATH THROUGH THE MEDIA AND KNEW NOTHING REGARDING THE EVACUATION OF HIS RESIDENCE. BIN AL-SHIBH STATED THAT PRIOR TO HIS RETURN TO GERMANY IN EARLY 2001, ABU HAFS AL-MASRI TASKED HIM TO FIND A PHYSICIST WHO WOULD BE WILLING TO HELP AL-QA';IDA. BIN AL-SHIBH SAID HE NEVER FOUND A PHYSICIST TO ASSIST AL-QA'IDA BECAUSE HE DID NOT LOOK FOR ONE. ████████████ SEE ████████████ DATED 9 JULY 2004, FOR PREVIOUS REPORTING ON BIN AL-SHIBH'S COMMENTS ON ABU HAFS AL-MASRI'S TASKING TO RECRUIT A PHYSICIST IN GERMANY.)

  - (S/███/NF) Furthermore, Ramzi's reliability was questioned in the very first report from him ████████████ which stated:

DURING A 13 SEPTEMBER 2002 INITIAL CUSTODIAL INTERVIEW, AL-QA'IDA OPERATIVE RAMZI BIN AL-SHIBH AKA UBAYDAH DENIED HAVING ANY KNOWLEDGE OF PLANNED FUTURE TERRORIST OPERATIONS. BIN AL-SHIBH WAS UNCOOPERATIVE THROUGHOUT THE INTERVIEW, APPEARED TO FABRICATE SOME DETAILS, AND WITHHELD SIGNIFICANT INFORMATION ON RELEVANT SUBJECTS.

(S/██████/NF) UPON FURTHER CUSTODIAL INTERVIEWS, THE SENIOR OPERATIVE RETRACTED HIS STATEMENTS REGARDING THE INVOLVEMENT OF TWO SAUDI AL-QA'IDA MEMBERS IN POSSIBLE ATTACKS AGAINST U.S. VEHICLES IN JEDDAH.

- E. (S/██████/NF) **Muhammad Sayyid Ibrahim.** The *Study* notes, based on █████████ 1347 ████████████████ that Ibrahim "retracted claims he had made about meeting with a senior al-Qa'ida leader... because 'interrogators forced him to lie.'" However, claiming to be "forced to lie" is a known counter-interrogation technique that is not unique to CIA's program. Only two days later ████████ 1365 ████████████ recorded that:

  [IBRAHIM] CLAIMED THAT HE WAS PREPARED TO START TELLING THE TRUTH AFTER WARNINGS THAT HIS SITUATION WOULD CONTINUE TO DETERIORATE IF HIS UP AND DOWN ANTICS OF THE PAST WEEK CONTINUED. [HE] BEGAN TO RESPOND TO QUESTIONING BY INTERROGATORS AND SUBSTANTIVE EXPERT [NAME REDACTED], VOLUNTEERING BACKGROUND TO SUPPORT MANY OF HIS POINTS, APPEARING TO STRAIN ON OCCASION TO COME UP WITH A NAME OR TO RECALL DETAILS OF A CONVERSATION, AND OCCASIONALLY IDENTIFYING AREAS WHERE HE HAD PROVIDED FALSE INFORMATION IN THE PAST.

  - (S/██████/NF) Information from Ibrahim was disseminated with the standard caveats.

- F. (S/██████/NF) **Hambali.** The *Study* notes only that "Hambali stated that he fabricated information"; no specifics are given. An example of a corrected version of a Hambali report is ████████████████ which contained the following language:

  THIS REPORT IS BEING REISSUED TO PROVIDE ADDITIONAL DETAILS OBTAINED DURING LATE NOVEMBER 2003 DEBRIEFINGS, SEE PARAGRAPH 11. IN LATE NOVEMBER, THE DETAINEE REVERSED PREVIOUS STATEMENTS AND CLAIMED THAT HE HAD NOT ATTEMPTED TO RECRUIT ABDUL KHOLIQ TO ASSIST IN DEVELOPING OR ACQUIRING WMD, NOR HAD HE AND YAZID SUFAAT EVER DISCUSSED WMD WITH KHOLIQ.

  ████████████████████ WE ARE CONTINUING TO REVIEW THE BELOW ACCOUNTING FROM THE DETAINEE AND WILL PROVIDE FURTHER DETAILS AS THEY BECOME AVAILABLE.) DURING LATE NOVEMBER 2003 DEBRIEFINGS, THE DETAINEE CLAIMED THAT HE FABRICATED PREVIOUS INFORMATION CONCERNING THE INVOLVEMENT OF ABDUL KHOLIQ IN AL-QA'IDA'S EFFORTS TO ACQUIRE AND/OR DEVELOP WMD. SPECIFICALLY, THE DETAINEE STATED THAT HE HAD TWICE MET WITH KHOLIQ, SUBJECT OF PARAGRAPHS 3 AND 5, BUT THAT THESE MEETINGS TOOK PLACE IN SEPTEMBER 1999, VICE 2000. IN ADDITION, THE DETAINEE STATED THAT HE AND YAZID SUFAAT DID NOT USE

EITHER VISIT TO EVALUATE KHOLIQ AS A POTENTIAL WMD ACCOMPLICE OR TO DISCUSS WMD, BUT RATHER HAD ONLY VISITED KHOLIQ TO TALK ABOUT BUSINESS OPPORTUNITIES. FINALLY, THE DETAINEE RECANTED ON THE INFORMATION CONTAINED IN PARAGRAPHS 4, 5, AND 6, STATING THAT HE HAD FABRICATED THE DISCUSSION OF SARIN GAS, TALK OF SETTING UP A LAB WITH ABDUL KHOLIQ, AND HIS PRIOR CLAIM THAT SUFAAT THOUGHT THAT KHOLIQ WAS "VERY CLOSE," IN TERMS OF CAPABILITIES, TO WHAT THEY NEEDED TO ESTABLISH WMD PRODUCTION. THE DETAINEE ALSO CLAIMED HE FABRICATED THE INFORMATION CONTAINED IN PARAGRAPH 10.)

- (S/ /NF) **Khalid Shaykh Muhammad.** With regard to Jaffar al-Tayyar, Majid Khan, and the Heathrow and gas station plots, the *Study* notes, based on ████████ 10906 (20 Mar 03), that "...MUKHTAR RECANTED HIS PREVIOUS ASSERTIONS THAT AL-TAYYAR IS/WAS INVOLVED IN THE HEATHROW OPERATION AND THE MAJID KHAN PLOT TO BLOW UP GAS STATIONS..." The study also quoted ████████ 10894 (22 Jun 03), which stated that "[KHALID SHYAKH MUHAMMAD] ALSO ADMITTED THAT HIS DECISION TO INCLUDE JAFFAR AL-TAYYAR IN THE MAJID ((KHAN)) PLOT INSIDE THE UNITED STATES...WAS A COMPLETE FABRICATION." Revised information on the Heathrow plot was disseminated in ████████

    DURING A CUSTODIAL INTERVIEW ON 18 MARCH 2003, MUKHTAR PROVIDED ADDITIONAL INFORMATION ON THE OPERATIVES HE IDENTIFIED TO PARTICIPATE IN THE ATTACK ON HEATHROW AIRPORT....ALTHOUGH MUKHTAR PREVIOUSLY STATED THAT JAFAR AL-((TAYYAR)) WAS INVOLVED IN THE LONDON CELL, HE RETRACTED THIS ASSERTION....

    o Revised information on the gas station plot was disseminated in ████████

    MUKHTAR REITERATED THAT HIS MAIN PLAN FOR MAJID KHAN WAS TO PURSUE THE PLOT OF BLOWING UP SEVERAL GASOLINE STATIONS IN THE UNITED STATES. HOWEVER, MUKHTAR ADMITTED THAT, IN FACT, HE NEVER INTENDED FOR AL-QA'IDA OPERATIVE JAFFAR AL-((TAYYAR)) TO PARTICIPATE IN THESE OPERATIONS.

    o With regard to Abu Issa, and Black Muslims in Montana: the *Study* states that Khalid Shaykh Muhammad recanted statements that he directed Abu Issa to convert Black Muslims in Montana. The report cites ████████ 12198 (3 Jul 03) as the source of that information. The revised information was disseminated in ████████ and ████████

    REGARDING THE ALLEGATION THAT ISSA HAD MENTIONED BLACK MUSLIM CONVERTS WITH FAMILY IN MONTANA WHO WORKED AS BODYGUARDS FOR SHAYKH ((ABU HAMZA AL-MASRI)), THE DETAINEE CONFIRMED THAT ISSA TOLD HIM ABOUT THE BODYGUARDS, AND SAID THAT HE BELIEVED THIS CAME UP WHEN HE SUGGESTED ISSA FIND SOMEONE IN THE UNITED KINGDOM WHO COULD HELP HIM SET UP THE MULTIPLE INCENDIARY DEVICES HE HAD CONCEIVED IN HIS PLAN. THE DETAINEE SAID THERE WAS NO

CONNECTION BETWEEN THE BODYGUARDS MENTIONED BY ISSA AND MONTANA.

THE DETAINEE CLARIFIED THAT HE DID NOT ASK ISSA TO RECRUIT AFRICAN-AMERICAN MUSLIMS IN MONTANA, BUT RATHER ISSA MENTIONED HE KNEW AN AFRICAN-AMERICAN MUSLIM IN MONTANA THROUGH HIS CONTACTS IN THE UNITED KINGDOM. THE DETAINEE SAID HE WAS ORIGINALLY CONFUSED ABOUT THIS ISSUE.

(U) **Conclusion 12: The CIA provided inaccurate information to the Department of Justice on the way in which interrogations were conducted, the conditions of confinement, and the effectiveness of the CIA's enhanced interrogation techniques. The Department of Justice relied on CIA's factual representations to support its conclusions that the program was consistent with U.S. statutes, the U.S. Constitution, and U.S. treaty obligations, and warned the CIA that if facts were to change, its legal conclusions might not apply.**

(S//OC/NF) CIA did not consistently or intentionally provide inaccurate information to DOJ. While stronger communication and coordination between CIA and DOJ's Office of Legal Counsel (OLC) would have enabled OLC's legal guidance to reflect more up-to-date factual information, we found no evidence that any information was known to be false when it was provided or that additional or more frequent updates would have altered OLC's key judgments.

- (S//OC/NF) For example, prior to issuance of OLC's 1 August 2002 opinion, CIA represented that "[enhanced techniques] will not be used with substantial repetition" as applied to any one detainee. As the program evolved, in certain exceptional cases—particularly involving the waterboard, which was applied to three detainees—the number of repetitions was inconsistent with this assertion. However, OLC made clear that the precise number of applications of the waterboard did not contravene OLC's guidance. The *Study* itself, summarizing a 2004 memorandum from OLC to the CIA IG, states:

  > The memorandum explained that the Attorney General had expressed the view that the legal principles in the OLC opinion would allow the same techniques to be used on detainees other than Abu Zubaydah and that the repetitions in the use of the waterboard on Khalid Shaykh Muhammad and Abu Zubaydah did not contravene the principles underlying the August 2002 opinion.

(S//OC/NF) Similarly, the *Study* emphasizes that in seeking initial legal guidance from OLC regarding interrogation techniques, CIA represented that it believed Abu Zubaydah was al-Qa'ida's third- or fourth-ranking leader. The *Study* alleges that CIA learned Zubaydah was not actually a formal member of al-Qa'ida prior to issuance of the August 2002 opinion, and failed to share this new information with DOJ. The implication is that had this information been made available, the guidance provided would have been different. While we acknowledge the Agency should have kept OLC more fully informed, neither the documents cited in the *Study* nor CIA's contemporaneous analytic judgments support the *Study's* conclusion.

- (S//OC/NF) As a threshold matter, the *Study* incorrectly claims that CIA's view of Abu Zubaydah's importance to al-Qa'ida was based solely on a single source who recanted. In fact, CIA had multiple threads of reporting indicating that Zubaydah was a dangerous terrorist, close associate of senior al-Qa'ida leaders, and was aware of critical logistical and operational details of the organization, whether or not he held formal rank in al-Qa'ida. Analysts did not alter their fundamental assessment of Zubaydah's intelligence value as a result of anything said or later recanted by the single source cited by the *Study*.

- (S//OC/NF) Moreover, it is important to note that there are no facts suggesting that the conclusions in the August 2002 opinion were dependent on CIA's representation about Abu Zubaydah's rank. In fact, the Attorney General later extended the opinion to other detainees for which no such representations were made. In 2003 he explicitly reaffirmed that the "legal principles reflected in DOJ's specific original advice could appropriately be extended to allow use of the same approved techniques (under the same conditions and subject to the same safeguards) to other individuals besides the subject of DOJ's specific original advice."

- (U//~~FOUO~~) More generally, the *Study* seems to misunderstand the role of OLC and its interaction with CIA. OLC is not an oversight body, and it does not act as a day-to-day legal advisor for any executive agency. Further, OLC does not "approve" executive agency activities. Instead, when requested and otherwise appropriate, OLC provides legal guidance and analysis to executive agencies on specific questions of law applicable to specific and defined sets of facts. It then is incumbent upon Executive agencies to apply OLC legal guidance to their activities. In doing so, agencies, including CIA, will often apply the legal guidance provided in a particular OLC memorandum to other similar factual scenarios. It is neither practical nor required for an agency to seek prior OLC legal review of all possible factual scenarios.

(~~TS/~~ ▓▓▓▓▓▓▓▓▓ ~~NF~~) In other instances cited by the *Study*, new or different information was only discovered *after* the issuance of applicable DOJ opinions. For example, the *Study* notes that CIA sought and obtained from DOJ authorization to use enhanced interrogation techniques on Janat Gul based on what turned out to be fabricated source reporting. As the *Study* itself acknowledges, however, this fabrication was not discovered until "[a]fter the CIA's use of its enhanced interrogation techniques on Gul."

(~~S//OC/NF~~) The *Study* mischaracterizes as inaccurate certain other representations CIA provided to DOJ by either omitting or inaccurately describing the surrounding context.

- (~~S//OC/NF~~) With regard to Abu Zubaydah, the *Study* claims that CIA's representation to OLC that it was "certain" Abu Zubaydah was withholding information on planned attacks was inaccurate, pointing to an "interrogation team" cable in which the team describes their objective as merely to *ensure* Abu Zubaydah was not holding back. The *Study*, however, neglects to relate critical elements later in the cable that go on to say that "[t]here is information and analysis to indicate that subject has information on terrorist threats to the United States"; and "[h]e is an incredibly strong willed individual which is why he has resisted this long".

- (~~S//OC/NF~~) The *Study* also notes that CIA inaccurately informed OLC in September 2004 that Ahmed Khalfan Ghailani was believed to have intelligence on individuals trained for an attack and may have been involved in attack plotting, despite "an email sent almost a month before the OLC letter indicat[ing] that this was speculation." The email referenced states only that Ghailani's specific role in operational planning was unclear, and then goes on to add that, "[i]n particular, Ghailani may know the identities and locations of operatives who trained in Shkai. He also may know aliases and intended destinations for these operatives...." Read in full, the underlying email fully supports CIA's representation regarding the intelligence Ghailani was believed to possess.

- (~~S//OC/NF~~)The *Study* points to alleged misstatements by CIA in late 2005 and early 2006 regarding conditions of confinement. It asserts CIA inaccurately represented that certain conditions—such as constant light, white noise, and the shaving of detainees—

were used for security purposes when, in fact, the record indicates they were also used for other purposes related to interrogation. These assertions take CIA's representations out of context, as they originated from communications with OLC regarding which measures would be *necessary* for security purposes, without excluding any other ancillary purposes they might serve. Indeed, we were unable to find any representation by CIA that security was the sole purpose of these measures. Moreover, in April 2006, CIA sought to specifically clarify this issue with OLC when it became clear this concept was not well understood. Responding to a draft OLC opinion, CIA stated, "Overarching issue. This opinion focuses exclusively on the use of these conditions for the security of the installation and personnel. However, these conditions are also used for other valid reasons, such as to create an environment conducive to transitioning captured and resistant terrorists to detainees participating in debriefings."

(U//FOUO) Finally, the *Study* generally alleges that representations made to OLC prior to its May 30, 2005 opinion regarding the importance of intelligence obtained as a result of the program in thwarting various terrorist plots were inaccurate. The Agency's refutation of charges that it misrepresented the value of program-derived intelligence is presented in Appendix B.

(U//FOUO) CIA at all times sought to obtain legal guidance from DOJ based on the best information then available. Nevertheless, it is clear the Agency could and should have taken greater steps to support the integrity of the process and guarantee transparency, both in fact and in appearance, by occasionally revisiting its factual representations and updating them as necessary—even when doing so would not have had a practical impact on the outcome.

> **(U) Conclusion 13: The CIA actively impeded Congressional oversight of the CIA detention and interrogation program. In 2002, the CIA avoided and denied then-Chairman Bob Graham's oversight requests for additional information about the program, and later resisted efforts by then-Vice Chairman John D. Rockefeller IV to investigate the program. The CIA restricted briefings of the CIA interrogation program to the Chairman and Vice Chairman of the Senate Select Committee on Intelligence until September 6, 2006, the day the President of the United States publicly acknowledged the program. Prior to that time, the CIA declined to answer all questions from other Committee members. Once the full membership of the Committee was briefed, the CIA continued to impede Committee oversight by restricting the members' staff from being "read-in" to the program, delaying and denying the provision of information on the program, and refusing to respond to formal Committee questions for the record. Information the CIA did provide on the operation and effectiveness of the CIA detention and interrogation program was largely inaccurate from 2002 through at least 2011. The CIA Director nonetheless represented that the CIA detention and interrogation program was "fully briefed" to "every member of our Intelligence Committees," relaying to foreign government leaders that therefore the interrogation program was not a CIA program, but "America's program." Ultimately, the Committee and both the Senate and the House of Representatives rejected the CIA program in bipartisan legislation.**

(TS/~~███████████~~NF) We disagree with the *Study's* conclusion that the Agency actively impeded Congressional oversight of the CIA detention and interrogation program. We believe the record demonstrates that CIA leaders made a good faith effort to keep oversight committee leaders fully briefed on the program within the strict limits on access that had been set by the White House. Within these parameters, Agency records indicate a fairly consistent engagement with Congressional oversight in the period prior to the public acknowledgment of the program. As discussed in our response to Conclusion 9, we also disagree with the assessment that the information CIA provided on the effectiveness of the program was largely inaccurate. Finally, we have reviewed DCIA Hayden's testimony before SSCI on 12 April, 2007 and do not find, as the *Study* claims, that he misrepresented virtually all aspects of the program, although a few aspects were in error.

(TS/~~███████████~~NF) CIA acknowledges that it did not share all available information concerning the program with all members of the Committees—especially prior to 6 September, 2006—but this was in keeping with the guidance provided by the White House. Under the National Security Act of 1947 as amended, Section 503(c) (2), the President sets the parameters for how much information on covert action programs is shared with the Congress; CIA does not determine such access. While all oversight committee members were informed of the existence of the program, the White House decided that information on the enhanced interrogation techniques would be restricted to the chairman and the ranking minority members of the oversight committees, along with up to two additional staffers on each committee. Within this framework, the records show an effort to keep congressional oversight informed of developments, as a few key examples indicate.

- (TS/~~███████████~~NF) In total, CIA briefed SSCI members or staff on rendition, detention, or interrogation issues more than 35 times from 2002-2008. CIA provided more than 30 similar briefings to HPSCI members or staff during the same time period and provided more than 20 notifications.

- (TS/███████████NF) CIA began using enhanced techniques while Congress was in its August 2002 recess. The first briefing of HPSCI leadership followed on 4 September while SSCI leaders received the same briefing on 27 September. Both briefings for leaders covered background on the authorities to use the techniques, the coordination which had taken place with DoJ and the White House, a description of the enhanced techniques which had been employed, and some discussion of the intelligence that had been acquired.

- (TS/███████████NF) CIA's Inspector General was informed of a case of a deviation from approved techniques and of the death of Gul Rahman on 21 and 22 January 2003 respectively. CIA briefed those incidents to DoJ on 24 January and underscored its intention to notify the new leadership of the oversight committees as part of a previously planned briefing on interrogation practices. These briefings took place on 4 and 5 February, and covered what had happened in both cases, what intelligence was being collected in the debriefings, a detailed discussion of enhanced techniques, and CIA's intention to destroy tapes of the interrogation sessions.

- (TS/███████████NF) CIA's Inspector General initiated a review of CIA's counterterrorism detention and interrogation activities in January 2003. The review was completed in May 2004 and he and senior CIA officers briefed the results to the HPSCI and SSCI leadership on 13 and 15 July respectively. The HPSCI session lasted two hours and contemporaneous notes indicate it evolved into an in-depth discussion of the practical, political, legal, and moral issues involved. The Inspector General followed up with separate briefings for the SSCI leadership in early March 2005 on the cases and projects pending in his office.

- (TS/███████████NF) The leadership of both oversight committees were briefed in March 2005. The topics ranged from the legal justifications for enhanced techniques, internal controls and safeguards, the approach that was taken to employing the techniques, and interrogation results.

(U//FOUO) We disagree with the *Study's* contention that limiting access is tantamount to impeding Congressional oversight. The *Study* cites a number of examples to bolster its contention; these involve points of process, refusal to provide documents, and selective provision of information to shape legal opinions. We assess all contain inaccuracies.

- (U//FOUO) Conclusion 13 does not reflect mutually agreed upon past or current practices for handling restricted access programs. Indeed, the Committee codified, as part of the FY12 Intelligence Authorization Act, the practice of briefing sensitive matters to just the Chairman and Ranking Member, along with notice to the rest of the Committee that their leadership has received such a briefing.

- (U//FOUO) We also disagree with the *Study's* contention that not "reading-in" additional Committee staffers in the post-2006 period equates to actively impeding oversight. Restricting staff access was consistent with current and long-standing practice as regards sensitive covert action programs.

- (U/~~FOUO~~) The *Study's* statement that CIA denied Members' requests for a copy of the OLC Memoranda is incorrect. CIA did not have the authority to provide those memoranda to the Committee. The President and the Attorney General determine whether to grant direct access. In lieu of providing the memoranda, however, Acting Assistant Attorney General Bradbury testified and provided information about the OLC memoranda.

(~~TS/~~ ███████████████ ~~NF~~) Finally, we disagree with the *Study's* claim that DCIA Hayden's testimony before SSCI on 12 April 2007 misrepresented virtually all aspects of the program. The testimony contained some inaccuracies, and the Agency should have done better in preparing the Director, particularly concerning events that occurred prior to his tenure. However, there is no evidence that there was any intent on the part of the Agency or Director Hayden to misrepresent material facts. DCIA Hayden sought in the statements made during this session to discuss the history of the program, the safeguards that had been built into it, and the way ahead.

- (U/~~FOUO~~) Consistent with our response to Conclusion 9, we maintain that his characterization of the intelligence derived from the program as having helped the US disrupt plots, save lives, capture terrorists and, as a supplementary benefit, better understand the enemy, was correct.

- (~~TS/~~ ███████████████ ~~NF~~) In his statement for the record, DCIA Hayden noted as an example of a safeguard CIA had built into the program that all those involved in the questioning of detainees are carefully selected and trained. We concede that prior to promulgation of DCIA guidance on interrogation in January 2003 and the establishment of interrogator training courses in November of the same year, not every CIA employee who debriefed detainees had been thoroughly screened or had received formal training. After that time, however—the period with which DCIA Hayden, who came to the Agency in 2005, was most familiar—the statement is accurate.

- (~~TS/~~ ███████████████ ~~NF~~) DCIA Hayden stated that "punches" and "kicks" were not authorized techniques and had never been employed and that CIA officers never threatened a detainee or his family. Part of that assertion was an error. The DCIA would have been better served if the Agency had framed a response for him that discussed CIA's policy prohibiting such conduct, and how the Agency moved to address unsanctioned behavior which had occurred (including punches and kicks) and implement clear guidelines. He could have also reported that CIA's Inspector General investigated these incidents and recommended reviews of the employees' conduct as warranted. Several employees were removed from the program for the use of unsanctioned techniques.

- (~~TS/~~ ███████████████ ~~NF~~) Director Hayden also expressed his view that CIA would not have been able to obtain the intelligence it did from 30 detainees who underwent enhanced interrogation techniques if the Agency had been restricted to the Army Field Manual alone. CIA's current view, as described elsewhere in our response, is that it is inherently unknowable whether the Agency could have acquired the same information without the use of enhanced techniques. That does not, however, suggest that Director Hayden sought to mislead when he expressed his opinion.

- (TS/▮▮▮▮▮▮▮▮▮▮▮▮▮▮/NF) We acknowledge that the location of the "blacksites" was withheld from the full Committee. As DCIA Hayden and others made clear, however, CIA was not authorized to share that information.

- (S//NF//OC) We disagree with the *Study's* claim that DCIA Hayden misled Congress on the videotapes. As noted above, CIA officials in January 2003 notified the leadership of both Congressional oversight committees of the existence of tapes of interrogations and of CIA's intent to destroy them. We acknowledge that DCIA did not volunteer past information on CIA's process of videotaping the interrogation sessions or of the destruction of the tapes, but note that by the time hearing took place, HPSCI and SSCI leaders had been notified of the tapes' destruction and had access to the 2004 CIA IG report that spoke in detail concerning the tapes' existence.

> (C//OC/NF) **Conclusion 14: The CIA's Office of Public Affairs and senior CIA leadership coordinated to share classified information on the CIA detention and interrogation program to select members of the media to counter public criticism and avoid potential Congressional action to restrict the CIA's detention and interrogation authorities and budget. Much of the information the CIA provided to the media on the operation and effectiveness of the CIA detention and interrogation program was inaccurate. It was the policy of the CIA not to submit crimes reports on potential disclosures of classified information to the media when the CIA's Office of Public Affairs and the CIA leadership had sanctioned the cooperation with the media.**

(C//OC/NF) CIA did occasionally engage with the media on the RDI program, but the *Study* is wrong in asserting that it did so for the purpose of avoiding oversight or that there was a coordinated, systemic public relations campaign to garner support for the program. The Office of Public Affairs' (OPA) records from this period are fragmentary, but the documents that are available, as well as the recollections of those working in OPA at the time, indicate that the vast majority of CIA's engagement with the media on the program was the result of queries from reporters seeking Agency comment on information they had obtained *elsewhere.* As a result, the primary purpose of these interactions—as with many of our interaction with the media--was to persuade reporters to safeguard as much sensitive intelligence as possible and to minimize inaccuracies that might reflect badly on the US Government.

(C//OC/NF) The Agency makes decisions to engage with journalists on press stories or book projects on a case-by-case basis after a review of the risks and potential benefits to the US Government, including the opportunities to mitigate or limit the disclosure of classified information. In general, when reporters come to OPA with stories on classified programs and sources and methods, Director OPA (D/OPA) will consult with CIA leadership and those components whose operational equities are at stake.

- (C//OC/NF) When faced with a reporter who already has classified information in hand, there are a number of potential options, including asking the reporter to hold the story or remove specific information, which sometimes has the effect of providing an off-the-record acknowledgement of the sensitive information; steering the reporter away from incorrect information that impinges on sources and methods without confirming any other information; providing a balanced perspective via a broad overview that does not provide additional detail; and declining to comment.

(C//OC/NF) During this period, CIA's interaction with the media involved examples that fell into each of these categories. The Agency consistently tried to protect classified programs and, if necessary, provide context that would allow the program to be put into context. As is always the case, the reporters and their management ultimately decided what information to publish.

(C//OC/NF) The supporting text to Conclusion 14 focuses on a single interaction between the CIA and the media in 2005, as evidence of a CIA plan to make unauthorized releases of classified information in order to increase public support for the program and blunt any Congressional opposition to program activities that could arise. The *Study's* account of this interaction omits key facts. We acknowledge that some CIA officers, including then-Director Porter Goss, met with Tom Brokaw of NBC news in April, 2005. Although Agency records from the period are incomplete, the documentary record we do have as well as our conversations with former officers strongly indicate that it was NBC that initiated contact with the Agency, requesting information as part of a one-hour documentary to be hosted by Mr. Brokaw on the global war on terrorism.

- (C//OC/NF) The record shows a careful effort to create talking points for both the Director and the Deputy Director of CTC that referenced previously disclosed or reported material, with citations for each item to public sources such as the 9-11 Commission Report, court documents, and periodicals. We found no materials showing discussions about making first-time, classified disclosures.

- (C//OC/NF) The *Study* cites a portion of an electronic "chat" between the Deputy Director of CTC and another officer, construing it as evidence that the Agency intended to provide classified information to NBC in an effort to "sell" the program publically. As a threshold matter, the informal comments of any one CIA officer do not constitute Agency policy with regard to media interactions. More importantly, a review of the complete chat transcript and contemporaneous emails that were made available to the Committee shows that the officers were discussing the talking points mentioned above, which describe previously disclosed information relating to the program.

- (U) A review of the NBC broadcast, cited by the *Study*, shows that it contained no public disclosures of classified CIA information; indeed, *the RDI program was not discussed*.

(C//OC/NF) We also disagree with the Study's allegation that the information that we provided to the public regarding the value of the intelligence derived from the program was inaccurate. Our response to Conclusion 9 makes clear that CIA's representations, as reflected in President Bush's 2006 speech, were, with one exception, accurate.

(C//OC/NF) Conclusion 14 is incomplete with regard to its discussion of CIA policy on unauthorized disclosures. With regard to intelligence activities, Agency regulations empower the Director of Public Affairs, with the approval of one of the Agency's top three leaders (DCIA, DDCIA, and EXDIR), to authorize the disclosure of information to the media. With regard to information related to covert action, authorization rests with the White House. When such authorizations occur, there is self-evidently no need for a crimes report as the disclosure is fully in accord with the law.

- (TS/ ████████████ NF) Records on the drafting of an unrealized public "rollout" of the RDI program, cited by the *Study*, are incomplete. But any such rollout would have been, by definition, an authorized disclosure implemented at the direction of and in concert with the White House, which owns all covert action programs. It would be nonsensical to file a crimes report on this or similar properly authorized disclosures.

> **(S//OC/NF)** Conclusion 15: The CIA's management and operation of the detention and interrogation program was deeply flawed. Despite the importance and significance of the authorities granted to the CIA to detain individuals outside of established law enforcement or military structures, the CIA did not keep accurate records on those it detained, placed individuals with no experience or training in senior detention and interrogation roles, and had inadequate linguistic and analytical support to conduct effective questioning of CIA detainees. The CIA also selected personnel to carry out sensitive detention and interrogation activities who had documented personal and professional problems which called into question the suitability of their participation in a sensitive CIA program, as well as their employment with the CIA and eligibility for access to classified information.

(TS/███████████████NF) We agree that the Agency made serious missteps in the management and operation of the program in its early days, as we discuss in Conclusion 1. However, by focusing almost exclusively on CIA's early efforts in █████████and at█████ we believe the *Study* significantly overstates CIA's shortcomings in managing the RDI program as a whole.

(TS/███████████████NF) As noted in our response to Conclusion 1, on September 12, 2001, CIA was unprepared to take on the operation of a worldwide detention program. It lacked key resources and expertise—particularly language-trained officers and personnel knowledgeable about detention facility management or interrogation. As CIA surged officers to the field in█████████the Agency's natural inclination was to focus on operations, analysis, and plot disruption. But even allowing for this mission-focused predisposition and the inherent difficulties█████████████CIA failed to focus sufficient attention on creating standard operating procedures to manage detention facilities, provide officers in the field the resources they needed, or begin to keep adequate records until early 2003. As a direct consequence of these failings, CIA's operation of ███████████████was marred by serious flaws.

- (TS/███████████████NF) In the earliest days of the program, CIA officers were unsure which CIA component was responsible for managing the█████facility,███████
  █████████████████████████████ Multiple components at Headquarters monitored the facility, but no one actively "owned" it. There is no justification for this confusion, and its existence represents a failure of management. CIA leadership should have made clear from the outset which component and chain of command bore unambiguous responsibility for█████and its detainees.

- (S//OC/NF) As the IG previously noted in its 2004 Special Review of the program, Headquarters officials did not act swiftly to respond to the field's concerns about inadequate staffing levels. As a result of staffing shortfalls, during the early months of █████some detainees were not being questioned because the Agency lacked a sufficient number of debriefers in country. Moreover, CIA asked some officers to take on responsibilities for which they were neither prepared nor trained.

- (S//OC/NF) As a result of these severe shortfalls, a junior, "first tour" officer in █████████was asked to assume responsibilities for detainee interrogations only weeks after his arrival there. As the *Study* and two IG reports observed, that officer was later

41

involved in the death of detainee Gul Rahman at ███████ Delegating management of the ███████ facility and detainee affairs in ███████ to a first tour officer was not a prudent managerial decision given the risks inherent in the program. The Agency could have and should have brought in a more experienced officer to assume these responsibilities. The death of Rahman, under conditions that could have been remediated by Agency officers, is a lasting mark on the Agency's record.

(S//OC/NF) While we acknowledge these shortcomings, the *Study* fails to take note of significant improvements implemented at ███████ following Rahman's death, as well as the far more stringent standards governing interrogations and safety applied at later detention sites. Headquarters established CTC's Renditions and Detentions Group CTC/RDG as the responsible entity for all CIA detention and interrogation sites in December 2002, removing any latent institutional confusion. CTC/RDG sent its first team to ███████ to debrief and interrogate detainees that same month, and the team immediately established procedures for requesting approval for enhanced techniques. These procedures were further institutionalized following promulgation of the DCI's Detention and Interrogation Guidelines in January 2003. With the exception of water dousing and the use of a wooden dowel behind the knees of a detainee employed by the lead HVT interrogator (who was removed from the program as a consequence of employing the latter in July 2003), these adjustments eliminated the use of improvised techniques, which were criticized extensively in the 2004 IG's *Special Review* and in its investigation report on Gul Rahman's death, as they are in the *Study*.

- (TS/███████NF) There were inherent limitations on Agency efforts to upgrade ███████ Its location ███████ made it difficult to implement facilities upgrades to bring it more in line with sites like ███████ ███████ The program continued to face challenges in identifying sufficient, qualified staff—particularly language-qualified personnel—as requirements imposed by Agency involvement in Iraq increased. However, the first Quarterly Review of Confinement Conditions mandated by the 31 January 03 DCIA Guidelines on the Conditions of Confinement, produced in April 2003, cited significant improvements at ███████ including space heaters, sanitation and hygiene enhancements, as well as better nutrition for the detainee population.

(S//OC/NF) Indeed, from January 2003 through 2005 the program as a whole continuously improved. Certification of officers involved in interrogations continued; procedures and confinement conditions continued to be refined and upgraded. This is reflected in the CIA IG's 2005 audit of the program, which concluded that the overall program for operating detention and interrogation facilities was effective and that standards, guidelines, and recordkeeping were generally sufficient. As occasional errors occurred over the remaining life of the program, they were reviewed by supervisors and IG investigations, and sometimes resulted in accountability boards or, in appropriate cases, referrals to the Department of Justice.

(TS/███████NF) In ███████ was eventually closed in accord with planning begun in ███████ and necessitated by the site's inherent limitations with respect to operational security. ███████ CIA decided that the risks of operating ███████ outweighed the benefits of having a place to intern detainees who could no longer be housed in ███████

███ The decision to close ██████████
reflected a maturation of CIA's approach to risk management in the program and better prioritization of longer term detention challenges.

(S//OC/NF) The *Study* omits important additional facts and context relating to its critique of Agency recordkeeping and the selection of officers with questionable professional and personal track records to perform interrogations and other sensitive program tasks.

(S//OC/NF) First, the decline in reporting over time on the use of enhanced techniques, which the *Study* characterizes as poor or deceptive recordkeeping, actually reflects the maturation of the program. In early 2003, a process was put in place whereby interrogators requested permission in advance for interrogation plans. The use of these plans for each detainee obviated the need for reporting in extensive detail on the use of specific techniques, unless there were deviations from the approved plan. Moreover, the use of certain techniques declined over time; the list of approved techniques dropped from a high of 13 in 2004 to six in 2007. The waterboard was not used after March 2003.

(S//OC/NF) Second, the *Study* implies that Agency managers knowingly sent ██████ individuals to the field, highlighting ███████████ officers with problematic service or personal histories. Overall, more than ███ officers were part of this program over its life. The vast majority were solid performers and were well trained. ████████████████████████████████████ some of the ███ officers mentioned in the *Study*—█████████████████████████ should have been excluded—much of the derogatory information was not in fact available to senior managers making assignments ██████ ████████████████████████

(S//OC/NF) For example, the junior officer assigned to oversee ████████ was not placed in his position by a formal Headquarters assignment panel, but was given his responsibilities as a consequence of an on-the-scene decision by ████ COS ████████ operating in a resource-constrained environment, ██

• ██

(S//OC/NF) **Conclusion 16: CIA officers and contractors involved in the CIA detention and interrogation program known to have violated CIA policy were rarely held accountable by the CIA, including those CIA officers who used unauthorized interrogation techniques against CIA detainees. Significant events, to include the death and injury of detainees and the detention of individuals who did not meet the legal standard to be held by the CIA, did not result in appropriate organizational lessons learned or effective corrective actions.**

(S//OC/NF) Our review of Conclusion 16 did indicate significant shortcomings in CIA's handling of accountability for problems in the conduct and management of CIA's RDI activities. However, the *Study* lays out two supporting arguments that are best assessed separately, because we agree—and have expanded on—the first, but the second appears unfounded.

- (S//OC/NF) The first argument is that in some important cases involving clearly evident misconduct, the CIA did not in the end sufficiently hold officers accountable even after full investigation and adjudication.[9] We largely concur, although we would take the *Study's* argument one step further. The *Study* focuses on the inadequate consequences meted out for line officers who acted contrary to policy in conducting interrogations in the field or in providing the rationale for captures from CTC. To us, an even more compelling concern is that the Agency did not sufficiently broaden and elevate the focus of its accountability efforts to include the more senior officers who were responsible for organizing, guiding, staffing, and supervising RDI activities, especially in the beginning.

- (S//OC/NF) The Conclusion's second supporting argument is that there were many more instances of improper actions for which some form of accountability exercise should have been conducted but was not. We found problems with the factual basis for this argument.

(S//OC/NF) **Accountability Outcomes.** CIA's RDI activities engendered a significant number of accountability-related actions. The IG, often in response to CIA referrals, conducted at least 29 investigations of RDI-related conduct, plus two wide-ranging reviews of the program. Many cases were investigated by the IG and found to be without merit. Of the cases which were found to be supported by the facts, one involved the death of an Afghan national who was beaten by a contractor. The individual involved was prosecuted by the Department of Justice and convicted on a felony charge. Another case involved a contractor who slapped, kicked, and struck detainees when they were in military custody. Shortly after the IG concluded its investigation of that case, the contractor was terminated from the CIA, had his security clearances revoked, and was placed on a contractor watchlist.

(S//OC/NF) In addition to IG investigations and criminal prosecutions—including an omnibus three-year investigation of all RDI activity by a DoJ special prosecutor, which involved the review of more than 100 detainee cases, involving those in both Agency and DoD custody—CIA convened six accountability proceedings, either at the directorate or higher level, from 2003 to

---

[9] The *Study's* main boldface conclusion states that those known to have violated policy were "*rarely* held accountable," but the first line of the discussion that follows states categorically that CIA "*did not* hold individuals accountable for abuses in the CIA detention and interrogation program" (emphasis added). For purposes of our response, and in light of the substantial documentation demonstrating the existence of numerous accountability exercises, we will assume that the authors intended to allege that we only "rarely" held officers accountable.

2012. These reviews assessed the performance of 30 individuals (staff officers and contractors), and 16 were deemed accountable and sanctioned. [10]

(S//OC/NF) Although considerable attention was paid to cases of wrongdoing, we acknowledge that, particularly in the cases cited in the *Study's* Conclusion, the narrow scope of CIA's accountability efforts yielded outcomes that are, in retrospect, unsatisfying in view of the serious nature of the events. Most egregiously, we believe that CIA leaders erred in not holding anyone formally accountable for the actions and failure of management related to the death of **Gul Rahman** at ███████ in 2002. We understand the reasoning underlying CIA management's decision to overturn an accountability board recommendation that would have imposed sanctions on the least experienced officer involved. The most junior in the chain of command should not have to bear the full weight of accountability when larger, systemic problems exist and when they are thrust into difficult battlefield situations by their supervisors and given a risky and difficult task and little preparation or guidance. Still, it is hard to accept that a CIA officer does not bear at least some responsibility for his or her actions, even under trying circumstances.

- (S//OC/NF) Moreover, deciding to minimize the punishment for a junior officer should not have been the end of the matter. CIA had an affirmative obligation to look more deeply into the leadership decisions that helped shape the environment in which the junior officer was required to operate, to examine what could have been done better, and to determine what responsibility, if any, should be fixed at a more senior level.

(TS/███████████████NF) In the case of **Khalid al-Masri** , our view of the accountability exercise is more mixed. As discussed in our response to Conclusion 18, the Agency applied the wrong interpretation of the MoN standard and plainly took too long to remediate its mistake. In that instance, an accountability review was undertaken and then-DCIA Hayden took significant steps to improve Agency practices in the wake of the error, directing that the Acting General Counsel review the legal guidance provided to CTC regarding renditions. The Director further called for a zero-based review of the operations officers and managers who were required to make analytic targeting judgments to determine the appropriate level of formal analytic training these officers needed to be effective in discharging their duties. That review was done, and it resulted in improved training for officers engaged in targeting work.

- (S//OC/NF) Nonetheless, we concede that it is difficult in hindsight to understand how the Agency could make such a mistake, take too long to correct it, determine that a flawed legal interpretation contributed, and in the end only hold accountable three CTC attorneys, two of whom received only an oral admonition.

---

[10] In the RDI-related reviews, some of the officers assessed as accountable received disciplinary actions including one and two year prohibitions on promotion or any form of monetary recognition. Disciplinary actions at the level of Letters of Reprimand or above are permanently maintained in the security files of the disciplined officers. Other officers received oral admonitions and letters of warning; these individuals were those with a lesser degree of involvement in the matters under review. Some of the officers assessed as accountable were either not recommended for disciplinary action or recommended for lesser disciplinary actions, due to mitigating factors that included whether these officers had been provided appropriate guidance from CIA Headquarters; had sought, but not received, adequate guidance; or were not found to have acted with malice.

(S//OC/NF) Accountability was more robust with regard to the incident in which an officer sought to frighten **Abd al-Rahim al-Nashiri** by threatening him with an unloaded handgun and a powerdrill. The senior officer present, who authorized use of the gun and drill as fear-inducers, retired ███████████ and was therefore beyond the reach of meaningful discipline. The subordinate officer involved, who had exhibited poor judgment but had obtained his supervisor's permission, received a letter of reprimand, was blocked from receiving pay increases or promotions for two years, suspended without pay for a week, and removed from the program.

- (S//OC/NF) However, we found no indication that the accountability process looked beyond the specific actions of these two officers to determine accountability for any management shortcomings related to such issues as the suitability of the officers involved or the paucity of guidance—the incident occurred prior to dissemination of DCI's formal guidance on interrogation techniques—under which they were operating.

(S//OC/NF) Although we do not believe it would be practical or productive to revisit any RDI-related case so long after the events unfolded, looking forward the Agency should ensure that leaders who run accountability exercises do not limit their sights to the perpetrators of the specific wrongful action, but look more broadly at management responsibility and look more consistently at any systemic issues. At a minimum, no board should cite a broader issue as a mitigating factor in its accountability decision on an individual without addressing that issue head on, provided it remains practical to do so.

- (U//FOUO) In that regard we must note that such boards are sometimes encumbered by the excessive length of time that can lapse between the offending action and the convening of the board. Boards begun years after an event struggle just to sort out the basic facts, and they are not well positioned to expand the scope of inquiry or remedy management issues long in the past. Unfortunately, this problem can defy ready solution, because when it occurs, a contributing factor may be the time required for the DoJ to investigate and decide whether to prosecute any offenses.

(S//OC/NF) Although we judge that the outcomes of these accountability exercises were inadequate, at least in scope, the record does show that, contrary to the claim in Conclusion 16, CIA often learned much from its mistakes and took corrective action. As we have discussed in responses to various *Study* conclusions, Gul Rahman's death catalyzed significant improvements in the organization, management, and conduct of the program. CIA made other significant adjustments in response to various internal and external reviews and investigations. For example, in response to the 2004 IG *Special Review*, CIA further refined its detention and interrogation guidelines; made improvements in CTC detainee record keeping; reviewed staffing plans for RDI facilities; issued additional Headquarters instructions to Chiefs of Station on their RDI responsibilities; worked to further ensure the timely dissemination of intelligence collected from detainees; and reviewed options available for eventual disposition of CIA detainees. The documentary record shows clearly that CIA took the recommendations seriously and that senior CIA leadership directed, and monitored, remedial actions as they were implemented.

(U//FOUO) **Alleged Additional Offenses**. As noted above, we were not persuaded by the *Study's* argument that there were multiple accountable offenses that CIA ignored. For instance, the *Study* alleges that 16 detainees were subjected to enhanced techniques without written authorization, and that officers participated in the use of enhanced techniques with at least eight detainees without having received approval to do so. As discussed in our response to Conclusion 20, the *Study* is wrong on both counts and falls short in its attempt to make the case that greater accountability was warranted. No more than seven detainees received enhanced techniques prior to written Headquarters approval; the *Study* miscounts because it confuses the use of standard techniques that did not require prior approval at the time they were administered with enhanced techniques that did.

- (S//OC/NF) One of the seven was Gul Rahman; in the other cases no accountability review was warranted because of a variety of mitigating factors, such as the fact that the unauthorized techniques in question did not differ greatly from those which Headquarters had already approved, Headquarters approved use of the techniques shortly after their use, or the existence of evidence indicating that there was no intent to mislead Headquarters or to substantively alter the approved interrogation plans.

- (S//OC/NF) With regard to the participation of insufficiently trained interrogators, in reaching its total the *Study* ignores the fact that interrogators were required, as a predicate to receiving certification, to participate in the application of enhanced techniques under the supervision of an already-certified instructor. As a result, an accountability review would have been inappropriate.

(TS/██████████, NF) Similarly, the *Study* claims that 26 individuals were detained even though they did not meet the requisite MoN standard. As our response to Conclusion 18 makes clear, the precise number, while the subject of much debate, was far fewer. The *Study's* count rests on a lack of appreciation for the evolving nature of intelligence and the real-world realities of the battlefield.

- (TS/██████████ NF) The fact that the intelligence case for detaining an individual is later shown to be less powerful than originally thought does not, in itself, render the original reasonably well-founded decision to detain "wrongful," and therefore deserving of accountability review. Most notably, we observe that in decisions to detain within the context ██████████████████████████ which represent a large percentage of the 26 cases cited by the *Study*— evidence indicates the MoN standard was in fact met. The decisions were prompted by a reasonable belief that an individual was "planning terrorist activities" or represented a "serious threat of violence or death to U.S persons." When it subsequently learned that a given detainee did not, in fact, meet this standard, CIA's general course of action was to remedy the error, release the detainee, and provide cash payments for lost wages and inconvenience.

(S//OC/NF) **Conclusion 17: The CIA improperly used two private contractors with no relevant experience to develop, operate, and assess the CIA detention and interrogation program. In 2005, the contractors formed a company specifically for the purpose of expanding their detention and interrogation work with the CIA. Shortly thereafter, virtually all aspects of the CIA's detention and interrogation program were outsourced to the company. By 2006, the value of the base contract with the company with all options exercised was in excess of $180 million. In 2007, the CIA signed a multi-year indemnification agreement protecting the company and its employees from legal liability.**

(U//FOUO) We agree that CIA should have done more from the outset to ensure there was no conflict of interest—either apparent or actual—in the role performed by the contractors selected to assist with the program. However, we disagree that the contractors lacked important and relevant experience, that we "outsourced" or somehow lost governmental control over the program, or that the Agency erred in entering into a relatively commonplace indemnification agreement with the contractors' company.

(TS/   NF) Over the course of the detention and interrogation effort, the roles performed by   included interrogations, assessment of detainees' psychological fitness for interrogation, as well as assessment of the effectiveness of particular interrogation techniques, among other responsibilities. They performed these functions as part of an interrogation team in which decision-making authority rested with a CIA staff officer. As the *Study* correctly points out, the propriety of the wide-ranging nature of the psychologists' roles—particularly their involvement in 1) performing interrogations, 2) assessing the detainees' psychological fitness, and 3) assessing the techniques' effectiveness—raised concerns and prompted considerable discussion and deliberation within CIA.

- (S//OC/NF) As a result of these internal deliberations and reviews relating to the propriety of permitting one individual to play the dual role of psychologist and interrogator, CIA management promulgated guidance on the scope of the contractor psychologists' involvement in individual interrogations. On 30 January 2003, CIA Headquarters affirmed that CIA policy was to ensure that no contractor could issue the psychological assessment of record and that the staff psychologist responsible for this assessment could not be serving in a role which included the application of interrogation techniques on the same detainee nor focus their support on assisting the interrogators for the purpose of the interrogation instead of the detainee's psychological health.[11]

- (TS/   NF) In practice, by April 2003, staff psychologists had taken over almost all of the provision of support to the RDI program. As it concerned   however, the appearance of impropriety continued, albeit to a lesser degree, because they were occasionally asked to provide input to assessments on detainees whom they had not interrogated. CIA's policy on this score changed in May 2004, limiting them to an interrogation role only.

---

[11] DIRECTOR

- (S//OC/NF) We acknowledge that the Agency erred in permitting the contractors to assess the effectiveness of enhanced techniques. They should not have been considered for such a role given their financial interest in continued contracts from CIA.

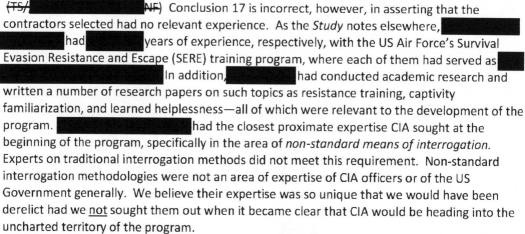

(TS/███████████NF) Conclusion 17 is incorrect, however, in asserting that the contractors selected had no relevant experience. As the *Study* notes elsewhere,█████████ ██████had██████years of experience, respectively, with the US Air Force's Survival Evasion Resistance and Escape (SERE) training program, where each of them had served as██ █████████████ In addition,████████ had conducted academic research and written a number of research papers on such topics as resistance training, captivity familiarization, and learned helplessness—all of which were relevant to the development of the program. ██████████████had the closest proximate expertise CIA sought at the beginning of the program, specifically in the area of *non-standard means of interrogation*. Experts on traditional interrogation methods did not meet this requirement. Non-standard interrogation methodologies were not an area of expertise of CIA officers or of the US Government generally. We believe their expertise was so unique that we would have been derelict had we <u>not</u> sought them out when it became clear that CIA would be heading into the uncharted territory of the program.

(TS/███████████NF) Conclusion 17's assertion that we "outsourced" the program is likewise flawed. Although the company that the two psychologists formed,████████████ ██████████ did take on a fairly comprehensive set of responsibilities, including interrogation services, security teams for facilities, and training, all of that work was closely managed by CIA staff officers pursuant to policy guidelines and oversight from Headquarters managers. Their role also served as tacit acknowledgement that interrogating detainees and managing internment facilities would not be a long-term CIA core mission.

- (TS/███████████NF) The *Study's* citation of the value of████contract is requires clarification. Although the value of the contract would have been in excess of $180 million if all options had been exercised, in fact the firm was actually paid about $81 million by the time the contract was terminated in 2009.

(TS/███████████NF) The *Study* implies that there was something unusual and nefarious in CIA's indemnification of████which protected the company and its employees from legal liability arising out of their work on the RDI program. In fact, the need and value of indemnification provisions for private corporations that assist the Government in achieving its national security priorities are widely recognized, including in the Detainee Treatment Act and the FISA Amendments Act. Without such agreements, it would be difficult and ultimately more expensive to find quality firms willing to take on difficult tasks that bear greater than usual legal risk.

- (TS/███████████NF) The terms of the indemnification agreement with████ ensured that it was in the Government's best interest. The agreement set a overall monetary cap, and excluded indemnification for gross negligence or intentional misconduct, lost profits, damages to reputation, or any legal fees or fines resulting from a final adjudication of guilt of any criminal offense in any US federal or state court.

(TS/███████████NF) Finally, the *Study* notes that CIA employees were lured away to work for████ That is true, but this phenomenon was not unique to that firm. Government wide, the surge in capacity needed to fight the war on terrorism was heavily dependent on the services of a variety of contractors, which created a strong demand for cleared personnel and, for too many of our employees, an irresistible financial lure. Indeed, the resulting loss of talent and the morale problems created when employees saw colleagues resign one day and return the next at higher pay became sufficiently acute that in 2007 CIA issued regulations that imposed an 18-month waiting period on CIA employees returning as contractors if they resigned but did not retire.

(S//OC/NF) **Conclusion 18: The CIA consistently represented in classified settings and to the public that the CIA had detained fewer than 100 individuals. This information was inaccurate. A review of CIA records found that the CIA detained at least 119 individuals, including at least 26 individuals who did not meet the requirements for CIA detention. Those detained inappropriately included individuals deemed innocent of any wrongdoing, including an "intellectually challenged" man whose detention was used solely as leverage against his brother, individuals who were intelligence sources, and individuals whom the CIA assessed to be connected to al-Qaida solely due to information fabricated by a CIA detainee being subjected to the CIA's enhanced interrogation techniques.**

(TS/███████████████████NF) CIA agrees that it should have been able to provide, and the Committee had reason to expect, better record keeping with regard to the number of individuals detained under CIA's authorities in paragraph 4 of the 2001 MoN. Moreover, CIA acknowledges that it detained at least six individuals who failed to meet the proper standard for detention, and waited too long, in too many cases, to release detainees when we determined they did not meet that standard. However, we believe the *Study* applies too much hindsight in reaching its conclusion that 26 individuals were wrongly detained, ignoring key facts that, at the time, drove rational CIA decision-making.

(S//OC/NF) Over the life of the program, CIA had difficulty accurately articulating how many individuals were in the program, largely due to two factors:

- (TS/███████████████NF) *Evolving standards for counting detainees and defining what it meant to be an RDI program detainee.* Throughout the program's history, CIA failed to promulgate sufficiently clear definitional standards for determining which detainees should be formally counted as falling within it. Through at least 2009, CIA generally utilized a definition of "RDI program" detainees as those held by CIA following the decision in December 2002 to consolidate formal control over all detention and interrogation activities under CTC/RDG. That meant that detainees who were housed at ██████ prior to that date, for example, were not counted as part of "the program." That was so even where paragraph 4 of the MON was the basis for CIA's involvement in the detention.[12]

- (TS/███████████████NF) *Poor record keeping relating to when MoN authorities were invoked and when detainees entered and left CIA custody.* Many of the appropriate records are either absent or inadequate, especially during the 2002-2003 period. In too many instances, CIA lacks documentation explaining the rationale for detention under the MoN or clear records showing detainee movements and dates of custody.

(S//OC/NF) While the Agency should certainly have done much better in accounting for the total of detainees and in making representations as to their number, we do not agree with the *Study's* implication that our failure was intentional or that the discrepancy was substantively meaningful, in that it does not impact the previously known scale of the program. It remains

---

[12] (S//OC/NF) We address Director Hayden's decision to maintain that the number of CIA detainees was less than 100, despite emerging information to the contrary, in our response to Conclusion 8.

true that approximately 100 detainees were part of the program; not 10 and not 200. The *Study* leaves unarticulated what impact the relatively small discrepancy might have had on policymakers or Congressional overseers.

(TS/███████████████ NF) With regard to "wrongfully detained" individuals, we acknowledge that there were cases in which errors were made. One important source of error was that the Agency's lawyers sometimes reached different conclusions about the correct legal standard for detention—a state of affairs that should never have been allowed to develop. This issue was examined in detail in the OIG Report of Investigation relating to the rendition and detention of Abu Khalid al-Masri. From the outset, CIA should have clearly defined the standard for placing a detainee in CIA custody and required a clear statement of that correct standard, as well as an outline of the supporting intelligence case, in cables which approved renditions and subsequent detentions. Instead, confusion about the correct legal standard occasionally prevailed.

- (TS/███████████████ NF) Some CIA officers believed that if a potential detainee had access to information about a high-value target the MoN standard was satisfied, while others focused (correctly) on the MoN language requiring a "continuing, serious threat of violence or death to U.S. persons and interests or who are planning terrorist activities." OGC management should have worked closely to clarify the basic standard and regularly review its application.

- (TS/███████████████ NF) A review that resulted from the accountability board charged with assessing the improper detention of al-Masri showed that other individuals detained under the incorrect MoN standard would, in fact, have met the correct standard had it been applied. Nevertheless, the al-Masri case remains a blemish on CIA's record of accurately interpreting and working within its counterterrorism authorities.

(TS/███████████████ NF) We do not agree with the *Study's* assumption that every detainee who was ultimately released due to a change in our assessment of whether or not he met the MoN standard should be considered to have been "wrongfully" detained. Many detention decisions were reasonable under the MoN standard at the time they were made.

- (TS/███████████████ NF) For example, the *Study* highlights several cases in which CIA is alleged to have wrongfully detained individuals in ████ settings ███ ████████ Two such examples involve the "mentally challenged" brother of a Hezb-I Islami Gulbuddin (HIG) facilitator who were captured together along with explosives and communications gear, and a detainee who was captured by the U.S. Military for using a satellite phone and turned over to CIA. Another example not cited concerned a Saudi national who was detained on the spot ████████ while he was videotaping ████ ██ in a casing effort that he admitted was at the direction of a senior al-Qa'ida commander in the FATA.

- (TS/███████████████ NF) The MoN standard allowed for persons who were planning terrorist attacks to be captured and detained, and given the context of the battlefield environment we believe detention was a reasonable approach in all of these cases. We also note that in the case of the "mentally challenged" brother, the detainee was removed from CIA custody in a matter of weeks after it had been conclusively determined that he did not have any knowledge of his brother's HIG activities. He was released by the U.S. military shortly thereafter.

(S//OC/NF) Moreover, the *Study* highlights a number of cases, particularly in 2002 through late 2003—a period during which there were significant concerns about follow-on attacks against the homeland—where we acknowledge CIA occasionally accepted compelling sole-sourced intelligence cases for detaining individuals in an effort to be sure that all possible was being done to thwart attack planning. At the time, the national priority was preventing attacks.

- (S//OC/NF) For example, in March 2003 we assessed that Khalid Shaykh Muhammad (KSM) had moved to a more cooperative posture as his interrogation progressed. When he provided actionable information and what we assessed as well-sourced intelligence indicating that two individuals posed "continuing, serious threats to U.S. persons and interests," we took action to detain them. In the end, KSM admitted that he fabricated the derogatory information on these individuals, and they were released. But their detention can only be considered "wrongful" after the fact, not in the light of credible information available at the time and in a context in which plot disruption was deemed an urgent national priority.

(TS/ ███████████████ NF) ████████████████████ Overall, we believe that continuing re-evaluations of detainees' status in light of new information are in fact indicative of a functioning "safety valve." The *Study* notes several cases in which detainees were released after new, exculpatory information came to light. In some cases, information that had led to the initial detention of certain individuals was later recanted; in others, forensic testing revealed incidents of mistaken identity or comprehensive debriefings led CIA to conclude that certain detainees did not meet the MoN standard.

- That said, the Agency frequently moved too slowly to release detainees. Of the 26 cases cited by the *Study*, we adjudicated only three cases in less than 31 days. Most took three to six months. CIA should have acted sooner.

(TS/█████████NF) **Conclusion 19:** The interrogation of CIA detainees and the conditions of their confinement were more brutal than previously known. The CIA's enhanced interrogation techniques, as employed individually and in combination, diverged significantly from CIA representations to the Department of Justice. The waterboarding technique was physically severe, inducing convulsions and vomiting, with one detainee becoming "completely unresponsive, with bubbles rising through his full, open mouth." Later, internal CIA records detail how the waterboard evolved into a "series of near drownings." In addition, the use of the CIA's enhanced interrogation techniques continued against CIA detainees despite the detainees experiencing disturbing hallucinations and warnings from CIA medical personnel that the interrogation techniques could exacerbate injuries. The CIA doused and submerged detainees in ice-cold water. The conditions of confinement at CIA detention sites varied, but one CIA detention facility was described as a "dungeon," where CIA detainees were kept in complete darkness and constantly shackled in isolation cells with only a bucket to use for human waste. At times, the detainees were walked around naked and were shackled with their hands above their heads. A CIA detainee at one CIA detention site died of suspected hypothermia. At least four CIA detainees were subjected to rectal rehydration or feeding without medical cause. The technique was described by CIA personnel as effective in helping to "clear a person's head" and getting a detainee to talk.

(S//OC/NF) We acknowledge that the *Study* has identified instances, discussed below, when CIA erred in applying individual techniques and agree that conditions at ████ particularly in its early days, were unacceptable and fell below those established at later detention sites. However, as we have noted in our response to several other conclusions, the *Study* consistently fails to distinguish between the early days at ████ and the rest of CIA's RDI efforts. Many of the *Study's* other examples and characterizations relating to allegedly "brutal" use of enhanced techniques lack clarifying detail or are incorrect. Most importantly, we found no evidence to support the charge that the facts relating to confinement conditions or the application of enhanced techniques were previously unknown or undisclosed to NSC and DOJ officials or to oversight committees.

- (S//OC/NF) The detention and interrogation regimen, including enhanced techniques and their expanded use after initial DOJ approvals in 2002, was briefed to NSC and DOJ officials and to oversight Committee leaders. The record shows that HPSCI and SSCI leaders, for example, were briefed on the program and enhanced techniques—including their expanded use—on 10 occasions between the Fall of 2002 and September 2003. In addition, most of the material contained in Conclusion 19 was investigated by the OIG and included in a *Special Review*, an audit, and several OIG Reports of Investigation published between 2004-2006, all of which were disseminated to oversight committee leaders and, in appropriate cases, referred to DOJ.

(U//FOUO) Nor does the record support the *Study's* claims with regard to the following enhanced technique-related issues:

(S//OC/NF) **Hallucinations:** The *Study* alleges that the use of sleep deprivation exceeded the intended limits as represented to DOJ, resulting in a high incidence of hallucinations. In fact, hallucinations were rare in the RDI program, and when they occurred medical personnel intervened to ensure a detainee would be allowed a period of sleep. Medical literature overwhelmingly supported the conclusion that the adverse effects of acute sleep deprivation could be reversed with relatively short periods of rest or sleep. A review of the cases cited in the *Study* indicates that short periods of sleep effectively addressed the hallucinations and that the detainees were conscious of the fact that they had hallucinated.

(S//OC/NF) **Water Dousing:** The *Study* asserts that CIA Headquarters provided no guidance on the use of water dousing until 2004. This is incorrect. In fact, CIA Headquarters provided guidance via cable traffic on water dousing as early as March 2003 and the technique was also part of OMS' draft guidelines dated September 2003. It was considered the most coercive of the standard techniques in use until early 2004, when allegations made by Mustafa al-Hawsawi were reported to OIG and investigated. At that time, given the risk that the technique could be misused, it was added to the list of enhanced techniques.

- (S//OC/NF) While it is reasonable to question the propriety of employing water dousing with cold water at the ███████ facility at which Gul Rahman died, likely due to hypothermia, it is important to note that the technique was employed after the first few months at ███████ in rooms heated to a minimum of 65 degrees in order to prevent possible harm.

(S//OC/NF) **Rectal Rehydration:** The *Study* alleges that that CIA used rectal rehydration techniques for reasons other than medical necessity. The record clearly shows that CIA medical personnel on scene during enhanced technique interrogations carefully monitored detainees' hydration and food intake to ensure HVD's were physically fit and also to ensure they did not harm themselves. Dehydration was relatively easy to assess and was considered a very serious condition. Medical personnel who administered rectal rehydration did not do so as an interrogation technique or as a means to degrade a detainee but, instead, utilized the well-acknowledged medical technique to address pressing health issues. A single flippant, inappropriate comment by one CIA officer concerning the technique, quoted in *the Study*, is not evidence to the contrary.

- (S//OC/NF) The technique was deemed safer than using IV needles with noncompliant detainees and was considered more efficient than a naso-gastric tube.

- (S//OC/NF) With respect to Majid Khan, in contrast to the *Study's* account, our records indicate Khan removed his naso-gastric tube, which posed the risk of injury and other complications. Given this dangerous behavior, rectal rehydration was considered the most appropriate means of addressing the potential harm Khan might inflict on himself.

(S//OC/NF) **Waterboard.** We acknowledge that the Agency's use of the waterboard—particularly as it was applied to KSM, who was adept at resisting the technique—deviated from representations originally made by CIA to OLC in 2002. CIA recognized this and, in 2003, sought to reaffirm the OLC guidance. As detailed in our response to Conclusions 12, the result was that DOJ reviewed the issue and affirmed that the deviations did "not contravene the principles" of the original OLC opinion.

- (S//OC/NF) Without commenting on the wisdom or propriety of the waterboard or any other technique, and while acknowledging that the accounts of waterboarding contained in the *Study* certainly depict the application of a harsh interrogation regimen, we believe it important the record be clear: CIA utilized the waterboard on only three detainees. The last waterboarding session occurred in March 2003.

(~~TS/~~▮▮▮▮▮▮▮▮▮▮▮▮▮~~NF~~) We agree with aspects of the *Study's* assertion that, in two instances, CIA used enhanced techniques which could have exacerbated injuries sustained by detainees during capture. As acknowledged in our response to Conclusion 20, techniques (walling and cramped confinement) that had not been previously approved by Headquarters were applied to two Libyan detainees who had foot injuries. In the cases involving those detainees, Abu Hazim and 'abd al-Karim, Headquarters ultimately approved the techniques the following month as components of revised interrogation plans. Agency officers erred by proceeding without Headquarters approval –and even after obtaining approvals, it strikes us as unwise to have placed Hazim in a position that necessitated weight-bearing on his one healthy leg.

- ~~(S//OC/NF)~~ That said, a review of the relevant cable traffic indicates that CIA medical personnel were on scene and worked with the interrogators and support personnel in a sustained effort directed at preventing these pre-existing injuries from worsening.

~~(S//OC/NF)~~ Finally, as discussed in several other responses to conclusions, we agree with the *Study's* assessment that confinement conditions at ▮▮▮▮▮ were harsher than at other facilities and were deficient in significant respects for a few months prior to the death of Gul Rahman in late 2002. After his death, CIA took steps to consolidate responsibility for the facility at Headquarters and moved quickly to improve conditions. Although conditions at the facility remained sub-optimal throughout its existence, significant improvements at the site prompted two SSCI staff members who visited the facility in late 2003 to compare it favorably with military facilities at Bagram and Guantanamo Bay. In fact, one remarked that ▮▮▮▮▮ was "a markedly cleaner, healthier, more humane and better administered facility." ▮▮▮▮▮ was decommissioned in 2004 in favor of a newer facility which incorporated many of the lessons learned from managing the program in ▮▮▮▮▮▮ as well as from RDI program facilities in other countries.

(S//OC/NF) **Conclusion 20: CIA personnel frequently used interrogation techniques that had not been reviewed by the Department of Justice or approved by CIA Headquarters. The CIA regularly subjected CIA detainees to nudity, abdominal slaps, dietary manipulation, and cold water dousing, prior to seeking advice from the Department of Justice on the legality of the techniques. At least 16 detainees were subjected to the CIA's enhanced interrogation techniques without authorization from CIA Headquarters. In at least eight detainee interrogations, CIA officers participated in the use of the CIA's enhanced interrogation techniques without the approval of CIA Headquarters.**

(S//OC/NF) We agree that there were instances in which CIA used inappropriate and unapproved interrogation techniques, particularly at the program's outset. Overall, however, we believe that the *Study* overstates the number of instances of unauthorized use of enhanced techniques as well as the number of non-certified individuals whom it alleges wrongfully participated in interrogations. The *Study* also overlooks the fact that, subsequent to CIA's efforts to organize and consolidate its detention and interrogation efforts into one Headquarters-managed program, the Agency worked to ensure that allegations of wrongdoing were reported to management, the Office of Inspector General, and/or the Department of Justice (DOJ), as appropriate.

- (U//FOUO) Moreover, while it would have been prudent to seek guidance from OLC on the complete range of techniques prior to their use, we disagree with any implication that, absent prior OLC review, the use of the "unapproved" techniques was unlawful or otherwise violated policy.

(S//OC/NF) The *Study's* assertion that 16 detainees were subjected to enhanced techniques without authorization from CIA Headquarters seems founded on a misunderstanding of the facts. The *Study* arrives at this number largely by conflating *standard* interrogation techniques that did not require prior approval with *enhanced* interrogation techniques that did. Some of this confusion is understandable, as over time, the term "standard" techniques was eliminated and some techniques which were initially classified as "standard" eventually were reclassified as "enhanced."

(TS/███████████NF) The *Study* correctly identifies seven instances in which detainees were subjected to individual techniques which were not approved in advance and included in their interrogation plans. In several of these, however, Headquarters had approved interrogation plans for the detainees utilizing other enhanced techniques. For instance, our review of contemporaneous cable traffic indicates that, at ██████Libyans Abu Hazim and 'abd al-Karim appear to have been subjected to walling without prior approval. Muhammad Umar 'Abd al-Rahman , also known as "Asadallah," and 'abd al-Karim appear to have been subjected to cramped confinement without prior Headquarters approval. ██████detainee Ramzi bin al-Shibh appears to have been subjected to the use of the facial hold technique without prior approval. In these cases, other previously approved enhanced techniques were also used.

- (TS/███████████NF) In the cases involving Abu Hazim and 'abd al-Karim, Headquarters approved the techniques the following month as components of revised interrogation plans. In the case of Ramzi bin al-Shibh, a cable exchange 18 days after he was subjected to the facial hold indicated Headquarters support for the use of the technique so long as necessary medical personnel were on scene.

(S//OC/NF) However, nine of the *Study's* examples describe the application, not of enhanced techniques, but of techniques that were classified at the time as standard. The DCI Guidelines for the Conduct of Interrogation, issued in January 2003, explicitly required prior written approval in advance for use of enhanced techniques, but the guidelines did not require such approvals for the use of standard techniques. While sleep deprivation, nudity, bathing, water dousing, and dietary manipulation were later reclassified as enhanced techniques, they were defined as standard techniques not requiring prior approval at the time relevant to the examples cited in the *Study*. As a consequence, it is misleading to assert that either officers or CIA's management of the RDI program erred by failing to obtain prior written approvals.

(TS/███████████NF) We also believe it is important to note that half of the 16 examples cited in the *Study* concern detainees who were held at █████prior to 3 December 2002, before█████formal transition to RDG supervision and subsequent imposition, in January 2003, of guidance on standardized program techniques and approval processes for detention and interrogation operations in ████████ The 2004 OIG *Special Review* catalogued the use of unapproved and inappropriate techniques at ██████from September through December 2002, and we have acknowledged serious shortcomings at ██████in several of our responses to *Study* conclusions. However, after the standard was approved and communicated in January 2003, interrogation operations at ██████were generally in line with the guidance— with some isolated exceptions identified in the *Study* and described elsewhere in our response.

(S//OC/NF) The *Study* also asserts that CIA officers employed water dousing even though CIA Headquarters offered no guidance on the technique until January 2004. That is incorrect. We identified several Headquarters cables dated as early as 2 March 2003 which contained clear instruction on conditions required in order to apply water dousing in a safe and sanctioned manner. Subsequent Headquarters-originated cables were also located dating to June 2003, which classified the application of the technique as a "standard" technique. In September 2003, draft OMS guidelines also discussed water dousing as a standard technique and provided guidance to OMS personnel on its safe application.

(S//OC/NF) The *Study* further asserts that in "at least eight" interrogations, officers participated without approval of CIA Headquarters. We are unable to locate and identify within the *Study* all eight instances to which the underlying text of Conclusion 20 refers. We presume the allegation is intended to reference interrogations involving non-certified officers. In reaching this conclusion, the *Study* appears to rely upon information taken out of context and, in other cases, simply fails to provide supporting evidence.

- (TS/███████████NF) The *Study* alleges that "CIA Headquarters approved the use of the CIA's enhanced interrogation techniques against Ridha al-Najjar at a ██████ ██████despite the fact that the CIA officers applying the techniques had never been trained in the use of the CIA enhanced interrogation techniques." Specifically, the *Study* goes on to assert that the officer used "sleep deprivation, sound, and other techniques" with Ridha al-Najjar ████████████████████ As with the examples the *Study* cites above, these techniques were not defined at the time as enhanced interrogation techniques requiring prior approval. Further, the *Study* itself acknowledges that the officer in question attended the *first* iteration of interrogation training that was offered in November 2002.

- (S//OC/NNF) The *Study* asserts that a CIA officer who was not specifically approved to use interrogation techniques during the debriefing of a detainee in early 2003 "participated in multiple interrogations" in which enhanced interrogation techniques were used and in which a certified interrogator participated. However, the *Study* itself specifically notes that the "cables do not specify whether [the officer] performed any of the interrogation techniques." There was never any requirement that officers be certified in order to be merely *present* when interrogation techniques were used. The certification requirement applied only to those individuals employing the techniques without supervision. In fact, in order to become certified, officers were required to observe the use of interrogation techniques as well as to use them with a detainee under the supervision of a certified interrogator.

- (S//OC/NF) Similarly, the *Study* asserts that in May 2003, ████ trained and qualified CIA officers applied enhanced interrogation techniques to a detainee under the supervision of a certified interrogator but without prior CIA Headquarters approval. The facts are otherwise, as the interrogation plan from the field—which was approved by Headquarters—specifically noted that these ████ CIA officers would employ the techniques under the supervision of the certified interrogator.

(S//OC/NF) Finally, the *Study* asserts that interrogation techniques used with Abu Zubaydah subsequent to the August, 2002 OLC Memorandum differed from those represented to OLC prior to the memorandum and that CIA did not notify DOJ regarding these differences. The *Study* also asserts that after the 2002 memorandum, CIA used four interrogation techniques not yet reviewed by OLC. While we disagree with any implication that, absent prior OLC review, the use of particular techniques was unlawful or otherwise violated policy, we assess that the risks of this program would have been better managed by limiting ourselves to techniques defined and reviewed in advance by OGC and OLC.

(U) **Examples of CIA Representations of the Value of Intelligence Acquired From Detainees**

Overview

(U//FOUO) As discussed in our response to Conclusion 9 (see Tab B), we conducted a careful review of the *Study's* 20 examples of the value of the information obtained as a result of CIA's RDI effort. As we did in that response, we note here that in commenting on the value of the information derived from detainees, we are not arguing in favor of the decision to use the enhanced techniques to which these detainees were subjected. We are not endorsing those techniques, we are not making an "ends-justify-the-means" case for them, nor are we implying that those techniques were the only way to obtain the information from detainees. We only are assessing the accuracy of CIA's representations in response to the *Study's* allegations that those representations were false.

(U//FOUO) Based on our review, we concluded that all the examples fit within and support the Agency's overall representations that information obtained from CIA interrogations produced unique intelligence that helped the US disrupt plots, capture terrorists, better understand the enemy, prevent another mass casualty attack, and save lives. In some of the Agency's representations, however, CIA failed to meet its own standards for precision of language and we acknowledge that this was unacceptable. However, even in those cases, we found that the actual impact of the information acquired from interrogations was significant and still supported CIA's overall judgments about the value of the information acquired from detainees.

(U//FOUO) **Summary of the 20 Examples**. In one of the 20 examples (#2), we found that CIA mischaracterized on several occasions, including in prominent representations such as President Bush's 2006 speech, the impact of information on specific terrorist plotting acquired from a set of CIA interrogations.

- (U//FOUO) CIA said the information "helped stop a planned attack on the US Consulate in Karachi," when the Agency should have said it "revealed ongoing attack plotting against the US official presence in Karachi that prompted the Consulate to take further steps to protect its officers."

(U//FOUO) There were four examples (#1,# 3, #5, and #17) in which CIA used imprecise language or made errors in some of its representations that, although deeply regrettable, did not significantly affect the thrust of those representations.

(U//FOUO) In another four examples, we found single, isolated representations in which CIA was imprecise in describing the relative impact of the information or the manner in which it was acquired.

- (U//FOUO) In two of these examples (#13 and #18), CIA made mistakes that caused the IG to incorrectly describe in its 2004 *Special Review* the precise role that information acquired from KSM played in the detention of two terrorists involved in plots against targets in the US. These were not "frequently cited" or "repeatedly represented" as the *Study* claims. Numerous other representations of one of these cases were accurate; we found no other representations for the other.

- (U//FOUO) In two examples (#9 and #10), we found a one-time error not noted in the *Study*. In a set of talking points prepared for DCIA, CIA incorrectly said enhanced interrogation techniques played a role in acquiring two important pieces of information about KSM. In the Agency's other representations, including our most prominent, we stated correctly that this information was acquired during initial interviews of Abu Zubaydah.

(U//FOUO) In the other 11 examples, we determined that CIA's representations were consistently accurate, in contrast to the *Study*, which claims the Agency misrepresented them all.

1. (U) The Dirty Bomb Plot/Tall Buildings Plots and/or the Capture/Arrest of Jose Padilla

"(S//OC/NF) There was intelligence in CIA databases independent of the CIA interrogation program to fully identify Jose Padilla as a terrorist threat and to disrupt any terrorist plotting associated with him."

(S/ ▆▆▆ /NF) **CIA's representations that Abu Zubaydah's information allowed us to identify US citizen Jose Padilla as an al-Qa'ida operative tasked to carry out an attack in the US were largely accurate. We acknowledge that it took us too long to stop making references to his infeasible "Dirty Bomb" plot and to consistently and more accurately cite him as a terrorist directed to attack high rise apartment buildings. Despite the imprecision of our language, we continue to assess it was a good example of the importance of intelligence derived from the detainee program.**

(S/ ▆▆▆▆ /NF) CIA believes the *Study* overstates the value and clarity of reporting on Jose Padilla in CIA databases prior to Abu Zubaydah's debriefings. As it played out at the time, the combination of a suspicious traveler report ▆▆▆▆▆▆▆▆▆▆▆▆▆▆▆▆▆▆▆▆▆ and Abu Zubaydah's information allowed us to identify Padilla and the threat he posed. Abu Zubaydah revealed this information after having been subjected to sleep deprivation, which would be categorized as an enhanced interrogation technique once the program was officially underway.

- (S/ ▆▆▆ NF) The first report—unremarkable at the time—▆▆▆▆▆▆▆▆▆▆ identifying Padilla as a "possible illegal traveler" using a US passport, prompting CIA ▆▆▆▆▆ to request traces on him.[1] In a follow-up cable on Padilla's co-traveler, later identified as Binyam Muhammad, ▆▆▆▆▆▆▆▆▆▆▆▆▆▆▆▆▆▆▆ speculated in the final paragraph that ▆▆▆▆▆▆ passed the names of the travelers because they had concerns about "possible terrorist activity."[2] Contrary to the *Study's* statement that "CIA *knew* Jose Padilla...was suspected by the Pakistani Government of being engaged in possible terrorist activity,"[3] the actual cable reads, "At this juncture, ▆▆▆ *does not know* if there is more to these trace requests other than a desire to root out illegal travelers or suspected terrorist [sic]."[4] (emphasis added)

- (S/ ▆▆▆ NF) The importance of that report only became apparent ten days later, when Abu Zubaydah described a terrorist plot by two individuals matching ▆▆▆ descriptions of Padilla and Muhammad.[5] ▆▆▆▆▆▆ immediately linked the reports and ▆▆▆▆▆▆▆▆▆▆▆▆ Muhammad, who was already in Pakistani police custody for using a fake passport.[6][7] Within two days, and based on the Abu Zubaydah report, the CIA ▆▆▆▆▆▆▆▆[8] alerted other USG agencies to the threat,[9][10] ▆▆▆▆▆▆▆▆▆▆▆▆[11]

- (S/ ▆▆▆ NF) We judge that both reports were important; CIA would not have known the operatives' true names without the report ▆▆▆▆ and Abu Zubaydah's subsequent information added the context necessary to make this report stand out as something more than a routine "illegal traveler" report, which was particularly important due to the absence of Jose Padilla's name in any CIA records.

- (S//OC/NF) The *Study* cites "significant intelligence"[12] available on Padilla independent of CIA detainee information, but the only documents—aside ▆▆▆▆ suspicious traveler report—that mention his name were two internal State Department emails about a suspicious passport request in 2001; these emails were not in CIA databases.. All other citations included only general descriptors—such as his nationality or the languages he spoke—but did not provide his name. The most detailed report was an undisseminated document in FBI's possession that contained Padilla's birth date, alias, and language skills. Contrary to the *Study's* claim—which was based on a personal email containing a recollection of an FBI officer—a review of CIA databases reveals no record of this document. We did, however, find documentation indicating the FBI official who believed the CIA provided the document had confused the operation where this document was recovered with a separate operation, likely explaining the error in the *Study*. [13]

(S//OC/NF) The *Study* also claims Abu Zubaydah had already provided the "Dirty Bomb" plot information to FBI interrogators prior to undergoing CIA interrogation, but this is based on an undocumented FBI internal communication and an FBI officer's recollection to the Senate Judiciary Committee seven years later. While we have considerable information from FBI debriefings of Abu Zubaydah, we have no record that FBI debriefers acquired information about such an al-Qa'ida threat.

- (S//OC/NF) The *Study* also states that enhanced techniques were only established after Abu Zubaydah revealed the information on Padilla, implying that enhanced techniques could not have played a role in Abu Zubaydah's description of Padilla. This is technically accurate because enhanced techniques had not been formally designated as such until after Padilla was arrested. However, Abu Zubaydah had been subjected to sleep deprivation prior to revealing the information to CIA or FBI. Thus, CIA correctly represented Abu Zubaydah's description of Jose Padilla as an example of information provided after an individual had been subjected to enhanced interrogation techniques.

(S//OC/NF) We assess to this day that Padilla was a legitimate threat who had been directed to use his training in Afghanistan, funding from al-Qa'ida, and US passport to put together a plan to attack tall residential buildings. It took us until 2007 to consistently stop referring to his association with the "Dirty Bomb" plot—a plan we concluded early on was never operationally viable.

2. (U) The Karachi Plots

(S//OC/NF) *"A review of CIA records found the CIA interrogation program and the CIA's enhanced interrogation techniques—to include the waterboard—played no role in the disruption of the Karachi Plot(s). CIA records indicate that the Karachi Plot(s) was thwarted by the arrest of operatives and the interdiction of explosives* ███

(S//NF) **CIA acknowledges that on several occasions, including in prominent representations such as President Bush's 2006 speech, we mischaracterized the impact of the reporting we acquired from detainees on the Karachi plots. We said the information "helped stop a planned attack on the US Consulate in Karachi," when we should have said it "revealed ongoing attack plotting against the US official presence in Karachi that prompted the Consulate to take further steps to protect its officers."**

(S//OC/NF) Pakistan's arrest on 29 April 2003 of al-Qa'ida operatives Ammar al-Baluchi and Khallad Bin Attash disrupted an al-Qa'ida plot to attack the US Consulate in Karachi. However, that was only one of several "Karachi plots." Ammar and Khallad provided new information on other attack plans in Karachi after entering CIA custody and undergoing enhanced interrogation techniques. [14]

- (S//OC/NF) Ammar on 29 April told ████████████████████ that he planned to attack the US Consulate using an explosives-filled helicopter and claimed the attack was still in the nascent stages. On 11 May he told ████████████████████████ that there were no current plans to attack the Consulate.[15][16] During his first interrogation session in CIA custody and after enhanced techniques commenced, he revealed that the plan was to use a motorcycle bomb and a car bomb in a single, coordinated attack at the end of May or early June, and he pointed to the location on the Consulate's perimeter wall where the attack would occur.[17][18][19]

- (S//OC/NF) Khallad repeatedly denied knowing of any operations in Pakistan ████████████ ███████ After his transfer to CIA custody on 17 May—and after being subjected to enhanced techniques—he admitted the plotting details Ammar had provided and claimed that Khalid Shaykh Muhammad (KSM) had approved the US Consulate plot in February.[20]

- (S//OC/NF) During CIA interrogations, Ammar and Khallad admitted they were also planning to attack a Consular vehicle using a motorcycle bomb, Westerners at the Karachi airport, and a neighborhood where Westerners lived.[21][22] CIA representations about the value of this reporting should have made clear that it caused the US and Pakistan to take additional security measures related to those targets, including relocating ████████████ officers and working with the State Department's Regional Security Office (RSO) to increase physical security in the neighborhood. However, we have no information specifically indicating whether the additional Karachi plotting was disrupted by those measures, by Pakistan's detention of Ammar, Khallad, and other extremists, or by other unknown factors.

(S//OC/NF) *"CIA had information regarding the Karachi terrorist plotting as early as September 11, 2002."*

(S//OC/NF) The plots disrupted with the arrest and interrogation of Ammar and Khallad were separate from the plot referenced in the so-called "perfume letter," which we obtained on 11 September 2002

6

during ▆▆▆▆ raid on an al-Qa'ida safehouse in Karachi. The letter contained coded references to operations, but CIA did not understand the codes until KSM explained them during interrogation. [a][2324]

- (S//OC/NF) On 5 March 2003—after initial enhanced techniques but before waterboarding—KSM explained that the word "perfume" referred to types of conventional explosives, not poisons as CIA interpreted originally; that "animals" was not a reference to chemical or poison tests, but to vehicles; and that the word "hotels" referred to actual hotels in Karachi, which he then identified. [252627]

- (S//OC/NF) Khallad on 17 May 2003 confirmed that the plot against Karachi hotels, which KSM said the letter referenced, was disrupted on 11 September 2002, but that Ammar intended to use the explosives he had stashed for that operation to target the US Consulate. [28]

---

[a] CIA cable traffic shows that before KSM's debriefings in March 2003, analysts believed the "perfume letter" authorized a chemical or poison attack against an unknown target. [aa]

3. (U) The Second Wave Plot

"(U) The CIA Interrogation Program played no role in the "disruption" of the "Second Wave" plotting and the identification of the al-Ghuraba group."

(S/▮▮▮▮▮/NF) CIA continues to assess that the capture of Southeast Asia-based al-Qa'ida operations planner Hambali in 2003, which resulted in large part from information obtained from Khalid Shaykh Muhammad (KSM) (see Example 8), was a critical factor in the disruption of al-Qa'ida's plan to conduct a "Second Wave" attack involving multiple airplanes crashing into buildings on the US West Coast. Based on our understanding of al-Qa'ida's persistence in the pursuit of plots and KSM's own assessment, we judge that Hambali remained capable of directing the plot at the time of his arrest, even though other operatives involved in the plan had been arrested in 2002. We agree with the *Study* that some of our representations incorrectly claimed that we first "learned" of the overall plot and a related cell of students through CIA interrogations, but despite our imprecision, we continue to assess this was a good example of the importance of intelligence derived from the detainee program.

(S//OC/NF) CIA continues to assess that information obtained from CIA interrogations of KSM helped us disrupt plotting for a "Second Wave" aircraft attack on the US West Coast by identifying Hambali's role in the plot and by giving us information that helped lead to his capture and the detention of a group of students who almost certainly were slated to be part of the same plot.[b] In turn, Hambali provided information during our interrogations of him that helped us understand the purpose of the students whom he had selected and sent to Karachi.

- (S/▮▮▮▮▮/NF) ▮▮▮▮▮ detainee Masran bin Arshad in early 2002 first told ▮▮▮▮▮▮▮▮▮ about al-Qa'ida's plot to attack the US West Coast, his involvement in it, and several individuals participating.

- (S//OC/NF) The following year we learned of Hambali's involvement from KSM, who provided this information after having undergone enhanced interrogation techniques in CIA detention. KSM stated in June 2003 that while his own efforts with this plan ended with the arrest of Masran, he believed Hambali—whose efforts he had enlisted—could still successfully execute an aerial attack in the future, suggesting a variation of the plot could still have been underway.[29] KSM also admitted he had tasked Hambali to recruit other non-Arab passport-holders to serve as pilots for the plot.

- (S//OC/NF) CIA at the time already sought to detain Hambali due to his role as a senior al-Qa'ida figure in the group's Southeast Asian network, and knowledge of his role in the plot only strengthened our resolve to locate and capture him.

- (S/▮▮▮▮▮/NF) After his arrest in mid-August 2003 (see Example 8), Hambali quickly admitted to having been associated with Masran's cell, conceded more details of his involvement, and by early September had confessed that KSM had asked him to choose four people for a suicide operation involving individuals associated with the original Masran plot.[303132]

- (S//OC/NF) When faced with news of Hambali's detention, KSM provided information on the role played by Hambali's brother, Pakistan-based Gun Gun Ruswan Gunawan. Gunawan was

---

[b] For a more detailed account of Hambali's capture in 2003, please see Example Study #8, page 17.

subsequently detained by ███████████████ based at least in part on KSM's intelligence, and he told us of a group of al-Qa'ida-associated students whom Hambali had selected and sent to Karachi.

██

- (S//OC/NF) Hambali, after having undergone enhanced techniques in CIA detention, admitted he had hand-picked these students in response to KSM's request and that some were being groomed as pilots for unspecified al-Qa'ida operations.[36] Hambali did subsequently recant this statement, claiming he made it to satisfy his interrogators and relieve the pressure of enhanced techniques. We continue to assess his original revelation was correct, however, based on KSM's claim that he tasked Hambali to identify and train pilots, Hambali's verification of this claim in multiple instances, and the students' interest in aircraft and aviation.[3738]

(S//OC/NF) The Study's conclusion that KSM's information played no role in disrupting the attack appears to rest on the assumption that a change to any one element of a plot—such as the capture of an operative or exposure of an attack method—would have derailed the entire plan. In reality, al-Qa'ida has demonstrated its willingness and ability to adapt its plans, especially for is most ambitious operations, in response to unexpected developments.

- (S//OC/NF) KSM admitted to having already adjusted his plans following some of the arrests, noting that he identified a new operative—Masran—to replace one of the arrested original three, Zacharias Moussaoui. He also stated that while his own efforts with this plan ended with the arrest of Masran, he believed Hambali—whose efforts he had enlisted—could still successfully execute a future aerial attack.

- (S████████████NF) The Study highlights the arrest of Richard Reid in December 2001 and Masran's claim that this arrest and the revelation of al-Qa'ida's use of explosives in shoes derailed the plot, prior to any detainee reporting.[41] We would note, however, that KSM discussed with Masran after Reid's arrest a planned attack using the specific "method of Richard Reid,"[42] and that other al-Qa'ida operatives until at least 2004 continued to plan to use variations of this technique.

(S//OC/NF) The Study correctly points out that we erred when we represented that we "learned" of the Second Wave plotting from KSM and "learned" of the operational cell comprised of students from Hambali. We knew about the overall plotting well before KSM's arrest, although he gave us important information that helped us disrupt Hambali's role in it. The student cell was arrested because of information provided by Hambali's brother ███████████████ who had been arrested due in part to information obtained from KSM. Information obtained from KSM and Hambali after enhanced techniques revealed the significance of the cell in the context of the Second Wave plotting.

4. (S//NF) The UK Urban Targets Plot and/or the Capture/Arrest of Dhiren Barot, aka Issa al-Hindi

"(S//OC/NF) *The intelligence that led to Issa al-Hindi's true name, his capture, and the uncovering of his UK plotting came from intelligence sources unrelated to the CIA detention and interrogation program.*"[43]

(TS   NF) CIA accurately represented that Khalid Shaykh Muhammad (KSM) provided the initial lead to a UK-based al-Qa'ida operative named Dhiren Barot, aka Issa al-Hindi, whom KSM had tasked to case US targets. That information allowed us to identify this Issa as Barot and ultimately led British authorities to arrest him. In arguing that CIA already had what it needed to identify and arrest Barot, the *Study* confuses two different extremists using the name Issa and cites intelligence that was not operationally useful absent KSM's information, or was gathered because of his information.

(S//OC/NF) CIA continues to assess that information KSM provided in March 2003 after the application of enhanced interrogation techniques was vital to the identification and capture of Dhiren Barot, aka Issa al-Hindi, aka Issa al-Britani, a UK-based terrorist whom KSM had tasked to collect information on US targets. The *Study's* key finding hinges on the availability of information about Issa and his activities on behalf of al-Qa'ida prior to KSM's March 2003 debriefings. However, the documentation cited in the *Study* as evidence CIA had prior to KSM's debriefings refers to the wrong person, was acquired after KSM's debriefings, or was so vague that it was of no use until KSM put it into context. References to information acquired later—which accurately described the right person—fail to note that the information was only pursued in response to KSM's debriefings.

- (S   NF) The *Study* cites 2002 reporting from detainees [   ] at Guantanamo Bay on an Issa from Britain linked to KSM and plotting in the UK, but each of those reports actually referred to Sajid Badat, a different UK extremist also known as Issa.[44] The Guantanamo Bay detainees—one of whom photo identified Badat as "Issa"—served in a small cell with Badat in Qandahar.[45] The detainee [   ] described an Issa who attended the Arab Studies Institute in Qandahar in 1999, where he translated for several Westerners, also consistent with Badat.[46][47]

- (S//OC/NF) The *Study* inaccurately characterizes information the CIA acquired in September 2003— regarding the *correct* Issa (Barot)—as "CIA information acquired in 1999."[48][49] This reporting, which links Issa to another UK extremist, addresses events in 1999, but was collected [   ] in 2003 in response to the KSM debriefings.

- (S//OC/NF) The *Study* rightfully credits interviews of two individuals in FBI and DOD custody as playing an important role in advancing and focusing the investigation, but it fails to note that these interviews (conducted in May 2003) and the specific questions asked were a direct result of reporting disseminated from KSM in March 2003.[50]

(S//OC//NF) The *Study* highlights and mischaracterizes two pieces of information in CIA's intelligence holdings from 1999 and 2000, which CIA in June 2003 found in hindsight to reference a book Issa wrote, but this information did not name him or link him to any threat.[51][52] These bits of information were of no apparent consequence until KSM commented that Issa had "authored a well-known book about the jihad in Kashmir,"[53] which allowed [   ] to prioritize identifying this book and its author as a lead to Issa, thus putting these otherwise obscure references into useful context.

- (S//OC/NF) The first piece of information the *Study* cites was contained in a set of more than 30 intelligence reports containing hundreds of pages of documents seized on a Pakistani raid of an al-

Qa'ida-linked establishment in 1999. In one seized email, the author cites the name and topic of Issa's book, but identifies the author only as an Afghanistan-trained British convert writing about Hindu atrocities in Kashmir.[54]

- (S//OC/NF) The second piece of information is a 105-page financial document seized during a raid in the UK, in which Issa's book is listed on the invoice in a bookstore run by UK extremist Moazzem Begg.[55] The document includes only the book's title and no further information to identify Issa.

(S//OC/NF) The push to identify Issa's true name and location came in response to KSM's unique and accurate information on his tasking of Issa in 1999 or 2000 to travel to the United States to collect information on economic targets in New York for al-Qa'ida—and that Bin Ladin had sat privately with Issa to impart the same tasking.[56][57] One of the key avenues of inquiry that KSM's information prompted involved Issa's links to the UK-based "Hubaib Group," which KSM reportedly used to contact and send money to Issa.

- (S/███/NF) KSM claimed the group was led by Abu Khubayb,[58][59] and, based on the disseminated reports CIA shared with UK ███████████████████████████ was able to identify Abu Khubayb as UK-based extremist Babar Ahmed.[60]

- (S/███/NF) This information enhanced British investigative scrutiny of Babar Ahmed and his group and ultimately enabled ███ identification in early 2004[61] of a cousin of Babar Ahmed. That cousin turned out to be Abu Talha al-Pakistani, a senior al Qa'ida facilitator whom KSM in 2002 had tasked to assist with attacking London's Heathrow Airport.

(S/███████/NF) The *Study* accurately characterizes Abu Talha al-Pakistani's July 2004 arrest ██████ and subsequent debriefings ██████████████████ as having proved invaluable to our overall understanding of Issa's activities and the threat he posed, suggesting we did not need CIA detainee reporting to learn of Issa's UK plotting. The *Study* fails to recognize that Abu Talha's arrest—a case CIA frequently cited as a success of the detainee program—would not have happened if not for reporting from CIA-held detainees.

- (S//OC/NF) In an effort to uncover information about plotting against Heathrow Airport, the CIA questioned Ammar al-Baluchi, KSM, and Khallad bin Attash about personalities who could be involved, and all three highlighted Abu Talha al-Pakistani.[62][63][64] In all cases, the information was provided after the commencement of enhanced techniques.

- (S//OC/NF) When Hassan Gul was later in CIA custody, he provided a more current update on Abu Talha's activities. Gul reported that Abu Talha was working on some external operation and had sought out the new external operations chief following the arrests of KSM, Ammar, and Khallad.[65][66]

- (S/███/NF) Given the threat implications of this reporting, the USG and UK authorities made identifying and disrupting Abu Talha a top priority. Through ████ KSM-spurred investigation of the Abu Khubayb/Babar Ahmed group, by early 2004 ██████ █████ Pakistani Mohammed Naim Noor Khan as possibly being the operative known as Abu Talha. CIA ██████████████████████ ██████ worked with relevant sources to locate him, ultimately leading to his capture ██████ ██████

(S/███/NF) Information from KSM also played a role in confirming the identity of an Issa candidate once he was located by UK authorities. While we were pursuing Abu Talha ██████████████

7172

5. (U) The Capture/Identification/Arrest of Iyman Faris

"(U) *The intelligence that led to the identification of Iyman Faris was unrelated to the CIA detention and interrogation program.*"[73]

(S//NF) CIA most often represented accurately that Khalid Shaykh Muhammad's (KSM) information enhanced the FBI's understanding of the role of Iyman Faris, a US-based extremist whom KSM tasked to support an attack against the Brooklyn Bridge. In a few cases, we incorrectly stated or implied that KSM's information led to the investigation of Faris, but we should have stated that his reporting informed and focused the investigation. Nonetheless, we continue to assess it was a good example of the importance of intelligence derived from the detainee program.

(S//OC/NF) We have reviewed our representations and assess that most of them accurately capture the contribution made by information obtained from interrogations of KSM. We most often represented this case as follows:

- (S//OC/NF) "KSM described an Ohio-based truck driver whom the FBI identified as Iyman Faris, and who was already under suspicion for his contacts with al-Qa'ida operative Majid Khan. The FBI and CIA shared intelligence from interviews of KSM, Khan, and Faris on a near real-time basis and quickly ascertained that Faris had met and accepted operational taskings from KSM on several occasions." This statement is accurate and appeared in representations to the Department of Justice, the White House, the SSCI, and CIA finished intelligence production.

(S//OC/NF) In a small number of other representations, we imprecisely characterized KSM's information as having "led" to the investigation of Iyman Faris, rather than more accurately characterizing it as a key contribution to the investigation. For example, our officers' statements—as reflected in the 2004 Inspector General's (IG) *Special Review*—that KSM's information "led to the investigation and prosecution of Iyman Faris" were inaccurate. The specific chain of events was:

- (S/████NF) FBI identified Faris on 5 March 2003 as one resident of a house that received a suspicious phone call, prompting FBI to open preliminary inquiries—and on 11 March, a full field investigation—into the residents.[74][75][76] During 11-14 March debriefings, Pakistani extremist Majid Khan ████████████████████ photo-identified Faris as an extremist who worked as a truck driver, kept multiple girlfriends, lived in the Midwest, and wanted to work on a business project with his father.[77][78][79] Khan did not know Faris' true name or implicate him in any al-Qa'ida plotting.

- (S/████NF) On 18 March, CIA disseminated KSM's photo-identification and description of Faris as an Ohio-based truck driver who was very interested in business, kept multiple girlfriends, and whom he had tasked with procuring machine tools for a potential attack against a US suspension bridge.[80][81] KSM's information allowed debriefers to confront Majid Khan, who then provided much greater detail on Faris' terrorist ties.[82]

- (S/████NF) FBI on 20 March conducted a previously planned interview with Faris, and—armed with the information revealed by KSM and Majid Khan—asked Faris to begin discussing his ties with KSM and al-Qa'ida plotting in the US. FBI submitted further questions to CIA to be used with KSM "to advance the interview with Faris," and noted FBI's appreciation for the close collaboration on the case.[83]

(S//OC/NF) We do not agree with the *Study's* claim that, "CIA records indicate there was significant intelligence on Iyman Faris and targeting of suspension bridges acquired prior to—and independently of—the CIA detention and interrogation program." [84]

- (S//OC/NF) The *Study's* accompanying intelligence chronology includes only one non-detainee report that references suspension bridges, and that reference was to West Coast suspension bridges (the Iyman Faris plot was against the Brooklyn Bridge).

- (S//OC/NF) The FBI's earlier investigation of Iyman Faris—cited by the *Study* as evidence of available intelligence on him—was opened and closed in 2001 and not disseminated in CIA channels. The first reference to him in CIA records is on 6 March 2003, and it states, ████ surfaced no [search results] on Iyman Faris." [85]

6. (S//NF) The Capture/Identification/Arrest of Sajid Badat

"(S//OC/NF) The CIA Detention and Interrogation Program produced no unique intelligence leading to the identification and arrest of Sajid Badat."

(S//OC/NF) CIA accurately represented that Khalid Shaykh Muhammad's (KSM) information was central to our efforts to identify and enable British liaison to arrest Sajid Badat, an al-Qa'ida operative who originally planned to conduct a shoe bomb attack aboard an airplane. KSM was the first to tell us there was a second shoe bomber and that he remained at large, and he provided sufficient details to allow CIA and British authorities to identify Badat. Fragmentary information implied a second shoe bomber existed before KSM's detention, but this information was either inconclusive or not available to CIA.

(S//OC/NF) CIA assesses that detainees, particularly KSM, did provide unique intelligence that helped lead to the identification of Sajid Badat as the would-be second shoe bomber and his subsequent arrest by UK authorities in 2003.

(S//OC/NF) The *Study's* finding on Badat hinges on the premise that investigations of existing intelligence eventually would have led to a similar outcome—the identification and arrest of Badat in the UK and the recovery of his shoe bombs—even if we had never received the intelligence from KSM. As a matter of course, we cannot rule out any hypothetical possibility. In reality, though, KSM's reporting was central to the investigations that led to Badat's arrest.

- (S//OC/NF) The *Study* states that by 14 January 2002, the FBI investigation of Richard Reid found Reid "had an unidentified partner who allegedly backed out of the operation at the last minute."[86] There is no reference to this possibility in official communications between FBI and CIA, nor did it exist in any searchable CIA data repositories prior to KSM's reporting.

- (S//OC/NF) In response to FBI information that a "Badad Sajid" from the UK was linked to Richard Reid and was one of 13 persons characterized by a ▮▮▮▮ detainee as "involved in operations targeting American interests,"[87] CIA in summer 2002 noted that "Sajid" may be identifiable with one Sajid Badat, on whom we had little existing derogatory reporting.[88] At this time we were following many disparate individuals who were allegedly threatening US interests, and there was nothing at the time on Badat to lead us to prioritize him over the others or to tie him to a shoe bomb plot.

- (S//OC/NF) The *Study* accurately highlights a body of reporting from detainees not in CIA custody— disseminated prior to KSM's arrest—that collectively described a British al-Qa'ida operative of Indian descent known as "Issa" who was linked to KSM, was probably involved in operations in the UK, and was a Richard Reid associate. In hindsight, it is reasonable to assess that we should have included Badat on the list of potential matches for this unknown individual, but our review of the records indicates no one had suggested Badat could be a candidate for this Issa until KSM's reporting. In addition, no one suggested a link to Reid's shoe bombing attempt.

- (S//OC/NF) The fact that the ▮▮▮▮▮▮▮▮▮▮▮▮ as late as August 2003 was only able to locate a poor quality photo of Sajid Badat belies the notion that Badat was well on his way to being identified as important and disrupted in advance of KSM's reporting.

15

(S//OC/NF) KSM was the first person to provide—in March 2003, after having undergone enhanced interrogation techniques in CIA custody—a detailed and authoritative narrative of al-Qa'ida development of and plans to use shoe bombs operationally.[89][90][91] KSM's narrative included the fact that there was a second shoe bomber still at large who was a close associate of Richard Reid and who was also from the United Kingdom; KSM provided a detailed description of Reid's mystery partner to include the fact that he was known by the operational alias name of Issa.[92]

- (S//OC/NF) KSM was explicit that there was a second pair of shoe bombs unaccounted for, a fact that was not available in any other reporting at the time.[93]

- (S//OC/NF) KSM's reporting also clearly distinguished between, and thereby focused investigations of, two al-Qa'ida operatives known as Issa al-Britani—one turning out to be Badat, the other Dhiren Barot aka Issa al-Hindi.[94] No other single source had the same degree of knowledge about both individuals—including their compartmented operational activities for al-Qa'ida.

- (S/▮▮▮▮/NF) Once ▮▮▮▮▮▮ were able to locate and provide to CIA a high quality photograph of Badat on 3 September 2003, KSM identified it with "100 percent certainty" as the Issa he had described as Reid's partner and would-be shoe bomber.[95] KSM's identification of Badat was more important than others who also recognized the photograph—including one who identified the photo a day before KSM did—because only KSM at the time had characterized this Issa as a partner to Reid and as a would-be shoe bomber.

7. (U) The Heathrow/Canary Wharf Plotting

"(U) The CIA Interrogation Program played no role in the disruption of the Heathrow and Canary Wharf plotting."

(S//OC/NF) CIA disagrees with the *Study's* assessment that we incorrectly represented that information derived from interrogating detainees helped disrupt al-Qa'ida's targeting of Heathrow Airport and Canary Wharf in London, including in President Bush's 2006 speech on the Program. Detainee reporting, including some which was acquired after enhanced interrogation techniques were applied, played a critical role in uncovering the plot, understanding it, detaining many of the key players, and ultimately allowing us to conclude it had been disrupted. It is a complex story, however, and we should have been clearer in delineating the roles played by different partners.

- (S/███ NF) As we highlight in our response to Example 11, the information provided by Abu Zubaydah played a key role in the capture of Ramzi Bin al-Shibh. It was from Bin al-Shibh, ███ ████████ that we first heard of Khalid Shaykh Muhammad's (KSM) plot to attack Heathrow. In our custody, Bin al-Shibh told us how he learned of the attack along with where preparations stood and KSM's contingency plans to scale back the plot if necessary, to keep it viable.[96]

- (S/███ NF) Zubaydah's reporting also contributed to KSM's arrest—a point we note in our response to Example 12—as did information provided by Bin al-Shibh██████ By all accounts, KSM's arrest was the action that most disrupted the plot.

- (S/███ NF) CIA obtained updated information from KSM about the plot to attack Heathrow Airport and Canary Wharf after he had been subjected to enhanced techniques, including the information on the individual managing the plot, Abu Talha al-Pakistani.

- (S/███ NF) CIA lacked reporting on Abu Talha prior to March 2003 and first learned of his specific role in the plot from debriefing KSM; al-Qa'ida operatives Ammar al-Baluchi and Khallad Bin Attash during interrogations in CIA custody later corroborated KSM's information.[97] KSM admitted to tasking Abu Talha in 2002 to conduct surveillance of Heathrow Airport's security and to gather time tables of flights there. He added that it was Abu Talha who first raised Canary Wharf as a potential target.[98]

- (TS/██████ NF) KSM also was responsible for helping us identify two potential operatives—known only as Abu Yusef and Abu Adil—whom al-Qa'ida had deployed to the United Kingdom by early 2002 and whom KSM wanted to tap for a role in a future Heathrow operation. The pair was unwitting of KSM's intent to direct them against Heathrow—an example of al-Qa'ida's tight compartmentation of external attack plans—and had fallen out of contact with KSM's lieutenants, but we assess they remained potential threats until their full identification by UK authorities.

- (S/███ NF) Based in part on our intelligence, ████████ detained Abu Talha—an action that strengthened our confidence at the time that the plot was disrupted. ██████ he acknowledged he had been working to advance the plot and had briefed it to Hamza Rabi'a, al-Qa'ida's chief of external operations. Rabi'a, however, assessed the plot had been compromised by KSM's arrest, and Abu Talha abandoned the effort.

(S//OC/NF) While we assess detainee reporting did play a key role in disrupting the Heathrow plot, it is a complex story, and we should have been more precise at times in laying out our argumentation. Our operational success was based both on information we acquired from detainees after they had been subjected to enhanced techniques as well as information gleaned from ███████████████ in response to questions we had provided. In reviewing the array of representations we made on this subject, there are a few in which we mentioned only one aspect of the story instead of providing a better sense of the richness of the effort. In these cases, we should either have used more representative examples or, better, provided a fuller accounting.

8. (U) The Capture of Hambali

~~(S//OC/NF)~~ A review of CIA records found that CIA representations that KSM's reporting led to or played a role in the capture of Hambali are inaccurate. The review concluded there was sufficient intelligence in CIA databases acquired independently of the CIA detention and interrogation program to capture Hambali on August 11, 2003."

~~(S//NF)~~ **CIA accurately cited Khalid Shaykh Muhammad's (KSM) reporting as a crucial link in a chain of events that led to the capture of Hambali. KSM provided information on an al-Qa'ida operative named Zubair, we shared that lead with Thai authorities, they detained Zubair, and he gave actionable information that helped us identify Hambali's location. Although we had some other information linking Zubair to al-Qa'ida's Southeast Asian network, the record shows clearly that it was KSM's information that caused us to focus on him as an inroad to Hambali, so we continue to assess this is a good example of the importance of intelligence derived from detainee reporting in helping to capture other terrorists.**

~~(S//OC/NF)~~ CIA continues to assess that KSM's reporting played a role in the capture of Hambali on 11 August 2003. Other information acquired independently of the CIA detention and interrogation program contributed as well, but KSM's information was an important piece of the puzzle.

- ~~(S/████NF)~~ Majid Khan ████████████████████ in early March said he had delivered money to a "Zubair" in Thailand in December 2002.[99] While we had some reporting on Zubair and his connections to al-Qa'ida's Southeast Asian network, we did not have sufficient information to focus us on him or lead us to view him as an inroad to Hambali until KSM told us in mid-March that he had tasked Khan to deliver the money to unnamed individuals working for Hambali.[100] This information allowed us to connect Zubair to Hambali.[101]

- ~~(TS/███████████NF)~~ Thai ████████████████████ detained Zubair on 8 June.

- ~~(S//OC/NF)~~ During ████ debriefings, Zubair reported on the ████████████ and corroborated reporting on the ████████████████ ████████████ This information when combined with reporting from other sources to form a complete picture of Hambali's status was critical in helping[108] identify Hambali's general location and led to his arrest on 11 August ████████

19

9. (U) The Identification of KSM as the Mastermind of the 11 September 2001 Attacks

"(S//OC/NF) *There is no evidence to support the statement that Abu Zubaydah's information—obtained prior to using the CIA's enhanced interrogation techniques—was uniquely important or played any 'vital' role in the identification of KSM as the 'mastermind' of the 9/11 attacks. This information had been collected independent of the CIA detention and interrogation program and was acquired prior to the detention of the CIA's first detainee."*

(S//OC/NF) **CIA assesses that Abu Zubaydah's admission that Khalid Shaykh Muhammad (KSM) was the mastermind of the 9/11 attacks remains an example of important detainee information. None of the intelligence that preceded Abu Zubaydah's remarks characterized KSM as *the* mastermind of the attacks or provided the same level of clarity on his role. Our records indicate we accurately represented this example seven times. We acknowledge that in one instance—a supporting document for a set of DCIA talking points for a meeting with the President—we mischaracterized the information as having been obtained after the application of enhanced interrogation techniques. We also note that the *Study* incorrectly cites how we used the word "vital" in reference to Abu Zubaydah's information.**

(S//OC/NF) CIA assesses Abu Zubaydah's information was "important" because it was the most authoritative, detailed account of KSM's role, which, for the first time, singled him out from others involved in the plot as the "mastermind." The *Study's* assertion that we characterized this information as "vital" is incorrect.

- (S//OC/NF) The word "vital" was used in President Bush's 2006 CIA-vetted speech when he said "Zubaydah disclosed Khalid Sheikh Mohammed, or KSM, was the mastermind behind the 9/11 attacks and used the alias Mukthar. This was a vital piece of the puzzle that helped our intelligence community pursue KSM." In this context, "vital" refers to the connection between KSM and the alias Mukthar, which did significantly contribute to our pursuit of KSM.

(S//OC/NF) Immediately after the 11 September 2001 attacks, CIA officers debated whether KSM might be involved, or if Abu Zubaydah had conceived of and directed the plot. Cable traffic from November 2001 to April 2002—just before Abu Zubaydah's arrest—shows that CIA had reserved a definitive assessment of KSM's role until it received concrete reporting from a credible source.

- (S//OC/NF) Indeed, between October and January, CIA described KSM as "one of the individuals considered the potential mastermind;"[109] "one of the top candidates for having been involved in the planning for the 11 September attacks;"[110] and "one of the leading candidates to have been a hands-on planner in the 9/11 attacks."[111] Alec Station on 12 April described KSM as a "financier" of the attacks.[112]

(S//OC/NF) The *Study* cites five references to KSM that preceded Abu Zubaydah's information. Two of these references are speculative e-mails, one is a vague reference in the 9/11 Commission Report, and two are intelligence reports that did not describe the extent of KSM's role in the same manner as Abu Zubaydah or single out KSM as the "mastermind" of the attack.

- (S//OC/NF) A CIA officer in September 2001 e-mailed another officer speculating that KSM was "one of the individuals who had the capability" to conduct the attacks, and a similar e-mail in October 2001 indicated an officer "believe[d] KSM may have been the mastermind," but that more proof was needed.

- (S//OC/NF) The referenced text from the 9/11 Commission Report does not cite primary source information; it simply repeats the same internal speculations.

- (S//OC/NF) The first of the two intelligence reports indicates KSM was one of three people who had "originated" the "command and planning," along with Abu Zubaydah and an "American" who was with Abu Zubaydah.[113] The report did not distinguish KSM from the other two as the mastermind.

- (S//OC/NF) The second intelligence report only says that KSM supervised the "final touches" of the operation.[114]

10. (U) The Identification of KSM's "Mukhtar" Alias

"(U) While Abu Zubaydah did provide information on KSM's alias—prior to the initiation of the CIA's enhanced interrogation techniques to FBI interrogators—this intelligence was corroborative of information already collected and known by CIA."

(S//OC/NF) We continue to assess that Abu Zubaydah's information was a critical piece of intelligence. The *Study* is correct that CIA already had an intelligence report that Khalid Shaykh Muhammad (KSM) was using the nickname "Mukhtar" before Abu Zubaydah told us about it. Our review indicates, however, that analysts overlooked this report, and we cannot confidently conclude it would have ended the debate regardless. It is clear that CIA only made a definitive determination that KSM was "Mukhtar" after receiving the information from Abu Zubaydah. We should note that CIA made this representation twice—in the President's 2006 speech and in a supporting document for a set of DCIA talking points for a meeting with the President. The speech made clear that the information was acquired during an initial interview. In the talking points, we mistakenly claimed the information was acquired after Abu Zubaydah had undergone enhanced interrogation techniques.

(S//OC/NF) We acknowledge the *Study* is correct that CIA had an intelligence report that identified KSM as "Mukhtar" prior to Abu Zubaydah's information. We have reviewed our records, and we have concluded that our officers simply missed the earlier cable. We can find no instance in which the report spurred an analytic debate about "Mukhtar's" identity. In view of the debate that was underway at the time over multiple reports mentioning "Mukhtar," however, we cannot confidently conclude that this report would have ended the debate because much of the information we had on "Mukhtar" seemed inconsistent with an al-Qa'ida mastermind.

- (TS   NF) The details about "Mukhtar's" activities reflected in signals intelligence before March 2002 portrayed him as a document facilitator or someone procuring or disseminating video tapes and arranging travel documents.

- (TS   NF) In addition, CIA also knew from signals intelligence that there were several different "Mukhtars" linked to al-Qa'ida, making it more difficult to confidently link Mukhtar to KSM.[115] A CIA cable on 9 April 2002 acknowledged this. The cable, titled "Possible Identification of Khalid Shaykh Muhammad," noted that "we were particularly interested in the information Abu Zubaydah provided on 'Mukhtar'," and indicated that we would be combing through the SIGINT to see which Mukhtars we now could line up as KSM. [116][117]

11. (U) The Capture of Ramzi Bin al-Shibh

"(S//OC/NF) *A review of CIA records found no connection between Aby Zubaydah's reporting on Ramzi Bin al-Shibh and Ramzi Bin al-Shibh's capture.*"

"(S//OC/NF) *CIA records indicate that Abu Zubaydah did provide information on Ramzi Bin al-Shibh, however, there is no indication that Abu Zubaydah provided information on Bin al-Shibh's whereabouts. Further, while Abu Zubaydah provided information on Bin al-Shibh while being subjected to the CIA's enhanced interrogation techniques, he provided similar information to FBI interrogators prior to the initiation of the CIA's enhanced interrogation techniques.*"

(S//OC/NF) **CIA accurately represented that Abu Zubaydah's information helped lead to the arrest of Ramzi Bin al-Shibh, but we should have more clearly explained the contribution his reporting made to this operation. Abu Zubaydah provided information on how to contact another al-Qa'ida member. We passed that information to Pakistani authorities, who used it to set up a broad sting operation that fortuitously netted Bin al-Shibh. Bin al-Shibh's capture would not have occurred that day without Abu Zubaydah's information; it is a good example of how intelligence-driven operations against terrorist networks can yield results that exceed the intended target of the specific operation.**

(S//OC/NF) CIA assesses that Abu Zubaydah provided key information that "helped lead to the capture of Ramzi Bin al-Shibh." It is true that Abu Zubdaydah provided no information specifically on Bin al-Shibh's whereabouts, but as the *Study* explicitly acknowledges, he did provide information on another al-Qa'ida facilitator that prompted Pakistani action that netted Bin al-Shibh. Although Bin al-Shibh was not the target of the raid, his capture is a good example of how information obtained from detainees led to actions that had a greater impact on the group than one might have expected from any single piece of information.

- (S//OC/NF) Abu Zubaydah stated that if he personally needed to reach Hassan Gul, he would contact ██████████████████████ We provided this information to Pakistani authorities, who then interviewed ████████ and ██████████████████ which ultimately led them to an apartment linked to Gul.[118][119][120][121][122]

- (S/████████NF) ████████████████████████████████ raided the apartment on 10 September 2002 and detained Gul's brother-in-law, who provided information on Gul's safe houses in Karachi. ████ arrested Bin al-Shibh at one of these safe houses the next day.[123]

(S//OC/NF) The *Study's* own concluding paragraph on the capture of Ramzi Bin al-Shibh accurately explains this chain of events. The *Study's* concluding paragraph reads:

> (S//OC/NF) "*It is possible that the sourcing for CIA claims that 'as a result of EITs' Abu Zubaydah provided information that 'played a key role in the ultimate capture of Ramzi Bin al-Shibh [sic],' is related to Abu Zubaydah's information that Hassan Gul could be located through* ████████████ *While* ████████████ *did not provide information on Gul's whereabouts,* ████████ *led Pakistani officials to an apartment once rented by Gul. While surveillance of this apartment led to the capture of unrelated individuals, raids resulting from the interviews of one of these individuals led to the unexpected capture of Ramzi Bin al-Shibh.*"

(S//OC/NF) Finally, the *Study* states that Abu Zubaydah "provided similar information to FBI interrogators prior to the initiation of the CIA's enhanced interrogation techniques." This is incorrect.

Abu Zubaydah's unique information concerning his contact with Hassan Gul was collected on 20 August 2002, after he had been subjected to enhanced interrogation techniques.

12. (U) The Capture of KSM

"~~(S//OC/NF)~~ *A review of CIA operational records results in no indication that information from Abu Zubaydah, Ramzi Bin al-Shibh, or any other detainee, contributed to KSM's capture.*"

~~(S//OC/NF)~~ **CIA correctly represented that detainee reporting helped us capture Khalid Shaykh Muhammad (KSM). The** *Study* **says that a unilateral CIA source led us to KSM and that detainee reporting played no role. However, the** *Study* **fails to note that detainees gave us the critical information on KSM ▆▆▆▆▆ that allowed us to understand that our source knew ▆▆▆▆▆**

~~(S▆▆▆▆▆NF)~~ CIA should have been more precise in laying out the role that the various elements of the program played in this complicated case, but we stand by the assessment that detainee information contributed to KSM's capture. We assess that information provided by Abu Zubaydah—after the commencement of enhanced interrogation techniques —helped lead to the capture of Ramzi Bin al-Shibh (see Example 11).[c] CIA subsequently obtained key insights from Bin al-Shibh and ▆▆▆▆▆ ▆▆▆▆▆ related to KSM ▆▆▆▆▆ which allowed CIA to redirect a source that led us to KSM's location. ▆▆▆▆▆

[124]

- ~~(S//OC/NF)~~ Bin al-Shibh told ▆▆▆▆▆ likely on 21 September 2002, that "the best way to find KSM is to find KSM ▆▆▆▆▆ 'Ammar' who is also in Karachi."[125] On 24 September, Bin al-Shibh photo-identified FBI Most Wanted fugitive Ali Abdul Aziz Ali—a primary financier of the 9/11 attacks—as "Amar al-Baluchi," and clarified that he had a "very close relationship with KSM," and "would know how and where to contact KSM."[126] Alec Station on 30 September highlighted Bin al-Shibh's photo-identification as a "breakthrough."[127] [128][129]d

- ~~(S▆▆▆▆▆NF)~~ ▆▆▆▆▆ officers on ▆▆▆▆▆ used that information to ▆▆▆▆▆
  [130]

~~(S//OC/NF)~~ The detainees' information on ▆▆▆▆▆ ▆▆▆▆▆ ▆▆▆▆▆ Although fortuitous, this information helped CIA to redirect the source ▆▆▆▆▆ in an effort to locate KSM. [131]

~~(S//OC/NF)~~ The *Study* claims it was this unilateral source, not detainees, who first identified ▆▆▆▆▆ ▆▆▆▆▆ This is an incorrect repetition of an error made by a CIA officer in a cable in 2003.

- ~~(S//OC/NF)~~ CIA officers in late 2001 did show the source ▆▆▆▆▆ [132][133]

---

[c] For a more detailed account of Ramzi Bin al-Shibh's arrest, please see Example 11, page 21.

25

13. (U) The Capture of Majid Khan

"(S//OC/NF) The CIA repeatedly represented that the CIA interrogation program, and/or the CIA's enhanced interrogation techniques, resulted in critical, otherwise unavailable intelligence, related to...the capture of Majid Khan."

(S//NF) **CIA mistakenly provided incorrect information to the Inspector General (IG) that led to a one-time misrepresentation of this case in the IG's 2004** *Special Review.* **This mistake was not, as it is characterized in the "Findings and Conclusions" section of the** *Study,* **a "repeatedly represented" or "frequently cited" example of the effectiveness of CIA's interrogation program. CIA accurately described the importance of Khalid Shaykh Muhammad's (KSM) information in the Majid Khan case in a number of finished analytic reports and briefings before and after the** *Special Review.*

(S//OC/NF) Broadly disseminated DI finished intelligence, as well as briefings and materials provided to the SSCI, the White House, the Department of Justice, and the American public—both before and after the *Special Review*—included accurate representations regarding Majid Khan's importance.

(S//OC/NF) The standard language we used to describe Majid Khan did not imply KSM's information played a role in his capture and instead focused on the importance of his information as a building block that led to other operational successes. For example, a typical representation stated:

> *"KSM provided information about an al-Qa'ida operative, Majid Khan, who he was aware had recently been captured. KSM—possibly believing the detained operatives was "talking" admitted to having tasked Majid with delivering a large sum of money to individuals working for another senior al-Qa'ida associate. In an example of how information from one detainee can be used in debriefing another detainee in a "building block" process, Khan—confronted with KSM's information about the money—acknowledged that he delivered the money to an operative named Zubair and provided Zubair's physical description and contact number."*

14. (U) The Thwarting of the Camp Lemonier Plotting

"(U) A review of CIA records found that the plotting against Camp Lemonier was not "stopped" because of information acquired from the CIA detention and interrogation program."

(S//OC/NF) CIA assesses that its representations related to this plot—most notably the CIA-vetted statement in President Bush's 2006 speech that "Terrorists held in CIA custody have also provided information that *helped* stop the planned strike on US Marines at Camp Lemonier in Djibouti" (emphasis added)—were accurate. We did not represent that we initially learned of the plot from detainees, or that it was disrupted based solely on information from detainees in CIA custody.

(S//OC/NF) Some information came from detainees in CIA custody, ███████████████████ ████████████████████████████ No single detainee's information or arrest stopped this plot. Rather, a series of events—several of which were related to CIA's detainee program—helped disrupt it.

- (S//OC/NF) According to Khalid Shaykh Muhammad (KSM), his arrest in March 2003 (which we note in Example 12 resulted in part from information provided by Ramzi Bin al-Shibh) prevented him from transferring 30,000 euros from al-Qa'ida in Pakistan to al-Qa'ida in East Africa leaders, some of whom were plotting the Camp Lemonier attack. [134][135] Funding shortages were cited repeatedly by detainees and in ██████████████ as a reason for the Camp Lemonier plot's delays.

- (TS██████████NF) In March 2004, ████████████████████ based information from a clandestine source—detained and rendered to CIA custody the primary facilitator for al-Qa'ida's Camp Lemonier plot, Guleed Hassan Ahmed, who had cased the Camp on behalf of al-Qa'ida. [136] Guleed provided details about the plot and al-Qa'ida's Somali support network, which drove CIA's targeting efforts. [137][138][139][140]

- (S//OC/NF) We combined Guleed's information with other reporting to build a more detailed targeting picture of al-Qa'ida's East Africa network, helping us to locate ████████████ several other al-Qa'ida couriers, some of whom had been tasked with transferring additional funding to the network. [141][142][143][144][145][146]

(S//OC/NF) We agree with the *Study* that we had threat reporting against Camp Lemonier prior to the March 2004 detention and rendition of one of the plot's key facilitators, but we believe the earliest reports cited in the *Study* have no relation to this plot.

- (S██████████NF) The *Study* states, "CIA first learned of this terrorist threat from ████████████ as early as January 2003." [147] The *Study* cites a PDB article based on ████████████ ██████ but that report was later recalled after being revealed to be a fabrication. [148]

- (S//OC/NF) The *Study* cites a Terrorist Advisory from March 2003 that states, "US forces stationed at Camp Lemonier in Djibouti also could be targeted." [149] This reference, however, was not based on specific intelligence reporting and is actually focused on a different al-Qa'ida cell based in Kenya, which was targeting sites primarily in Kenya or Tanzania. The reference to Djibouti in this context was an analytic assessment that Djibouti was a potential target given its US Military presence. A later Djibouti-specific section in the same report focused on a local Somali group and never mentions plot leader Abu Talha al-Sudani or his Somalia-based cell.

- (S̶ ███████ N̶F̶) Moreover, the *Study* cites ████████████████████████ information noting that a local Somali group planned to hijack an aircraft and crash it into the base.[150] This threat was later found to be unrelated to the al-Qa'ida plot against Camp Lemonier.[151][152]

15. (U) The Assertion that Detainee Reporting Helped Validate Sources

"(TS█████████████NF) *The CIA represented to policymakers over several years that information acquired from CIA detainees helped validate CIA sources. CIA records indicate that these CIA representations are based on the CIA's experience with one CIA detainee, Janat Gul. The CIA representations omit key contextual information, including that the CIA subjected Janat Gul to the CIA's enhanced interrogation techniques based on single-source CIA humint reporting that the CIA later concluded was fabricated, and that the CIA officers doubted the credibility of the source prior to Gul's interrogation.*"

(S//OC/NF) **CIA frequently cited one particular example of information from a detainee that helped us validate a source because it was the clearest and most consequential case in which what we learned from a detainee interrogation caused us to take steps that revealed the source had fabricated a highly concerning threat. There have been many other occasions when information obtained from detainees has helped us determine how best to use, question, and evaluate the veracity of our sources. We acknowledge that this information was a supplementary benefit to the program, the primary purpose of which was to capture disrupt plots, save lives, and remove senior al-Qa'ida leaders from the battlefield.**

(TS█████████████NF) CIA has used reporting from numerous detainees in addition to Janat Gul to vet, task, and corroborate information from countless sources of intelligence. These encompass human sources, other detainees, signals intelligence, and al-Qa'ida's ████communications. We often cited the case of Janat Gul, who was arrested in June 2004 for his facilitation activities on behalf of senior al-Qa'ida leaders, because it was a clear cut example of source validation that resulted from detainee information regarding an important alleged threat. The *Study* incorrectly implies that our use of this example was disingenuous because we already had doubts about the credibility of the source's report. The source told us that he met Janat Gul in 2004 and acquired information on plans for a high-profile attack to occur in the United States before the US Presidential elections.

- (TS█████████████NF) Although some officers raised questions about this information—as often occurs, especially with sensational intelligence—CIA wrote numerous finished intelligence products citing the information before learning it was fabricated, indicating that CIA took it seriously even as we worked to resolve the inconsistencies.[153][154][155][156]

- (TS█████████████NF) A body of intelligence reporting contributed to the plausibility of the information. Other sources were reporting on al-Qa'ida attack preparations, and Hassan Gul told CIA interrogators in January 2004 about al-Qa'ida's compartmented external operations training program in Pakistan's tribal areas. At the time of his arrest, CIA believed based on a body of intelligence that Gul facilitated for al-Qa'ida's senior-most leaders, placing him in a position to know details of the group's operational plans. Moreover, CIA had corroborated other aspects of the source's reporting.[157][158][159][160][161][162][163][164][165][166][167][168][169][170][171]

- (TS█████████████NF) Janat Gul's claim that the source never met the al-Qa'ida finance chief— who the source said told him about the pre-election threat—was vital to CIA's assessment and handling of the case. CIA officers assessed Gul was cooperating during his interrogations by that time, leading CIA to ████████the source on the meeting and the plot, which he ultimately recanted.[172][173]

- (TS⬛⬛⬛⬛⬛NF) Gul was not the only CIA detainee to help CIA vet the source's information. CIA detainee Sharif al-Masri, who also knew the source and arranged to have ⬛⬛⬛⬛⬛ ⬛⬛⬛⬛⬛⬛⬛⬛⬛ also provided information that reinforced CIA's decision to ⬛⬛⬛ the source.[174][175]

(S⬛⬛⬛⬛NF) CIA officers routinely use detainee reporting as an integral part of our tradecraft to help validate sources and array against the larger base of all-source reporting on al-Qa'ida's activities, leadership, and locations. For example, CIA in 2005 questioned Abu Faraj al-Libi—after he underwent enhanced interrogation techniques —on his access to Bin Ladin after a sensitive clandestine source, whose access and past reporting were by that time well established, claimed that Abu Faraj told him he was present with Bin Ladin when the leader filmed a video statement that aired in October 2004.

- (S⬛⬛⬛⬛NF) A CIA cable on 2 August 2005 shows that nearly a year later analysts were struggling to corroborate the information, which was important to understanding Bin Ladin's associates and their access to him. Abu Faraj adamantly denied the claim and later gave information about how he received the videotape from Bin Ladin's courier, which allowed us to assess that the source's information was incorrect.

- (S⬛⬛⬛⬛NF) CIA in 2009 published an Intelligence Assessment titled "Hunting Usama Bin Ladin: What We Have Learned from Senior Al-Qa'ida Detainees (S/NF)," which contains the judgment— ultimately validated by what we learned at his Abbottabad compound—that Bin Ladin probably did not meet face to face even with his most senior lieutenants after he fled Afghanistan, citing the information from Abu Faraj and other information acquired from detainees in CIA custody. [176][177][178][179][180][181][182][183][184][185][186][187][188][189][190][191][192][193][194][195][196]

16. (U) Arrest and Identification of Uzhair and Saifullah Paracha

"(S//OC/NF) *The CIA also repeatedly represented that the CIA interrogation program, and/or the CIA's enhanced interrogation techniques, resulted in critical, otherwise unavailable intelligence related to...the arrests of Uzhair and Sayf al-Rahman Paracha. A review of CIA records found [this] representation to be inaccurate.*"[197]

(TS,████████NF) CIA continues to assess that Khalid Shaykh Muhammad's (KSM) identification of Pakistani businessman Saifullah Paracha, an al-Qa'ida contact whom KSM was trying to use to smuggle explosives into the United States, was a success resulting from detainee reporting. KSM's information spurred FBI action against Paracha; prompted FBI to question his son, Uzhair; and allowed analysts to focus on the <u>right</u> Saifullah Paracha.

(S//OC/NF) Reporting from interrogations of KSM was directly and uniquely responsible for the arrests of Saifullah Paracha and his son Uzhair Paracha, both of whom KSM claimed had agreed to facilitate an al-Qa'ida plan to smuggle explosives into the United States.[198] In a 26 March 2003 cable, the FBI stated that it had taken action with regard to Saifullah and Uzhair based on KSM's debriefing disseminated 25 March.[199][200]

- (S//NF) The FBI immediately watchlisted Saifullah and Uzhair and searched domestic immigration and law enforcement databases for details on their locations and activities. The FBI determined Saifullah was located in Pakistan but was able to arrest Uzhair in New York on 31 March.[201]

-
  206 207 208

(S//OC/NF) The *Study's* finding that CIA possessed sufficient information to identify and detain Saifullah Paracha without reporting from KSM is incorrect. We had fragmentary information suggesting that someone by the name of Saifullah Paracha might be of interest to us as a possible accomplice in an al-Qa'ida overseas financial scheme. However, we did not know which among the many people who have that name around the world to focus upon. We did not know he was involved in a potential attack on the US until KSM told us Saifullah and his son agreed to smuggle explosives into the US. The FBI found the son in New York, in their words, "based on this reporting."

(S//OC/NF) The *Study* says that Saifullah Paracha was already "well-known to the IC prior to the capture of KSM,"[209] but the only clear link the *Study* cites between Paracha and terrorist plotting is actually a reference to a <u>different</u> Saifullah Paracha.[210] All other references are either too vague or indirect to have been meaningful without detainee reporting, refer to a nascent investigation of terrorist use of a Paracha-affiliated business to mask financial transfers, or in many cases, also refer to a different Saifullah Paracha.

- (S//OC/NF) The *Study* refers to a Saifullah Paracha who had links to Mir Aimal Kansi, the terrorist who killed two people outside CIA Headquarters in 1993.[211][212][213] However, the Saifullah Paracha KSM reported on was more than 25 years younger and not connected to Mir Aimal Kansi.[214][215]

- (S//OC/NF) The *Study* cites a "link" between Paracha and Abu Zubaydah, because Paracha's name appeared among hundreds of other names in documents confiscated in the Abu Zubaydah raid.

31

While the CIA passed Paracha's name and information on his ties to a Karachi, Pakistan-based company with a New York office to the FBI,[216] the Bureau did not report any further information of interest concerning Paracha until after KSM's debriefings.[217][218][219][220]

(S//OC/NF) The *Study* cites two other pieces of information on Paracha that it claims are representative of reporting available independent of the CIA detention and interrogation program. Neither report was noteworthy without KSM's information.

- (S//OC/NF) One is an indirect connection to Paracha's business in Pakistan that Committee staff found in an undisseminated FBI case file. It was not available to CIA at the time and would not have linked Paracha to an al-Qa'ida operation independent of KSM's information in any case. The other report is ▮▮▮▮▮▮▮▮▮▮▮▮ of Majid Khan before he was rendered ▮▮▮▮▮▮ to US custody, but the report included few details and was disseminated just _after_ KSM provided the information that allowed us to identify Paracha.

17. (U) Critical Intelligence Alerting the CIA to Ja'far al-Tayyar

"(S//OC/NF) The CIA made repeated claims that the use of the CIA's enhanced interrogation techniques resulted in 'key intelligence' from Abu Zubaydah and KSM on an operative named Ja'far al-Tayyar—later identified as Adnan el-Shukrijumah. These CIA representations omit key contextual facts."

(S//OC/NF) CIA continues to assess that information from detainees in CIA custody—specifically Khalid Shaykh Muhammad (KSM) and Abu Zubaydah—that was obtained after they were subjected to enhanced interrogation techniques was important to identifying Ja'far al-Tayyar. We acknowledge there were cases in which we either made a factual error or used imprecise language, but these mistakes were not central to our representations and none invalidates our assessment that detainee reporting provided key intelligence on this important terrorist.

The "key contextual facts" that the *Study* claims CIA omitted are incorrect:

"(S//OC/NF) The Intelligence Community was interested in the Florida-based Adnan al-Shukrijumah prior to the detention of the CIA's first detainee."

(S//OC/NF) The only reference to Shukrijumah in CIA holdings prior to 2003 was a request for traces from FBI and a CIA response that stated, "A search of our Agency's records found no identifiable information on...Adnan Gulshair el-Shukri Jumah."[221] To support its claim, the *Study* cites a US District Court case file—which was not in CIA databases—that mentions Shukrijumah due to his association with a Florida-based extremist.[222]

"(S//OC/NF) Abu Zubaydah provided information on a KSM associate named Ja'far al-Tayyar to FBI agents in May 2002, prior to being subjected to the CIA's enhanced interrogation techniques."

(TS̶̶̶̶̶̶̶̶̶̶̶̶NF) Abu Zubaydah's information in May 2002 came after being subjected to sleep deprivation. Although sleep deprivation was not officially designated an enhanced technique in 2002, it was classified as such in 2005. This information was an initial step toward identifying the right Ja'far al-Tayyar, but we were not able to do so until KSM provided more detailed reporting.[223][224][225]

(S//OC/NF) The *Study* implies that CIA had substantial information on Ja'far al-Tayyar by noting that we produced "a targeting study" on him in January 2003, prior to KSM's detention. However, that study was titled, "Targeting Study: Finding the Right Ja'far al-Tayyar,"[226] and the first paragraph stated, "Unfortunately, many extremists use the name of Ja'far al-Tayyar, which can be translated as 'Jafar the Pilot.' Headquarters research has identified several distinct Ja'far al-Tayyars. We very much want to confirm the locations of each of these Jafars."[227]

"(S//OC/NF) CIA personnel distrusted KSM's reporting on Ja'far al-Tayyar—stating KSM fabricated information and had included al-Tayyar 'into practically every story, each time with a different role.'"

(S//OC/NF) KSM's inconsistencies did not lead CIA officers to discount al-Tayyar's importance. The cited cable, when taken in context says, "We believe this [deception] could indicate that KSM is trying to protect al-Tayyar, and we intend to focus more strongly on [al-Tayyar]."[228] Our focus on al-Tayyar over the years—particularly when coupled with detainee reporting and documents seized at Bin Ladin's compound in Abbottabad—has helped us better understand his important role in al-Qa'ida's terror operations and his involvement in several unrealized plots.[229][230][231][232]

"(S//OC/NF) Other CIA detainee reporting differed from KSM's reporting."

(S//OC/NF) Discrepancies between KSM and other detainee accounts of al-Tayyar, who is one of al-Qa'ida's most security-conscious and reclusive operatives,[233] were to be expected from detainees with varying degrees of access to him. Furthermore, the *Study's* basis for this criticism consists of two personal emails, a single detainee report, and an NCTC product from its "Red Team," which is charged with providing analysis that is contrary to widely held analytic positions. Terrorism analysts are trained to question their judgments and to openly express disagreement, especially when there is conflicting information. However, there has always been a strong interest in al-Tayyar, and there is consensus that he has become a leading figure in al-Qa'ida's external operations.

"(S//OC/NF) CIA records indicate that KSM did not know al-Tayar's true name and that it was Jose Padilla—in military custody and questioned by the FBI—who provided al-Tayar's true name as Adnan el-Shukrijumah."

(S//OC/NF) While KSM did not know al-Tayyar's true name, his biographic description was sufficient for FBI to identify Adnan el-Shukrijumah as a likely candidate. In addition, the FBI knew to ask Padilla about al-Tayyar's true name because KSM told CIA debriefers that he would know it.

(S//OC/NF) In reviewing this case, we did identify occasions when CIA's language either was not as precise as it should have been or we made factual errors.

- (S//OC/NF) Sometimes we said KSM called al-Tayyar the "next Muhammad Atta." This was an imprecise paraphrase of KSM, who actually described al-Tayyar as having similar education and Western experience as Muhammad Atta and considered him as the "next emir" for an attack in the United States. KSM did not call al-Tayyar "the next Muhammad Atta."

- (S//OC/NF) In some of the early representations, we incorrectly stated al-Tayyar fled the United States in response to the FBI investigation, although he had in fact already departed the United States by this time.

18. (S///NF) The Identification and Arrest of Salih al-Marri

"(S//OC/NF) The CIA repeatedly represented that the CIA interrogation program, and/or the CIA's enhanced interrogation techniques, resulted in critical, otherwise unavailable intelligence, related to...the arrest of Salih al-Marri."

"(S//OC/NF) Reporting from KSM as a result of the lawful use of EITs played no role in the arrest of Salih al-Marri."

(S//OC/NF) CIA mistakenly provided incorrect information to the Inspector General (IG) that led to a one-time misrepresentation of this case in the IG's 2004 *Special Review*. This mistake was not, as it is characterized in the "Findings and Conclusions" section of the *Study*, a "repeatedly represented" or "frequently cited" example of the effectiveness of CIA's interrogation program. We are unable to identify other cases in which we link al-Marri's arrest to CIA detainee reporting.

(S⬛⬛⬛NF) With respect to the merits of this case, however, we would note that reporting from Khalid Shaykh Muhammad (KSM) was responsible for clarifying the role that al-Marri—on whom we previously had no concrete information—played for al-Qa'ida as a sleeper operative in the US.

- (S⬛⬛⬛/NF) Prior to KSM's detention on 1 March 2003, CIA and FBI were aware of al-Marri's links to al-Qa'ida and strongly suspected him of having a nefarious objective[234] in the Peoria, Illinois area near the time the FBI arrested him in December 2001. Both agencies, however, lacked detailed reporting to confirm these suspicions or more fully understand al-Marri's specific role for al-Qa'ida until KSM discussed him. [235][236][237]

- (S⬛⬛⬛NF) KSM during CIA debriefings in March 2003 identified a photograph of al-Marri as an individual whom he had ordered to travel to the US as a sleeper operative shortly before the 9/11 attacks.[238] KSM claimed that he intended for al-Marri to help other al-Qa'ida operatives in the US prior to unspecified follow-on operations, to explore the possibility of hacking into US banks, and to receive funds for the 9/11 hijackers—all of which put into context the fragmentary information previously available.

19. (S//NF) The Collection of Critical Tactical Intelligence on Shkai, Pakistan

"(TS ███████████ NF) *The CIA represented to policymakers over several years that 'key intelligence' was obtained from the use of the CIA's enhanced interrogation techniques that revealed Shkai, Pakistan to be 'a major al-Qa'ida hub in the tribal areas,' and resulted in 'tactical intelligence* ███████ ████████████████ *Shkai, Pakistan.' These CIA representations are based on the CIA's experience with one CIA detainee, Hassan Ghul [sic]. While CIA records indicate that Hassan Ghul did provide information on Shkai, Pakistan, a review of CIA records also found that (1) this information was provided prior to Hassan Ghul being subjected to CIA interrogation techniques; and (2) the CIA assessed that information provided by Ghul confirmed earlier reporting that the Shkai valley of Pakistan served as al-Qa'ida's command and control center after the group's 2001 exodus from Afghanistan."*

(S//OC/NF) CIA correctly reported that senior al-Qa'ida facilitator Hassan Gul's information about a small town in Pakistan's tribal areas called Shkai was critical, ███████████ ████████████████████████████ **We never represented that Shkai was previously unknown to us or that Gul only told us about it after he was subjected to enhanced interrogation techniques . We said that after these techniques were used, Gul provided "detailed tactical intelligence." That intelligence differed significantly in granularity and operational** ███ **from what he provided before enhanced techniques. As a result of his information, we were able to make a persuasive case** █████████████████████████

(TS ███████ NF) CIA continues to assess that the information derived from Hassan Gul after the commencement of enhanced techniques provided new and unique insight into al-Qa'ida's presence and operations in Shkai, Pakistan. [239] Before Gul's capture in January 2004, sources of varying credibility gave general information about the town's importance as an emerging al-Qa'ida safehaven, but Gul's debriefings were the most definitive first-hand account of the identities, precise locations, and activities of senior al-Qa'ida members in Shkai at that time. [240] As a result of the information Gul provided, █████████

████████████████████████████

(TS ████████ NF) As the *Study* notes, Gul showed signs of cooperation immediately following his capture; before undergoing enhanced techniques, he did give us some detail about the activities and general whereabouts of al-Qa'ida members in Shkai. Nonetheless, interrogators judged that he was not yet cooperative enough to be debriefed by subject matter experts and requested the use of enhanced techniques. [241] After being subjected to enhanced techniques, he provided more granular information when, for example, he sat down with ██████ experts and pointed to specific locations where he met some of the senior al-Qa'ida members we were trying to find. The intelligence derived from Gul's debriefings yielded information that continues to undergird our analysis of al-Qa'ida's activities in Pakistan's tribal areas.

- (TS ██████████ NF) Gul revealed his understanding that then little-known al-Qa'ida operative Hamza Rabi'a had taken over as the group's lead attack coordinator after 9/11 mastermind Khalid Shaykh Muhammad's capture in 2003, and was using facilities in Shkai to train operatives for attacks outside Pakistan. [242] He also used ████████████ to pinpoint a Shkai residence where he claimed to have met senior al-Qa'ida leader 'Abd al-Hadi al-Iraqi. He said the facility was called the "Bachelor House" and that several unmarried men associated with al-Qa'ida lived there, ████████████ ████████ [243]

- (TS̶ ███████████ N̶F̶) Gul also used ███████ to give more details about the Bachelor House, another facility owned by a local al-Qa'ida supporter dubbed "The Ida Khan Complex," and a separate compound used by a group of al-Qa'ida-aligned Uzbeks. He also described the group's evacuation plans in the event of Pakistani military operations.[244]

- (TS̶ ███████████ N̶F̶) The granularity of Gul's information—coupled with ██████████████ ██████████ significantly bolstered CIA analysts' confidence about al-Qa'ida's disposition in the region, and revealed how the group was using Shkai as a venue to plot attacks against the West, including possible US interests.[245]

(TS̶ ███████████████ N̶F̶) Senior US officials during the winter and spring of 2004 presented the Agency's analysis of Gul's debriefings and other intelligence about Shkai ██████████████████ ██████████████████████████████

- (TS̶ ███████████████ N̶F̶) CIA Headquarters in February 2004 sent a cable to ██████████ titled *Eyes Only: Transmittal of Shkai Pre-brief Package for DCI Meeting with* ████████████ ████████ which outlined how CIA's analysis of ██████████ and detainee reporting—including Gul's—crystallized the Agency's understanding of al-Qa'ida's robust operational hub in Shkai.[247]

- (TS̶ ███████████████ N̶F̶) Days later, CIA Headquarters sent ██████████████ a cable for passage to ██████████████ offering the Agency's latest assessment of Shkai. The cable explicitly cited Gul as the source of the information, and included a comprehensive list—including ██████████████ of buildings, compounds, and other facilities tied to the group in Shkai.[248][249][250][251]

20. (U) Information on the Courier that Led to the UBL Operation

"(S//OC/NF) A review of CIA records found that much of the critical intelligence on Abu Ahmed [sic] al-Kuwaiti was acquired prior to—and independently of—the CIA detention and interrogation program."

(S//OC/NF) **CIA correctly represented that detainee reporting helped us identify Usama Bin Ladin's courier, Abu Ahmad al-Kuwaiti. The** *Study* **incorrectly characterizes the intelligence we had on Abu Ahmad before acquiring information on him from detainees in CIA custody as "critical." That intelligence was insufficient to distinguish Abu Ahmad from many other Bin Ladin associates until additional information from detainees put it into context and allowed us to better understand his true role and potential in the hunt for Bin Ladin.**

(S//OC/NF) Information from detainees in CIA custody on Abu Ahmad's involvement in delivering messages from Bin Ladin beginning in mid-2002 fundamentally changed our assessment of his potential importance to our hunt for Bin Ladin. That information prompted us to question other detainees on his role and identity and to review previous reporting. CIA combined this information with reporting from detainees ▮▮▮▮▮▮▮▮▮ signals intelligence, and reporting from clandestine sources to build a profile of Abu Ahmad's experiences, family, and characteristics that allowed us to eventually determine his true name and location. The other intelligence that the *Study* characterizes as "critical" did not distinguish Abu Ahmad from others who had some level of access to Bin Ladin, especially before 9/11.

(TS▮▮▮▮▮▮▮▮NF) Detainees in CIA custody Ammar al-Baluchi and Hassan Gul offered vital insights into Abu Ahmad's role.

- (S//OC/NF) Ammar, after undergoing enhanced interrogation techniques, was the first detainee to reveal what apparently was a carefully guarded al-Qa'ida secret—that Abu Ahmad served as a courier for messages to and from Bin Ladin.[252] Before that, we had only general information ▮▮▮▮▮▮▮▮▮▮▮▮▮▮▮▮▮▮▮▮that Abu Ahmad had interacted with Bin Ladin before the group's retreat from Tora Bora, Afghanistan in late 2001, when Bin Ladin was relatively accessible to a number of al-Qa'ida figures.

- (TS▮▮▮▮▮▮▮NF) Gul, while in CIA custody—before undergoing enhanced techniques—speculated that Abu Ahmad could be one of three people with Bin Ladin and speculated that Abu Ahmad may have handled Bin Ladin's needs, including sending messages to his gatekeeper, Abu Faraj al-Libi.[253]

- (TS▮▮▮▮▮▮▮NF) After undergoing enhanced techniques, Gul stated that Abu Ahmad specifically passed a letter from Bin Ladin to Abu Faraj in late 2003 and that Abu Ahmad had "disappeared" from Karachi, Pakistan in 2002. This information was not only more concrete and less speculative, it also corroborated information from Ammar that Khalid Shaykh Muhammad (KSM) was lying when he claimed Abu Ahmad left al-Qa'ida in 2002.

(S//OC/NF) Even after undergoing enhanced techniques, KSM lied about Abu Ahmad, and Abu Faraj denied knowing him.[254][255][256] A cable in the aftermath of Abu Faraj's debriefing[257] indicates that this dissembling immediately raised our suspicions, and it would eventually strengthen our assessment that Abu Ahmad was an important potential inroad to Bin Ladin, which is reflected in analytic products and targeting cables beginning in 2007.[258]

- (TS █████████████ OC/NF) Ammar and Gul both said Abu Ahmad worked directly for Abu Faraj as of mid-2002.[259260]

- (TS █████████████ NF) KSM denied that Abu Ahmad delivered letters from Bin Ladin and claimed that Abu Ahmad left al-Qa'ida in 2002.[261] Ammar, however, claimed KSM had told him that Abu Ahmad continued to deliver letters from Bin Ladin after 2002—a point that Gul corroborated.[262]

(S//OC/NF) Detainees in CIA custody helped confirm Abu Ahmad's true identity. We first obtained a partial true name for Abu Ahmad from a detainee ██████████████ but that detainee claimed Abu Ahmad died in 2001.[263] CIA later discovered through signals intelligence, a clandestine source, and other detainees—in CIA ████████ custody—that the ███████ detainee had confused Abu Ahmad with his deceased brother. Once we learned that Abu Ahmad was most likely alive, we were able to use the partial true name to acquire additional information ████████████████████████ ██ Detainees in CIA custody provided additional pieces of the puzzle.

- (TS █████████ NF) Detainee Abu Yasir al-Jazari told CIA interrogators that Abu Ahmad mixed "Pakistani words" with Arabic. A native Arabic and Pashtu speaker, ████████—████████ ████████████████████—spoke with a speech impediment that made it sound as if he were mixing the two languages, ████████████ This information helped CIA ████████ assess that the ███████ living at the compound in Abbottabad was Abu Ahmad.[264265]

- (TS █████ NF) Ahmad Ghailani during a CIA interrogation said that Abu Ahmad's first child was a daughter born around 2002, which matched information from ████████████ about individuals at the Abbottabad compound.[266]

(S//OC/NF) Insights from detainees in CIA custody into Bin Ladin's security practices and family increased CIA's confidence that Bin Ladin could be residing at the compound in Abbottabad.

- (S//OC/NF) Khallad Bin Attash and other detainees in CIA custody[267] confirmed Bin Ladin after fleeing Afghanistan would not meet face-to-face with al-Qa'ida members, had few bodyguards, relied on a small group of individuals native to the area to carry messages and handle daily chores, would not leave the house, and did not relocate frequently—all of which matched circumstances at the compound.[268269270271272273274275]

- (TS █████████████ NF) Sharif al-Masri and KSM speculated during CIA interrogations that Bin Ladin's youngest wife, Amal, probably was with Bin Ladin,[276277278279280] and Sharif indicated he passed a letter intended for another Bin Ladin wife, Siham, along with a letter for Bin Ladin to Abu Faraj, suggesting they were at least near each other. These observations helped ███ identify family members at the Abbottabad compound.

(S//OC/NF) CIA has never represented that information acquired through its interrogations of detainees was either the first or the only information that we had on Abu Ahmad. We have reported—and continue to assess—that the information we acquired from them significantly advanced our understanding of Abu Ahmad beyond the other intelligence cited in the *Study*.

- (S █████ NF) Zubair al-Ha'ili's comment ████████ interrogators in 2002 that Abu Ahmad was one of several "close associates of Usama Bin Ladin," was not sufficient to distinguish Abu Ahmad from many other al-Qa'ida members who knew Bin Ladin at the time. Similarly, we assess Riyadh the

Facilitator's claim that Abu Ahmad traveled to meet Bin Ladin refers to a meeting before 11 September 2001, when numerous al-Qa'ida members had access to Bin Ladin.

- (S//OC/NF) Abu Ahmad's interactions with Bin Ladin's son Sa'ad—which the *Study* suggests were another "critical" piece of intelligence—were not unusual because Sa'ad worked under KSM as a facilitator; he also relied on KSM to send messages to his father. Similarly, Abu Ahmad's involvement in operational planning with KSM did not suggest that he was facilitating for Bin Ladin.

- (TS███████NF) Abu Ahmad in 2002 stopped using the phone number and the email address the *Study* cites as "critical" information in our possession. The IC has never linked the phone number to any of Bin Ladin's known locations in Peshawar, Swat/Shangla, Haripur or Abbottabad, nor linked the email account to any of Abu Ahmad's communications after 2002.

(TS███████████████NF) It is impossible to know in hindsight whether we could have obtained from Ammar, Gul, and others the same information that helped us find Bin Ladin without using enhanced techniques, or whether we eventually would have acquired other intelligence that allowed us to successfully pursue the Abu Ahmad lead or some other lead without the information we acquired from detainees in CIA custody. However, the information we did obtain from these detainees played a role—in combination with other important streams of intelligence—in finding the al-Qa'ida leader.

---

[1] [CIA | ██████ 10972 | | 12 April 2002 | | | | | (S/ ████ NF) |]

[2] [CIA | ████ 10976 | | 12 April 2002 | | | | | (S/ ████ NF) |]

[3] [Other | SSCI Report, Volume 2, Part 1, Page 382 | | 13 Dec 2012 | | | | | (TS/ ████████ NF) |]

[4] [CIA | ████ 10976 | | 12 April 2002 | | | | | (S/ ████ NF) |]

[5] [CIA | ALEC ████████ | 22 Apr 2002 | | | | | (S/ ████ NF) |]

[6] [CIA | ████ 11036 | | 22 Apr 2002 | | | | | (S/ ████ NF) |]

[7] [CIA ████████████████████████████ | | | | (S//NF) |]

[8] [CIA | ████ 11058 | | 23 Apr 2002 | | | | | (S/ ████ NF) |]

[9] [CIA | ████ 78390 | | 25 Apr 2002 | | | | | (S/ ████ NF) |]

[10] [CIA | ████ 11070 | | 25 April 2002 | | | | | (S/ ████ NF) |]

[11] [CIA | ALEC ████████████████ | | | | (S/ ████ NF) |]

[12] [Other | SSCI Report, Volume 2, Part 1, Pages 376 | | 13 Dec 2012 | | | | | (TS/ ████████ NF) |]

[13] [Other | SSCI Report, Volume 2, Part 1, P. 395, Citation 1867 | | 13 December 2012 | | | | | (TS/ ████████ NF)] The citation refers to two documents, the first being a Department of Justice summary of chronology on Jose Padilla. This document (on page 2, paragraph 3), cites Padilla's "Mujahideen Identification Form" as having been "recovered by FBI in Pakistan in a box of documents containing approximately 180 such applications." This identification form, as cited in FBI WASH 101514Z, item 4, as a "pledge sheet" was acquired by LEGAT ████ on 15 December 2001, as the SSCI Report cites. It does not say how FBI acquired these documents, but states they were originally collected in a raid on 8 December 2001 at "an Arab office (NFI) Kandahar." We have been unable to locate any records of this document entering CIA possession. Reports at this time also were often stored in CIA facilities, because they were secure, but FBI maintained possession of them to preserve chain of custody for use in legal cases. This may have applied to this document. The *Study* then cites a July 2007 personal email from a CIA officer describing a meeting with an FBI officer recalling the raids over five years later. The FBI officer mistakenly recollected that the pledge sheet was collected during the 24 November 2001 raid against Salim Ahmad Salim Hamdan. This raid was against two vehicles, not an Arab office. Documents in this raid were disseminated by ████████ before passing them to FBI, but there is no record of Padilla's pledge sheet appearing in this documentation. The FBI officer's confusion over which raid the specific document came from probably explains why the SSCI Report claimed the document was "obtained in Afghanistan by the CIA." CIA has no record of having possession of this document between its 8 December 2001 recovery by the US military and its 15 December 2001 acquisition by the FBI.]

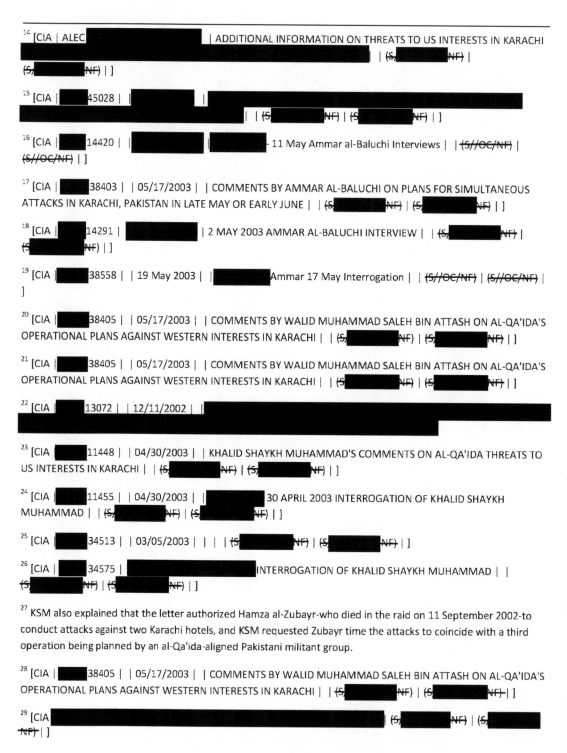

[14] [CIA | ALEC ███████████ | ADDITIONAL INFORMATION ON THREATS TO US INTERESTS IN KARACHI ████████████████████ | (S/ ███ NF) | (S/ ███ NF) |]

[15] [CIA | ███ 45028 | | ██████ | ████████████████████ | (S/ ███ NF) | (S/ ███ NF) |]

[16] [CIA | ███ 14420 | | ████████████ | ██████ - 11 May Ammar al-Baluchi Interviews | | (S//OC/NF) | (S//OC/NF) |]

[17] [CIA | ███ 38403 | | 05/17/2003 | | COMMENTS BY AMMAR AL-BALUCHI ON PLANS FOR SIMULTANEOUS ATTACKS IN KARACHI, PAKISTAN IN LATE MAY OR EARLY JUNE | | (S/ ███ NF) | (S/ ███ NF) |]

[18] [CIA | ███ 14291 | ████████ | 2 MAY 2003 AMMAR AL-BALUCHI INTERVIEW | | (S/ ███ NF) | (S/ ███ NF) |]

[19] [CIA | ███ 38558 | | 19 May 2003 | | ████████ Ammar 17 May Interrogation | | (S//OC/NF) | (S//OC/NF) |]

[20] [CIA | ███ 38405 | | 05/17/2003 | | COMMENTS BY WALID MUHAMMAD SALEH BIN ATTASH ON AL-QA'IDA'S OPERATIONAL PLANS AGAINST WESTERN INTERESTS IN KARACHI | | (S/ ███ NF) | (S/ ███ NF) |]

[21] [CIA | ███ 38405 | | 05/17/2003 | | COMMENTS BY WALID MUHAMMAD SALEH BIN ATTASH ON AL-QA'IDA'S OPERATIONAL PLANS AGAINST WESTERN INTERESTS IN KARACHI | | (S/ ███ NF) | (S/ ███ NF) |]

[22] [CIA | ███ 13072 | | 12/11/2002 | | ████████████████████████]

[23] [CIA ███ 11448 | | 04/30/2003 | | KHALID SHAYKH MUHAMMAD'S COMMENTS ON AL-QA'IDA THREATS TO US INTERESTS IN KARACHI | | (S/ ███ NF) | (S/ ███ NF) |]

[24] [CIA ███ 11455 | | 04/30/2003 | | ██████ 30 APRIL 2003 INTERROGATION OF KHALID SHAYKH MUHAMMAD | | (S/ ███ NF) | (S/ ███ NF) |]

[25] [CIA | ███ 34513 | | 03/05/2003 | | | | (S/ ███ NF) | (S/ ███ NF) |]

[26] [CIA | ███ 34575 | ██████████████ INTERROGATION OF KHALID SHAYKH MUHAMMAD | | (S/ ███ NF) | (S/ ███ NF) |]

[27] KSM also explained that the letter authorized Hamza al-Zubayr-who died in the raid on 11 September 2002-to conduct attacks against two Karachi hotels, and KSM requested Zubayr time the attacks to coincide with a third operation being planned by an al-Qa'ida-aligned Pakistani militant group.

[28] [CIA | ███ 38405 | | 05/17/2003 | | COMMENTS BY WALID MUHAMMAD SALEH BIN ATTASH ON AL-QA'IDA'S OPERATIONAL PLANS AGAINST WESTERN INTERESTS IN KARACHI | | (S/ ███ NF) | (S/ ███ NF) |]

[29] [CIA ████████████████████████████ | (S/ ███ NF) | (S/ ███ NF) |]

56 [CIA ███████████████████ | | | | (S//NF) |]

57 [CIA ███████████████████ | | | | (S//NF) |]

58 [CIA ███████████████████ | | | | (S//NF) |]

59 [CIA ████████████████ | | | | (S/███████NF) |]

60 [CIA ██████████ | | | | (S/██████NF) |]

61 [CIA ████████████████ | | | | (S/███████NF) |]

62 [CIA ███████████████████ | | | | (S//NF) |]

63 [CIA ██████████████████ | | | | (S//NF) |]

64 [CIA ██████████████████ | | | | (S/███████NF) |]

65 [CIA ████████████████████ | | | | (S/██████NF) |]

66 [CIA ████████████████████ | | | | (S/██████NF) |]

67 ████████████████████████

68 ███████████████████████

69 ███████████████████████

70 ███████████████████████████████

71 ███████████████████████████████

72 ███████████████████████████████

73 [Other | SSCI Report Volume 2, Part 2, Page 600 | | 13 Dec 2012 | | | | (TS███████████NF) |]

74 [CIA | ALEC██████████████ | | | | (S/██████████NF) |]

75 [FBI | FBI WASH 092137Z | | 9 March 2003 | | | | (S//OC/NF) |]

76 [FBI | FBI WASH 190653Z | | 19 March 2003 | | | | (S//OC/NF) |]

77 [CIA | ████13758 | ████████████ | | | | (S/████████NF) |]

78 [CIA | ████13765 | ████████████ | | | | (S/████████NF) |]

79 [CIA | ████13785 | ████████████ | | | | (S/████████NF) |]

80 [CIA | ALEC████████ | 18 Mar 2003 | | | | (S/███████NF) |]

81 [CIA ████████████████████████ | | | | (S//NF) |]

82 [CIA ████13826 | | 19 Mar 2003 | | | | (S/██████████NF) |]

83 [FBI | FBI WASH 040537Z | | 4 Apr 2003 | | | | (S//OC/NF) |]

84 [Other | SSCI Report Volume 2, Part 2, Page 605 | | 13 Dec 2012 | | | | (TS/██████████████NF) |]

[85] [CIA | ALEC ███████ | 6 March 2003 | | | | | (S, ██████ NF) |]

[86] The source the *Study* cites containing this statement was an internal CIA sitrep compiled daily by 4:30pm at the time for counterterrorism seniors at CIA; the reference to the Reid investigation came on page 10 of 15 pages of updates that day and must have come via some informal communication from FBI that was not otherwise documented.

[87] The *Study* references FBI WASHINGTON DC130555Z dated 13 July 2002 and FBI WASHINGTON DC152151Z dated 16 July 2002. The only other relevant communication was FBI WASHINGTON DC281958Z dated 29 August 2002, which was a follow-on to the others and indicated in relevant part that Belgian authorities "contacted the Leicester Constabulary in the UK [about Badad Sajid] and were told by officers in the Constabulary that Sajid was out of the country (NFI)."

[88] CIA advised FBI that the SajidBadat with whom Sajid might be identifiable was from Gloucester England, and his name and date-of-birth had appeared on a list of 68 persons characterized as "suspected of involvement in terrorist financing" provided ████████████████ in October 2001. Otherwise there were no further references to Badat's name or variants thereof in CIA reporting until August 2003. ██████████████████
██

[89] [CIA ████████████████████████████ | (S//NF) | (S//NF) |]

[90] [CIA ██████████████████████████████ | (S/ ██████ NF) | (S/ NF) |]

[91] [CIA ██████████████████████████████ | (S, ██████ NF) | (S/ NF) |]

[92] KSM initially reported Reid's partner's alias as "Talha," not Issa, when he provided his shoe bomb narrative on 20 March 2003. KSM later corrected himself on 11 May 2003 and confirmed the operative's alias was in fact Issa. We note that KSM's correction came soon after the arrest of his nephew, Ammar al-Baluchi, on 29 April 2003, and assess KSM may have corrected this information knowing that Ammar had communicated with Issa on KSM's behalf and could refute KSM's initial claim that he went by the name Talha. This change was reflected in a reissue of the intelligence report, ████████████████

[93] [CIA ██████████████████████ | 314/15752-03 | | (S//NF) | (S//NF) |]

[94] [CIA ██████████████████████ | 315/31329-03 | | (S, ██████ NF) | (S NF) |]

[95] The provision of this photograph ████████████████████████████████ dated 03 September 2003. KSM's identification was reported in ██████ 12806 dated 10 September 2003 and highlighted in Alec ████████

[96] [CIA ██████████████████████████████ | | (S//OC-NF) | (S//OC-NF) |]

[97] See CIA's response to the SSCI report's finding on Issa al-Hindi for further details on the essential role information from detainees in CIA custody played in sparking efforts to identify, track, capture, ██████ Abu Talha al-Pakistani.

[98] See ██████████████████████ and ████████████████████

[99] [CIA ██████ 13678 | | ██████████ | | | | | (S, ██████ NF) |]

[100] [CIA ████████████████████████████ | (S//NF) | (S//NF) |]

[101] [CIA ██████ 81697 | ████████████ | | | | (S//NF) |]

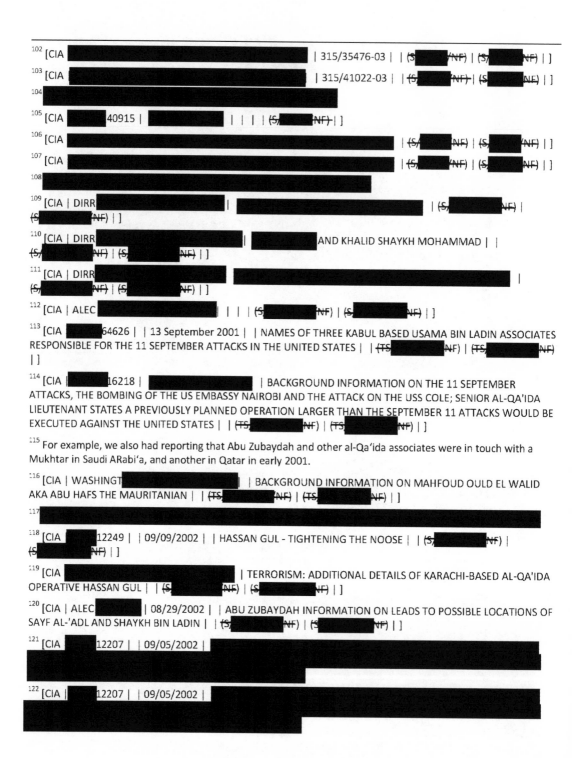

102 [CIA ███████████████████████ | 315/35476-03 | | (S████NF) | (S████NF) |]

103 [CIA ████████████████████ | 315/41022-03 | | (S████NF) | (S████NF) |]

104 ████████████████████

105 [CIA ████ 40915 | ████████ | | | | (S████NF) |]

106 [CIA ████████████████████████████ | (S████NF) | (S████NF) |]

107 [CIA ████████████████████████████ | (S████NF) | (S████NF) |]

108 ████████████████████████

109 [CIA | DIRR████████████████ | ████████████ | (S████NF) | (S████NF) |]

110 [CIA | DIRR████████████████ | ████ AND KHALID SHAYKH MOHAMMAD | | (S████NF) | (S████NF) |]

111 [CIA | DIRR████████████████ | ████████████████ | (S████NF) | (S████NF) |]

112 [CIA | ALEC ████████████████ | | | | (S████NF) | (S████NF) |]

113 [CIA ████ 64626 | | 13 September 2001 | | NAMES OF THREE KABUL BASED USAMA BIN LADIN ASSOCIATES RESPONSIBLE FOR THE 11 SEPTEMBER ATTACKS IN THE UNITED STATES | | (TS████NF) | (TS████NF) |]

114 [CIA ████ 16218 | ████████████████ | BACKGROUND INFORMATION ON THE 11 SEPTEMBER ATTACKS, THE BOMBING OF THE US EMBASSY NAIROBI AND THE ATTACK ON THE USS COLE; SENIOR AL-QA'IDA LIEUTENANT STATES A PREVIOUSLY PLANNED OPERATION LARGER THAN THE SEPTEMBER 11 ATTACKS WOULD BE EXECUTED AGAINST THE UNITED STATES | | (TS████NF) | (TS████NF) |]

115 For example, we also had reporting that Abu Zubaydah and other al-Qa'ida associates were in touch with a Mukhtar in Saudi ARabi'a, and another in Qatar in early 2001.

116 [CIA | WASHINGT████████████████ | BACKGROUND INFORMATION ON MAHFOUD OULD EL WALID AKA ABU HAFS THE MAURITANIAN | | (TS████NF) | (TS████NF) |]

117 ████████████████████████████████

118 [CIA ████ 12249 | | 09/09/2002 | | HASSAN GUL - TIGHTENING THE NOOSE | | (S████NF) | (S████NF) |]

119 [CIA ████████████████████ | TERRORISM: ADDITIONAL DETAILS OF KARACHI-BASED AL-QA'IDA OPERATIVE HASSAN GUL | | (S████NF) | (S████NF) |]

120 [CIA | ALEC ████████ | 08/29/2002 | | ABU ZUBAYDAH INFORMATION ON LEADS TO POSSIBLE LOCATIONS OF SAYF AL-'ADL AND SHAYKH BIN LADIN | | (S████NF) | (S████NF) |]

121 [CIA ████ 12207 | | 09/05/2002 | ████████████████████████

122 [CIA ████ 12207 | | 09/05/2002 | ████████████████████

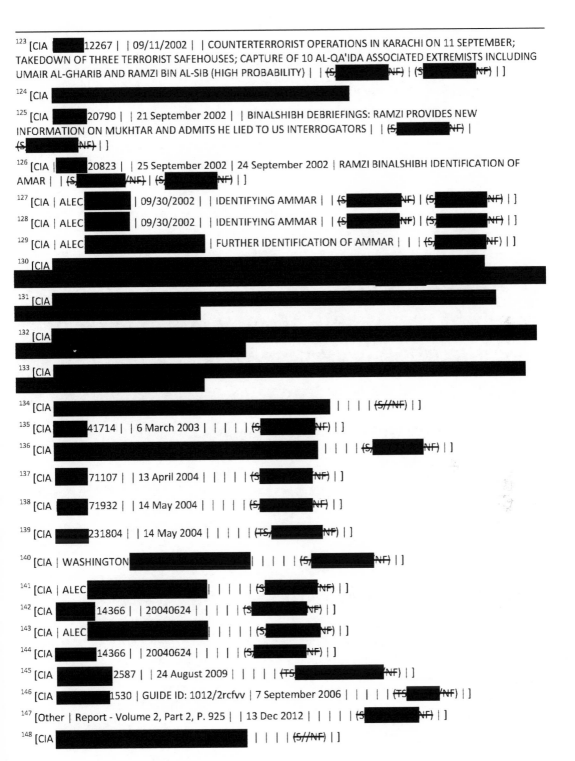

123 [CIA ████ 12267 | | 09/11/2002 | | COUNTERTERRORIST OPERATIONS IN KARACHI ON 11 SEPTEMBER; TAKEDOWN OF THREE TERRORIST SAFEHOUSES; CAPTURE OF 10 AL-QA'IDA ASSOCIATED EXTREMISTS INCLUDING UMAIR AL-GHARIB AND RAMZI BIN AL-SIB (HIGH PROBABILITY) | | (S██████NF) | (S███████NF) |]

124 [CIA ████████████████████████

125 [CIA ████ 20790 | | 21 September 2002 | | BINALSHIBH DEBRIEFINGS: RAMZI PROVIDES NEW INFORMATION ON MUKHTAR AND ADMITS HE LIED TO US INTERROGATORS | | (S██████NF) | (S████NF) |]

126 [CIA | ████ 20823 | | 25 September 2002 | 24 September 2002 | RAMZI BINALSHIBH IDENTIFICATION OF AMAR | | (S████NF) | (S████NF) |]

127 [CIA | ALEC ████ | 09/30/2002 | | IDENTIFYING AMMAR | | (S██████NF) | (S████NF) |]

128 [CIA | ALEC ████ | 09/30/2002 | | IDENTIFYING AMMAR | | (S██████NF) | (S████NF) |]

129 [CIA | ALEC ████████ | FURTHER IDENTIFICATION OF AMMAR | | | (S████NF) |]

130 [CIA ████████████████████████████████████

131 [CIA ████████████████████████████████

132 [CIA ████████████████████████████████

133 [CIA ████████████████████████

134 [CIA ████████████████ | | | | (S//NF) |]

135 [CIA ████ 41714 | | 6 March 2003 | | | | | (S████NF) |]

136 [CIA ████████████████████ | | | | (S████NF) |]

137 [CIA ████ 71107 | | 13 April 2004 | | | | | (S████NF) |]

138 [CIA ████ 71932 | | 14 May 2004 | | | | | (S████NF) |]

139 [CIA ████ 231804 | | 14 May 2004 | | | | | (TS████NF) |]

140 [CIA | WASHINGTON████████ | | | | | (S████NF) |]

141 [CIA | ALEC ████████ | | | | | (S████NF) |]

142 [CIA ████ 14366 | | 20040624 | | | | | (S████NF) |]

143 [CIA | ALEC ████████ | | | | | (S████NF) |]

144 [CIA ████ 14366 | | 20040624 | | | | | (S████NF) |]

145 [CIA ████ 2587 | | 24 August 2009 | | | | | (TS████NF) |]

146 [CIA ████ 1530 | GUIDE ID: 1012/2rcfvv | 7 September 2006 | | | | | (TS████NF) |]

147 [Other | Report - Volume 2, Part 2, P. 925 | | 13 Dec 2012 | | | | | (S████NF) |]

148 [CIA ████████████████ | | | | (S//NF) |]

149 [CIA | WASHINGT█████████████ | | | | (TS█████████NF) |]

150 [CIA █████████████████████ | | | | (S//NF) |]

151 [CIA ████████████████████████ | | | | (S████████NF) |]

152 [CIA ████████████████████████ | | | | (S████████NF) |]

153 [CIA | CTC 2004-30098HC | | 6 August 2004 | | The Homeland Plot: What We Still Need to Learn | | (TS████████NF) | (TS████████NF) |]

154 [CIA | CTC 2004-30064H | GUIDE ID: 1012/41rb1j | 12 July 2004 | | Al-Qa'ida Aiming for Homeland Strike Ahead of US Election: The Origins of the Plot | | (S████████NF) | (S████████NF) |]

155 [CIA | CTC 2004-3011H | | 15 September 2004 | | Time is Running Out to Stop Al-Qa'ida's Attack on the Homeland | | (S████████NF) | (S████████NF) |]

156 [CIA | CTC 2005-30001H | GUIDE ID: 1012/6shg | 8 January 2005 | | Al-Qa'ida's Efforts Against the US Homeland: Persistent and Resilient | | (TS████████NF) | (TS████████NF) |]

157 [CIA | ████████03023 | ████████████ | PLANS TO STRIKE THE UNITED STATES | | (S████████NF) | (S████████NF) |]

158 [CIA ██ | (S████████NF) | (S████NF) |]

159 [CIA ██ | (S████████NF) | (S████NF) |]

160 [CIA ██ | (S████████NF) | (S████NF) |]

161 [CIA ██ | (S████NF) | (S████NF) |]

162 [CIA ██ | (S████NF) | (S████NF) |]

163 [CIA ██ | (S//NF) | (S//NF) |]

164 [CIA ██ | (S████NF) | (S████NF) |]

165 [CIA ██ | (S████NF) | (S████NF) |]

166 [CIA ██ | (S████NF) | (S████NF) |]

167 [CIA ██ | (S████NF) | (S████NF) |]

168 [CIA ██ | (S████NF) | (S████NF) |]

169 [CIA ██ | (S//NF) | (S//NF) |]

170 [CIA ████4267 | | 170646Z SEP 04 | | ████████████████████ | (S████████NF) | (S████████NF) |]

171 [CIA ████████03023 | ████████████ | PLANS TO STRIKE THE UNITED STATES | | (S████████NF) | (S████████NF) |]

172 [CIA | HEADQUAR███████████████04 |████████████████████████████████ |███████████| (S███████NF) | (S███████NF) |]

173 [CIA | HEADQUAR███████████████ |████████████████████████████████ |███| (S███████NF) | (S███████NF) |]

174 [CIA | HEADQUAR███████████ |██████████████████████████████████ |███████| (S███████NF) | (S███████NF) |]

175 [CIA██████1369 |██ | (S//OC/NF) | (S//OC/NF) |]

176 [CIA████████03023 |████████████████| PLANS TO STRIKE THE UNITED STATES | | (S███████NF) | (S███████NF) |]

177 [CIA██ | (S███████NF) | (S███████NF) |]

178 [CIA██ | (S███████NF) | (S███████NF) |]

179 [CIA██ | (S███████NF) | (S███████NF) |]

180 [CIA██ | (S███████NF) | (S███████NF) |]

181 [CIA██ | (S███████NF) | (S███████NF) |]

182 [CIA██ | (S//NF) | (S//NF) |]

183 [CIA██ | (S███████NF) | (S███████NF) |]

184 [CIA██ | (S███████NF) | (S███████NF) |]

185 [CIA██ | (S███████NF) | (S███████NF) |]

186 [CIA██ | (S███████NF) | (S███████NF) |]

187 [CIA██ | (S███████NF) | (S███████NF) |]

188 [CIA██ | (S//NF) | (S//NF) |]

189 [CIA | CTC 2004-30098HC | | 6 August 2004 | | The Homeland Plot: What We Still Need to Learn | | (TS███████NF) | (TS███████NF) |]

190 [CIA | CTC 2004-30064H | GUIDE ID: 1012/41rb1j | 12 July 2004 | | Al-Qa'ida Aiming for Homeland Strike Ahead of US Election: The Origins of the Plot | | (S███████NF) | (S███████NF) |]

191 [CIA | CTC 2004-3011H | | 15 September 2004 | | Time is Running Out to Stop Al-Qa'ida's Attack on the Homeland | | (S███████NF) | (S███████NF) |]

192 [CIA | CTC 2005-30001H | GUIDE ID: 1012/6shg | 8 January 2005 | | Al-Qa'ida's Efforts Against the US Homeland: Persistent and Resilient | | (TS███████NF) | (TS███████NF) |]

193 [CIA | HEADQUAR███████████████04 |████████████████████████████████ |███████| (S███████NF) | (S███████NF) |]

¹⁹⁴ [CIA | HEADQUAR████████████ | ████████████ ██████ | (S█████████NF) | (S█████NF) |]

¹⁹⁵ [CIA | HEADQUAR████████████ | ████████ | (S█████NF) | (S█████NF) |]

¹⁹⁶ [CIA ████ 1369 | ████████ | ████████ (S//OC/NF) | (S//OC/NF) |]

¹⁹⁷ [Other | SSCI Report Executive Summary, Page 26 of 95 | | 13 Dec 2012 | | | | | (TS████████NF) |]

¹⁹⁸ [CIA ███████████████████████ | | | | (S//NF) |]

¹⁹⁹ [CIA ███████████████████████ | | | | (S█████NF) |]

²⁰⁰ [FBI | FBI WASH 261909Z | | 26 March 2003 | | | | | (S//OC/NF) |]

²⁰¹ [FBI | FBI WASH 312109Z | | 1 April 2003 | | | | | (S//OC/NF) |]

²⁰² ████████████████████████████████

²⁰³ ████████████████████████████████

²⁰⁴ [CIA ███████████████████ | | | | (S█████NF) |]

²⁰⁵ ████████████████████████████████

²⁰⁶ ████████████████████████████████

²⁰⁷ ████████████████████████████████

²⁰⁸ ████████████████████████████████

²⁰⁹ [Other | SSCI Report, Volume 2, Part 2, Page 958 | | 13 December 2012 | | | | | (TS█████NF) |]

²¹⁰ [Other | SSCI Report Volume 2, Part 2, Page 957 | | 13 Dec 2012 | | | | | (TS█████NF) |]

²¹¹ [Other | SSCI report, Volume 2, Part 2, Page 958 | | 2012 Dec 13 | | | | | (TS█████/NF) |]

²¹² [CIA | ████ 872897 | | 4 March 1993 | | | | | (S,█████NF) |]

²¹³ [CIA | ████ 67622 | | 10 March 1993 | | | | | (S█████NF) |]

²¹⁴ [CIA | CIA WASH █████████ | | | | (S//OC/NF) |]

²¹⁵ [Other | SSCI Report Volume 2, Part 2, Page 960-961 | | 13 Dec 2012 | | | | | (TS█████/NF) |]

²¹⁶ [CIA ████ 231584 | | 30 April 2002 | | | | | (S//OC/NF) |]

²¹⁷ [FBI | FBI WASH 271529Z | | 27 March 2003 | | | | | (S//OC/NF) |]

²¹⁸ [CIA ████ 13890 | ███████████ | | | | (S█████NF) |]

²¹⁹ [FBI | Case file ████████████████ | | | | | (S█████NF) |]

²²⁰ [FBI | Case file ████████████████ | | | | | (S█████/NF) |]

²²¹ [CIA ████ 771087 | | 9 October 2001 | | | | | (S█████NF) |]

²²² [Other | Report, Volume 2, Part 2, Page 975 | | 13 December 2012 | | | | | (TS█████/NF) |]

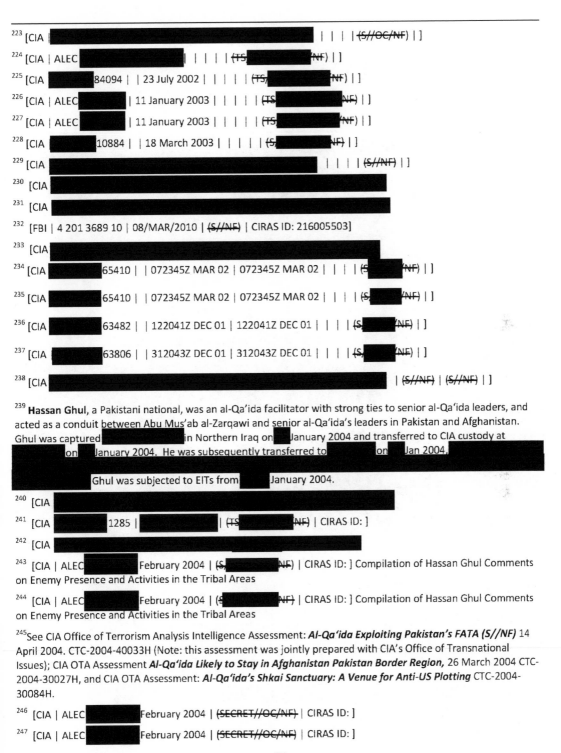

223 [CIA █████████████████████ | | | | (S//OC/NF) |]

224 [CIA | ALEC ███████████ | | | | | (TS ██████ NF) |]

225 [CIA ██████ 84094 | | 23 July 2002 | | | | | (TS ██████ NF) |]

226 [CIA | ALEC ██████ | 11 January 2003 | | | | | (TS ██████ NF) |]

227 [CIA | ALEC ██████ | 11 January 2003 | | | | | (TS ██████ NF) |]

228 [CIA ██████ 10884 | | 18 March 2003 | | | | | (S ██████ NF) |]

229 [CIA ████████████████████████ | | | | (S//NF) |]

230 [CIA ███████████████████████████

231 [CIA ██████████████████████████

232 [FBI | 4 201 3689 10 | 08/MAR/2010 | (S//NF) | CIRAS ID: 216005503]

233 [CIA █████████████████████████

234 [CIA ██████ 65410 | | 072345Z MAR 02 | 072345Z MAR 02 | | | | (S ██████ NF) |]

235 [CIA ██████ 65410 | | 072345Z MAR 02 | 072345Z MAR 02 | | | | (S ██████ NF) |]

236 [CIA ██████ 63482 | | 122041Z DEC 01 | 122041Z DEC 01 | | | | (S ██████ NF) |]

237 [CIA ██████ 63806 | | 312043Z DEC 01 | 312043Z DEC 01 | | | | (S ██████ NF) |]

238 [CIA ██████████████████████████ | (S//NF) | (S//NF) |]

239 **Hassan Ghul**, a Pakistani national, was an al-Qa'ida facilitator with strong ties to senior al-Qa'ida leaders, and acted as a conduit between Abu Mus'ab al-Zarqawi and senior al-Qa'ida's leaders in Pakistan and Afghanistan. Ghul was captured █████████████ in Northern Iraq on ██ January 2004 and transferred to CIA custody at ████████████ on ██ January 2004. He was subsequently transferred to ██████████ on ██ Jan 2004, ██ Ghul was subjected to EITs from ██████ January 2004.

240 [CIA ████████████████████████

241 [CIA ██████ 1285 | ██████████ | (TS ██████ NF) | CIRAS ID:]

242 [CIA ███████████████████████

243 [CIA | ALEC ██████ February 2004 | (S ██████ NF) | CIRAS ID:] Compilation of Hassan Ghul Comments on Enemy Presence and Activities in the Tribal Areas

244 [CIA | ALEC ██████ February 2004 | (S ██████ NF) | CIRAS ID:] Compilation of Hassan Ghul Comments on Enemy Presence and Activities in the Tribal Areas

245See CIA Office of Terrorism Analysis Intelligence Assessment: *Al-Qa'ida Exploiting Pakistan's FATA (S//NF)* 14 April 2004. CTC-2004-40033H (Note: this assessment was jointly prepared with CIA's Office of Transnational Issues); CIA OTA Assessment *Al-Qa'ida Likely to Stay in Afghanistan Pakistan Border Region,* 26 March 2004 CTC-2004-30027H, and CIA OTA Assessment: *Al-Qa'ida's Shkai Sanctuary: A Venue for Anti-US Plotting* CTC-2004-30084H.

246 [CIA | ALEC ██████ February 2004 | (SECRET//OC/NF) | CIRAS ID:]

247 [CIA | ALEC ██████ February 2004 | (SECRET//OC/NF) | CIRAS ID:]

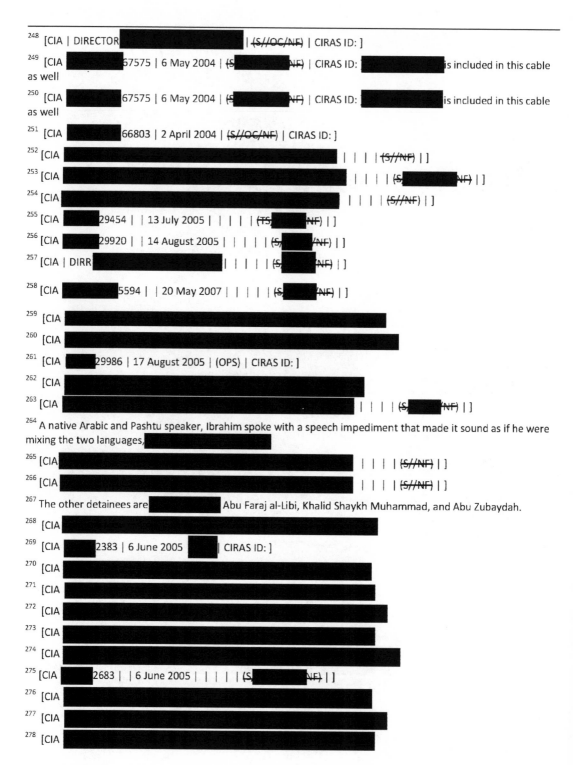

248 [CIA | DIRECTOR █████████████ | (S//OC/NF) | CIRAS ID:]

249 [CIA ██████ 67575 | 6 May 2004 | (S██████NF) | CIRAS ID: ██████████ is included in this cable as well

250 [CIA ██████ 67575 | 6 May 2004 | (S██████NF) | CIRAS ID: ██████████ is included in this cable as well

251 [CIA ██████ 66803 | 2 April 2004 | (S//OC/NF) | CIRAS ID:]

252 [CIA ███████████████████████ | | | | (S//NF) |]

253 [CIA ███████████████████████ | | | | (S██████NF) |]

254 [CIA ███████████████████████ | | | | (S//NF) |]

255 [CIA ████ 29454 | | 13 July 2005 | | | | | (TS██████NF) |]

256 [CIA ████ 29920 | | 14 August 2005 | | | | | (S██████NF) |]

257 [CIA | DIRR ██████████████ | | | | | (S██████NF) |]

258 [CIA ████ 5594 | | 20 May 2007 | | | | | (S██████NF) |]

259 [CIA ██████████████████████████]

260 [CIA ██████████████████████████]

261 [CIA ████ 29986 | 17 August 2005 | (OPS) | CIRAS ID:]

262 [CIA ████████████████████████]

263 [CIA ██████████████████████ | | | | (S██████NF) |]

264 A native Arabic and Pashtu speaker, Ibrahim spoke with a speech impediment that made it sound as if he were mixing the two languages, ████████████

265 [CIA ████████████████████████ | | | | (S//NF) |]

266 [CIA ████████████████████████ | | | | (S//NF) |]

267 The other detainees are ██████████ Abu Faraj al-Libi, Khalid Shaykh Muhammad, and Abu Zubaydah.

268 [CIA ████████████████████████]

269 [CIA ████ 2383 | 6 June 2005 ████ | CIRAS ID:]

270 [CIA ████████████████████████]

271 [CIA ████████████████████████]

272 [CIA ████████████████████████]

273 [CIA ████████████████████████]

274 [CIA ████████████████████████]

275 [CIA ████ 2683 | | 6 June 2005 | | | | | (S██████NF) |]

276 [CIA ████████████████████████]

277 [CIA ████████████████████████]

278 [CIA ████████████████████████]

[279] [CIA ██████████████████████████████████

[280] [CIA ██████████████████████████████████

THE
MINORITY
REPORT

MINORITY VIEWS OF VICE CHAIRMAN CHAMBLISS, SENATORS BURR, RISCH, COATS, RUBIO, AND COBURN[*]

June 20, 2014

[[Revised for Redaction on December 5, 2014]][†]

---

[*] When these minority views were initially written in response to the original Study approved by the United States Senate Select Committee on Intelligence on December 13, 2012, the following members of the Committee signed on to them: Vice Chairman Chambliss joined by Senators Burr. Risch. Coats, Blunt, and Rubio.

[†] [[Please note that the double-bracketed text in this document is new explanatory text necessitated by substantive modifications to the Study's Executive Summary and Findings and Conclusions that were made *after* our June 20, 2014, Minority Views were submitted to the Central Intelligence Agency for the declassification review. We also note that these Minority Views are in response to, and at points predicated upon, the research and foundational work that underlie the Study's account of the CIA Detention and Interrogation Program. These Views should not be treated as an independent report based upon a separate investigation, but rather our evaluation and critique of the Study's problematic analysis, factual findings, and conclusions.]]

TABLE OF CONTENTS

MINORITY VIEWS OF VICE CHAIRMAN CHAMBLISS, SENATORS BURR, RISCH, COATS, RUBIO, AND COBURN[1]

(U) EXECUTIVE SUMMARY

(U) In March 2009, the Senate Select Committee on Intelligence ("SSCI" or "Committee") decided, by a vote of 14-1, to initiate a *Study of the Central Intelligence Agency's Detention and Interrogation Program,* (the Study).[2] On August 24, 2009, Attorney General Eric Holder decided to re-open the criminal inquiry related to the interrogation of certain detainees in the Central Intelligence Agency's (CIA) Detention and Interrogation Program ("the Program" or "the Detention and Interrogation Program").[3] Shortly thereafter, the minority withdrew from active participation in the Study when it determined that the Attorney General's decision would preclude a comprehensive review of the Program, since many of the relevant witnesses would likely decline to be interviewed by the Committee. Three years later, on August 30, 2012, Attorney General Holder closed the criminal investigation into the interrogation of certain detainees in the Detention and Interrogation Program.[4] At the end of the 112th Congress, on December 13, 2012, the Committee approved the adoption of the Study's three-volume report, executive summary, and findings and conclusions by a vote of 9-6.[5] On April 3, 2014, by a vote of 11-3, the Committee approved a motion to send updated versions of the Study's executive summary and findings and conclusions to the President for declassification review.[6]

(U) The latest version of the updated Study is a [[6,682]]-page interpretation of documents that, according to the CIA, has cost the American taxpayer more than 40 million dollars and diverted countless CIA analytic and support resources.[7] Contrary to the Terms of Reference, the Study does not offer any recommendations for improving intelligence interrogation practices, intelligence activities, or covert actions. Instead, it offers 20 conclusions,

---

[1] The following members of the Committee signed on to the minority views drafted in response to the original Study approved by the United States Senate Select Committee on Intelligence on December 13, 2012: Vice Chairman Chambliss joined by Senators Burr, Risch, Coats, Blunt, and Rubio. [[Please note that the double-bracketed text in this document is new explanatory text necessitated by substantive modifications to the Study's Executive Summary and Findings and Conclusions that were made *after* our June 20, 2014, Minority Views were submitted to the Central Intelligence Agency for the declassification review. We also note that these Minority Views are in response to, and at points predicated upon, the research and foundational work that underlie the Study's account of the CIA Detention and Interrogation Program. These Views should not be treated as an independent report based upon a separate investigation, but rather our evaluation and critique of the Study's problematic analysis, factual findings, and conclusions.]]

[2] SSCI Transcript, *Business Meeting to Discuss and Revote on the Terms of Reference for the Committee's Study of the CIA's Detention and Interrogation Program,* March 5, 2009, p. 10 (DTS 2009-1916).

[3] DOJ, *Attorney General Eric Holder Regarding a Preliminary Review into the Interrogation of Certain Detainees,* August 24, 2009, p. 1.

[4] *See* DOJ, *Statement of Attorney General Eric Holder on Closure of investigation into the Interrogation of Certain Detainees,* August 30, 2012. p. 1.

[5] SSCI Transcript, *Business Meeting to Consider the Report on the CIA Detention and Interrogation Program,* p. 74 (DTS 2013-0452).

[6] SSCI Transcript, *Hearing to Vote on Declassification of the SSCI Study of the CIA's Detention and Interrogation Program,* April 3, 2014, pp. 8-9 (DTS 2014-1137).

[7] CIA, Letter from V. Sue Bromley, Associate Deputy Director, November 6, 2012, p. 1 (DTS 2012-4143).

I

many of which attack the CIA's integrity and credibility in developing and implementing the Program. Absent the support of the documentary record, and on the basis of a flawed analytical methodology, these problematic claims and conclusions create the false impression that the CIA was actively misleading policy makers and impeding the counterterrorism efforts of other federal government agencies during the Program's operation.

(U) THE STUDY'S FLAWED PROCESS

(U) We begin with an examination of the procedural irregularities that negatively impacted the Study's problematic claims and conclusions. First, the Committee's decision not to interview key witnesses led to significant analytical and factual errors in the original and subsequent updated versions of the Study. Second, over the objection of the minority, the Committee did not provide a copy of the draft Study to the Intelligence Community for initial fact-checking prior to the vote to adopt the Study at the end of the 112th Congress. Third, Committee members and staff were not given sufficient time to review the Study prior to the scheduled vote on December 13, 2012. Fourth, the Committee largely ignored the CIA's response to the Study on June 27, 2013, which identified a number of factual and analytical errors in the Study. Fifth, during the summer and early fall of 2013, SSCI majority staff failed to take advantage of the nearly 60 hours of meetings with some of the CIA personnel who had led and participated in the CIA's study response. Instead of attempting to understand the factual and analytical errors that had been identified by the CIA, the majority staff spent a significant portion of these meetings criticizing the CIA's study response and justifying the Study's flawed analytical methodology. Sixth, the production and release of the updated Study was marred by the alleged misconduct of majority staff and CIA employees in relation to a set of documents known as the "Panetta Internal Review." Finally, Committee members and staff were not given sufficient time to review the updated Executive Summary and Findings and Conclusions prior to the scheduled vote on April 4, 2014.

(U) With the exception of the decision not to interview relevant witnesses, most, if not all, of these procedural irregularities could have been avoided. As will be seen below, the updated Study still contains a significant number factual inaccuracies and invalid claims and conclusions. We believe that many of these problems could have been corrected if the Committee had simply adhered to our established procedural precedents for a report of this importance.

(U) THE STUDY'S PROBLEMATIC ANALYSIS

(U) We found a number of analytical deficiencies in the Study beginning with an inadequate discussion of the context that led to the implementation and operation of the CIA's Detention and Interrogation Program. Also, as an oversight body, this Committee reviews the Intelligence Community's analytic products with an expectation that they will follow certain analytic integrity standards. While these standards do not technically apply to this Committee's oversight products, the values behind these standards are useful in assessing our own analytic tradecraft. When applied to the Study, these standards were helpful in identifying some of the Study's general analytic deficiencies concerning objectivity, independence from political considerations, timeliness, the use of all available intelligence sources, and consistency with proper standards of analytic tradecraft.

(U) Inadequate Context

(U) The Study does very little to provide the context in which the CIA's Detention and Interrogation Program was initiated and operated. It is entirely silent on the surge in terrorist threat reporting that inundated the Intelligence Community following the September 11, 2001, terrorist attacks by al-Qa'ida. It also makes no mention of the pervasive, genuine apprehension about a possible second attack on the United States that gripped the CIA in 2002 and 2003. During our review of the documentary record, we could clearly discern a workforce traumatized by the thousands of lives lost as a result of the September 11, 2001, terrorist attacks, but also galvanized by the challenge of working to ensure such an attack never occurred again.

(U) Inadequate Objectivity

(U) With respect to the standard of objectivity, we were disappointed to find that the updated Study still contains evidence of strongly held biases. John Brennan emphasized this point prior to his confirmation as the Director of the CIA, when he told Vice Chairman Chambliss that, based on his reading of the originally approved Executive Summary and the Findings and Conclusions, the Study was "not objective" and was a "prosecutor's brief," "written with an eye toward finding problems." We agree with Director Brennan's assessments. We also agree with the criticism he relayed from Intelligence Community officials that it was written with a "bent on the part of the authors" with "political motivations."

(U) We found that those biases led to faulty analysis, serious inaccuracies, and misrepresentations of fact in the Study. For example, the Study states, "At no time during or after the aggressive interrogation phase did Abu Zubaydah provide the information that the CIA enhanced interrogation were premised upon, specifically, 'actionable intelligence about al-Qa'ida operatives in the United States and planned al-Qa'ida lethal attacks against U.S. citizens and U.S. interests.'"[8] Specifically, our review of the documentary record revealed that Abu Zubaydah provided actionable intelligence, after he was subjected to "aggressive" interrogation in April[9] and August[10] 2002, that helped lead to the capture of Ramzi bin al-Shibh and other al-Qa'ida associates during the Karachi safe house raids conducted on September 10-11, 2002. These captures effectively disrupted the al-Qa'ida plot to bomb certain named hotels in Karachi, Pakistan, that had been selected because they were frequented by American and German guests.

(U) The Study's lack of objectivity is also evidenced by the uneven treatment of key U.S. officials throughout the report, attacking the credibility and honesty of some, while making little mention of others. For example, former Director George Tenet led the CIA at the outset of the Program, during a period the Study contends was characterized by mismanagement. Tenet authorized the enhanced interrogation techniques, and if the Study is to be believed, headed an

---

[8] SSCI Study, Volume I, March 31, 2014, p. 146.

[9] *See* SSCI Minority Views of Vice Chairman Chambliss joined by Senators Burr, Risch, Coats, Rubio, and Coburn, June 20, 2014, p. 33.

[10] *See* CIA, ▮▮▮▮ 10586, August 4, 2002, pp. 2-5.

organization that withheld information from and misled policymakers in the executive branch and Congress. He is mentioned 62 times in the updated version of the Study's Executive Summary. By comparison, former Director Michael Hayden—who joined the CIA in 2006, after all but two detainees entered the Program and the most severe EITs were no longer in use—is mentioned over 200 times in the Executive Summary and disparaged numerous times. Notably, he was also the only Director to brief the Program to all members of the congressional oversight committees.

(U) Indications of Political Considerations

(U) Ideally, oversight reports should not be distorted or altered with the intent of supporting or advocating a particular policy, political viewpoint, or specific audience."[11] We found indications of political considerations within the Study. For example, the Study uses out-of-context quotes from certain minority members to suggest incorrectly that they supported certain positions taken by the Study. The Study omits additional comments by these same members which contradict the out-of-context statements.

(U) Lack of Timeliness

(U) The analytic integrity standard of timeliness centers on the need to effectively inform key policy decisions. The same could be said for intelligence oversight reports. The updated version of the Study was released for declassification review on April 3, 2014—more than five years after the Terms of Reference were approved. No version of the Study, updated or otherwise, has ever contained any recommendations. Moreover, there are no lessons learned, nor are there any suggestions of possible alternative measures. This absence of Committee recommendations is likely due to the fact that the key policy decisions about the CIA's Detention and Interrogation Program were decided by President Obama in 2009. Since it does little to effectively inform current policymakers, we found that the Study is not timely.

(U) Inadequate Use of Available Sources of Intelligence

(U) Despite the millions of records available for the Study's research, we found that important documents were not reviewed and some were never requested. We were surprised to learn that the e-mails of only 64 individuals were initially requested to support the review of a program that spanned eight years and included hundreds of government employees. Committee reviews of this magnitude typically involve interviewing the relevant witnesses. Here, these relevant witnesses were largely unavailable due to the Attorney General's decision to re-open a preliminary criminal review in connection with the interrogation of specific detainees at overseas locations. When DOJ closed this investigation in August 2013, however, the Committee had a window of opportunity to invite these relevant witnesses in for interviews, but apparently decided against that course of action. The lack of witness interviews should have been a clear warning flag to all Committee members about the difficulty of completing a truly "comprehensive" review on this subject.

---

[11] Intelligence Community Directive Number 203, *Analytic Standards* (effective June 21, 2007), p. 2.

(U) Poor Standards of Analytic Tradecraft

(U) We found numerous examples of poor analytic tradecraft in the Study. There were instances where the Study did not accurately describe the quality and reliability of the sources of information supporting its analysis. For example, the Study states that a review by the CIA Inspector General (IG) "uncovered that additional unauthorized techniques were used against" a detainee, but the Inspector General report actually said it "heard allegations" of the use of unauthorized techniques and said, "[F]or all of the instances, the allegations were disputed or too ambiguous to reach any authoritative determination about the facts."[12] The Study rarely included caveats about uncertainties or confidence in its analytic judgments. Many of the Study's conclusions and underlying claims are offered as matters of unequivocal fact. As an example, the Study asserts "CIA officers conducted no research on successful interrogation strategies during the drafting of the [Memorandum of Notification], nor after it was issued."[13] Proving a negative is often very difficult, and in this particular case it is difficult to understand how such an absolute assertion can be made without interviewing the affected witnesses or even citing to one documentary source that might support such a claim.

(U) The Study also engaged in little alternative analysis of its claims and conclusions. In many respects, these minority views provide this necessary alternative analysis. For example, the Study is replete with uncited and absolute assertions like "there is no indication in CIA records that Abu Zubaydah provided information on bin al-Shibh's whereabouts."[14] Our review of the documentary record revealed that Abu Zubaydah did provide locational information about bin al-Shibh. As discussed below, Zubaydah made four separate photographic identifications of bin al-Shibh and placed him in Kandahar, Afghanistan, during the November to December 2001 timeframe and provided sufficient information for interrogators to conclude that bin al-Shibh was subsequently with Khalid Shaykh Mohammad (KSM) in Karachi, Pakistan.[15]

(U) Finally, we found instances where claims were supported more by rhetorical devices than sound logical reasoning. For example, in support of the Study's conclusion that the CIA's use of enhanced interrogation techniques were not effective, the Study stated:

> At least seven detainees were subjected to the CIA's enhanced interrogation techniques almost immediately after being rendered into CIA custody, *making it impossible to determine* whether the information they provided could have been obtained through non-coercive debriefing methods."[16]

---

[12] *Compare* SSCI Study, Volume I, March 31, 2014, p. 229 *with* CIA Office of Inspector General, *Special Review: Counterterrorism Detention and Interrogation Activities (September 2001 - October 2003)*, May 7, 2004, p. 41 (DTS 2004-2710). [[This tradecraft error was partially corrected in the November 26, 2014, version of the Executive Summary by editing the offending sentence to read, "The Office of Inspector General later *described* additional *allegations* of unauthorized techniques used against . . . ." (emphasis added). *Compare* SSCI Study, Executive Summary, April 3, 2014, p. 67 *with* SSCI Study, Executive Summary, December 3, 2014, p. 70.]]

[13] SSCI Study, Volume I, March 31, 2014, p. 20.

[14] SSCI Study, Executive Summary, December 3, 2014, p. 318.

[15] *See* SSCI Minority Views of Vice Chairman Chambliss joined by Senators Burr, Risch, Coats, Rubio, and Coburn, June 20, 2014, pp. 37-38.

[16] SSCI Study, Findings and Conclusions, April 3, 2014, p. 2 (emphasis added). [[This false reasoning was tempered in the December 3, 2014, version of the Executive Summary by editing the sentence to read, "CIA

V

This statement is a rhetorical attempt to persuade the reader that non-coercive techniques may have been equally or even more successful than the enhanced techniques. It is little more than an appeal to unknowable facts and is not based upon logical reasoning.[17]

(U) ERRONEOUS STUDY CONCLUSIONS

(U) Despite the fact that the CIA response and the summer staff meetings essentially validated our criticisms of the original Study, it appears that the updated version of the Study largely persists with many of its erroneous analytical and factual claims. We have used these past eleven weeks to update our own Minority Views and focus our attention on eight of the Study's most problematic conclusions.

(U) Conclusion 1 (The CIA's use of enhanced interrogation techniques was not effective)

(U) This updated conclusion asserts that the "CIA's use of enhanced interrogation techniques was not an effective means of acquiring intelligence or gaining cooperation from detainees."[18] The Study attempts to validate this conclusion by relying upon four faulty premises. The first faulty premise is that "seven of the 39 CIA detainees known to have been subjected to the CIA's enhanced interrogation techniques produced no intelligence while in CIA custody."[19] If true, that means that 82 percent of detainees subjected to enhanced interrogation techniques produced some intelligence while in CIA custody, which is better than the 57.5 percent effectiveness rate of detainees not subjected to enhanced interrogation techniques. Regardless, these statistics do not provide any real insight on the *qualitative* value of the intelligence information obtained. The true test of effectiveness is the value of *what* was obtained—not how much or how little was obtained.

(U) We have already discussed the second faulty premise, which involves a rhetorical appeal to ignorance based on the fact that at least seven detainees were subjected to enhanced interrogation techniques almost immediately after coming into the CIA's custody. Such speculation is not helpful in assessing whether the enhanced interrogation techniques were effective.

(U) The third faulty premise of this ineffective techniques conclusion focuses on the fact that "multiple" detainees subjected to enhanced interrogation techniques "fabricated information, resulting in faulty intelligence."[20] Our documentary review also found that "multiple" detainees

---

detainees who were subjected to the CIA's enhanced interrogation techniques were usually subjected to the techniques immediately after being rendered to CIA custody. Other detainees provided significant accurate intelligence prior to, or without having been subjected to these techniques." *Compare* SSCI Study, Findings and Conclusions, April 3, 2014, p. 2 *with* SSCI Study, Findings and Conclusions, December 3, 2014, p. 2.]]

[17] For a more detailed analysis of this unsupported claim, *see infra*, SSCI Minority Views of Vice Chairman Chambliss joined by Senators Burr, Risch, Coats, Rubio, and Coburn, December 5, 2014, p. 22.

[18] SSCI Study, Findings and Conclusions, December 3, 2014. The first and second conclusions in the updated Findings and Conclusion had been combined in Conclusion 9 of the original Study.

[19] SSCI Study, Findings and Conclusions, December 3, 2014, p. 2. The assertion of "produced no intelligence" as used by the Study reflects that the interrogations of these detainees resulted in no intelligence reports.

[20] SSCI Study, Findings and Conclusions, December 3, 2014, p. 2.

who were not subjected to enhanced interrogation techniques also provided fabricated information to their interrogators. The only real inference that can be drawn from these facts is that detainees fabricated information regardless of whether they were subjected to enhanced interrogation.

(U) The final faulty premise used in support of this "effectiveness" conclusion was that "CIA officers regularly called into question whether the CIA's enhanced interrogation techniques were effective, assessing that the use of the techniques failed to elicit detainee cooperation or produce accurate intelligence."[21] While the *opinions* of these unidentified CIA officers may happen to coincide with the Study's first conclusion, there were at least three other CIA officials who held the opposite view—Directors Tenet, Goss, and Hayden.

(U) Conclusion 2 (CIA's Justification for EITs Rested on Inaccurate Effectiveness Claims)

(U) Conclusion 2 states, "[t]he CIA's justification for the use of its enhanced interrogation techniques rested on inaccurate claims of their effectiveness."[22] While our review of the documentary record did reveal some instances of inaccurate effectiveness claims by the CIA, we found that many of the Study's claims related to this conclusion were themselves inaccurate. We reviewed 17 of the 20 cases studies that the Study relies upon to support this flawed conclusion. We examined these case studies in logical groupings (e.g., related to information provided by Abu Zubaydah) using chronological order rather than the Study's confusing "primary" and "secondary" effectiveness representations. This approach helped us better understand how the intelligence resulting from these detainee interrogations was used by the CIA to disrupt terrorist plots and identify, capture, and sometimes prosecute other terrorists.

(U) The Study developed an analytical methodology to examine the effectiveness of the information obtained from the CIA's Detention and Interrogation Program that we found to be both confusing and deeply flawed. Usually, effectiveness is measured by establishing performance metrics that require the collection of pertinent data and the subsequent analysis of such data. For example, in the context of counterterrorism such metrics might include: (1) increased understanding of terrorist networks; (2) identification of terrorists and those providing material support; (3) terrorist captures; (4) terrorist interrogations; (5) disruption of terrorist operations and financing; (6) disruption of terrorist recruitment; (7) reduction in terrorist safe-havens; (8) development of counterterrorism assets; (9) intelligence gathering of documents, computer equipment, communications devices, etc.; (10) improved information sharing; and (11) improved foreign liaison cooperation against terrorism. Such metrics could then be compared against the information provided by CIA detainees to assess the relative effectiveness of the Program.

(U) Instead of performance metrics, the Study's analytical methodology creates artificial categories that are used to *exclude* certain detainee information from being considered in an effectiveness assessment of the Program. For example, if the Study found that a detainee subjected to enhanced interrogation had provided similar information during an earlier non-

---

[21] SSCI Study, Findings and Conclusions, December 3, 2014, p. 2.
[22] SSCI Study, Findings and Conclusions, December 3, 2014, p. 2.

enhanced interrogation, then such information could not be used for assessing the effectiveness of the program. This category appears to have been developed in an attempt to exclude much of the intelligence information provided by Abu Zubaydah after he was subjected to enhanced interrogation in August 2002, since some of the information Abu Zubaydah provided during those interrogations was similar to information he had provided prior to August. However, it turns out that this category is largely inapplicable to Abu Zubaydah's case, because he was subjected to enhanced interrogation by the CIA when he was released from the hospital on April 15, 2002.[23]

(U) Another category of information that the Study's flawed analytical methodology excludes is corroborative information. If a detainee subjected to enhanced interrogation provided information that was already available to the CIA or other elements of the Intelligence Community from another source, then the methodology dictates that such information cannot be considered to support a CIA effectiveness representation. This result occurs even in situations in which the detainee's information clarified or explained the significance of the prior information. Another exclusion category applies if the Study determined that there was no causal relationship between the information obtained from a detainee after the use of enhanced interrogation and the operational success claimed by the CIA. In these case studies, we often found documentary evidence that supported direct causal links between such detainee information and the operational success represented by the CIA. The final category excludes detainee information about terrorist plots when there was a subsequent assessment by intelligence and law enforcement personnel that such plots were infeasible or never operationalized.

(U) This flawed analytical methodology often forced the Study to use absolute language such as, "no connection," "no indication," "played no role," or "these representations were inaccurate." Our review of the documentary record often found valid counter-examples that disproved such absolute claims. We also found that when we invalidated the claims in the initial case studies, there was often a cascading effect that further undermined claims in the subsequent case studies. Here we summarize the claims for the case studies we examined and our alternate analysis of those claims.

(U) *The Identification of Khalid Shaykh Mohammad as the Mastermind of the 9/11 Attacks and His "Mukhtar" Alias*

(TS███████████NF) We combined our analysis of these two case studies because they share common facts and analytical issues. The Study claims that "[o]n at least two prominent occasions, the CIA represented, inaccurately, that Abu Zubaydah provided [information identifying KSM as the mastermind of 9/11] after the use of the CIA's enhanced interrogation techniques."[24] We found that neither of the occasions cited with respect to the "Mastermind of 9/11" information were "prominent." The first occasion was not even a CIA representation, but rather a mistake made by the Department of Justice in one of its legal opinions.[25] The second occasion involved a set of November 2007 documents and talking points

---

[23] *See infra*, SSCI Minority Views of Vice Chairman Chambliss joined by Senators Burr, Risch, Coats, Rubio, and Coburn, December 5, 2014. pp. 33-37.

[24] SSCI Study, Executive Summary, December 3, 2014, p. 312.

[25] *See* SSCI Study. Executive Summary, December 3, 2014, p. 313, n.1748.

for the CIA Director to use in a briefing with the President. Although these briefing materials did contain some erroneous information about KSM's interrogation, the Study fails to demonstrate whether this erroneous information was actually briefed to the President during that timeframe.[26]

(TS███████NF) The Study also claims that "[i]n at least one instance in November 2007 . . . the CIA asserted that Abu Zubaydah identified KSM as 'Mukhtar' after the use of the CIA's enhanced interrogation techniques."[27] However, this instance is no more "prominent" than the above "mastermind" occasion, because it was contained in the same November 2007 briefing materials used by the CIA Director to brief the President.[28] Again, the Study fails to demonstrate whether this erroneous information was actually briefed to the President during this timeframe.

(TS███████NF) The Study's third claim in relation to this case study is that "[t]here is no evidence to support the statement that Abu Zubaydah's information—obtained by FBI interrogators prior to the use of the CIA's enhanced interrogation techniques and while Abu Zubaydah was hospitalized—was uniquely important in the identification of KSM as the 'mastermind' of the 9/11 attacks."[29] We found considerable evidence that the information Abu Zubaydah provided identifying KSM as "Mukhtar" and the mastermind of 9/11 was significant to CIA analysts, operators, and FBI interrogators. Both the Congressional Joint Inquiry into the 9/11 Attacks and the 9/11 Commission discussed the importance of this information to the Intelligence Community in understanding KSM's role in the attacks and in the al-Qa'ida organization.

(U) *The Thwarting of the Dirty Bomb/Tall Buildings Plot and the Capture of Jose Padilla*

(TS███████NF) The Study falsely claims that "[a] review of CIA operational cables and other CIA records found that the use of the CIA's *enhanced interrogation techniques played no role* in the identification of 'Jose Padilla' or the thwarting of the Dirty Bomb or Tall Buildings plotting. CIA records indicate that: . . . (3) Abu Zubaydah provided this information to FBI officers who were using rapport-building techniques, in April 2002, more than three months *prior* to the CIA's 'use of DOJ-approved enhanced interrogation techniques,' . . ."[30] However, CIA records clearly indicate that during the time period when FBI agents and CIA officers were working together in rotating, round-the-clock shifts, some of the interrogation techniques used on Abu Zubaydah included *nudity,*[31] *liquid diet,*[32] *sensory deprivation,*[33] and

---

[26] *See* DCIA Talking Points: Waterboard, 06 November 2007, pp. 1-3. This document was sent to DCIA on November 6 in preparation for a meeting with the President.

[27] SSCI Study, Executive Summary, December 3, 2014, p. 315.

[28] *See* DCIA Talking Points: Waterboard, 06 November 2007, pp. 1-3.

[29] SSCI Study, Executive Summary, December 3, 2014, p. 313.

[30] SSCI Study, Executive Summary, December 3, 2014, pp. 229-31 (emphasis added).

[31] SSCI Transcript, *Staff Interview of FBI Special Agent Ali Soufan*, April 28, 2008, p. 22. (DTS 2008-2411).

[32] *See* CIA, ███ 10090, April 21, 2002, p. 5.

[33] *See* CIA, ███ 10116, April 25, 2002, pp. 3-4; CIA, ███ 10016, April 12, 2002, pp. 4-5.

extended sleep deprivation.[34] Specifically, sleep deprivation played a significant role in Abu Zubaydah's identification of Jose Padilla as an al-Qa'ida operative tasked to carry out an attack against the United States. Abu Zubaydah provided this information to FBI agents during an interrogation session that began late at night on April 20, 2002, and ended on April 21, 2002. Between April 15, 2002 and April 21, 2002, *Abu Zubaydah was deprived of sleep for a total of 126.5 hours (5.27 days) over a 136 hour (5.6 day) period—while only being permitted several brief sleep breaks between April 19, 2002 and April 21, 2002, which totaled 9.5 hours.* Thus, all information provided by Abu Zubaydah subsequent to his return from the hospital on April 15, 2002, was obtained during or after the use of enhanced interrogation techniques and cannot be excluded from supporting the CIA's effectiveness representations under the Study's flawed analytical methodology. Over the course of his detention, Abu Zubaydah provided 766 sole-source disseminated intelligence reports.[35]

(U) *The Capture of Ramzi bin al-Shibh*

(TS█████████NF) The Study claims, "[a] review of CIA records found *no connection* between Abu Zubaydah's reporting on Ramzi bin al-Shibh and Ramzi bin al-Shibh's capture. . . . While CIA records indicate that Abu Zubaydah provided information on Ramzi bin al-Shibh, there is *no indication* that Abu Zubaydah provided information on bin al-Shibh's whereabouts. Further, while Abu Zubaydah provided information on bin al-Shibh while being subjected to the CIA's enhanced interrogation techniques, *he provided similar information* to FBI interrogators *prior* to the initiation of the CIA's enhanced interrogation techniques."[36]

(TS█████████NF) CIA records demonstrate that Abu Zubaydah was subjected to enhanced interrogation techniques during two separate periods in April 2002 and August 2002. During these timeframes, Abu Zubaydah made several photographic identifications of Ramzi bin al-Shibh and provided information that bin al-Shibh had been in Kandahar at the end of 2001, but was then working with KSM in Karachi, Pakistan. More important, Abu Zubaydah provided information about how he would go about locating Hassan Ghul and other al-Qa'ida associates in Karachi. This information caused █████████ Pakistani authorities to intensify their efforts and helped lead them to capture Ramzi bin al-Shibh and other al-Qa'ida associates during the Karachi safe house raids conducted on September 10-11, 2002.

(U) *The Capture of Khalid Shaykh Mohammad*

(TS█████████NF) The Study claims "there are no CIA records to support the assertion that Abu Zubaydah, Ramzi bin al-Shibh, or any other CIA detainee played any role in

---

[34] *See* CIA, █████ 10094, April 21, 2002, p. 3; CIA, █████ 10071, April 19, 2002, p. 2; CIA, █████ 10091, April 21, 2002, p. 2. Dietary manipulation, nudity, and sleep deprivation (more than 48 hours) were also subsequently authorized as enhanced interrogation techniques by the Department of Justice. *See* Memorandum for John A. Rizzo, Senior Deputy General Counsel, Central Intelligence Agency, from Steven G. Bradbury, Principal Deputy Assistant Attorney General, Office of Legal Counsel, Department of Justice, May 30, 2005, *Re: Application of United States Obligations under Article 16 of the Convention Against Torture to Certain Techniques that May be Used in the Interrogation of High value Al Qaeda Detainees* (DTS 2009-1810, Tab-11).

[35] SSCI Study, Volume III, March 31, 2014, pp. 282-283.

[36] SSCI Study, Executive Summary, December 3, 2014, p. 318 (emphasis added).

X

the 'the planning and execution of the operation that captured Khalid Sheikh Mohammed.'"[37] However, information obtained from CIA detainee Abu Zubaydah was essential to furthering the CIA's understanding of KSM's role in the September 11, 2001, terrorist attacks and helped lead to the capture of Ramzi bin al-Shibh. The ███████████████████ interrogations of bin al-Shibh and DETAINEE R provided key insights about KSM███████████ Information produced through detainee interrogation was pivotal to the retention of a key CIA asset whose cooperation led directly to the capture of KSM.

(U) *The Disruption of the Karachi Hotels Bombing Plot*

(TS███████████████NF) The Study claims, "[T]he CIA's enhanced interrogation techniques—to include the waterboard—played no role in the disruption of the Karachi Plot(s)."[38] However, CIA documents show that key intelligence collected through the CIA's Detention and Interrogation Program, including information obtained after the use of enhanced interrogation techniques, played a major role in disrupting the Karachi hotels bombing plot. Specifically, Abu Zubaydah provided crucial information that helped lead to the successful ███ raids of the al-Qa'ida safe houses on September 11, 2002—the same raids that yielded the "perfume letter" and disrupted the Karachi hotels plot. Specifically, the ██████████ raids were the direct result of information provided by Abu Zubaydah on August 20, 2002, during his second period of enhanced interrogation.

(U) *The Heathrow and Canary Wharf Plots*

(TS███████████████NF) The Study asserts that "contrary to CIA representations, information acquired during or after the use of the CIA's enhanced interrogation techniques played no role in 'alert[ing]' the CIA to the threat to—or the 'disrupt[ing]' the plotting against—Heathrow Airport and Canary Wharf."[39] We found that the CIA interrogation program played a key role in disrupting the Heathrow and Canary Wharf plotting. Specifically, the Study itself twice concedes these plots were "fully disrupted" with the detentions of Ramzi bin al-Shibh, KSM, Ammar al-Baluchi, and Khallad bin Attash.[40] The Study then incorrectly asserts, "There are no CIA records to indicate that any of the detainees were captured as a result of CIA detainee reporting."[41] Information obtained from the CIA interrogation program played a key role in the capture of al-Shibh and KSM.[42] Also, Ramzi bin al-Shibh provided information about Ammar al-Baluchi and Abu Zubaydah provided information about Khallad bin Attash prior to their arrests.[43] The same detainee information that helped lead to the capture of these terrorists also played a key role in fully disrupting the Heathrow Airport and Canary Wharf plots.

---

[37] SSCI Study, Executive Summary, December 3, 2014, p. 327.

[38] SSCI Study, Executive Summary, December 3, 2014, p. 242.

[39] SSCI Study, Executive Summary, December 3, 2014, pp. 297-298.

[40] *See* SSCI Study, Executive Summary, December 3, 2014, pp. 295 and 299.

[41] SSCI Study, Executive Summary December 3, 2014, p. 299.

[42] *See* SSCI Minority Views of Vice Chairman Chambliss joined by Senators Burr, Risch, Coats, Rubio, and Coburn, December 5, 2014, pp. 37-41.

[43] *See* SSCI Minority Views of Vice Chairman Chambliss joined by Senators Burr, Risch, Coats, Rubio, and Coburn, December 5, 2014, pp. ██ and 47.

(U) *The Capture of Hambali*

(TS███████████████NF) The Study claims that "[a] review of CIA operational cables and other records found that information obtained from KSM during or after the use of the CIA's enhanced interrogation techniques played no role in the capture of Hambali."[44] However, CIA documents show that the interrogation of KSM and al-Qa'ida operative Zubair, during and after the use of enhanced interrogation techniques on both individuals, played a key role in the capture of Hambali. Specifically, CIA documents indicate it was the combination of reporting from KSM and Majid Khan that led to the efforts to find Hambali through Zubair. A CIA summary of Hambali's capture timeline states, while "numerous sources had placed Hambali in various Southeast Asian countries, it was captured al-Qa'ida leader KSM who put ███████ ██████████████████ on Hambali's trail"—contradicting the Study's claim that the KSM interrogation played "no role."[45]

(U) *The Thwarting of the Second Wave Plots and Discovery of the Al-Ghuraba Group*

(TS███████████████NF) The Study claims that, "[a] review of CIA operational cables and other documents found that the CIA's enhanced interrogation techniques played no role in the 'discovery' or thwarting of either 'Second Wave' plot. Likewise, records indicate that the CIA's enhanced interrogation techniques played no role in the 'discovery' of a 17-member 'cell tasked with executing the 'Second Wave.'"[46] However, we found that the CIA interrogation program played a key role in disrupting the "Second Wave" plot and led to the capture of the 17-member al-Ghuraba group. Specifically, the Study ignores that KSM, who had also been subjected to the CIA's enhanced interrogation techniques, provided information months earlier on this same group of JI students and their location in Karachi—information that helped lead to the capture of Gunawan himself. According to CIA information, while the CIA was already aware of Gunawan, "KSM's identification of his role as Hambali's potential successor prioritized his capture. Information from multiple detainees, including KSM, narrowed down [Gunawan's] location and enabled his capture in September 2003."[47] This information was excluded from the Study. Pakistani authorities arrested the members of the al-Ghuraba group during raids on ██████████████████████ A cable describing the arrests said ████ captured this cell based on the debriefings of captured senior al-Qa'ida operatives, who stated that some members of this cell were to be part of senior al-Qa[']ida leader Khalid Shaykh Muhammad (KSM)['s] [']second wave['] operation to attack the United States using the same modus operandi as was used in the September 11, 2001 attacks."[48]

---

[44] SSCI Study, Executive Summary, December 3, 2014, p. 305.

[45] CIA, *Hambali Capture/Detention Timeline*, no date, p. 6.

[46] SSCI Study, Executive Summary, December 3, 2014, p. 251. This claim has been modified from the version that appeared in the report that was approved by the Committee at the end of the 112th Congress. For example, it no longer claims that the CIA's interrogation program, excluding the use of enhanced interrogation techniques, did not play a role in the thwarting of the al-Ghuraba Group. It also substitutes the words "discovery *or* thwarting" in place of the original "identification *and* disruption." (emphasis added).

[47] CIA, Detainee Reporting Pivotal for the War Against Al-Qa'ida, June 1, 2005, p. 2 (DTS 2009-1387).

[48] CIA, CIA CABLE 52981. ██████████████

(U) *Critical Intelligence Alerting the CIA to Jaffar al-Tayyar*

(TS███████████████NF) The Study asserts that,

CIA representations [about detainee reporting on Jaffar al-Tayyar] also omitted
key contextual facts, including that . . . (2) CIA detainee Abu Zubaydah provided
a description and information on a KSM associate named Jaffar al-Tayyar to FBI
Special Agents in May 2002, prior to being subjected to the CIA's enhanced
interrogation techniques . . . and (5) CIA records indicate that KSM did not know
al-Tayyar's true name and that it was Jose Padilla—in military custody and being
questioned by the FBI—who provided al-Tayyar's true name as Adnan el-
Shukrijumah."[49]

(TS███████████████NF) On May 20, 2002, while in CIA custody, Abu Zubaydah
provided information on an associate of KSM by the name of Abu Jaffar al-Thayer. Abu
Zubaydah provided a detailed description of Abu Jaffar al-Thayer, including that he spoke
English well and may have studied in the United States.[50] The Study incorrectly claims that this
May 20, 2002, interrogation took place prior to the initiation of the CIA's enhanced interrogation
techniques.[51] Abu Zubaydah had already been subjected to an extended period of sleep
deprivation and other enhanced interrogation techniques during his interrogation between April
15, 2002 and April 21, 2002, about one month *prior* to his May 20 interrogation.[52]

(TS███████████████NF) The Study also cites as a key contextual fact omitted from
CIA representations that KSM did not know al-Tayyar's true name, and it was Jose Padilla, in
military custody and being questioned by the FBI, who provided al-Tayyar's true name as Adnan
el-Shukrijumah.[53] However, this omission was rendered moot because, as the Study itself notes
a few pages later,[54] the "FBI began participating in the military debriefings [of Padilla] in March
2003, *after KSM reported Padilla might know the true name of a US-bound al-Qa'ida operative
known at the time only as Jaffar al-Tayyar.* Padilla confirmed Jaffar's true name as Adnan El
Shukrijumah."[55]

(U) *The Arrest and Prosecution of Saleh al-Marri*

(TS███████████████NF) The Study correctly asserts, "The CIA represented to the
CIA Office of Inspector General that 'as a result of the lawful use of EITs,' KSM 'provided
information that helped lead to the arrests of terrorists including . . . Saleh Almari, a sleeper

---

[49] SSCI Study, Executive Summary, December 3, 2014, pp. 358-359.

[50] *See* FBI draft report of the interrogation of Abu Zubaydah, May 20, 2002, 5:25 p.m. to 8:40 p.m., p 3.

[51] *See* SSCI Study, Executive Summary, December 3, 2014, p. 362.

[52] *See infra,* SSCI Minority Views of Vice Chairman Chambliss joined by Senators Burr, Risch, Coats, Rubio, and
Coburn, December 5, 2014, pp. 33-36.

[53] *See* SSCI Study, Executive Summary, December 3, 2014, p. 359.

[54] *See* SSCI Study, Executive Summary, December 3, 2014, p. 365 (emphasis added).

[55] *See* CIA, *Briefing Notes on the Value of Detainee Reporting,* April 15, 2005, p. 3 (emphasis added); *See also CIA,*
ALEC████████March 24, 2003, p. 6 ("Our service has developed new information, based on leads from detained al-
Qa'ida operations chief Khalid Shaykh Muhammad (KSM), that al-Qa'ida operative Jafar al-Tayyar's true name is
Adnan Shukri Jumah and he could be involved in an imminent suicide attack in the United States").

operative in New York.'"[56] As the Study makes clear, al-Marri was not arrested based on information from KSM, and could not have been, because al-Marri was arrested in December 2001, before the detention of KSM in March 2003.[57]

(TS███████████████NF) In its response to the Study, the CIA concedes that the agency erred in describing detainee reporting as contributing to al-Marri's arrest. However, the agency stresses that KSM did provide valuable intelligence on al-Marri—intelligence that played a significant role in al-Marri's prosecution.[58] It was KSM who identified a photograph of al-Marri and described him as an al-Qa'ida sleeper operative sent to the United States shortly before 9/11. KSM said he planned for al-Marri, who "had the perfect built-in cover for travel to the United States as a student pursuing his advanced degree in computer studies at a university near New York," to serve as al-Qa'ida's point of contact to settle other operatives in the United States for follow-on attacks after 9/11.[59] KSM also said that al-Marri trained at the al-Faruq camp, had poisons training, and had offered himself as a martyr to bin Ladin.[60]

(TS███████████████NF) Prior to the information from KSM, al-Marri was charged with credit card fraud and false statements. After the information from KSM, al-Marri was designated as an enemy combatant. In 2009, after being transferred to federal court, al-Marri pled guilty to one count of conspiracy to provide material support to al-Qa'ida. In his plea, he admitted that he attended terrorist training camps and met with KSM to offer his services al-Qa'ida, who told him to travel to the United States before 9/11 and await instructions—*all information initially provided by KSM.*

(U) *The Arrest and Prosecution of Iyman Faris*

(U) The Study claims, "[o]ver a period of years, the CIA provided the 'identification,' 'arrest,' 'capture,' 'investigation,' and 'prosecution' of Iyman Faris as evidence for the effectiveness of the CIA's enhanced interrogation techniques. These representations were inaccurate."[61] The Study correctly points out that CIA statements implying that detainee information led to the "identification" or "investigation" of Iyman Faris were inaccurate. However, CIA, FBI, and Department of Justice documents show that information obtained from KSM after he was waterboarded led directly to Faris's arrest and was key in his prosecution.

(TS███████████████NF) On March 17 and 18, 2003, the CIA questioned KSM about Majid Khan's family and KSM stated that another Khan relative, whom he identified from a picture of Faris, was a "truck driver in Ohio."[62] On March 18, 2003, KSM told interrogators he tasked the truck driver to procure specialized machine tools that would be useful to al-Qaida in loosening the nuts and bolts of suspension bridges in the United States. KSM said he was

---

[56] SSCI Study, Executive Summary, December 3, 2014, p. 366.
[57] SSCI Study, Executive Summary, December 3, 2014, p. 366.
[58] See CIA Study Response, *Case Studies (TAB C)*, June 27, 2013, p. 35.
[59] CIA, WASHINGTON DC ███████████████
[60] *See* CIA, CIA WASHINGTON DC ███████████████
[61] SSCI Study, Executive Summary, December 3, 2014, p. 276-277.
[62] CIA, CIA CABLE 10886, March 18, 2003, pp 5-6.

XIV

informed by an intermediary that Faris could not find the tools.[63] This revelation would turn out to be a key piece of incriminating evidence against Iyman Faris. The Study excluded information found in CIA documents which shows that, immediately after obtaining information from KSM and Majid Khan regarding Faris, the CIA queried the FBI for "additional details" on Faris, "including a readout on his current activities and plans for FBI continued investigation."[64] The cable specifically noted that "KSM seems to have accurately identified" Faris from a photograph as the "truck driver in Ohio."[65]

(TS███████████NF) On March 20, 2003, the FBI picked up Faris for questioning and conducted a consent search of his apartment, seizing his laptop. When our staff asked the FBI why Faris was picked up, they cited the cables from CIA.[66] The FBI investigators went into this interview armed with the information revealed by KSM and Majid Khan, which enabled them to explore Faris's ties with KSM and al-Qa'ida plotting in the United States.[67] On May 1, 2003, Faris pled guilty to "casing a New York City bridge for al Qaeda, and researching and providing information to al Qaeda regarding the tools necessary for possible attacks on U.S. targets," *the exact terrorist activities described by KSM*. Ultimately, the CIA's representation concerning the identification and initial investigation of Faris is much less important than the details that led to his arrest and prosecution.

(U) *The Arrest and Prosecution of Uzhair Paracha and the Arrest of Saifullah Paracha*

(TS███████████NF) The Study asserts,"[t]he CIA represented that information obtained through the use of the CIA's enhanced interrogation techniques produced otherwise unavailable intelligence that led to the identification and/or arrest of Uzhair Paracha and his father Saifullah Paracha (aka, Sayf al-Rahman Paracha). These CIA representations included inaccurate information and omitted significant material information, specifically a body [of] intelligence reporting—acquired prior to CIA detainee reporting—that linked the Parachas to al-Qa'ida-related terrorist activities."[68]

(TS███████████NF) We found, however, that information obtained from KSM during his enhanced interrogation on March 25, 2003, about alleged explosives smuggling into the United States, attacks on U.S. gas stations, and related material support to al-Qa'ida, motivated the FBI to track down and arrest Uzhair Paracha in New York a few days later on March 31, 2003.[69] The Intelligence Community continued its pursuit of Saifullah, who was later arrested ██████████████ on July 6, 2003. Among other charges, Uzhair was successfully convicted on November 23, 2005, of providing material support to al-Qa'ida and sentenced to 30 years in prison. KSM's description of Uzhair's involvement in the gas station plots and his claim that Uzhair may have provided other logistical support for Majid's entry into

---

[63] CIA, CIA CABLE 10886, March 18, 2003, pp 5-6.
[64] CIA, ██████████████████ *Information from KSM on Majid Khan.*
[65] CIA, ██████████████████ *Information from KSM on Majid Khan.*
[66] Phone call from the FBI responding to minority staff questions from a document review, January 25, 2013.
[67] *See* CIA Study Response, *Case Studies (TAB C),* June 27, 2013, p. 13; FBI WASH 040537Z, April 4, 2003, p. 2.
[68] SSCI Study, Executive Summary, December 3, 2014, p. 352.
[69] CIA, DIRECTOR ██████████████

the United States was consistent with the press release's description of some of the evidence used during Uzhair's trial.[70]

(U) *Tactical Intelligence on Shkai, Pakistan*

(U) This case study is no longer as problematic as the version contained in the appendix to the original Findings and Conclusions section of the Study approved by the Committee during the 112th Congress. That appendix falsely accused the CIA of providing an inaccurate representation about the tactical intelligence acquired on Shkai, Pakistan, during the interrogations of Hassan Ghul after the use of enhanced interrogation techniques.[71] Fortunately, that appendix has been dropped from the Study's updated Findings and Conclusions and there is no claim in the updated version of the Study that the representation concerning Shkai, Pakistan, was inaccurate.

(U) *Thwarting of the Camp Lemonier Plotting*

(TS   NF) The Study claims, "[t]he CIA represented that intelligence derived from the use of CIA's enhanced interrogation techniques thwarted plotting against the U.S. military base, Camp Lemonier, in Djibouti. These representations were inaccurate."[72] We found, however that representations about the thwarting of an attack against Camp Lemonier in Djibouti, specifically President Bush's 2006 comments that "Terrorists held in CIA custody have also provided information that helped stop a planned strike on U.S. Marines at Camp Lemonier in Djibouti," were accurate and have been mischaracterized by the Study.[73] Specifically, contrary to the Study's assertions, the President did not attribute the thwarting of this plot exclusively to the use of enhanced interrogation techniques, but information from "[t]errorists held in CIA custody." In addition, the President never stated that the plot was disrupted exclusively because of information from detainees in CIA custody. The President was clear that information from detainees "helped" to stop the planned strike. This idea that detainee reporting builds on and contextualizes previous and subsequent reporting is repeated a few lines later in the speech, when the President makes clear, "[t]he information we get from these detainees is corroborated by intelligence . . . that we've received from other sources, and together this intelligence has helped us connect the dots and stop attacks before they occur."[74]

(U) *CIA Detainees Subjected to EITs Validated CIA Sources*

(TS   NF) The Study claims, "the CIA also represented that its enhanced interrogation techniques were necessary to validate CIA sources. The claim was based

---

[70] *See* DOJ, United States Attorney, Southern District of New York, *Pakistani Man Convicted of Providing Material Support to Al Qaeda Sentenced to 30 Years in Federal Prison,* July 20, 2006, p.2.

[71] SSCI Study, December 13, 2012, Findings and Conclusions, *Appendix: Details on CIA's Effectiveness Representations–Conclusion #9,* p. 92.

[72] SSCI Study, Executive Summary, December 3, 2014, p. 336.

[73] President George W. Bush, *Trying Detainees; Address on the Creation of Military Commissions,* Washington, D C., September 6, 2006.

[74] President George W. Bush, *Trying Detainees; Address on the Creation of Military Commissions,* Washington, D.C., September 6, 2006.

on one CIA detainee—Janat Gul—contradicting the reporting of one CIA asset."[75] Contrary to the Study's claim, the representations cited by the Study do not assert that enhanced interrogation techniques helped to validate sources. Rather, the representations only make reference to "detainee information" or detainee "reporting." Also contrary to the Study's claim, we found evidence in the documentary record where the CIA representations about Janat Gul also contained additional examples of source validation. Moreover, the three items of information that the Study asserts should have been included in the Janat Gul asset validation representations were not "critical" and their inclusion does not alter the fact that Gul's persistent contradiction of the asset's claims did help the CIA "validate" that particular asset.

(U) *The Identification of Bin Ladin's Courier*

(TS~~███████████~~NF) The Study asserts, "the 'tipoff' on Abu Ahmad al-Kuwaiti in 2002 did not come from the interrogation of CIA detainees and was obtained prior to any CIA detainee reporting."[76] However, CIA documents show that detainee information served as the "tip-off" and played a significant role in leading CIA analysts to the courier Abu Ahmad al-Kuwaiti. While there was other information in CIA databases about al-Kuwaiti, this information was not recognized as important by analysts until after detainees provided information on him. Specifically, a CIA paper in November 2007 noted that "over twenty mid to high-value detainees have discussed Abu Ahmad's ties to senior al-Qa'ida leaders, including his role in delivering messages from Bin Ladin and his close association with former al-Qa'ida third-in-command Abu Faraj al-Libi."[77] The report highlighted specific reporting from two detainees, Hassan Ghul and Ammar al-Baluchi, who both identified Abu Faraj al-Libi's role in communicating to bin Ladin through Abu Ahmad. It was this and similar reporting from other detainees that helped analysts realize Abu Faraj's categorical denials that he even knew anyone named Abu Ahmad al-Kuwaiti, "almost certainly were an attempt to protect Abu Ahmed," thus showing his importance.[78]

(TS~~███████████~~NF) The Study also asserts, "the most accurate information on Abu Ahmad al-Kuwaiti obtained from a CIA detainee [Hassan Ghul] was provided by a CIA detainee who had not yet been subjected to the CIA's enhanced interrogation techniques."[79] We found, however, that Detainees who provided useful and accurate information on Abu Ahmad al-Kuwaiti and bin Ladin had undergone enhanced interrogation prior to providing the information. Specifically, Ammar al-Baluchi, who appears to be the first detainee to mention Abu Ahmad al-Kuwaiti's role as a bin Ladin courier and a possible connection with Abu Faraj al-Libi, provided this information at a CIA black site during a period of enhanced interrogation.[80]

---

[75] SSCI Study, Executive Summary, December 3, 2014, p. 342.

[76] SSCI Study, Executive Summary, December 3, 2014, p. 389.

[77] CIA Intelligence Assessment, *Al-Qa'ida Watch, Probable Identification of Suspected Bin Ladin Facilitator Abu Ahmad al-Kuwaiti*, November 23, 2007, p. 2.

[78] CIA Intelligence Assessment, *Al-Qa'ida Watch, Probable Identification of Suspected Bin Ladin Facilitator Abu Ahmad al-Kuwaiti*, November 23, 2007, p. 2.

[79] SSCI Study, Executive Summary, December 3, 2014, p. 379.

[80] *See* CIA, WASHINGTON DC ███████████████ Ammar al-Baluchi attempted to recant his earlier description of Abu Ahmad as a Bin Ladin courier. CIA, DIRECTOR ██████████████████

(TS███████████NF) Additional CIA-fact checking explained that Ghul offered more details about Abu Ahmad's role after being transferred from COBALT and receiving enhanced interrogation. Specifically, the CIA stated:

> After undergoing enhanced techniques, Gul stated that Abu Ahmad specifically passed a letter from Bin Ladin to Abu Faraj in late 2003 and that Abu Ahmad had "disappeared" from Karachi, Pakistan in 2002. This information was not only more concrete and less speculative, it also corroborated information from Ammar that Khalid Shaykh Muhammad (KSM) was lying when he claimed Abu Ahmad left al-Qa'ida in 2002.[81]

Ghul stated that while he had "no proof," he believed that Abu Faraj was in contact with Abu Ahmad and that Abu Ahmad might act as an intermediary contact between Abu Faraj and Bin Ladin. Ghul said that this belief "made sense" since Abu Ahmad had disappeared and Ghul had heard that Abu Ahmad was in contact with Abu Faraj.[82] Months later, Ghul also told his interrogators that he knew Abu Ahmad was close to Bin Ladin, which was another reason he suggested that Abu Ahmad had direct contact with Bin Ladin as one of his couriers.[83]

(TS███████████NF) The role of other detainees who had undergone enhanced interrogation, but were believed to be untruthful about knowing Abu Ahmad al-Kuwaiti, was described by CIA analysts as being very significant in their understanding of the courier as well. CIA documents make clear that when detainees like Abu Zubaydah, KSM, and Abu Faraj al-Libi—who had undergone enhanced interrogation and were otherwise cooperative—denied knowing Abu Ahmad Kuwaiti or suggested that he had "retired," it was a clear sign to CIA analysts that these detainees had something to hide, and it further confirmed other detainee information that had tipped them off about the true importance of Abu Ahmad al-Kuwaiti.[84]

(U) Conclusion 6 (CIA Impeded Congressional Oversight)

(TS███████████NF) Conclusion 6 states: "[t]he CIA has actively avoided or impeded congressional oversight of the program."[85] In reality, the overall pattern of engagement with the Congress shows that the CIA attempted to keep the Congress informed of its activities. From 2002 to 2008, the CIA provided more than 35 briefings to SSCI members and staff, more than 30 similar briefings to HPSCI members and staff, and more than 20 congressional notifications.[86] Because the Study did not interview the participants in these restricted briefings, it is impossible to document how much information the CIA provided to Committee leadership during those briefings. Often, the Study's own examples contradict the assertion that the CIA tried to avoid its overseers' scrutiny. For example, the Study notes that the CIA reacted to Vice

---

[81] CIA Study Response, *Case Studies (TAB C)*, June 27, 2013, p. 38 (citing CIA, ████████████

[82] CIA, ████████████

[83] CIA, DIRECTOR ████████

[84] CIA, DIRECTOR ████████ CIA Center for the Study of Intelligence, *Lessons from the Hunt for Usama Bin Ladin*, dated September 2012, pp. 9-10 (DTS 2012-3826); CIA Intelligence Assessment, *Al-Qa'ida Watch, Probable Identification of Suspected Bin Ladin Facilitator Abu Ahmad al-Kuwaiti*, November 23, 2007, p. 2.

[85] SSCI Study, Findings and Conclusions, December 3, 2014, p. 5.

[86] CIA Study Response, *Conclusions (TAB B)*, June 27, 2013, p. 35.

XVIII

Chairman Rockefeller's suspicion about the agency's honesty by planning a detailed briefing on the Program for him.[87]

(TS███████████████NF) The Study claims, "[t]he CIA did not brief the Senate Intelligence Committee leadership on the CIA's enhanced interrogation techniques until September 2002, after the techniques had been approved and used."[88] We found that the CIA provided information to the Committee in hearings, briefings, and notifications beginning shortly after the signing of the Memorandum of Notification (MON) on September 17, 2001. The Study's own review of the CIA's representations to Congress cites CIA hearing testimony from November 7, 2001, discussing the uncertainty in the boundaries on interrogation techniques.[89] The Study also cites additional discussions between staff and CIA lawyers in February 2002.[90] The Study seems to fault the CIA for not briefing the Committee leadership until after the enhanced interrogation techniques had been approved and used. However, the use of DOJ-approved enhanced interrogation techniques began during the congressional recess period in August, an important fact that the Study conveniently omitted.[91] The CIA briefed HPSCI leadership on September 4, 2002. SSCI leadership received the same briefing on September 27, 2002.[92]

(TS███████████NF) The Study also asserts, "[t]he CIA subsequently resisted efforts by then-Vice Chairman John D. Rockefeller, IV, to investigate the program, including by refusing in 2006 to provide requested documents."[93] However, we determined that the CIA provided access to the documents requested. On January 5, 2006, the Director of National Intelligence's Chief of Staff wrote a letter to Vice Chairman Rockefeller which denied an earlier request for full Committee access to over 100 documents related to the Inspector General's May 2004 Special Review.[94] However, this denial of "full Committee access," did not mean that the documents were not made available to the CIA's congressional overseers. In fact, the Chief of Staff's letter stated, "Consistent with the provisions of the National Security Act of 1947, the White House has directed that specific information related to aspects of the detention and interrogation program be provided only to the SSCI leadership and staff directors."[95] The letter concluded by advising Vice Chairman Rockefeller that the documents "remain available for review by SSCI leadership and staff directors at any time through arrangements with CIA's Office of Congressional Affairs."[96]

---

[87] *See* SSCI Study, Executive Summary, December 3, 2014, p. 441.

[88] SSCI Study, Findings and Conclusions, December 3, 2014, p. 5.

[89] SSCI Study, Executive Summary, December 3, 2014, p. 437 n.2447. *See also* SSCI Transcript, *Briefing on Covert Action*, November 7, 2001, p. 56 (DTS 2002-0611).

[90] *See* SSCI Study, Executive Summary, December 3, 2014, p. 437; Email from: Christopher Ford, SSCI Staff, to: ███ Cleared SSCI staff; subject: Meeting yesterday with CIA lawyers on ███████ date: February 26, 2002 (DTS 2002-0925).

[91] *See* CIA Study Response, *Conclusions (TAB B)*, June 27, 2013, p. 36.

[92] CIA Study Response, *Conclusions (TAB B)*, June 27, 2013, p. 36.

[93] SSCI Study, Findings and Conclusions, December 3, 2014, pp. 5-6.

[94] SSCI Study, Executive Summary, December 3, 2014, p. 442.

[95] Letter from David Shedd to Andy Johnson, January 5, 2006 (DTS 2006-0373).

[96] Letter from David Shedd to Andy Johnson, January 5, 2006 (DTS 2006-0373).

(TS███████████NF) In support of this erroneous conclusion that the CIA impeded congressional oversight, the Study notes that the "CIA restricted access to information about the program from members of the Committee beyond the Chairman and Vice Chairman until September 6, 2006."[97] Although we agree that the full Committee should have been briefed much earlier, the CIA's limitation of access to sensitive covert action information is a long-standing practice codified in Section 503 of the National Security Act of 1947, as amended.

(TS███████████NF) The Study notes that the CIA briefed a number of additional Senators who were not on the Select Committee on Intelligence.[98] The National Security Act permits the President to provide senators with information about covert action programs at his discretion, without regard to Committee membership. Moreover, providing a briefing to inform key senators working on legislation relevant to the CIA's program is inconsistent with the narrative that the CIA sought to avoid congressional scrutiny.

(U) Conclusion 7 (CIA Impeded White House Oversight)

(U) Conclusion 7 states, "[t]he CIA impeded effective White House oversight and decision-making."[99] It is important to place this serious allegation within its proper context—the CIA's Detention and Interrogation Program was conducted as a covert action.[100] Covert action is the sole responsibility of the White House, a principle enshrined in law since the National Security Act of 1947. [101] The President, working with his National Security Staff, approves and oversees all covert action programs. The congressional intelligence committees also conduct ongoing oversight of all covert actions and receive quarterly covert action briefings. Given this extensive covert action oversight regime, this conclusion seems to imply falsely that the CIA was operating a rogue intelligence operation designed to "impede" the White House. We reject this unfounded implication.

(TS███████████NF) The Study asserts, "[a]ccording to CIA records, no CIA officer, up to and including CIA Directors George Tenet and Porter Goss, briefed the President on the specific CIA enhanced interrogation techniques before April 2006. By that time, 38 of the 39 detainees identified as having been subjected to the CIA's enhanced interrogation techniques had already been subjected to the techniques."[102] We found that the CIA records are

---

[97] SSCI Study, Findings and Conclusions, December 3, 2014, p. 6.
[98] *See* SSCI Study. Executive Summary, December 3, 2014. p. 443.
[99] SSCI Study. Findings and Conclusions. December 3, 2014, p. 6.
[100] *See* SSCI Study, Executive Summary. December 3, 2014. p. 11. "On September 17, 2001, six days after the terrorist attacks of September 11, 2001, President George W. Bush signed a covert action MON to authorize the Director of Central Intelligence (DCI) to '*undertake operations designed to capture and detain* persons who pose a continuing, serious threat of violence or death to U.S. persons and interests or who are planning terrorist activities.'" (emphasis added).
[101] In 1974, the Hughes-Ryan amendment to the Foreign Assistance Act of 1961 created the requirement for presidential "Findings" for covert action. The Intelligence Oversight Acts of 1980 and 1988 amended the Finding process, and the Intelligence Oversight Act of 1991 replaced Hughes-Ryan with the current Finding process. *See* William Daugherty, *Executive Secrets, Covert Action and the Presidency*. The University Press of Kentucky, 2004, pp. 92-98.
[102] SSCI Study. Findings and Conclusions, December 3, 2014, p. 6.

contradictory and incomplete regarding when the President was briefed, but President Bush himself says he was briefed in 2002, before any techniques were used.[103]

(TS███████████NF) The Study claims that, "[t]he information provided connecting the CIA's detention and interrogation program directly to [the "Dirty Bomb" Plot/Tall Buildings Plot, the Karachi Plots, Heathrow and Canary Wharf Plot, and the Identification/Capture of Iyman Faris] was, to a great extent, inaccurate."[104] We found, however, the information provided to the White House attributing the arrests of these terrorists and the thwarting of these plots to the CIA's Detention and Interrogation Program was accurate.[105]

(U) Conclusion 8 (CIA Impeded National Security Missions of Executive Branch Agencies)

(U) Conclusion 8 states, "[t]he CIA's operation and management of the program complicated, and in some cases impeded, the national security missions of other Executive Branch agencies."[106] As noted in the CIA response to the Study, "the National Security Council established the parameters for when and how CIA could engage on the program with other Executive Branch agencies."[107] The CIA was not responsible nor did it have control over the sharing or dissemination of information to other executive branch agencies or members of the Principals Committee itself. That responsibly rested solely with the White House.

(TS███████████NF) The Study claims, "[t]he CIA blocked State Department leadership from access to information crucial to foreign policy decision-making and diplomatic activities."[108] However, the Study does not provide any evidence that the CIA deliberately impeded, obstructed or blocked the State Department from obtaining information about the Program inconsistent with directions from the White House or the National Security Council. CIA officers were in close and constant contact with their State Department counterparts where detention facilities were located and among senior leadership to include the Secretary of State and the U.S. Deputy Secretary of State. For example, leading to the establishment of a facility in Country█ the Study notes that the chief of station (COS) was coordinating activities with the ambassador. Because the Program was highly compartmented, the ambassador was directed by the National Security Council not to discuss with his immediate superior at headquarters due to the highly compartmented nature of the covert action. Instead, the COS, sent feedback from the ambassador through CIA channels, to the NSC, whereby the Deputy Secretary of State with the knowledge of the Secretary, would discuss any issues or concerns with the ambassador in country.[109] While the process was less direct, the security precautions to protect sensitive information did not impede the national security mission of the State Department.

---

[103] See George W. Bush, *Decision Points*, Broadway Paperbacks, New York, 2010, p. 169.
[104] SSCI Study, April 1, 2014, Volume II, p. 446.
[105] See SSCI Minority Views of Vice Chairman Chambliss joined by Senators Burr, Risch, Coats, Rubio, and Coburn, June 20, 2014, *The Thwarting of the Dirty Bomb/Tall Buildings Plot and the Capture of Jose Padilla*, pp. 33-36; *The Thwarting of the Karachi Plots*, pp. 44-47; *The Heathrow and Canary Wharf Plots*, pp. 47-49; and *The Arrest and Prosecution of Iyman Faris*, pp. 58-60.
[106] SSCI Study, Findings and Conclusions, December 3, 2014, p. 7.
[107] CIA Study Response, *Conclusions (TAB B)*, June 27, 2013, p. 11.
[108] SSCI Study, Findings and Conclusions, December 3, 2014, p. 7.
[109] CIA CABLE ████████████ CIA CABLE ████████████ CIA CABLE ████████

(TS███████████████NF) The Study also claims, "[t]he CIA denied specific requests from FBI Director Robert Mueller, III, for FBI access to CIA detainees that the FBI believed was necessary to understand CIA detainee reporting on threats to the U.S. Homeland."[110] While the FBI's participation in the interrogation of detainees was self-proscribed, the Bureau was still able to submit requirements to the CIA and received reports on interrogations. Recognizing the need for FBI access to detainees, both agencies finalized a memorandum of understanding in the fall of 2003 that detailed how FBI ████████████████████████████████ agents would be provided access to detainees ████████████████████████"[111]

(TS███████████████NF) The Study asserts, "[t]he ODNI was provided with inaccurate and incomplete information about the program, preventing the ODNI from effectively carrying out its statutory responsibility to serve as the principal advisor to the President on intelligence matters."[112] We do not agree with this assertion. The updated Study treats this assertion differently than it did in the version that was adopted by the Committee during the 112th Congress. In the original Study, the assertion sought to dispute claims regarding the use of enhanced interrogation techniques and disruption of several plots. However, the updated Study drops the direct reference to coercive measures and instead focuses on the Detention and Interrogation Program in general.[113] The 2006 press release from the Office of Director of National Intelligence[114] does not reference the use of enhanced interrogation techniques, but states unequivocally: "The detention of terrorists disrupts—at least temporarily—the plots they were involved in." To assert that the detention and interrogation of terrorists did not yield intelligence of value is simply not credible.

(U) Conclusion 5 (CIA Provided Inaccurate Information to the Department of Justice)

(U) Conclusion 5 states, "[t]he CIA repeatedly provided inaccurate information to the Department of Justice, impeding a proper legal analysis of the CIA's detention and Interrogation Program."[115] Our analysis of the claims used in support of this conclusion revealed that many were themselves inaccurate or otherwise without merit.

(TS███████████████NF) The Study falsely claims that "CIA attorneys stated that 'a novel application of using the necessity defense' could be used 'to avoid prosecution of U.S. officials who tortured to obtain information that saved many lives.'"[116] We found that the draft CIA Office of General Counsel (OGC) legal appendix cited by the report contained a cursory discussion of the necessity defense that *did not* support the use of such defense in the context of the CIA's Detention and Interrogation Program.[117] Specifically, the claim here altered the

---

[110] SSCI Study, Findings and Conclusions, December 3, 2014, p. 7.
[111] SSCI Study, Volume I, March 31, 2014, p. 413.
[112] SSCI Study, Findings and Conclusions, December 3, 2014, p. 8.
[113] SSCI Study, Findings and Conclusions, December 3, 2014, p. 8.
[114] ODNI Press Release, September 6, 2006, "Information on the High Value Terrorist Detainee Program."
[115] SSCI Study, Findings and Conclusions, December 3, 2014, p. 4.
[116] SSCI Study, Findings and Conclusions, December 3, 2014, p. 5.
[117] *See* CIA Office of General Counsel draft *Legal Appendix: Paragraph 5--Hostile Interrogations: Legal Considerations for CIA Officers*, November 26, 2001, pp. 5-6 (CIA, Draft Appendix on Necessity Defense). This

meaning of the quoted text in draft legal appendix by separating portions of the text and inserting its own factually misleading text, which was not supported by the legal analysis, to achieve the following result: "*CIA attorneys stated that* a novel application of the necessity defense *could be used* to avoid prosecution of U.S. officials who tortured to obtain information that saved lives."[118] Fortunately, this erroneously doctored quotation only appears once in the Study—in this Conclusion.

(TS███████████████NF) Also in support of this conclusion, the Study makes a number of claims related to the accuracy of the information provided by the CIA about Abu Zubaydah to OLC. First, the Study asserts that the OLC "relied on inaccurate CIA representations about Abu Zubaydah's status in al-Qa'ida and the interrogation team's 'certain[ty]' that Abu Zubaydah was withholding information about planned terrorist attacks."[119] We found that the information relied upon by the Study to criticize the CIA's representations about Abu Zubaydah withholding information about planned terrorists attacks neglected to include important statements from within that same intelligence cable, which supported those representations by the CIA. Specifically, the Study cites an email from the CIA's interrogation team that included the sentence: "[o]ur assumption is the objective of this operation [the interrogation of Abu Zubaydah] is to achieve a high degree of confidence that [Abu Zubaydah] is not holding back actionable information concerning threats to the United States beyond that which [Abu Zubaydah] has already provided."[120] However, this carefully chosen text omits critical statements from later in the same cable: "[t]here is information and analysis to indicate that subject has information on terrorist threats to the United States" and "[h]e is an incredibly strong willed individual which is why he has resisted this long."[121]

(TS███████████NF) Second, the Study asserts the CIA assessment that Abu Zubaydah was the "third or fourth man" in al-Qa'ida was "based on single-source reporting that was recanted prior to the August 1, 2002, OLC memorandum."[122] The CIA was in possession of multiple threads of intelligence supporting Abu Zubaydah's prominent role in al-Qa'ida.[123] █

██ However, the level of detail that ████████████ had previously provided about Abu Zubaydah undermined his later attempts to retract his earlier admissions about his involvement in future terrorist attacks █

---

document is attached as Appendix IV to the SSCI Minority Views of Vice Chairman Chambliss joined by Senators Burr, Risch, Coats, Rubio, and Coburn. June 20, 2014. p. IV-1.

[118] SSCI Study, Findings and Conclusions, December 3, 2014, p. 5 (Erroneous text indicated by italics).

[119] SSCI Study, Findings and Conclusions, December 3, 2014, p. 5.

[120] CIA, [REDACTED] 73208, July 23, 2003, p. 3; Email from: CIA staff officer; to: [REDACTED], [REDACTED], ██████████; subject: Addendum from GREEN, [REDACTED] 73208 (231043Z JUL 02); date: July 23, 2004, at 07:56:49 PM. *See also* email from: [REDACTED]; to: [REDACTED]; subject: Re: Grayson SWIGERT and Hammond DUNBAR date: August 8, 21, 2002, at 10:21 PM.

[121] CIA, [REDACTED] 73208, July 23, 2003, p. 3; email from: CIA staff officer; to: [REDACTED], [REDACTED], ██████████subject: Addendum from GREEN, [REDACTED] 73208 (231043Z JUL 02); date: July 23, 2004, at 07:56 PM. *See also* Email from: [REDACTED]; to: [REDACTED]; subject: Re: Grayson SWIGERT and Hammond DUNBAR; date: August 8, 21, 2002, at 10:21 PM.

[122] SSCI Study, Executive Summary, December 3, 2014, p. 410 (emphasis added).

[123] *See* CIA Study Response, *Conclusions (TAB B)*, June 27, 2013, p. 32.

██████ and his denials about meeting with Abu Zubaydah.[124] Moreover, Abu Zubaydah himself admitted to at least one meeting with ████████████, which undermines ████████ denials about such meetings.[125]

(TS████████████████NF) Third, the Study incredibly claims that *"[t]he CIA later concluded that Abu Zubaydah was not a member of al-Qa'ida."*[126] We found that the one document cited by the Study did not support this unbelievable and factually incorrect assertion. Specifically, a text box in this cited intelligence product makes the following assertions:

> A common misperception in outside articles is that Khaldan camp was run by al-Qa'ida. Pre-911 September 2001 reporting miscast Abu Zubaydah as a "senior al-Qa'ida lieutenant," which led to the inference that the Khaldan camp he was administering was tied to Usama Bin Ladin . . . .

> Al-Qa'ida rejected Abu Zubaydah's request *in 1993* to join the group and that Khaldan was not overseen by Bin Ladin's organization.[127]

The Study fails to state that the interrogation of this supposed "non-member" resulted in 766 sole-source disseminated intelligence reports by the Study's own count.[128] Ironically, this intelligence product was written based on "information from detainees and captured documents"—including from Abu Zubaydah.[129]

(TS████████████████NF) In further support of this conclusion, the Study correctly asserts that "the CIA applied its enhanced interrogation techniques to numerous other CIA detainees without seeking additional formal legal advice from the OLC."[130] However, the CIA appropriately applied the legal principles of the August 1, 2002, OLC memorandum to other CIA detainees. Specifically, the fact that the CIA felt comfortable enough with OLC's August 1, 2002, legal opinion to apply the same legal principles to other detainees does not constitute an impediment to DOJ's legal analysis of the Program. In fact, the Attorney General later expressed the view that "the legal principles reflected in DOJ's specific original advice could appropriately be extended to allow use of the same approved techniques (under the same conditions and subject to the same safeguards) to other individuals besides the subject of DOJ's specific original advice."[131]

---

[124] *See* SSCI Minority Views of Vice Chairman Chambliss joined by Senators Burr, Risch, Coats, Rubio, and Coburn, June 20, 2014, p. 91.

[125] CIA, ALEC ████████████████ CIA, ALEC ████████████ Abu Zubaydah and ████████ accounts differ as to the location of this meeting(s).

[126] SSCI Study, Executive Summary, December 3, 2014, p. 410 (emphasis added).

[127] CIA, *Countering Misconceptions About Training Camps in Afghanistan, 1990-2001*, August 16, 2006, p. 2 (emphasis added).). This document is attached as Appendix I to the SSCI Minority Views of Vice Chairman Chambliss joined by Senators Burr, Risch, Coats, Rubio, and Coburn, June 20, 2014, p. I-1.

[128] *See* SSCI Study, Volume III, March 31, 2014, pp. 282-283.

[129] CIA, *Countering Misconceptions About Training Camps in Afghanistan, 1990-2001*, August 16, 2006, p. i (DTS 2006-3254).

[130] SSCI Study, Executive Summary, December 3, 2014, p. 411.

[131] *See* Memorandum from Jack Goldsmith III, Assistant Attorney General, Office of Legal Counsel, Department of Justice, to John Helgerson, Inspector General, Central Intelligence Agency, June 18, 2004, Addendum, p. 2 (DTS 2004-2730).

(TS███████████NF) The Study asserts that the CIA made inaccurate representations to DOJ that Janat Gul and Ahmed Khalfan Ghailani were high-value al Qaeda operatives with knowledge of a pre-election plot against the United States when seeking legal guidance on whether the use of four additional interrogation techniques might violate U.S. law or treaty obligations.[132] Contrary to the Study's claim, the CIA believed the representations to be true at the time it made them to the OLC. The CIA did not learn that some of these representations had been fabricated by a sensitive CIA source until months *after* OLC had approved the use of enhanced interrogation techniques against Janat Gul and Ahmed Khalfan Ghailani. Also, the Study claims that "the threat of a terrorist attack to precede the November 2004 U.S. election was found to be based on a CIA source whose information was questioned by senior CTC officials at the time. The same CIA source admitted to fabricating the information after ████████ in ████ October 2004."[133] However, the email relied upon by the Study does not support the proposition that senior CTC officials questioned the veracity of the sensitive CIA source. While the source did admit to fabricating information about a meeting that never occurred, the Study does not acknowledge that the Chief of Base believed that the source was "generally truthful" about his discussions on the pre-election threat, despite the source's ████████████████████████ on that issue.

(TS███████████NF) The Study also repeats its other claims that the CIA's "representations of 'effectiveness' were almost entirely inaccurate and mirrored other inaccurate information provided to the White House, Congress, and the CIA inspector general."[134] Based upon our examination of the "effectiveness" case studies, we assess that the CIA's Detention and Interrogation Program, to include the use of enhanced interrogation techniques, was effective and yielded valuable intelligence. The Study's exaggerated and absolute claims about inaccurate "effectiveness" representations by the CIA have been largely discredited by these minority views and the CIA's June 27, 2013, response to the Study. For the most part, we found that the CIA acknowledged those representations that were made in error or could have benefited from the inclusion of additional clarification.

(U) Conclusion 9 (CIA Impeded Oversight by CIA Office of Inspector General)

(U) Conclusion 9 states, "[t]he CIA impeded oversight by the CIA's Office of Inspector General."[135] However, we found that the Study itself is replete with examples that lead to the opposite conclusion—that the CIA did not significantly impede oversight by the CIA Office of the Inspector General (OIG). The law requires the CIA Inspector General to certify that "the Inspector General has had full and direct access to all information relevant to the performance of his function."[136] Yet, during the timeframe of the Program, the Inspector General certified in every one of its semiannual reports that it had "full and direct access to all CIA information

---

[132] *See* SSCI Study. Executive Summary. December 3. 2014. pp. 416-418.
[133] SSCI Study, Executive Summary, December 3, 2014, p. 417.
[134] SSCI Study, Executive Summary, December 3, 2014, p. 426.
[135] SSCI Study, Findings and Conclusions, December 3, 2014, p. 8.
[136] 50 U.S.C. 3517(d)(1)(D).

relevant to the performance of its oversight duties."[137] The law also requires the Inspector General to *immediately* report to the congressional intelligence committees if the Inspector General is "unable to obtain significant documentary information in the course of an investigation, inspection or audit . . . ."[138] Again, we are not aware of any such report being made to the SSCI during the relevant time period. We do know, however, that John Helgerson, the CIA Inspector General, testified before SSCI prior to the commencement of the SSCI's review of the CIA Detention and Interrogation Program in February 2007 and did not complain of access to Agency information.[139] Instead, he said that, during 2006, the IG took a comprehensive look at the operations of the CIA's Counterterrorism Center and conducted a separate comprehensive audit of detention facilities. General Helgerson also testified,

> [W]e look carefully at *all* cases of alleged abuse of detainees. The first paper of this kind that came to the Committee was in October 2003, not long after these programs had begun, when we looked at allegations of unauthorized interrogation techniques used at one of our facilities. It proved that indeed unauthorized techniques had been used. I'm happy to say that the processes worked properly. An Accountability Board was held. The individuals were in fact disciplined. The system worked as it should.

> On this subject, Mr. Chairman, I cannot but underscore that we also look at a fair number of cases where, at the end of the day, we find that we cannot find that there was substance to the allegation that came to our attention. We, of course, make careful record of these investigations because we think it important that you and others know that we investigate all allegations, some of which are borne out, some of which are not.[140]

(U) Another possible indicator of impeded oversight would be evidence that the CIA OIG was blocked from conducting or completing its desired reviews of the Program. The Study itself acknowledges the existence of at least 29 OIG investigations on detainee-related issues, including 23 that were open or had been completed in 2005.[141] We would also expect to see

---

[137] *See* CIA OIG, *Semi-Annual Report to the Director, Central Intelligence Agency.* July-December 2006, p. 5 (DTS 2007-0669); CIA OIG, *Semi-Annual Report to the Director, Central Intelligence Agency.* January-June 2006, p. 5 (DTS 2006-3195); CIA OIG, *Semi-Annual Report to the Director, Central Intelligence Agency.* July-December 2005, p. 5 (DTS 2006-0678); CIA OIG, *Semi-Annual Report to the Director. Central Intelligence Agency.* January-June 2005, p. 5 (DTS 2005-3140); CIA OIG, *Semi-Annual Report to the Director of Central Intelligence.* January-June 2004, p. 5 (DTS 2004-3307); and CIA OIG. *Semi-Annual Report to the Director of Central Intelligence.* January-June 2003, p. 5 (DTS 2003-3327); CIA Study Response, *Comments (TAB A),* June 27, 2013, pp. 4-6; and 10; and CIA Study Response, *Conclusions (TAB B),* June 27, 2013, pp. 7-9.
[138] 50 U.S.C. 3517(d)(3)(E).
[139] *See* SSCI Transcript, *Hearing on the Central Intelligence Agency Rendition Program.* February 14, 2007, p. 24 (DTS 2007-1337).
[140] SSCI Transcript, *Hearing on the Central Intelligence Agency Rendition Program,* February 14, 2007, p. 25 (DTS 2007-1337).
[141] SSCI Study, Volume I, April 1, 2014, p. 899 n.6257. The CIA asserts that the "OIG conducted nearly 60 investigations" related to the CIA's Detention and Interrogation Program and that the OIG found the initial allegations in 50 of these investigations to be unsubstantiated or did not make findings warranting an accountability review. Of the remaining 10 investigations, one resulted in a felony conviction, one resulted in the termination of a

indications in completed OIG reports that the investigation was hampered by limited access to documents, personnel, or site locations necessary for completing such investigations. Again, according to the OIG's own reports, we found evidence that the OIG had extensive access to documents, personnel, and locations. For example, in its May 2004 Special Review of the RDI program, the CIA OIG reported that it was provided more than 38,000 pages of documents and conducted more than 100 interviews, including with the DCI, the Deputy Director of the CIA, the Executive Director, the General Counsel, and the Deputy Director of Operations. The OIG made site visits to two interrogation facilities ████████████ and reviewed 92 videotapes of the interrogation of Abu Zubaydah. The CIA IG's 2006 Audit is another good example of extensive access to documents, personnel, and locations. During this audit, the OIG not only conducted interviews of current and former officials responsible for CIA-controlled detention facilities, but it also reviewed operational cable traffic in extremely restricted access databases, reports, other Agency documents, policies, standard operating procedures, and guidelines pertaining to the detention program. The OIG also had access to the facilities and officials responsible for managing and operating three detention sites. The OIG was able to review documentation on site, observe detainees through closed-circuit television or one-way mirrors, and the IG even observed the transfer of a detainee aboard a transport aircraft. They even reviewed the medical and operational files maintained on each detainee in those locations.[142]

(U) Conclusion 10 (The CIA Released Classified Information on EITs to the Media)

(U) Conclusion 10 asserts, "[t]he CIA coordinated the release of classified information to the media, including inaccurate information concerning the effectiveness of the CIA's enhanced interrogation techniques."[143] This conclusion insinuates that there was something improper about the manner in which the CIA managed the process by which information about the Detention and Interrogation Program was disclosed to the media. We found the National Security Council Policy Coordinating Committee determined that the CIA would have "the lead" on the "Public Diplomacy issue regarding detainees."[144]

(U) The Study also repeats one of its main faulty claims—that the CIA released inaccurate information about the Program's effectiveness. Our examination of the record revealed that the CIA's disclosures were authorized and that the CIA's representations about the Program were largely accurate. Specifically, we found that the Study's flawed analytical methodology cannot negate the reality that the CIA's Detention and Interrogation Program set up an effective cycle of events whereby al-Qa'ida terrorists were removed from the battlefield, which had a disruptive effect on their current terrorist activities and often permitted the Intelligence Community to collect additional intelligence, which, in turn, often led back to the

contractor and the revocation of his security clearances, and six led to Agency accountability reviews. CIA Study Response, *Conclusions (TAB B)*, June 27, 2013, p. 7.
[142] "CIA-controlled Detention Facilities Operated Under the 17 September 2001 Memorandum of Notification," July 14, 2006, APPENDIX A, page 1-2, DTS 2006-2793.
[143] SSCI Study, Findings and Conclusions, December 3, 2014, p. 8.
[144] Email from: ████████ to: CIA attorney; subject: Brokaw interview: Take one; date: April 15, 2005, at 1:00 PM.

capture of more terrorists. We also found, with a few limited exceptions, that the CIA generally did a good job in explaining the Program's accomplishments to policymakers.

(U) CONCLUSION

The CIA called the detention program a "crucial pillar of US counterterrorism efforts, aiding intelligence and law enforcement operations to capture additional terrorists, helping to thwart terrorist plots, and advancing our analysis of the al-Qa'ida target."[145] We agree. We have no doubt that the CIA's detention program saved lives and played a vital role in weakening al-Qa'ida while the Program was in operation. When asked about the value of detainee information and whether he missed the intelligence from it, one senior CIA operator ▮ ▮ told members, "I miss it every day."[146] We understand why.

---

[145] Detainee Reporting Pivotal for the War Against al-Qa'ida, June 1, 2005, p. i.
[146] ▮ Chambliss, ▮ conversation between SSCI members and CIA officers, ▮

MINORITY VIEWS OF VICE CHAIRMAN CHAMBLISS,
SENATORS BURR, RISCH, COATS, RUBIO, AND COBURN[1]

(U) INTRODUCTION

(U) In January 2009, as one of his first official acts, President Obama issued three Executive orders relating to the detention and interrogation of terror suspects, one of which ended the Central Intelligence Agency's (CIA) Detention and Interrogation Program ("the Program" or "the Detention and Interrogation Program"). At the same time, there were ongoing calls from critics of the Program for the appointment of a special committee or independent commission to review the Program and "hold accountable" those involved. Against this backdrop, in March 2009, the Senate Select Committee on Intelligence ("SSCI" or "Committee") decided, by a vote of 14-1, to initiate a *Study of the Central Intelligence Agency's Detention and Interrogation Program,* hereinafter "the Study," and adopt Terms of Reference.[2] While most minority members supported the Study in the hope that a fair, objective, and apolitical look at the Program could put calls for an "aggressive"[3] and burdensome Commission to rest and might result in thoughtful and helpful recommendations for detention and interrogation policy going forward, Senator Chambliss was the sole Committee member to vote against the Committee conducting this review.[4] He believed then, as today, that vital Committee and Intelligence Community resources would be squandered and the Committee's ability to conduct effective intelligence oversight would be jeopardized by looking in the rear-view mirror and debating matters that were, in practice, already settled by Congress, the executive branch, and the Supreme Court.

(U) Indeed, by the time the Study began, Congress had passed two separate acts directly related to detention and interrogation issues, specifically the Detainee Treatment Act of 2005 (DTA) and the Military Commissions Act of 2006 (MCA). The executive branch had terminated the CIA's program, ordered the closure of the Guantanamo Bay, Cuba, detention facility within one year, directed a review of detention and interrogation policies, and required that—except for the use of authorized, non-coercive interrogation techniques by federal law enforcement

---

[1] When these minority views were initially written in response to the original Study approved by the United States Senate Select Committee on Intelligence on December 13, 2012, the following members of the Committee signed on to them: Vice Chairman Chambliss joined by Senators Burr, Risch, Coats, Blunt, and Rubio. [[Please note that the double-bracketed text in this document is new explanatory text necessitated by substantive modifications to the Study's Executive Summary and Findings and Conclusions that were made *after* our June 20, 2014, Minority Views were submitted to the Central Intelligence Agency for the declassification review. We also note that these Minority Views are in response to, and at points predicated upon, the research and foundational work that underlie the Study's account of the CIA Detention and Interrogation Program. These Views should not be treated as an independent report based upon a separate investigation, but rather our evaluation and critique of the Study's problematic analysis, factual findings, and conclusions.]]

[2] SSCI Transcript, *Business Meeting to Discuss and Revote on the Terms of Reference for the Committee's Study of the CIA's Detention and Interrogation Program,* March 5, 2009, pp. 10-11 (DTS 2009-1916).

[3] *See e.g.,* SSCI Transcript, *Business Meeting to Discuss the Committee's Investigation of the CIA's Detention and Interrogation Program,* February 11, 2009, p. 69 (DTS 2009-1420) (description by Majority member of potential commission on this matter).

[4] SSCI Transcript, *Business Meeting to Discuss and Revote on the Terms of Reference for the Committee's Study of the CIA's Detention and Interrogation Program,* March 5, 2009, p. 10 (DTS 2009-1916).

1

agencies—future interrogations be conducted in accordance with the U.S. Army Field Manual on Interrogation. The Supreme Court had decided *Rasul v. Bush*, 542 U.S. 466 (2004), *Hamdi v. Rumsfeld*, 542 U.S. 507 (2004), *Hamdan v. Rumsfeld*, 548 U.S. 557 (2006), and *Boumediene v. Bush*, 553 U.S. 723 (2008), which established that detainees were entitled to habeas corpus review and identified certain deficiencies in both the DTA and MCA.

(U) Nonetheless, a majority of Committee members agreed to review the Program, and after its inception, the Study proceeded in a bipartisan manner until August 24, 2009, when Attorney General Eric Holder announced that the Department of Justice (DOJ) had re-opened a preliminary review into whether federal criminal laws were violated in connection with the interrogation of specific detainees at overseas locations.[5] Once the Attorney General made this announcement, the minority correctly predicted that the criminal investigation would frustrate the Committee's efforts to conduct a thorough and effective review of the Program. Absent a grant of immunity, key CIA witnesses would likely follow the inevitable and understandable advice of counsel and decline to participate in any Committee interviews or hearings. This situation would make it very difficult for the Committee to comply with one of the key requirements in the Terms of Reference adopted for the Study, which specifically called for interviews of witnesses and testimony at hearings.

(U) Without interviews, the Study was essentially limited to a cold document review with more questions likely raised than answered. Although in a prior, related review of the destruction of CIA's interrogation video tapes, the Committee had wisely suspended its own review rather than forego interviews or potentially jeopardize a criminal investigation, inexplicably, this precedent was not followed in the case of the Study. When Chairman Feinstein decided to continue the Study despite these impediments to a full and accurate review, then-Vice Chairman Bond informed her that he had directed the minority staff to withdraw from further active participation.

(U) On August 30, 2012, Attorney General Holder announced the closure of the criminal investigation into the interrogation of certain detainees in the Detention and Interrogation Program.[6] This provided the Committee a window of opportunity to invite relevant witnesses in for interviews, but that course of action was not pursued.

(U) THE STUDY'S FLAWED PROCESS

(S) Now, five years later, the minority's prediction has come to pass. With the decision not to conduct interviews, the latest version of the Study is a [[6,682]]-page interpretation of documents that, according to the CIA, has cost the American taxpayer more than 40 million dollars and diverted countless CIA analytic and support resources.[7] After expending tens of thousands of Committee and CIA staff working hours, this Study does not even offer *a single*

---

[5] DOJ. *Attorney General Eric Holder Regarding a Preliminary Review into the Interrogation of Certain Detainees*, August 24, 2009, p. 1.
[6] *See* DOJ, *Statement of Attorney General Eric Holder on Closure of investigation into the Interrogation of Certain Detainees*, August 30, 2012, p. 1.
[7] CIA, Letter from V. Sue Bromley, Associate Deputy Director, November 6, 2012, p. 1 (DTS 2012-4143).

recommendation for improving our intelligence interrogation practices—even though the Terms of Reference expressly contemplated both findings and recommendations.[8] Rather, the Study purports to serve intelligence oversight interests by proffering 20 questionable and inflammatory conclusions attacking the CIA's integrity and credibility in developing and implementing the Program. To us, this Study appears to be more of an exercise of partisan politics than effective congressional oversight of the Intelligence Community.

(U) It is important to understand that the Executive Summary and the Findings and Conclusions which the Committee recently sent to the executive branch for a declassification review are not the same documents that were approved by the Committee during the 112th Congress or even at the April 3, 2014, declassification review business meeting. The original Executive Summary had 282 pages; the updated business meeting version had 479 pages; and the updated version transmitted to President Obama had 488 pages. Conversely, the original Findings and Conclusions shrank down from 95 pages to 31-page updated business meeting version, only to shrink further to the 20-page updated version that was transmitted to the President. The 20 conclusions originally approved by the Committee during the 112th Congress are not the same as the 20 conclusions sent for declassification review. For example, two of the original conclusions—Conclusions 2 and 11—were dropped and two other conclusions—Conclusions 9 and 19—were split in a manner that kept the total number of conclusions at 20. Although some remnants of Conclusions 2 and 11 can still be found in the Study, we believe that these conclusions were properly dropped as headline conclusions. While there have been numerous and repeated calls for the declassification of the Study since it was adopted on December 13, 2012,[9] these individuals and groups did not understand that they were calling for the release of a report that was still being re-written more than 15 months after it was first approved by the Committee.

(U) Failure to Interview Witnesses

(U) Although the Study asserts that it "is the most comprehensive review ever conducted of the CIA's Detention and Interrogation Program,"[10] it began to experience serious problems when the Attorney General decided to re-open the criminal inquiry into the Program in 2009. The Attorney General's decision resulted in the Committee's inability to interview key witnesses during the pendency of that inquiry and led to significant analytical and factual errors in the

---

[8] *See* SSCI Review of the Central Intelligence Agency's Detention and Interrogation Program (SSCI Study). December 13. 2013 (SSCI Study), Volume I, pp. 1214-1215.

[9] On December 12, 2012, 26 retired generals and admirals urged the Committee to adopt the Study and make it public with as few redactions as possible. In early January 2013, Senators Feinstein, Levin, and McCain criticized the movie *Zero Dark Thirty* for its portrayal of the decade-long hunt for Usama Bin Ladin, because they believed it suggested that information obtained by torturing al-Qa'ida detainees aided in locating him. On November 26, 2013, the American Civil Liberties Union filed a lawsuit under the Freedom of Information Act to compel the CIA to release the SSCI Study and the CIA's June 27, 2013, response. On December 13, 2013, the Center for Victims of Torture released a statement supporting the release of the Study signed by 58 retired generals and admirals, national security experts, foreign policy experts, and religious leaders.

[10] SSCI Study, Executive Summary, December 3, 2014, p. 9. It would be more precise to assert that the SSCI Study is the most comprehensive *documentary* review ever conducted of the CIA's Detention and Interrogation Program.

3

original and subsequently updated versions of the Study, a point we made in our original minority views and one that was strongly echoed in the CIA response.

(U) In a *Washington Post* opinion piece published on April 10, 2014, the current and former Chairmen of the Senate Select Committee on Intelligence admitted that:

> Although the committee was not able to conduct new interviews, it had access to and used transcripts from more than 100 interviews conducted by the CIA inspector general and other agency offices while the program was ongoing and shortly after it ended. Many of these transcripts were from interviews of the same people the committee would have talked to, with answers to the same questions that would have been asked. This included top managers, lawyers, counterterrorism personnel, analysts, interrogators and others at the CIA.[11]

While these statements are true and might lead someone to infer that these interview transcripts may have been adequate substitutes for conducting new interviews of these key personnel, the Study itself appears to reach the opposite conclusion:

> There are no indications in CIA records that any of the past reviews attempted to independently validate the intelligence claims related to the CIA's use of its enhanced interrogation techniques that were presented by CIA personnel in interviews and documents. As such, no previous review confirmed whether the specific intelligence cited by the CIA was acquired from a CIA detainee during or after being subjected to the CIA's enhanced interrogation techniques or if the intelligence acquired was otherwise unknown to the United States government ("otherwise unavailable"), and therefore uniquely valuable.[12]

We suppose that this critique is leveled against the CIA IG Special Report, at least in part, because the special report concluded that:

> The detention of terrorists has prevented them from engaging in further terrorist activity, and their interrogation has provided intelligence that has enabled the identification and apprehension of terrorists, warned of terrorist plots planned for the United States and around the world, and supported articles frequently used in the finished intelligence publications for senior policymakers and war fighters. *In this regard, there is no doubt that the Program has been effective.* Measuring the effectiveness of EITs, however, is more subjective process and not without some concern.[13]

The CIA OIG Special Report also noted that George Tenet, the Director of Central Intelligence (DCI), said he believed, "the use of EITs has proven to be extremely valuable in obtaining

[11] http://www.washingtonpost.com/opinions/the-senate-report-on-the-cias-interrogation-program-should-be-made-public/2014/04/10/eeeb237a-c0c3-11e3-bcec-b7fee10e9bc3_story.html.
[12] SSCI Study, Executive Summary, December 3, 2014, p. 179.
[13] CIA, Office of Inspector General, *Special Review: Counterterrorism Detention and Interrogation Activities. (September 2001 – October 2003)*, May 7, 2004, p. 85 (DTS 2004-2710) (emphasis added).

enormous amounts of critical threat information from detainees who had otherwise believed they were safe from any harm in the hands of Americans."[14]

(U) The Study cannot have it both ways. Either the CIA IG Special Review interview transcripts were adequate substitutes for new interviews or they were not. Conclusion 9 of the Study states that the "CIA impeded oversight by the CIA's Office of Inspector General."[15] Specifically, the Study alleges that "[d]uring the OIG reviews, CIA personnel provided OIG with inaccurate information on the operation and management of the CIA's Detention and Interrogation Program, as well as on the effectiveness of the CIA's enhanced interrogation techniques."[16] This conclusion seems to establish that the prior interview transcripts were inadequate substitutes for new interviews. While we do not agree with Conclusion 9, or any of the other conclusions examined in these views, it seems pretty clear that the lack of new interviews has prevented the Committee from conducting the comprehensive review that was envisioned in the original Terms of Reference. Unlike the Study, we are willing to acknowledge that our own analysis in these views was similarly hampered by the inability to interview key personnel who might be able to shed light on any documentary inconsistencies or inaccurate interpretations. Regardless, we remain convinced that the minority's non-partisan decision to withdraw from further active participation in the Study was the correct decision.

(U) Insufficient Member Review of the Approved Study

(U) Our concerns about the quality of the Study's analysis drove our efforts, before and during the Committee's business meeting on December 13, 2012, to implore the majority to give members sufficient opportunity to review the Study and submit it for review and comment by the Intelligence Community prior to a vote. Unfortunately, members were only given a little over three weeks to review the 2,148 pages released in the last tranche of the draft Study prior to the vote for adoption at the scheduled business meeting. This material provided the first look at the majority's analysis of the effectiveness of the interrogation program and became the core of the report adopted by the Committee. This last tranche contained nearly all of the most consequential analysis and—with the 282-page Executive Summary and the 95-pages of Findings and Conclusions provided to members for the first time just *three days* prior to the business meeting—comprised 40 percent of the adopted Study. The *day before* the December 13, 2012, business meeting, the Committee members received another "final version" of the report that made extensive changes to Study text, including the conclusions.[17] This unreasonably short time-period to review thousands of pages of text essentially precluded the possibility of formulating and offering amendments to the Study—had such an opportunity even been afforded to our Committee members.

---

[14] CIA Office of Inspector General, *Special Review: Counterterrorism Detention and Interrogation Activities (September 2001 – October 2003)*. May 7, 2004, p. 88-89 (DTS 2004-2710).

[15] SSCI Study, Findings and Conclusions, December 3, 2014, p. 8.

[16] SSCI Study, Findings and Conclusions, December 3, 2014, p. 8.

[17] *See* SSCI Transcript, *Business Meeting to Consider the Report on the CIA Detention and Interrogation Program*, December 13, 2012, p. 25 (DTS 2013-0452).

(U) Aside from the sheer volume of the material, underlying the request for more time was the fact that almost all of the source material used to write the Study was located 40 minutes from Capitol Hill and thus not readily accessible to members and staff during the busiest month of the 112th Congress, when the Committee was simultaneously working on the Study, the Intelligence Authorization Act for Fiscal Year 2013, Foreign Intelligence Surveillance Act reauthorization, and its review of the Benghazi attacks. Nevertheless, the Chairman denied the Vice Chairman's request both prior to, and during, the Committee's business meeting for more time to review the draft Study.

(U) Insufficient Initial Fact Checking

(U) The 2,148-page tranche release, which specifically addressed the intelligence acquired from the Program and the CIA's representations regarding the effectiveness of the Program, also made serious allegations attacking the honesty and integrity of the CIA as an institution and of many of its senior and junior officers. In preparing this part of the Study, the majority selected 20 cases in which they claim the CIA inaccurately described information acquired from the interrogation program. This is ironic, since we found the Study itself consistently mischaracterized CIA's analysis. In each of these 20 cases, the Study absolutely and categorically dismissed any correlation previously drawn by the CIA between the Detention and Interrogation Program and the capture of terrorists, thwarting of terrorist plots, or the collection of significant intelligence. There is no ambiguity in the Study's indictment: in every one of these cases, the CIA and its officers lied—to Congress, to the White House, to the Department of Justice, and ultimately to the American people.

(U) We believe that the serious nature of these original conclusions required, as the Committee has done in the past with reports of such magnitude, submitting the Study to the Intelligence Community for review and comment before the vote. This deviation not only hampered the Committee's efforts to approve a factually accurate report, but it deprived the Intelligence Community of its traditional opportunity to provide important feedback to the Committee prior to the approval of the Study. Moreover, the near absence of any timely interviews of relevant Intelligence Community witnesses during the course of this Study was a warning flag that should have signaled the increased need for initial fact-checking prior to the Study's adoption.

(U) The Committee has a long-standing practice of sending reports to the executive branch for review dating back to the Church Committee reports in 1975.[18] More recently, in 2004, the Committee provided the draft report on the *U.S. Intelligence Community's Prewar Intelligence Assessments on Iraq* to the Intelligence Community for fact-checking. The Committee wanted to ensure that a report of that magnitude, which purported to tell the Intelligence Community why years of analysis on Iraq's weapons of mass destruction programs was wrong, needed to be unquestionably accurate and not subject to challenge by the Intelligence Community. Only after the Intelligence Community provided its feedback and after the Committee held a hearing with the Director of Central Intelligence to give him the chance to

---

[18] *See* Loch K. Johnson, *A Season of Inquiry: The Senate Intelligence Investigation.* University Press of Kentucky, Lexington, 1985, p. 108.

comment on the record, did the Committee vote on the report. Thus, both the Committee and the Intelligence Community had a full and fair opportunity to review and check the report before a vote and before members provided additional or minority views. Also, unlike this Study, the Committee had conducted over 200 interviews with Intelligence Community witnesses who, over the course of a year, provided the investigative staff with information, insight, and clarification that could not be found in the documents alone.

(U) Unfortunately, in spite of a specific request at the December 2012 business meeting to follow these precedents, the majority refused to do so. Adhering to our established precedent for a report of this importance would have sent a clear signal to the entire Intelligence Community that the Committee's primary goal was to provide an accurate accounting of the Detention and Interrogation Program. Had the CIA been allowed to do so, the Study could have been modified, if necessary, or if not, members would at least have had the benefit of understanding the CIA's perspective prior to casting their votes. Yet, because the Committee approved the Study as final, before the Study had been sent to the Intelligence Community for review, the CIA was placed in the unenviable position—not of fact-checking—but of critiquing the Study of its own oversight Committee. In doing so, the Committee significantly undermined and diminished its own credibility.

(U) The CIA Response

(U) On June 27, 2013, the CIA provided a 130-page response to the original Study approved during the 112th Congress. The CIA also provided a two-page response to our initial minority views.[19] The purpose of the CIA response was to focus "on the Agency's conduct of the RDI program, in the interest of promoting historical accuracy and identifying lessons learned for the future, with the ultimate goal of improving the Agency's execution of other covert action programs."[20] The CIA noted, however, that a comprehensive review of the Study's almost 6,000 pages was an impossible task given the time allotted. They chose to concentrate their efforts on the Study's 20 conclusions and that part of the Study that assessed the value of the information derived from the CIA's RDI activities. When the CIA was able to review certain portions of the Study in detail, it found that the Study's accuracy "was encumbered as much by the authors' interpretation, selection, and contextualization of the facts as it was by errors in their recitation of the facts, making it difficult to address its flaws with specific technical correction."[21]

(U) Consistent with our own observations, the CIA response found that, while the Study has all the appearances of an authoritative history of the CIA's Detention and Interrogation Program and contains an impressive amount of detail, it fails in significant and consequential ways to correctly portray and analyze that detail. The CIA attributed these failures to two basic limitations on the authors: (1) a methodology that relied exclusively on a review of documents with no opportunity to interview participants; and (2) an apparent lack of familiarity with some of the ways the CIA analyzes and uses intelligence.[22]

---

[19] We modified these minority views based upon the CIA's input.

[20] CIA Study Response. *Comments (TAB A)*, June 27, 2013, p. 1.

[21] CIA Study Response, *Comments (TAB A)*, June 27, 2013, pp. 1-2.

[22] CIA Study Response. *Comments (TAB A)*, June 27, 2013, p. 2.

(U) Unlike the Study, the CIA response actually offered eight specific recommendations for improving future covert actions: (1) improve management's ability to manage risk by submitting more covert action programs to the special review process currently used ▓▓▓▓ ▓▓▓▓ (2) better plan covert actions by explicitly addressing at the outset the implications of leaks, an exit strategy, lines of authority, and resources; (3) revamp the way in which CIA assesses the effectiveness of covert actions; (4) ensure that all necessary information is factored into the selection process for officers being considered for the most sensitive assignments; (5) create a mechanism for periodically revalidating Office of Legal Counsel guidance on which the Agency continues to rely; (6) broaden the scope of accountability reviews; (7) improve recordkeeping for interactions with the media; and (8) improve recordkeeping for interactions with Congress.[23] We believe the CIA should implement these recommendations.

(U) The Summer Meetings

(U) During the summer and early fall of 2013, SSCI staff spent about sixty hours with CIA personnel who had led and participated in the preparation of the CIA's response to the Study. The purpose of these meetings was to discuss factual discrepancies and areas of disagreement between the SSCI Study and the CIA Study Response. These exchanges would have been much more productive if they had occurred *before* the Study was approved by the Committee in December 2012.

(U) The majority staff did not start these sessions with discussions about the substance of the Study or the CIA's response. Rather, they began by spending an inordinate amount of time questioning the CIA personnel about the process by which the CIA had prepared its response to the Study. Eventually, the discussions turned to more substantive issues. Prior to each session, the majority staff typically determined the order in which the Study conclusions would be discussed. Although the CIA and minority staff expressed repeated interest in discussing some of the more problematic conclusions and underlying "effectiveness" case studies, the majority staff proceeded with discussions of the least controversial portions of the Study.

(U) Our staff reported to us that the general tenor of these sessions was "unpleasant." Instead of giving the CIA an opportunity to help improve the Study by explaining the errors and factual inaccuracies identified in their response, the majority staff spent the vast majority of these sessions in "transmit" rather than "receive" mode. When the discussions finally turned to the "effectiveness" case studies, the majority staff spent a significant portion of the remaining time explaining its "methodology" and reading large portions of the report into the record. The CIA initially made arrangements to have certain key analysts participate in these discussions to help the Committee understand the meaning of certain parts of the historical documentary record. Unfortunately, these analysts were often kept waiting outside of the meeting room while the majority staff plowed through its set agenda with the senior CIA personnel. Some of those waiting analysts never received an opportunity to participate. Seeing the writing on the wall, the lead CIA personnel eventually stopped bringing the pertinent analysts along, which did not seem

---

[23] CIA Study Response. *Comments (TAB A)*. June 27, 2013, pp. 17-18.

to concern the majority staff. The most problematic case studies were summarily discussed in just a few hours during the very last session.

(U) Given the unproductive manner in which these meetings were conducted, the Committee missed a significant opportunity to improve its Study through a better understanding of the CIA's analytical and operational practices that produced the documentary record upon which the Study was based. We commend the CIA personnel who patiently and professionally participated in these unproductive sessions and thank them for their dedicated service to our Nation.

(U) The Clash Over the Panetta Review

(U) On January 15, 2014, Chairman Feinstein and Vice Chairman Chambliss met with the Director of the Central Intelligence Agency (CIA), John Brennan, at his urgent request. At this meeting, Director Brennan disclosed that the CIA conducted a "search"[24] of a CIA computer network used by the Committee. The CIA established this network at a CIA facility in 2009 pursuant to written agreements between the Committee and then-Director Leon Panetta. It is the understanding of the Committee that the CIA conducted the "Panetta Internal Review" for the purpose of summarizing for CIA leadership the contents of documents likely to be reviewed by the Committee during its review.

(U) As evidenced by repeated unauthorized disclosures in the news media, the production and release of the Study has been marred by the alleged misconduct of CIA employees and majority staff as it pertains to the so-called "Panetta Internal Review." Regardless of differences of opinion and policy, the relationship between the CIA and this Committee should not have escalated to this level of embarrassment and provocation. It is one of the most delicate oversight relationships in the Federal government and must be treated as such at all times. It would be a shame if this incident tarnished the reputation of the Committee or the CIA to such a degree that the normally constructive cooperation between the CIA and the Committee is scarred beyond repair.

(U) Typically, matters such as these are handled discreetly through the accommodation process and would involve internal investigations or joint inquiries. These options were not available in this situation. Presently, the Department of Justice, the CIA Inspector General, and the U.S. Senate Sergeant at Arms are conducting ongoing investigation into these matters. Nonetheless, for the purpose of these Views, it is worth noting the following observations:

(U) First, Committee majority staff knowingly removed the Panetta Internal Review, a highly classified, privileged CIA document, from a CIA facility without authorization and in clear violation of the existing agreed-upon procedures by the Committee and the CIA.

---

[24] The 2009 written agreement permitted CIA access to the network for technical support, but at the time of this writing, the forensic details of the CIA "search" are unknown.

(U) Second, although the Committee certainly needs to understand the facts and circumstances of whether the CIA acted inappropriately when it allegedly "searched" a Committee shared drive on certain CIA computers, this issue is separate and distinct from the earlier incident involving the unauthorized removal of the Panetta Internal Review document from the CIA facility. The subsequent "search" does not excuse or justify the earlier staff behavior or vice versa.

(U) Third, the Panetta Internal Review document that was brought back to Committee spaces was not handled in accordance with Committee protocols. Committee Rule 9.4 states, "Each member of the Committee shall at all times have access to all papers and other material received from any source." It appears that the existence, handling, and the majority's possession of this privileged document were not disclosed to the minority for months, and might never have been revealed but for the public disclosures about the document which led to the January meeting with Director Brennan.

(U) Finally, given the CIA's repeated assertions of privilege concerning the document since the January meeting with Director Brennan, at no time has a minority member or staff handled the document or reviewed its contents.

(U) The Declassification Review Business Meeting

(U) The majority's practice of providing insufficient time for member review of the report's contents was repeated just prior to the Committee's April 3, 2014, business meeting to consider whether to send the report to the executive branch for a declassification review. On April 1, 2014, updated versions of the Study's three volume report, totaling 6,178 pages, were made available on a Committee shared drive. The majority staff did not release its third updated versions of the Executive Summary and Findings and Conclusions *until the day before the business meeting*. Finally, *four days after the business meeting*, the Chairman transmitted to President Obama one last revised version of the updated Executive Summary and Findings and Conclusions.[25]

(U) THE STUDY'S PROBLEMATIC ANALYSIS

(U) As previously discussed, the flawed process used for the approval of the original Study and this updated version resulted in numerous factual errors. These factual errors were further compounded by the Study's numerous analytical shortfalls, which ultimately led to an unacceptable number of incorrect claims and invalid conclusions. This section will generally highlight many of the analytical shortcomings we found in the Study. The next section will then specifically examine some of the Study's most problematic conclusions, including our analysis of the factual premises, claims, and flawed analytical methodology upon which many of these faulty conclusions were based.

---

[25] The citations to the updated Executive Summary and Findings and Conclusions in these minority views have been revised to match up with the versions that were transmitted to the President. The citations to the updated three-volume report are keyed to the versions that were placed on the Committee's shared drive.

(U) When this Committee reviews the Intelligence Community's analytic products, it does so with the expectation of adherence to certain analytic integrity standards.[26] These standards "act as guidelines and goals for analysts and managers throughout the Intelligence Community who strive for excellence in their analytic work practices and products."[27] Although these specific analytic standards do not technically apply to this Committee's oversight reporting, the aspirational analytical values they represent are applicable to the Committee's analytical expectations for its own oversight work product. The examples offered in this section illustrate some of the Study's general analytic deficiencies concerning objectivity, independence from political considerations, timeliness, the use of all available intelligence sources, and consistency with proper standards of analytic tradecraft. These examples also serve as a useful backdrop for our specific analysis and critique of some of the Study's erroneous conclusions and claims.[28]

(U) Inadequate Context

(TS█████████NF) We begin, however, with a review of the context in which the CIA Program was initiated and operated. Although there is no specific, Intelligence Community analytic standard addressing context, it is important in any analysis or report to provide appropriate context so that the reader is able to understand why events transpired as they did. The Study does very little to provide such context—it is entirely silent on the surge in terrorist threat reporting that inundated the Intelligence Community following the September 11, 2001, terrorist attacks by al-Qa'ida, and it makes no mention of the pervasive, genuine apprehension about a possible second attack on the United States that gripped the CIA in 2002 and 2003. Rather, the Study begins by coldly describing the September 17, 2001, covert action Memorandum of Notification (MON) signed by the President authorizing the CIA to detain "persons who pose a continuing, serious threat of violence or death to U.S. persons and interests or who are planning terrorist activities," as if the attacks that had killed nearly 3,000 Americans just six days prior, were incidental to the extraordinary authorities granted under the MON, and all other events described in the Study.[29] They were not. In our collective view, to depict judgments and decisions arising from the administration of this program as having been made in a vacuum, or somehow in isolation of these events, is both unrealistic and unfair.

(U) During our review of the materials provided by the CIA for the Study, we could clearly discern a workforce traumatized by an intelligence failure that had left thousands of Americans dead, but also galvanized by the challenge of working on the frontline to ensure such an attack never occurred again. In the early years of this effort, there were constant threats of new attacks, and endless leads to track down. CIA and other Intelligence Community personnel worked relentlessly, day in and day out, to follow up on every one.

---

[26] In 2004, the SSCI was instrumental in including in the Intelligence Reform and Terrorism Prevention Act, P.L. 108-458, a provision mandating that the Director of National Intelligence "ensure the most accurate analysis" by implementing policies and procedure "to encourage sound analytic tradecraft."

[27] Intelligence Community Directive Number 203, *Analytic Standards* (effective June 21, 2007), p. 1.

[28] *See* Intelligence Community Directive Number 203, *Analytic Standards* (effective June 21, 2007), p. 2.

[29] *See* SSCI Study, Executive Summary, December 3, 2014, p. 11.

(U) There is no doubt that the CIA Program—executed hastily in the aftermath of the worst terrorist attack in our Nation's history—had flaws. The CIA has admitted as much in its June 27, 2013, response to the Study. However, the Study's conclusion that the use of enhanced interrogation techniques was ineffective does not comport with a massive documentary record that clearly demonstrates a series of significant counterterrorism operational successes. That same documentary record also undercuts the Study's flawed conclusions that the CIA "impeded" congressional and executive branch oversight of the Program, as well as the counterterrorism and diplomatic missions of other federal entities. Our review of the record revealed this conclusion—one the Study twists itself in knots to avoid—that the CIA Program was a vital source of critical intelligence that led to the detention of multiple terrorists and helped keep America safe.

(U) Whether the CIA should operate a clandestine detention program and whether it is in America's interests to interrogate suspected terrorists using methods beyond those in the U.S. Army Field Manual are valid questions worthy of serious debate. Unfortunately, the utility of Study's considerable work product in such a debate is seriously undermined by its disregard of the Program's historical context and its reliance upon an unrealistic analytical methodology, which appears to have been designed to exclude from consideration any inconvenient facts not fitting within the Study's preconceived view that such enhanced methods produced nothing of intelligence value. Although there are a number of findings in the Study with which we agree, our own review of the documentary record compelled us to focus our discussion in these minority views on these inconvenient facts that invalidate much of the revisionist history that is being advocated by many of the Study's findings and conclusions.

(U) Inadequate Objectivity

(TS███████████NF) The standard of objectivity requires that analysts perform their analytic functions from an unbiased perspective—analysis "should be free of emotional content, give due regard to alternative perspectives, and acknowledge developments that necessitate adjustments to analytic judgments."[30]

(TS███████████NF) We were disappointed to find the updated version of the Study still contains evidence of strongly held biases by the authors—a point emphasized by John Brennan prior to his confirmation as the Director of the CIA, when he told Vice Chairman Chambliss that, based on his reading of the originally approved Executive Summary and the Findings and Conclusions, the Study was "not objective" and was a "prosecutor's brief," "written with an eye toward finding problems." We still agree with Director Brennan's assessments. We also agree with the criticism he relayed from Intelligence Community officials that it was written with a "bent on the part of the authors" with "political motivations." We similarly found these problems, but more importantly, we found that those biases were not only present, but they resulted in faulty analysis, serious inaccuracies, and misrepresentations of fact in the Study.

---

[30] Intelligence Community Directive Number 203, *Analytic Standards* (effective June 21, 2007), p. 2.

(TS███████████████NF) For example, there were instances when detainees told their interrogators that they had provided everything they knew or denied that they were terrorists, and the Study seems to take them at their word. In June 2002, Abu Zubaydah told his interrogators, "What I have, I give it all . . . I have no more."[31] The Study seems to have bought into this lie when it subsequently concluded, "At no time during or after the aggressive interrogation phase did Abu Zubaydah provide the information that the CIA enhanced [interrogations] were premised upon, specifically, 'actionable intelligence about al-Qa'ida operatives in the United States and planned al-Qa'ida lethal attacks against U.S. citizens and U.S. interests.'"[32]

(TS███████████████NF) In fact, Abu Zubaydah did provide actionable intelligence that helped disrupt planned al-Qa'ida lethal attacks against U.S. citizens and interests following his June 2002 denials of having more information. Although our review of the documentary record revealed that Abu Zubaydah's first period of "aggressive" interrogation actually began on April 15, 2002,[33] he certainly provided valuable intelligence *after* his second period of aggressive interrogation began on August 4, 2002.[34] For example, on August 20, 2002,[35] Abu Zubaydah provided information about how he would go about locating Hassan Ghul and other al-Qa'ida associates in Karachi. This information caused ████████ Pakistani authorities to intensify their efforts and helped lead them to capture Ramzi bin al-Shibh and other al-Qa'ida associates during the Karachi safe house raids conducted on September 10-11, 2002."[36] These arrests effectively disrupted a then ongoing plot to bomb certain named hotels in Karachi, Pakistan.[37] In April 2002, Khalid Shaykh Mohammad (KSM) confirmed the hotels plot had been directed against U.S. citizens and interests when he told his interrogators that the hotels had been selected because they were frequented by American and German guests.[38]

(TS███████████████NF) The Study's lack of objectivity is further illustrated in the acceptance as factual those CIA documents that support its findings and conclusions, and the dismissal of documents contradictory to its findings and conclusions as being "inaccurate" or "misrepresentations." For example, the Study cites to a finished intelligence product published in 2006 as support for its stunning claim that the "CIA later concluded that Abu Zubaydah was not a member of al-Qa'ida."[39] In fact, the product states: "Al-Qa'ida rejected Abu Zubaydah's request *in 1993* to join the group and that Khaldan was not overseen by Bin Ladin's organization."[40] The Study fails to state that the interrogation of this supposed "non-member" resulted in 766 sole-source disseminated intelligence reports by the Study's own count.[41]

---

[31] SSCI Study, Volume I, March 31, 2014, p. 113; CIA, ██████ 10487, June 18, 2002, p. 4.
[32] SSCI Study, Volume I, March 31, 2014, p. 146.
[33] *See infra*, p. 34.
[34] *See* CIA, ██████ 10586, August 4, 2002, pp. 2-5.
[35] *See* CIA, *Captures Resulting From Detainee Information: Four Case Studies*, November 26, 2003, p. 2; CIA, ALEC ██████ August 29, 2002, pp. 2-7.
[36] *See infra*, pp. 38-41.
[37] *See infra*, pp. 45-47.
[38] *See* [REDACTED] 34513, March 5, 2003, p. 2.
[39] SSCI Study, Executive Summary, December 3, 2014, p. 410 n.2301.
[40] CIA, *Countering Misconceptions About Training Camps in Afghanistan, 1990-2001*, August 16, 2006, p. 2 (DTS 2006-3254) (emphasis added).). This document is attached as Appendix I, *see infra*, p. I-1.
[41] *See* SSCI Study, Volume III, March 31, 2014, pp. 282-283.

Ironically, this intelligence product was written based on "information from detainees and captured documents"—including from Abu Zubaydah.[42]

(TS███████████NF) Another indication of the Study's lack of objectivity is its tendency to state its conclusions in such a manner as to be technically accurate, but factually misleading. For example, in the Executive Summary, the Study authors state,

> a review of CIA records found no connection between Abu Zubaydah's reporting on Ramzi bin al-Shibh and Ramzi bin al-Shibh's capture. CIA records indicate that Ramzi bin al-Shibh was captured unexpectedly—on September 11, 2002, when Pakistani authorities, ███████████, were conducting raids targeting Hassan Ghul in Pakistan."[43]

The implication is that none of the information Zubaydah provided pursuant after enhanced interrogation led to al-Shibh's capture. What is ignored here is the exact expression of Zubaydah's role in al-Shibh's apprehension, captured in a CIA internal communication, where it is made clear, "[Zubaydah's] knowledge of al-Qa'ida lower-level facilitators, modus operandi and safehouses, which he shared with us as a result of EITs . . . played a key role in the ultimate capture of Ramzi Bin al-Shibh."[44] Zubaydah's reporting on how to locate terrorists in Pakistan, by trying to find another terrorist, is what led to bin al-Shibh's arrest.[45]

(TS███████████NF) The Study's uneven treatment of key U.S. officials throughout the report, attacking the credibility and honesty of some, while making little mention of others, also lacked objectivity. For example, former Director George Tenet led the CIA at the outset of the Program, during a period the Study contends was characterized by mismanagement. Tenet authorized the enhanced interrogation techniques, and if the Study is to be believed, headed an organization that withheld information from and misled policymakers in the executive branch and Congress. He is mentioned 62 times in the updated version of the Study's Executive Summary. By comparison, former Director Michael Hayden joined the CIA in 2006, after all but two detainees entered the Program and the most severe EITs were no longer in use. He was also the only Director to brief the Program to all members of the congressional oversight committees. Yet, Director Hayden is mentioned 172 times in the Executive Summary, where he is disparaged numerous times. For example, in Conclusion 18, which alleges the CIA marginalized criticisms and objections concerning the Detention and Interrogation Program, the Executive Summary states: "CIA Director Hayden testified to the Committee that 'numerous false allegations of physical and threatened abuse and faulty legal assumptions and analysis in the [ICRC] report undermine its overall credibility.'"[46] The Study also states:

---

[42] CIA, *Countering Misconceptions About Training Camps in Afghanistan, 1990-2001*, August 16, 2006, p. i (DTS 2006-3254).

[43] SSCI Study, Executive Summary, December 3, 2014, p. 318.

[44] CIA Memo from Pavitt to CIA IG on Draft Special Review, February 27, 2004, pp. 13-14. For a more detailed examination of this issue, *see infra*, pp. 38-42.

[45] *See* CIA, ALEC ████ August 29, 2002, pp. 2-3; CIA, ALEC ████ September 11, 2002, p. 2.

[46] SSCI Study, Findings and Conclusions, December 3, 2014, p. 15.

After multiple Senators had been critical of the program and written letters expressing concerns to CIA Director Michael Hayden, Director Hayden nonetheless told a meeting of foreign ambassadors to the United States that every Committee member was 'fully briefed,' and that '[t]his is not CIA's program. This is not the President's program. This is America's program.'[47]

Beyond the imbalance with which some officials are treated in the Study, we are particularly concerned that such treatment will send the perverse message to future CIA Directors and the CIA that they will face less criticism if they keep information limited to only a few members.

(U) Indications of Political Considerations

(U) The analysis and products of the Intelligence Community are supposed to remain independent of political consideration, leaving policy and political determinations to the policymakers and politicians. It follows that, Intelligence Community analysts "should provide objective assessments informed by available information that are not distorted or altered with the intent of supporting or advocating a particular policy, political viewpoint, or audience."[48] Although some might think that this analytic standard would have little applicability to Congress, which is an inherently political body, in the context of congressional oversight of the Intelligence Community, our Committee was designed to function in a bipartisan manner. Thus, this analytical standard is useful in assessing whether a particular Committee oversight report was crafted in a bipartisan manner or suffers from indications of political considerations.

(TS███████NF) Far from being free of political consideration, the Study uses quotes from minority members out of context to suggest they supported positions in the Study, that they in fact did not, and entirely omits contradictory comments. For example, the Study selectively quotes from a February 11, 2009, meeting organized around the discussion of a report prepared by majority staff, evaluating the detention and interrogation of two detainees. The Study indicates that "a Committee staff" presented the report, and quotes Chairman Feinstein saying the review represented, "the most comprehensive statement on the treatment of these two detainees."[49] What the Study fails to note, however, is that Vice Chairman Bond clarified the draft was "the work of two majority staff members," and that neither he, "nor any minority staff was informed of the work going into the memo over the course of the last year." He also noted that the minority had offered some input, but had not been able to review the document thoroughly, or fact check it, and therefore did not view the report as a bipartisan document. Moreover, he noted that the minority staff had just received the remarks the majority staff had prepared, several points of which were subsequently disputed by minority staff during the meeting.[50]

(TS███████NF) The Study also claims that a minority member's comments during the meeting, "expressed support for expanding the Committee investigation to learn more

---

[47] SSCI Study, Executive Summary, December 3, 2014, p. 448.
[48] Intelligence Community Directive Number 203, *Analytic Standards* (effective June 21, 2007), p. 2.
[49] SSCI Study, Volume I, March 31, 2014, p. 1211.
[50] *See* SSCI Transcript, *Business Meeting to Discuss the Committee's Investigation of the CIA's Detention and Interrogation Program*, February 11, 2009, pp. 6-7 and 33-34 (DTS 2009-1420).

about the program."[51] In fact, the member was explaining to two majority members, who were already talking about declassifying a report they had just seen, why he would like to know a lot more "before I pass judgment" on the CIA officers described in the document. Suggesting doubt about the allegations in the document, he commented, "It's hard to believe, and I can't help but think that there isn't more here."[52]

(U) Lack of Timeliness

(U) The analytic integrity standard of timeliness is predicated on maximizing the impact and utility of intelligence, and it encourages the Intelligence Community to produce relevant analysis that effectively informs key policy decisions.[53] The "effectively informs" aspect of this notion means that intelligence products which are published too near to a decision point, let alone after it, are of diminishing or negligible value. This same susceptibility holds true for intelligence oversight reports.

(TS   NF) On January 22, 2009, President Obama issued Executive Order 13491, which required the CIA to "close as expeditiously as possible any detention facilities that it currently operates and . . . not operate any such detention facility in the future." The Executive Order prohibited any U.S. government employee from using interrogation techniques other than those in the Army Field Manual 2-22.3 on Human Intelligence Collector Operations.[54] The Terms of Reference for the Study were approved by the Committee on March 5, 2009.[55] However, the original Study was adopted by the Committee on December 13, 2012— approximately three years and nine months after the approval of the Terms of Reference.[56] On April 3, 2014—*more than five years after* the Terms of Reference were approved—the Committee sent updated versions of the previously approved Executive Summary and Findings and Conclusions to the executive branch for a declassification review.

(TS   NF) This Study purports to represent "the most comprehensive review ever conducted of the CIA's Detention and Interrogation Program."[57] Certainly, there is some utility in the exercise of studying an intelligence program so expansive and intricate, that the document production phase alone lasted more than three years, and produced more than six million pages of material.[58] Normally, a review of this magnitude might be expected to yield valuable lessons learned and best practices, which might then be applied to future intelligence

---

[51] SSCI Study, Volume I, March 31, 2014, p. 1213.

[52] SSCI Transcript, *Business Meeting to Discuss the Committee's Investigation of the CIA's Detention and Interrogation Program*, February 11, 2009, pp. 48-51 (DTS 2009-1420).

[53] *See* Intelligence Community Directive Number 203, *Analytic Standards* (effective June 21, 2007), p. 2.

[54] Executive Order 13491, "Ensuring Lawful Interrogation," January 22, 2009, Section 3(b), p. 2.

[55] *See* SSCI Transcript, *Business Meeting to Discuss and Revote on the Terms of Reference for the Committee's Study of the CIA's Detention and Interrogation Program*, March 5, 2009, p. 11 (DTS 2009-1916).

[56] *See* SSCI Transcript, *Business Meeting to Consider the Report on the CIA Detention and Interrogation Program*, December 13, 2012, p. 74 (DTS 2013-0452).

[57] SSCI Study, Executive Summary, December 3, 2004, p. 9. A more accurate statement would have been, "the most comprehensive *documentary* review ever conducted of the CIA's Detention and Interrogation Program."

[58] SSCI Study, Executive Summary, December 3, 2004, p. 9.

programs. However, no version of the Study has ever contained any recommendations.[59] Moreover, there are no lessons learned, nor are there any suggestions of possible alternative measures. This absence of Committee recommendations is likely due to the fact that the key policy decisions about the CIA's Detention and Interrogation Program were decided years ago by President Obama in 2009. Despite its massive size, the Study does little to effectively inform current policymakers, but rather makes a number of inaccurate historical judgments about the CIA's Program. For these reasons, we conclude that the Study is not timely.

(U) Inadequate Use of Available Sources of Intelligence

(U) Despite the millions of records available for the Study's research, we found that important documents were not reviewed and some were never requested. We were surprised to learn that the e-mails of only 64 individuals were requested to support the review of a program that spanned eight years and included hundreds of government employees. Committee reviews of this magnitude typically involve interviewing the relevant witnesses. Here, these relevant witnesses were largely unavailable due to the Attorney General's decision to re-open a preliminary criminal review in connection with the interrogation of specific detainees at overseas locations. When DOJ closed this investigation in August 2013, however, the Committee had a window of opportunity to invite these relevant witnesses in for interviews, but apparently decided against that course of action. The lack of witness interviews should have been a clear warning flag to all Committee members about the difficulty of completing a truly "comprehensive" review on this subject.

(U) Exhibits Poor Standards of Analytic Tradecraft

(U) Compounding its disconcerting analytic integrity challenges, the Study's content is littered with examples of poor analytic tradecraft, across several critical measures of proficiency for authoring intelligence products. Here we provide some examples of the Study's poor analytic tradecraft.

(U) *Inadequately Describes the Quality and Reliability of Sources*

(TS███████████NF) Analysis that adheres to Intelligence Community tradecraft standards properly describes the quality and reliability of sources. Analysis that misrepresents or misinterprets the quality of source material compromises the integrity of the resulting analysis. At points, the Study relies upon "draft talking points" documents as being authoritative.[60] Doing so raises questions about the credibility of the assessment being drawn based on such a source, because draft talking points are prepared by staff for a senior leader and it is often difficult to ascertain, absent interviews, whether all, some, or none of the information contained in talking points was even used by the senior leader.

---

[59] At least the CIA's June 27, 2013, response to the Study identified eight recommendations derived from the lessons it had learned related to the Detention and Interrogation Program. *See* CIA Study Response, *Comments (Tab A)*, June 27, 2013, pp. 16-17.
[60] SSCI Study, Executive Summary, December 3, 2014, pp. 143 and 196.

(TS █████████ NF) We found frequent examples of citations that pointed to documents that did not discuss the material in question, were taken out of context, or did not accurately reflect the contents of the cited source documents—in some cases changing the meaning entirely. For example, the Study states that a review by the CIA Inspector General (IG) "uncovered that additional unauthorized techniques were used against" a detainee, but the Inspector General report actually said it "heard allegations" of the use of unauthorized techniques and said, "For all of the instances, the allegations were disputed or too ambiguous to reach any authoritative determination about the facts."[61] In another case, the Study states: "By early October 2002, the CIA completed a search of the names identified in the 'perfume letter' in its databases and found most of the individuals who 'had assigned roles in support of the operation' were arrested by Pakistani authorities during the raids."[62] This inaccurate paraphrase is different from the actual language of the quote, which states, "it appears that most of the detainees arrested on [September 11, 2002], had assigned roles in support of the operation outlined in the 'perfume" letter."[63] After explaining that a detainee had already admitted that "purchasing perfumes" likely referred to purchasing or making poisons, the cable states that, "[O]ur concern over this letter is heightened because of the identities of the individuals involved in the operation it outlines."[64] The Study's inaccurate paraphrase appears to minimize the remaining threat, while the cable itself indicates heightened concern. In hindsight, it appears that while the September 11, 2002, safe house raids helped to derail the Karachi hotels plot, the threat evolved into a planned attack on the U.S. consulate in Karachi by Ammar al-Baluchi and Khallad bin Attash, who were not captured during the September 2002 safe house raids.[65]

(U) *Inadequate Caveats About Uncertainties or Confidence in Analytic Judgments*

(TS █████████ NF) Proper tradecraft requires that the strength of an analytic judgment should be expressed when appropriate, through confidence level statements and the identification of uncertainty. This is an important check on analytical judgments that provides a key safeguard for policy makers. Many of the Study's conclusions and underlying claims are offered as matters of unequivocal fact. As an example, the Study asserts "CIA officers conducted no research on successful interrogation strategies during the drafting of the MON, nor after it was issued."[66] Proving a negative is often very difficult, and in this particular case it is difficult to understand how such an absolute assertion can be made without interviewing the affected witnesses or even citing to one documentary source that might support such a claim.

[61] *Compare* SSCI Study, Volume I, March 31, 2014, p. 229, *with* CIA Office of Inspector General. *Special Review: Counterterrorism Detention and Interrogation Activities (September 2001 - October 2003)*, May 7, 2004, p. 41 (DTS 2004-2710). [[This tradecraft error was partially corrected in the November 26, 2014, version of the Executive Summary by editing the offending sentence to read, "The Office of Inspector General later *described* additional *allegations* of unauthorized techniques used against . . . ." (emphasis added). *Compare* SSCI Study, Executive Summary, April 3, 2014, p. 67 *with* SSCI Study, Executive Summary, December 3, 2014, p. 70.]]
[62] SSCI Study, Executive Summary, December 3, 2014, p. 242. The Study cites to CIA, ALEC 188560, October 3, 2002, but the quoted language actually appears in CIA, ALEC 188565, October 3, 2002, p. 2.
[63] CIA, ALEC ██████ October 3, 2002, p. 2.
[64] CIA, ALEC ██████ October 3, 2002, pp. 2-3.
[65] CIA, CIA CABLE 45028, ██████████ CIA, [CIA CABLE] 38405, May 17, 2003, p. 4-7. *See infra*, pp. 45-47.
[66] SSCI Study, Volume I, March 31, 2014, p. 20.

(U) *Inadequate Incorporation of Alternative Analysis Where Appropriate*

(TS███████████NF) Analysts are generally encouraged to incorporate alternative analysis into their production where they can. Sometimes this exercise helps identify weaknesses in the analysis or highlights intelligence collection gaps. The Study is replete with uncited and potentially unknowable assertions like "there is no indication in CIA records that Abu Zubaydah provided information on bin al-Shibh's whereabouts"[67] or "███████ never visited the site."[68] Alternate analysis would certainly have been helpful in disproving the first claim and may have been helpful in the determination of whether the second assertion could really be established by records alone. With respect to the first claim, Abu Zubaydah did provide locational information about bin al-Shibh. As discussed below, Zubaydah made four separate photographic identifications of bin al-Shibh and placed him in Kandahar, Afghanistan, during the November to December 2001 timeframe and provided sufficient information for interrogators to conclude that bin al-Shibh was subsequently with KSM in Karachi, Pakistan.[69] With respect to the absolute claim that ████████████ never visited a particular site, alternative analysis may have demonstrated a need for additional information beyond that contained in the documentary record. That alternative analysis may have counseled in favor of modifying the assertion to something like, "It appears that no ██████████ visited the site during that timeframe" or dropping the assertion in its entirety.

(U) *Based on Flawed Logical Argumentation*

(TS███████████NF) Proper tradecraft entails understanding of the information and reasoning underlying analytic judgments. Key points should be made effectively and supported by information and coherent reasoning. Substandard analysis presents unsupported assertions that appear contrary to the evidence cited or in violation of common sense. We found instances where claims were supported more by rhetorical devices than sound logical reasoning. For example, in support of the Study's conclusion that the CIA's use of enhanced interrogation techniques was not effective, the Study stated:

> At least seven detainees were subjected to the CIA's enhanced interrogation techniques almost immediately after being rendered into CIA custody, *making it impossible to determine* whether the information they provided could have been obtained through non-coercive debriefing methods."[70]

---

[67] SSCI Study, Executive Summary, December 3, 2014, p. 317.

[68] SSCI Study, Volume I, March 31, 2014, p. 227.

[69] *See infra*, p. 38.

[70] SSCI Study, Findings and Conclusions, April 3, 2014, p. 2 (emphasis added). [[This false reasoning was tempered in the December 3, 2014, version of the Executive Summary by editing the sentence to read, "CIA detainees who were subjected to the CIA's enhanced interrogation techniques were usually subjected to the techniques immediately after being rendered to CIA custody. Other detainees provided significant accurate intelligence prior to, or without having been subjected to these techniques." *Compare* SSCI Study, Findings and Conclusions, April 3, 2014, p. 2 *with* SSCI Study, Findings and Conclusions, December 3, 2014, p. 2.]]

This statement is a rhetorical attempt to persuade the reader that non-coercive techniques may have been equally or even more successful than the enhanced techniques. It is little more than an appeal to unknowable facts and is not based upon logical reasoning.[71]

(TS ███████████ **NF)** We also found instances where the Study undermined its own claims by citing to documents that contradicted those claims. For example, while discussing testimony given by then CIA Director Hayden on the Program, the Study states, "Hayden's testimony included *the representation that Abu Zubaydah had a religious basis for cooperating* after the use of the CIA's enhanced interrogation techniques . . .Research Note: *CIA records do not support this representation related to Abu Zubaydah* . . . ."[72] The Study also asserted, "Abu Zubaydah explained that he informed trainees at the training camp that "'no brother' should be expected to hold out for an extended time," and that captured individuals will provide information in detention. For that reason, the captured individuals, he explained, should "expect that the organization will make adjustments to protect people and plans when someone with knowledge is captured."[73] However, in the same intelligence report cited for the above proposition, Abu Zubaydah revealed, that as his conditions in CIA detention worsened,

> [H]e became increasingly concerned for his long-term wellbeing. *He said that this process eventually became an 'unbearable weight' that Allah would no longer require him to carry. Under these conditions, Allah would have mercy and forgive him* ('As Jesus forgave Peter for denying him three times') *for revealing to the Americans what he knew about al Qa'ida and the brothers.*[74]

This one admission by Abu Zubaydah, unexplainably omitted from the Study, completely contradicts the flawed logic of the Study's claim that religion played no role in his cooperation with the Americans. The criticism of Director Hayden here is unwarranted.

(U) ERRONEOUS STUDY CONCLUSIONS

(U) We were only given 60 days to prepare our initial minority views in response to the more than 6, 000-page Study, which was approved by the Committee at the end of the 112th Congress. In those initial views, we successfully endeavored to describe the major fallacies and problematic findings that we had time to identify in the Study. Despite the fact that the CIA response and the summer staff meetings essentially validated our criticisms of the original Study, it appears that the updated version of the Study largely persists with many of its erroneous analytical and factual claims. We have used these past eleven weeks to update our own minority views and focus our attention on eight of the Study's most problematic conclusions.[75]

---

[71] For a more detailed analysis of this unsupported claim, *see infra*, p. 22.
[72] SSCI Study, Volume 1, March 31, 2014, p. 1130 (emphasis added).
[73] SSCI Study, Executive Summary, December 3, 2014, p. 469 (citing CIA, ███ 10496, February 16, 2003, p. 2).
[74] CIA, ███ 10496, February 16, 2003. p. 3 (emphasis added).
[75] We will address these eight conclusions in the following order: (1) Conclusion 1; (2) Conclusion 2; (3) Conclusion 6; (4) Conclusion 7; (5) Conclusion 8; (6) Conclusion 5; (7) Conclusion 9; and (8) Conclusion 10.

(U) Conclusion 1 (The CIA's use of enhanced interrogation techniques was not effective)

(U) The first of these updated conclusions asserts that the "CIA's use of enhanced interrogation techniques was not an effective means of acquiring intelligence or gaining cooperation from detainees."[76] The Study attempts to validate this apparently absolute conclusion by relying upon a number of faulty premises.

(U) The first faulty premise is that "seven of the 39 CIA detainees known to have been subjected to the CIA's enhanced interrogation techniques produced no intelligence while in CIA custody."[77] This 18 percent "failure rate" statistic may encourage some readers to jump to the hasty judgment that enhanced interrogation techniques were not an effective means of acquiring intelligence, because they failed to produce intelligence from every detainee against whom they were used. Such a judgment seems unreasonable, given that, in most human endeavors, 100 percent success rates are pretty rare, especially in complex processes like the ones involved here. If the Study's statistic is true, then it is just as true that 32 of the 39 detainees subjected to enhanced interrogation techniques did produce some intelligence while in CIA custody. That is an "effectiveness" rate of 82 percent for obtaining intelligence from detainees who were subjected to enhanced interrogation techniques. While an 82 percent effectiveness rate in obtaining some information sounds pretty good, this claim suffers from the same analytical defect as the Study's 18 percent failure rate, in that it does not provide any real insight about the *qualitative* value of the intelligence information obtained. The true test of effectiveness is the value of *what* was obtained—not how much or how little was obtained.

(U) As long as we are considering quantitative assessments of whether detainee interrogations led to the creation of intelligence reports, it might be useful to look at the "failure" and "effectiveness" rates for those detainees who were not subjected to enhanced interrogation. Using some of the Study's own numbers, a total of 119 detainees were in the CIA's Detention and Interrogation Program. Of these detainees, the interrogations of 41 of them resulted in no disseminated intelligence reports.[78] If true, we can deduce that 80 detainees were not subjected to enhanced interrogation and that the interrogations of 34 of these same detainees resulted in no disseminated intelligence reports.[79] Turning to the failure rate first, 34 of 80 CIA detainees who were not subjected to enhanced interrogation techniques produced no intelligence while in CIA custody. That is a 42.5 percent failure rate, more than double the 18 percent failure rate for the detainees subjected to enhanced interrogation techniques. Conversely, 46 of 80 detainees who were not subjected to enhanced interrogation techniques produced some intelligence while in CIA custody. That is a 57.5 percent effectiveness rate, which is also considerably lower than the 82 percent effectiveness rate for the detainees subjected to enhanced interrogation.

---

[76] SSCI Study, Findings and Conclusions, December 3, 2014, p. 2. The first and second conclusions in the updated Findings and Conclusion had been combined in Conclusion 9 of the original Study.

[77] SSCI Study, Findings and Conclusions, December 3, 2014, p. 2. The assertion of "produced no intelligence" as used by the Study reflects that the interrogations of these detainees resulted in no intelligence reports.

[78] *See* SSCI Study, Volume II, April 1, 2014, pp. 420-421.

[79] Subtracting the 39 detainees subjected to enhanced interrogation from 119 total detainees equals 80 detainees not subjected to enhanced interrogation. We know that seven of the detainees subjected to enhanced interrogation resulted in no intelligence reports. Subtracting these seven from the 41 total detainees whose interrogation did not result in disseminated intelligence reports leaves 34 detainees whose information did not result in disseminated intelligence products, even though they were not subjected to enhanced interrogation.

(U) Unlike the above measures, there are some quantitative statistics in the Study that are useful in comparing the relative "productivity" of certain detainees. The Study estimates that a total of 5,874 sole source disseminated intelligence reports were produced from the interrogation of 78 of the 119 detainees. Of these, 4266 reports (72.6 percent) were produced from the interrogation of 32 of the 39 detainees subjected to enhanced interrogation.[80] Thus, 1608 reports (27.4 percent) were produced from the interrogation of 46 of the 90 detainees not subjected to enhanced interrogation.[81] The Study also credits Abu Zubaydah and KSM with 1597 (27.1 percent) of the total number of disseminated reports.[82] While these statistics cannot be used to assess the qualitative value of the specific intelligence in these disseminated reports, they do seem to provide insight into the CIA's perceived value of the information being produced by the detainees who were subjected to enhanced interrogation, especially Abu Zubaydah and KSM. Given that the vast majority of these intelligence reports came from detainees selected for enhanced interrogations, these statistics seem to indicate that the CIA was proficient at identifying those detainees who might possess information worthy of dissemination.

(U) The second faulty premise states:

> At least seven detainees were subjected to the CIA's enhanced interrogation techniques almost immediately after being rendered to CIA custody, *making it impossible to determine* whether the information they provided could have been obtained through non-coercive debriefing methods. By contrast, other detainees provided significant accurate intelligence prior to, or without having been, subjected to these techniques.[83]

(U) This premise is problematic for at least two reasons. First, the premise itself admits that it is based upon ignorance—we will never know whether less coercive techniques would have provided the same amount of intelligence from these seven detainees as was obtained by using enhanced interrogation. It is troubling that the very first conclusion in this Study is based, at least in part, upon an appeal to unknowable facts. Second, this appeal to ignorance is linked to an observation that other detainees provided "significant accurate intelligence" without having been subjected to enhanced interrogation, in an apparent effort to persuade us that the use of less coercive techniques might have also resulted in "significant accurate intelligence." While this second observation is factually correct, it is misleading. We know from our earlier examination of the "productivity" statistics that the group of detainees who were not subjected to enhanced interrogation only provided 27.4 percent of the disseminated intelligence reporting, which undercuts the very inference raised by this empty premise.

---

[80] *See* SSCI Study, Volume II, April 1, 2014, p. 421.

[81] Subtracting the 4,266 reports produced from the interrogation of detainees subjected to enhanced interrogation from the 5,874 total number of reports equals 1,608 reports (27.4 percent) produced from the interrogation of detainees not subjected to enhanced interrogation.

[82] *See* SSCI Study, Volume II, April 1, 2014, p. 421.

[83] SSCI Study, Findings and Conclusions, April 3, 2014, p. 2 (emphasis added). [[This false reasoning was tempered in the December 3, 2014, version of the Executive Summary by editing the sentence to read, "CIA detainees who were subjected to the CIA's enhanced interrogation techniques were usually subjected to the techniques immediately after being rendered to CIA custody. Other detainees provided significant accurate intelligence prior to, or without having been subjected to these techniques." *Compare* SSCI Study, Findings and Conclusions, April 3, 2014, p. 2 *with* SSCI Study, Findings and Conclusions, December 3, 2014, p. 2.]]

(U) The third faulty premise of this ineffective means conclusion focuses on the fact that "multiple" detainees subjected to enhanced interrogation techniques "fabricated information, resulting in faulty intelligence."[84] Like the first faulty premise, this premise only tells one side of the story. It implies that only detainees subjected to enhanced interrogation provided fabricated information. Not surprisingly, our review of the documentary record revealed that "multiple" detainees whose non-enhanced interrogations resulted in at least one sole source intelligence report also provided fabricated information to their interrogators.[85] Fabrication is simply not a good measure of "effectiveness," because detainees are often strongly motivated to protect the identities of their terrorist colleagues and the details of their terrorist operations. We train our own military personnel to resist against providing sensitive information to their captors during the inevitable interrogation process. We understand that such resistance may occasionally lead our personnel to provide fabricated information to their interrogators. This is an ancient and well-recognized occupational hazard of war.

(U) Another problematic aspect of this third faulty premise is that it ignores the fact that fabricated information can sometimes turn out to be highly significant. One of the best examples of this concept can be found in our discussion about how the courier who led us to Bin Ladin's hideout was finally located.[86] Specifically, many of the senior al-Qa'ida detainees lied to protect the identity and importance of Abu Ahmad al-Kuwaiti. Abu Zubaydah and Abu Faraj al-Libi both lied when they claimed that they did not know anyone named Abu Ahmad al-Kuwaiti. KSM fabricated a story that Ahmad had retired from al-Qa'ida. When compared against other detainee information, these fabrications were clear signals to CIA analysts that these three detainees were trying very hard to keep Ahmad hidden.[87]

---

[84] SSCI Study, Findings and Conclusions, December 3, 2014, p. 2.

[85] Our review examined the first 15 of the 46 detainees whose non-coercive interrogations had resulted in at least one sole-source intelligence report. See SSCI Study, Executive Summary, December 3, 2014, p. 462. We found documentary evidence supporting the proposition that 11 of these 15 detainees provided deceptive or fabricated information to their interrogators. The 11 deceptive detainees were: Zakariya (CIA, [CIA CABLE] 22576, ████████; CIA, CIA CABLE ████████ CIA, CIA CABLE ████████ Jamal Eldin Boudraa, (CIA, [CIA CABLE] 22576, ████████ CIA [CIA CABLE] 21520, ████████ Bashir Nasir Ali al-Marwalah (CIA, [CIA CABLE] 27298████████ CIA, CIA CABLE 13756, ████████Ha'il Aziz Ahmad al-Mithali (CIA, CIA CABLE 13756████████Musab Umar Ail al-Mudwani (CIA, CIA CABLE 13756████████ Shawqi Awad (CIA, CIA CABLE 15643████████ Umar Faruq, aka Abu al-Faruq al-Kuwaiti (CIA, CIA CABLE ████████ CIA, CIA CABLE 12313████████ CIA, [CIA CABLE] 28108████████ [DETAINEE R] (CIA, CIA CABLE ████████ Abd al-Rahim Ghulam Rabbani (CIA, CIA CABLE ████████; and Haji Ghalgi (CIA, CIA CABLE 191458;████████ We were unable to find documentary evidence supporting any deception or fabrication by the following four detainees: Abbar al-Hawari, aka Abu Sufiyan; Hassan bin Attash; Said Saleh Said, aka Said Salih Said; and Hayatullah Haqqani.

[86] See infra, pp. 73-76.

[87] See CIA, DIRECTOR ████████ CIA Center for the Study of Intelligence. Lessons from the Hunt for Usama Bin Ladin, dated September 2012, pp. 9-10 (DTS 2012-3826); CIA Intelligence Assessment, Al-Qa'ida Watch. Probable Identification of Suspected Bin Ladin Facilitator Abu Ahmad al-Kuwaiti, November 23, 2007, p. 2.

[87] See SSCI Study, Executive Summary, December 3, 2014, p. 378-379.

(U) The final faulty premise used in support of this "effectiveness" conclusion was that "CIA officers regularly called into question whether the CIA's enhanced interrogation techniques were effective, assessing that the use of the techniques failed to elicit detainee cooperation or produce accurate intelligence."[88] While the *opinions* of these unidentified CIA officers may happen to coincide with the Study's first conclusion, there were at least three other CIA officials who held the opposite view—Directors Tenet, Goss, and Hayden. DCI Tenet stated that he "firmly believes that the interrogation program, and specifically the use of EITs, has saved many lives." Tenet added that the use of the CIA's enhanced interrogation techniques was "extremely valuable" in obtaining "enormous amounts of critical threat information," and he did not believe that the information could have been gained any other way.[89] Director Goss told our Committee members that

> This program has brought us incredible information. It's a program that could continue to bring us incredible information. It's a program that could continue to operate in a very professional way. It's a program that I think if you saw how it's operated you would agree that you would be proud that it's done right and well, with proper safeguards."[90]

CIA Director Hayden also told our Committee that the CIA's interrogation Program existed "for one purpose–intelligence," and that the Program "is about preventing future attacks. . . . In that purpose, preventing attacks, disabling al-Qa'ida, this is the most successful program being conducted by American intelligence today."[91]

(U) In our opinion, the reasons cited by the Study to support this conclusion that the CIA's use of enhanced interrogation techniques was not an effective means of acquiring intelligence or gaining cooperation from detainees are largely invalid. The faulty premises upon which the conclusion is based are more rhetorical than analytical. Our review of the facts contained in the documentary record has led us to the opposite conclusion—that the CIA's Detention and Interrogation Program, including the use of enhanced interrogation, was an effective means of gathering significant intelligence information and cooperation from a majority of these CIA detainees. Our conclusion, however, should not be read as an endorsement of any of these particular enhanced interrogation techniques.

(U) Conclusion 2 (CIA's Justification for EITs Rested on Inaccurate Effectiveness Claims)

(U) Conclusion 2 states, "[t]he CIA's justification for the use of its enhanced interrogation techniques rested on inaccurate claims of their effectiveness."[92] The Study continues to rely upon 20 separate case studies to support this erroneous conclusion. In our

---

[88] SSCI Study, Findings and Conclusions, December 3, 2014, p. 2.
[89] Interview of George Tenet, by [REDACTED], [REDACTED], Office of the Inspector General, 8 September, 2003.
[90] SSCI Transcript, *Briefing by the Director of the Central Intelligence Agency Regarding CIA's Counterterrorism Operations and Detention, Interrogation, and Rendition Program*, March 15, 2006, p. 8 (DTS 2006-1308).
[91] SSCI Transcript, *Hearing on the Central Intelligence Agency Detention and Interrogation Program*, April 12, 2007, pp. 16-17 (DTS 2007-3158).
[92] SSCI Study, Findings and Conclusions, December 3, 2014, p. 2.

original minority views, we only had time to identify the significant flaws in seven of these case studies. Prior to our receipt of the June 27, 2013, CIA response, we identified significant problems with four more of the case studies. Ultimately, the CIA response validated our critique of the original seven case studies and identified additional issues with the remaining case studies. We have decided to address 17 of these case studies in our examination of this conclusion.[93] Although one may have individual views on the relative effectiveness of the enhanced interrogation techniques; it is important for the public to understand that these flawed case studies are insufficient to establish that the CIA's justification for the use of enhanced interrogation techniques rested upon inaccurate claims of their effectiveness.

(U) *The Study's Flawed Analytical Methodology*

(U) In general, the Study essentially refuses to admit that CIA detainees, especially CIA detainees subjected to enhanced interrogation techniques, provided intelligence information which helped the United States government and its allies neutralize numerous terrorist threats. On its face, this position does not make much sense, given the vast amount of information gained from these interrogations, the thousands of intelligence reports that were generated as a result of them, the capture of additional terrorists, and the disruption of the plots those captured terrorists were planning.

(U) We reviewed 17 of the 20 cases studies that the Study relies upon to support this flawed conclusion. We examined these case studies in logical groupings (e.g., related to information provided by Abu Zubaydah) using chronological order rather than the Study's confusing "primary" and "secondary" effectiveness representations. This approach helped us better understand how the intelligence resulting from these detainee interrogations was used by the CIA to disrupt terrorist plots and identify, capture, and sometimes prosecute other terrorists.

(U) The Study developed an analytical methodology to examine the effectiveness of the information obtained from the CIA's Detention and Interrogation Program that we found to be both confusing and deeply flawed. Usually, effectiveness is measured by establishing performance metrics that require the collection of pertinent data and the subsequent analysis of such data. For example, in the context of counterterrorism such metrics might include: (1) increased understanding of terrorist networks; (2) identification of terrorists and those providing material support; (3) terrorist captures; (4) terrorist interrogations; (5) disruption of terrorist operations and financing; (6) disruption of terrorist recruitment; (7) reduction in terrorist safe-havens; (8) development of counterterrorism assets; (9) intelligence gathering of documents, computer equipment, communications devices, etc.; (10) improved information sharing; and (11) improved foreign liaison cooperation against terrorism. Such metrics could then be compared against the information provided by CIA detainees to assess the relative effectiveness of the Program.

---

[93] We have combined the KSM as the "mastermind" of the September 11, 2001, terrorist attacks case study with the KSM "Mukhtar" alias case study. We did not have time to adequately address the Majid Khan, Sajid Badat, and Dhiren Barot case studies.

(U) Instead of performance metrics, the Study's analytical methodology creates artificial categories that are used to *exclude* certain detainee information from being considered in an effectiveness assessment of the Program. For example, if the Study found that a detainee subjected to enhanced interrogation had provided similar information during an earlier non-enhanced interrogation, then such information could not be used for assessing the effectiveness of the program. This category appears to have been developed in an attempt to exclude much of the intelligence information provided by Abu Zubaydah after he was subjected to enhanced interrogation in August 2002, since some of the information Abu Zubaydah provided during those interrogations was similar to information he had provided prior to August. However, it turns out that this category is largely inapplicable to Abu Zubaydah's case, because he was subjected to enhanced interrogation by the CIA when he was released from the hospital on April 15, 2002.[94]

(U) Another category of information that the Study's flawed analytical methodology excludes is corroborative information. If a detainee subjected to enhanced interrogation provided information that was already available to the CIA or other elements of the Intelligence Community from another source, then the methodology dictates that such information cannot be considered to support a CIA effectiveness representation. This result occurs even in situations in which the detainee's information clarified or explained the significance of the prior information. Another exclusion category applies if the Study determined that there was no causal relationship between the information obtained from a detainee after the use of enhanced interrogation and the operational success claimed by the CIA. In these case studies, we often found documentary evidence that supported direct causal links between such detainee information and the operational success represented by the CIA. The final category excludes detainee information about terrorist plots when there was a subsequent assessment by intelligence and law enforcement personnel that such plots were infeasible or never operationalized.

(U) This flawed analytical methodology often forced the Study to use absolute language such as, "no connection," "no indication," "played no role," or "these representations were inaccurate." Our review of the documentary record often found valid counter-examples that disproved such absolute claims. We also found that when we invalidated the claims in the initial case studies, there was often a cascading effect that further undermined claims in the subsequent case studies. Here we summarize the claims for the case studies we examined and our alternate analysis of those claims.

(U) *Our Analytical Methodology*

(U) Our analytical methodology simply focuses on the significant inherent weaknesses contained in the analytical categories of the Study's methodology. For example, in case studies where the Study claims there was no relationship between the use of enhanced interrogation techniques and the operational success, it often uses absolute language such as, "no connection," "no indication," "played no role," or "these representations were inaccurate." This greatly simplified our analytical task, because the main problem with absolute claims is that it usually only takes one valid counter-example to disprove the claim. We did not have too much difficulty

---

[94] *See infra,* pp. 33-36.

using the documentary record to: establish connections; find indications; identify the roles; and demonstrate the accuracy of certain representations. We suspect that this task would have been even easier if there had been an opportunity to speak to the relevant witnesses.

(U) The same can be said with respect to the Study's treatment of the "otherwise available categories." In these case study claims, the Study would point to documents that "provided similar information" or contained "corroborative" information. The usual problem with these claims is that they failed to analyze the weight and significance of the information provided by the particular detainee. We found documentary evidence indicating that the CIA often had not understood or properly exploited previously acquired intelligence information until after its significance was clarified by a particular detainee or detainees.

(U) Also, we were less inclined to dismiss the significance of certain plots and threats just because there was documentary evidence indicating that some intelligence professionals found them infeasible or had not yet become operational. Often, the most difficult part of a terrorist plot is getting the terrorists into a position where they can attack. If the terrorists are not neutralized, they have additional time to refine their plans, adjust to new targets, or gain access to better weapons and equipment. The evolving nature of the Karachi terrorist plots demonstrates this point quite well.[95]

(U) *Re-organization of the "Effectiveness" Case Studies*

(U) In general, we have tried to organize our analysis of these case studies sequentially into six logical and chronological groupings. For example, since Abu Zubaydah was the first CIA detainee subjected to enhanced interrogation techniques, we begin with the case studies which examine the significant intelligence information that he disclosed to his interrogators. Despite claims made by the Study, we found that, over time, information obtained from Abu Zubaydah was very useful in the subsequent interrogation of other detainees and sometimes even helped lead to the capture of other terrorists, which in turn, often disrupted developing terrorist plots.

(U) The next logical grouping of case studies centers geographically in Pakistan during the March 2002 through April 2003 time-frame and concerns the Intelligence Community's efforts to locate and capture the al-Qa'ida terrorists in that country. For example, we trace how Abu Zubaydah's information helped ▮▮▮▮▮▮ Pakistani authorities conduct important raids on several key safe houses in Karachi on September 10-11, 2002, which resulted in a treasure trove of collected physical evidence and intelligence information, as well as the capture of Ramzi bin al-Shibh, Abu Badr, Abdul Rahim Gulam Rabbani, Hassan Muhammad, Ali bin Attash, and other al-Qa'ida members. We turn next to the capture of KSM in Rawalpindi in March 2003 and then examine the various Karachi terrorist plots, which were largely neutralized by the September 2002 safe house raids, but were not finally disrupted until the capture of Ali Abdul Aziz Ali and Khallad bin Attash on April 29, 2003, in Karachi. This grouping ends with our discussion of the Heathrow and Canary Wharf Plots, which were fully disrupted with the captures of Ramzi bin al-Shibh, KSM, Ali Abdul Aziz Ali, and Khallad bin Attash.

---

[95] *See infra*, pp. 45-47.

27

(U) The third grouping takes us briefly to Southeast Asia and our analysis of how detainee information helped lead to the capture of Riduan Isamuddin, also known as "Hambali" in Thailand during August 2003, the disruption of the Second Wave plots, and the capture of his Al-Ghuraba Group in Karachi, Pakistan.

(U) Our fourth grouping consists of the case studies that primarily involved information provided by KSM. We begin with an analysis of four case studies where KSM provided helpful information during 2003: the critical intelligence on Jaffar al-Tayyar (also known as Adnan el-Shukrijumah); the arrest of Saleh al-Marri; the capture of Iyman Faris; and the identification and arrests of Uzhair and Saifullah Paracha.

(U) The fifth grouping examines three case studies that are factually unrelated but depend upon detainee information that was provided in 2004. The first involves the tactical intelligence provided on Shkai, Pakistan, by Hassan Ghul. The second involves the thwarting of the Camp Lemonier plotting in Djibouti and the third examines how CIA detainees subjected to enhanced interrogation provided information useful in the validation of CIA sources.

(U) Our final chronological group covers the identification of Usama Bin Ladin's courier. Here, we demonstrate that detainee information played a significant role in leading CIA analysts to the courier Abu Ahmad al-Kuwaiti, who in turn, led the Intelligence Community to Usama Bin Ladin.

(U) *The Domino Effect*

(U) Our reorganization of these case studies away from the Study's confusing primary and secondary "effectiveness representations" frame of reference into a more traditional chronological analytical framework clearly exposes the fatal flaw in the structure of the Study's current analysis. In essence, the Study's analysis resembles a very large and carefully lined-up set of dominoes. The claims made in those first few dominoes are absolutely crucial in maintaining the structure and validity of many of the claims made and repeated in the dominoes that follow. Our analysis demonstrates that the claims in these initial case studies are simply not supported by the factual documentary record. This led to an analytical chain reaction in which many of the Study's subsequent claims became invalid, in part, because of their dependence on the first few factually inaccurate claims.

(TS███████████NF) A good example of this "Domino Effect" is the factually incorrect claim made by the Study that the use of enhanced interrogation techniques played "no role" in the identification of Jose Padilla, because Abu Zubaydah provided the information about Padilla during an interrogation by FBI agents who were "exclusively" using "rapport-building" techniques against him more than three months prior to the CIA's "use of DOJ-approved enhanced interrogation techniques."[96] The facts demonstrate, however, that Abu Zubaydah had been subjected to "around the clock" interrogation that included more than four days of dietary manipulation, nudity, as well as a total of 126.5 hours (5.27 days) of sleep deprivation during the 136-hour (5.67 day) period by the time the FBI finished up the 8.5-hour interrogation shift which

---

[96] SSCI Study, Executive Summary, December 3, 2014, pp. 230-231 and 230 n.1315; *see infra*. pp.33-36.

28

yielded the identification of Jose Padilla.[97] Since these three enhanced interrogation techniques were used in combination with the FBI's "rapport building" technique during this particular interrogation, it is simply absurd to claim that they played "no role" in obtaining the information about Padilla from Abu Zubaydah. Consistent with the "Domino Effect" analogy, when this factually incorrect claim falls, it can no longer be cited as support for other claims. This specific factually incorrect claim, sometimes used in slightly different variations, is repeated at least 19 times throughout the Study.[98]

(U) Ultimately, our analysis of these case studies leads us to conclude that there are simply not enough "dominoes" left standing to support the Study's explosive conclusion—that the "CIA's justification for the use of its enhanced interrogation techniques rested on inaccurate claims of their effectiveness." It is very disappointing that the Study has leveled such serious accusations against the personnel involved in the CIA's Detention and Interrogation Program, when so many of the Study's own claims are demonstrably false.

(U) *The Identification of Khalid Shaykh Mohammad as the Mastermind of the 9/11 Attacks and His "Mukhtar" Alias*

Study Claim: (TS NF) **"On at least two prominent occasions, the CIA represented, inaccurately, that Abu Zubaydah provided [information identifying KSM as the mastermind of 9/11] after the use of the CIA's enhanced interrogation techniques."[99]**

(TS NF) **"In at least one instance in November 2007 . . . the CIA asserted that Abu Zubaydah identified KSM as 'Mukhtar' after the use of the CIA's enhanced interrogation techniques."[100]**

(TS NF) **"There is no evidence to support the statement that Abu Zubaydah's information—obtained by FBI interrogators prior to the use of the CIA's enhanced interrogation techniques and while Abu Zubaydah was hospitalized—was uniquely important in the identification of KSM as the 'mastermind' of the 9/11 attacks."[101]**

Fact: **(U) Neither of the occasions cited with respect to the "Mastermind of 9/11" information were "prominent." The first occasion was not even a CIA representation, but rather a mistake made by the Department of Justice in one of its legal opinions.[102] The second occasion was a set of November 2007 documents and talking points for the CIA Director to use in a briefing with**

---

[97] *See infra,* pp. 33-36.
[98] *See* SSCI Study, Executive Summary, December 3, 2014, pp. 209-210. 230, 230 n.1314, 234; SSCI Study, Volume I, March 31. 2014, pp. 624 and 636; and SSCI Study, Volume II, April 1, 2014, pp. 57, 75. 75 n.274. 79, 343, 349. 358, 409. 445 n.2245. 530, 532. 535. and 1089.
[99] SSCI Study, Executive Summary, December 3, 2014, p. 312.
[100] SSCI Study, Executive Summary, December 3, 2014, p. 315.
[101] SSCI Study, Executive Summary, December 3, 2014, p. 313.
[102] *See* SSCI Study. Executive Summary, December 3, 2014, p. 313, n.1748.

the President. **Although these briefing materials did contain some erroneous information about KSM's interrogation, the Study fails to demonstrate whether this erroneous information was "represented" to the President during that timeframe.**[103]

(U) The one instance where the CIA asserted that Abu Zubaydah identified KSM as "Mukhtar" after the use of enhanced interrogation techniques was contained in the same November 2007 briefing materials used by the CIA Director to brief the President.[104] **Again, the Study fails to demonstrate whether this erroneous information was "represented" to the President during this timeframe.**

(U) There is considerable evidence that the information Abu Zubaydah provided identifying KSM as "Mukhtar" and the mastermind of 9/11 was significant to CIA analysts, operators, and FBI interrogators. Both the Congressional Joint Inquiry into the 9/11 Attacks and the 9/11 Commission discussed the importance of this information to the Intelligence Community in understanding KSM's role in the attacks and in the al-Qa'ida organization.

(U) We have combined our analysis of these two case studies because they share common facts and analytical issues. The Study's claims with respect to the CIA's alleged misrepresentations about KSM's "Mukhtar" alias and being the mastermind of 9/11 are themselves inaccurate. Also, the Study's absolute claim that "there is no evidence" that Abu Zubaydah's information was uniquely important in the identification of KSM as the mastermind of 9/11 is contradicted by the documentary record and publicly available information.

(U) Our analysis of the Study's erroneous claims about the supposed CIA "representations" is dispositive. For the first "prominent" occasion, the Study mistakenly alleges that the CIA made an inaccurate representation about Abu Zubaydah providing information identifying KSM as the mastermind of 9/11 after the use of the CIA's enhanced interrogation techniques.[105] It turns out that this particular inaccurate representation *was not made by the CIA*, but rather was expressed in a written legal opinion by the Office of Legal Counsel at the Department Justice (DOJ).[106] The Study confirms its own mistake by pointing out that the CIA briefing notes provided to DOJ in support of their request for the OLC opinion *correctly stated*, "Within months of his arrest, Abu Zubaydah provided details about al-Qa'ida's organization structure, key operatives, and modus operandi. It was also Abu Zubaydah, *early in his detention,*

---

[103] *See* DCIA Talking Points: Waterboard, 06 November 2007, pp. 1-3. This document was sent to DCIA on November 6 in preparation for a meeting with POTUS.
[104] *See* DCIA Talking Points: Waterboard, November 6, 2007, pp. 1-3.
[105] *See* SSCI Study, Executive Summary, December 3, 2014, p. 312-313.
[106] *See* Memorandum for John A. Rizzo from Steven Bradbury, *Re: Application of United States Obligations Under Article 16 of the Convention Against Torture to Certain Techniques that May Be Used in the Interrogation of High Value al Qaeda Detainees*, May 30, 2005, p. 10.

who identified KSM as the mastermind of 9/11."[107] DOJ is accountable for this negligible mistake, not the CIA.

(S//OC/NF) With respect to the second "prominent" occasion, the CIA does admit that "in one instance—a supporting document for a set of DCIA talking points for a meeting with the President—we mischaracterized the information as having been obtained after the application of enhanced interrogation techniques."[108] However, while this information in Director Hayden's briefing materials about KSM was inaccurate, the Study fails to explain how the CIA supposedly "represented" these inaccuracies to the President or other executive branch officials during this November 2007 timeframe. Without talking to witnesses, we have no proof that any such inaccurate representation ever occurred. What we do know is that President Bush got this issue right in a speech that he delivered nearly a year before this particular error was inserted into Director Hayden's briefing materials. Specifically, President Bush said,

> After he recovered, Zubaydah was defiant and evasive. He declared his hatred of America. During questioning, he at first disclosed what he thought was nominal information—and then stopped all cooperation. Well, in fact the 'nominal' information he gave us turned out to be quite important. For example, Zubaydah disclosed Khalid Sheikh Mohammed—or KSM—was the mastermind behind the 9/11 attacks, and used the alias 'Muktar.'[109]

The President's speech is the "representation" that mattered most, regardless of whether the erroneous information in Director Hayden's briefing materials was discussed during a classified Presidential briefing one year later. We conclude that if there was any error here, it was harmless.

(S//OC/NF) The Study's claim in the second case study is essentially identical to the first, except that Director Hayden's briefing materials for the November 2007 meeting with the President contained an erroneous assertion that Abu Zubaydah identified KSM as "Mukhtar" after the use of the CIA's enhanced interrogation techniques.[110] Analytically, this is a distinction without a difference and we reach the same conclusion—if there was any error here, it was harmless.

(S//████//NF) Turning now to the Study's "no evidence" claim, numerous Intelligence Community documents show that Intelligence Community analysts believed that Zubaydah's information identifying KSM as the mastermind of 9/11 was important. Soon after the interrogation that revealed KSM as the mastermind of 9/11 and identification as "Mukhtar," the CIA disseminated an intelligence report, ███ within the Intelligence Community ██████

---

[107] Briefing Notes on the Value of Detainee Reporting, April 8, 2005, p. 5. (emphasis added)
[108] CIA Study Response, *Case Studies (TAB C)*, June 27, 2013, p. 20.
[109] President George W. Bush, *Trying Detainees: Address on the Creation of Military Commissions*, Washington, D.C., September 6, 2006.
[110] *See* SSCI Study. Executive Summary, December 3, 2014, p. 315.

██████ detailing the information.[111] Responses ██████████████ indicated they followed up and requested more information ██████ on him.[112]

(S//NF) Zubaydah's FBI interrogator Ali Soufan also described the information from Zubaydah on KSM as significant. In 2008, Soufan told Committee staff that when Zubaydah provided that information, "we had no idea at the time that Mukhtar was the KSM from 9/11. . . . Because we had been working so diligently on trying to figure out the puzzles of 9/11 and who is Mukhtar, and when Abu Zubaydah said that, I think the picture was complete."[113] On May 13, 2009, Soufan also told the Senate Judiciary Committee that prior to Zubaydah providing information on KSM's role as the mastermind of the 9/11 attacks, "we had no idea of KSM's role in 9/11 or of his importance in the al Qaeda leadership structure."[114]

(U) Moreover, a summary of the Program released publicly by the Director of National Intelligence in 2006 explained both the significance of this information and how other previously collected intelligence had not stood out to analysts until the information from Zubaydah. According to the summary, "during initial interrogation, Abu Zubaydah gave some information that he probably viewed as nominal. Some was important, however, including that KSM was the 9/11 mastermind and used the moniker "Mukhtar." This identification allowed us to comb previously collected intelligence for both names, opening up new leads to this terrorist plotter— leads that eventually resulted in his capture."[115]

(TS██████████NF) The Senate and House Intelligence Joint Inquiry Into the Intelligence Community Activities Before and After the Terrorist Attacks of September 11, 2001, adopted with the support of four members who also voted in favor of the Study, said that "although the Intelligence Community knew of KSM's support for terrorism since 1995 and later learned of his links to al-Qa'ida, he was not recognized as a senior al-Qa'ida lieutenant. In April 2002, the Intelligence Community learned that KSM and his group conceived the September 11 plot."[116] If there is any doubt that the report was referring to the information from Zubaydah, CIA operational cable traffic from April 2002 confirms: "[Abu Zubaydah] stated the idea of September 11 was conceived by [KSM] and his group."[117]

(U) The 9/11 Commission Report also made clear that the Intelligence Community did not recognize KSM's importance prior to 9/11. "KSM, who had been indicted in January 1996 for his role in the Manila air plot, was seen primarily as another freelance terrorist, associated with Ramzi Yousef."[118] The Commission noted that because KSM was being targeted for arrest, responsibility for tracking him was in CIA's Renditions Branch, which did not focus on analytic connections. "When subsequent information came, more critical for analysis than for tracking,

---

[111] *See* CIA, ██████████████████
[112] *See* CIA, ██████
[113] SSCI Transcript, *Staff Interview of FBI Special Agent Ali Soufan*, April 28, 2008 (DTS 2008-2411).
[114] Ali Soufan, Statement for the Record, before the United States Senate Committee on the Judiciary, May 13, 2009.
[115] Summary of the High Value Terrorist Detainee Program, Office of the Director of National Intelligence, p. 1.
[116] The Joint Inquiry Into the Intelligence Community Activities Before and After the Terrorist Attacks of September 11, 2001, December 2002, p. 310.
[117] CIA, ██████ 10065, April 18, 2002, p. 3.
[118] 9/11 Commission Report, p. 276.

no unit had the job of following up on what the information might mean."[119] As one of ten "Operational Opportunities" that were missed prior to 9/11, the Commission wrote, "August 2001, the CIA does not focus on information that Khalid Sheikh Mohammed is a key al Qaeda lieutenant or connect information identifying KSM as the 'Mukhtar' mentioned in other reports to the analysis that could have linked 'Mukhtar' with Ramzi Binalshibh and Moussaoui."[120] The 9/11 Commission adds:

> The final piece of the puzzle arrived at the CIA's Bin Ladin unit on August 28 [2001] in a cable reporting that KSM's nickname was Mukhtar. No one made the connection to the reports about Mukhtar that had been circulated in the spring. This connection might have also underscored concern about the June reporting that KSM was recruiting terrorists to travel, including to the United States. Only after 9/11 would it be discovered that Mukhtar/KSM had communicated with a phone that was used by Binalshibh, and that Binalshibh used the same phone to communicate with Moussaoui.[121]

(U) Finally, the 9/11 Commission notes that the information connecting KSM to the Binalshibh phone came from detainee interviews with Binalshibh in late 2002 and 2003 and with KSM in 2003, well after Abu Zubaydah identified KSM as Mukhtar and the 9/11 mastermind.[122] It is also worth noting that, like this information, all of the information for chapters 5 and 7 of the 9/11 Commission report, which explain what the Commission knew about al-Qa'ida's planning for the 9/11 attacks, "rel[ies] heavily on information obtained from captured al Qaeda members," mostly in CIA's interrogation program.[123]

(U) *The Thwarting of the Dirty Bomb/Tall Buildings Plot and the Capture of Jose Padilla*

Study Claim: (TS███████████NF) "A review of CIA operational cables and other CIA records found that the use of the CIA's enhanced interrogation techniques played no role in the identification of 'Jose Padilla' or the thwarting of the Dirty Bomb or Tall Buildings plotting. CIA records indicate that: . . . (3) Abu Zubaydah provided this information to FBI officers who were using rapport-building techniques, in April 2002, more than three months prior to the CIA's 'use of DOJ-approved enhanced interrogation techniques,' . . . ."[124]

Fact: (TS███████████NF) CIA records clearly indicate that sleep deprivation played a significant role in Abu Zubaydah's identification of Jose Padilla as an al-Qa'ida operative tasked to carry out an attack against

---

[119] 9/11 Commission Report, p. 276.
[120] 9/11 Commission Report, p. 356.
[121] 9/11 Commission Report, p. 277. The CIA acknowledged that this intelligence report identified KSM as "Mukhtar" prior to Abu Zubaydah's information. After reviewing its records, the CIA concluded that "our officers simply missed the earlier cable." CIA Study Response, *Case Studies (TAB C)*, June 27, 2013, p. 22.
[122] 9/11 Commission Report, Chapter 7, n.163.
[123] 9/11 Commission Report, p. 146.
[124] SSCI Study, Executive Summary, December 3, 2014, pp. 229-231.

the United States. Abu Zubaydah provided this information to FBI agents during an interrogation session that began late at night on April 20, 2002, and ended on April 21, 2002. Between April 15, 2002 and April 21, 2002, Abu Zubaydah was deprived of sleep for a total of 126.5 hours (5.27 days) over a 136 hour (5.6 day) period—while only being permitted several brief sleep breaks between April 19, 2002 and April 21, 2002, which totaled 9.5 hours.

(TS██████NF) This particular Study claim gives the false impression that enhanced interrogation techniques played no role in obtaining important threat information about Jose Padilla during the interrogation of Abu Zubaydah on April 20-21, 2002, and implies that such information was really just the result of the "rapport-building" techniques used by the FBI agents that evening.

(TS██████NF) The CIA documentary record is clear that Abu Zubaydah was subjected to an extended period of sleep deprivation and other enhanced interrogation techniques during his interrogation between April 15, 2002 and April 21, 2002.[125] Specifically, during this time period when FBI agents and CIA officers were working together in rotating, round-the-clock shifts, some of the interrogation techniques used on Abu Zubaydah included nudity,[126] liquid diet,[127] sensory deprivation,[128] and extended sleep deprivation.[129]

(TS██████NF) The sleep deprivation of Abu Zubaydah began on April 15, 2002.[130] By April 19, 2002, Abu Zubaydah had been subjected to 76 straight hours of sleep deprivation in the form of intensive interrogation sessions and his ability to focus on questions and provide coherent answers appeared to be compromised to a point where sleep was required.[131] Abu Zubaydah was allowed three hours of sleep at that time.[132] On April 20, 2002, the FBI began its late-night interrogation shift at approximately 10:30 p.m. with Abu Zubaydah and continued until about 7:00 a.m. the next morning. During that shift, Abu Zubaydah was given a two-hour sleep break; time for prayer, food, and water; and a medical check-up.[133] By April 21, 2002, the day he identified Jose Padilla as a terrorist inside the United States, CIA

---

[125] *See* CIA, ████ 10043, April 15, 2002, p. 2; CIA, ████ 10047, April 16, 2002, p. 2.

[126] SSCI Transcript, *Staff Interview of FBI Special Agent Ali Soufan*, April 28, 2008, p. 22. (DTS 2008-2411).

[127] *See* CIA, ████ 10090, April 21, 2002, p. 5.

[128] *See* CIA, ████ 10116, April 25, 2002, pp. 3-4; CIA, ████ 10016, April 12, 2002, pp. 4-5.

[129] *See* CIA, ████ 10094, April 21, 2002, p. 3; CIA, ████ 10071, April 19, 2002, p. 2; CIA, ████ 10091, April 21, 2002, p. 2. Dietary manipulation, nudity, and sleep deprivation (more than 48 hours) were also subsequently authorized as enhanced interrogation techniques by the Department of Justice. *See* Memorandum for John A. Rizzo, Senior Deputy General Counsel, Central Intelligence Agency, from Steven G. Bradbury, Principal Deputy Assistant Attorney General, Office of Legal Counsel, Department of Justice, May 30, 2005, *Re: Application of United States Obligations under Article 16 of the Convention Against Torture to Certain Techniques that May be Used in the Interrogation of High value Al Qaeda Detainees* (DTS 2009-1810, Tab-11).

[130] *See* FBI Letter to Pasquale J. (Pat) D'Amuro, Assistant Director, Counterterrorism Division, April 16, 2002, p. 2 ("The interview with ABU ZUBAYDA is continuing around the clock and we will advise you of any further information ASAP").

[131] *See* CIA, ████ 10071, April 19, 2002, p. 2.

[132] *See* CIA, ████ 10071, April 19, 2002, p. 2.

[133] *See* FBI Draft Report on Abu Zubaida interview session from approximately 10:30 p.m., April 20, 2002, to about 7:00 a.m., on April 21, 2002, p. 1.

records indicate that Abu Zubaydah had only been permitted several brief sleep breaks between April 19, 2002 and April 21, 2002, which only totaled 9.5 hours of sleep over a 136-hour period.[134] *That means Abu Zubaydah had been sleep deprived for a total of 126.5 hours (5.27 days) over a 136-hour (5.6 day) period by the time his FBI interrogators were finished with him at the end of that shift.*

(TS █████████ NF) A CIA chart, not included in the Study, which describes both the standard and enhanced techniques used on Abu Zubaydah, notes for April 21, 2002, "two sessions; sleep deprivation (136 hours)" under the heading "enhanced techniques."[135] Moreover, the FBI interrogator, identified in the press as █████████, who was questioning Zubaydah at the time he provided the Padilla information, told the OIG that "during the CIA interrogations Zubaydah 'gave up' Jose Padilla and identified several targets for future al-Qaeda attacks."[136] In other words, while Special Agent ████ obtained the information on Padilla, it was during a period that the FBI and CIA officers were using the CIA's techniques.

(TS █████████ NF) When the CIA and FBI interrogators entered the room late on the night of April 20, 2002, Abu Zubaydah was totally naked.[137] He had been subjected to at least four days of dietary manipulation and had been deprived of 126.5 hours of sleep during the past 136 hours.[138] According to FBI Special Agent Ali Soufan, they gave him a towel. They took some Coke and tea into the room and "started talking about different things." Sometime during the next morning, Abu Zubaydah "came back to his senses and he started cooperating again. And this is when he gave us Padilla."[139] Rather than concede that Abu Zubaydah was being subjected to a combination of at least three enhanced interrogation techniques while the FBI agents were using an additional rapport-building technique, the Study includes this perplexing footnote text: "While Abu Zubaydah was subjected to nudity and *limited* sleep deprivation prior to this date by the CIA, *he had been allowed to sleep* prior to being questioned by the FBI officers, who were *exclusively* using rapport-building interrogation techniques when the information was acquired."[140] Like the claim in this case study, this footnote is simply at odds with what really happened.

---

[134] *See* CIA, ████ 10094, April 21, 2002, p. 2; CIA *Assessment of the accuracy of facts stated in the SSCI Minority's response to the Study of the Central Intelligence Agency's Detention and Interrogation Program,* June 27, 2013, p. 1.

[135] CIA, *Interrogations Using Standard and Enhanced Techniques, Abu Zubaydah,* undated, p. 1.

[136] Department of Justice Inspector General, *A Review of the FBI's Involvement in and Observations of Detainee Interrogations in Guantanamo Bay, Afghanistan, and Iraq,* May 2008, p. 69 (DTS 2008-2188).

[137] *See* SSCI Transcript. *Staff Interview of FBI Special Agent Ali Soufan,* April 28, 2008, p. 22. (DTS 2008-2411).

[138] *See* CIA, ████ 10094, April 21, 2002, p. 2; CIA, ████ 10090, April 21, 2002, p. 5.

[139] SSCI Transcript, *Staff Interview of FBI Special Agent Ali Soufan,* April 28, 2008, p. 19. (DTS 2008-2411).

[140] SSCI Study, Executive Summary, April 3, 2014, p. 226 n.1292 (emphasis added). *But see* FBI Draft Report on Abu Zubaida interview session from approximately 10:30 p.m., April 20, 2002, to about 7:00 a.m., on April 21, 2002, p. 1. It appears from this draft report that Abu Zubaydah was permitted a two-hour sleep break sometime *during* the FBI shift, which seems to clearly demonstrate that the FBI interrogators were aware that Abu Zubaydah was being subjected to sleep deprivation. [[The December 3, 2014, revision of footnote 1292 in the April 3, 2014 version of the Executive Summary continues to misrepresent the events surrounding Abu Zubaydah's interrogation by editing the footnote to read, "While Abu Zubaydah was subjected to sleep deprivation and nudity prior to this date by the CIA, he had been allowed to sleep *shortly* prior to being questioned *on this matter* by the FBI *special agents,* who were exclusively using rapport-building interrogation techniques when this information was acquired

(TS███████████NF) There is no reasonable way to reconcile these facts with the claim that enhanced interrogation techniques played "no role" in Abu Zubaydah's identification of Jose Padilla. Sleep deprivation for 126.5 hours over a 136-hour period—which was hardly "limited"—was an enhanced interrogation technique regardless of whether the Department of Justice formally labeled it as such a couple of months later. The Study cannot dismiss the use of these enhanced interrogation techniques simply because they were used before the Department of Justice eventually approved them. The Study's assertion that the FBI was "exclusively" using rapport-building techniques fails to recognize the reality that this interrogation technique was used in combination with at least three other enhanced interrogation techniques. In judging what caused Abu Zubaydah to give up valuable intelligence, including information on Jose Padilla, it is impossible to separate or disaggregate enhanced interrogation techniques from rapport-building techniques after enhanced techniques are applied. Enhanced interrogation techniques are designed to compel detainees to cooperate with questioning and are used in conjunction with traditional questioning methods or interrogation techniques. The simple fact is that Abu Zubaydah gave up Padilla during that interrogation, after being subjected to enhanced interrogation techniques. It is simply not factually accurate for the Study to claim that Abu Zubaydah gave up the information on Padilla *before* he was subjected to enhanced interrogation techniques. Nor is it factually accurate to claim that enhanced interrogation techniques played no role in identifying Padilla as a terrorist threat.

(TS███████████NF) The direct refutation of this Study claim illustrates the Study's flawed analytical methodology. As we detail in many of the case studies below, Zubaydah provided much of the key initial information that caused the Intelligence Community to recognize the significance of certain events, future threats, terrorist networks, and even potential assets. The Study repeatedly and incorrectly alleges that the FBI obtained this information prior to the application of CIA's enhanced interrogation techniques.[141] As a result, this mistaken allegation is taken as a settled premise in the Study's analysis of other case studies and related issues, which has the practical effect of undermining the Study's analyses of those matters.

(TS███████████NF) Under its flawed methodology, the Study was able to disregard the significance of the large amount of information provided by Abu Zubaydah between April 15, 2002 and August 4, 2002, by incorrectly categorizing it as not being obtained from the use enhanced interrogation techniques. We now know that all of the information obtained from Abu Zubaydah on and after April 15, 2002, was provided *after* he had been subjected to enhanced interrogation. The practical result of this fact is that information obtained from Abu Zubaydah after April 15, 2002, can no longer be disregarded by the Study and must be factored into the assessment of the executive branch's effectiveness claims concerning the enhanced interrogation techniques along with the significant amount of important information obtained from Zubaydah following his second period of enhanced interrogation, which began on

---

from Abu Zubaydah (who was covered with a towel)." (emphasis added). *Compare* SSCI Study, Executive Summary, April 3, 2014, p. 226 n.1292 *with* SSCI Study, Executive Summary, December 3, 2014, p. 230. n.1315.]]
[141] *See* SSCI Study. Executive Summary. December 3. 2014. pp. 209-210, 230, 230 n.1314, 234; SSCI Study, Volume I, March 31, 2014, pp. 624 and 636; and SSCI Study, Volume II, April 1, 2014, pp. 57, 75. 75 n.274, 79, 343, 349, 358, 409, 445 n.2245, 530, 532, 535, and 1089.

August 4, 2002. Given the breadth of the information provided by Abu Zubaydah after April 15, 2002, and its attendant impact on subsequent intelligence efforts by the United States government and its allies, we conclude that this information supports the CIA's specific representations about the effectiveness of its Detention and Interrogation Program, including the use of enhanced interrogation techniques, in relation to the thwarting of the Dirty Bomb/Tall Buildings plot and the capture of Jose Padilla.

(U) *The Capture of Ramzi bin al-Shibh*

Study Claim: (TS̶̶̶̶̶̶̶̶̶̶NF) "A review of CIA records found no connection between Abu Zubaydah's reporting on Ramzi bin al-Shibh and Ramzi bin al-Shibh's capture.... While CIA records indicate that Abu Zubaydah provided information on Ramzi bin al-Shibh, there is no indication that Abu Zubaydah provided information on bin al-Shibh's whereabouts. Further, while Abu Zubaydah provided information on bin al-Shibh while being subjected to the CIA's enhanced interrogation techniques, he provided similar information to FBI interrogators prior to the initiation of the CIA's enhanced interrogation techniques."[142]

Fact: (TS̶̶̶̶̶̶̶̶̶NF) CIA records demonstrate that Abu Zubaydah was subjected to enhanced interrogation techniques during two separate periods in April 2002 and August 2002. During these timeframes, Abu Zubaydah made several photographic identifications of Ramzi bin al-Shibh and provided information that bin al-Shibh had been in Kandahar at the end of 2001, but was then working with KSM in Karachi, Pakistan. More important, Abu Zubaydah provided information about how he would go about locating Hassan Ghul and other al-Qa'ida associates in Karachi. This information caused ▮▮▮▮▮▮ Pakistani authorities to intensify their efforts and helped lead them to capture Ramzi bin al-Shibh and other al-Qa'ida associates during the Karachi safe house raids conducted on September 10-11, 2002.

(TS̶̶̶̶̶̶̶̶NF) The claim made in this case study relies, in part, upon the factually incorrect premise that Abu Zubaydah was not subjected to enhanced interrogation techniques until August 4, 2002.[143] As previously demonstrated, Abu Zubaydah was first subjected to the enhanced interrogation techniques of sleep deprivation, nudity, and dietary

---

[142] SSCI Study, Executive Summary, December 3, 2014, p. 318.
[143] *Compare* SSCI Study, Executive Summary, December 3, 2014, p. 323 *with supra*, pp. 33-36.

manipulation on April 15, 2002.[144] Abu Zubaydah's second period of enhanced interrogation, which included the use of the waterboard, began on August 4, 2002.[145]

(TS ███████████ NF) The Study also incorrectly claims that "there is no indication in CIA records that Abu Zubaydah provided information on bin al-Shibh's whereabouts."[146] While the CIA Study Response appears to concede this point unnecessarily,[147] CIA and FBI records establish that Abu Zubaydah did provide locational information about Ramzi bin al-Shibh. Specifically, he noted that he had seen bin al-Shibh in Kandahar, Afghanistan, at the end of 2001, and that he was aware that bin al-Shibh was presently working with KSM in Karachi, Pakistan.

(TS ███████████ NF) On April 18, 2002, during Abu Zubaydah's first period of enhanced interrogation, an FBI interrogator showed him a photograph of Ramzi bin al-Shibh. According to the FBI, Abu Zubaydah said that he knew the man in the photograph as "Ramzi bin al-Shiba" and that he had seen him with a group of Arabs shortly after a missile strike in Kandahar, Afghanistan, on the house of Taib Agha, Mullah Omar's secretary.[148] This information appears to place bin al-Shibh in Kandahar in the November 2001 timeframe, roughly five months prior to this interview with Abu Zubaydah. On June 2, 2002, the FBI again showed Abu Zubaydah a photograph of bin al-Shibh. This time Abu Zubaydah provided some additional information, stating that he knew this man as "Al-Sheeba," whom he saw with KSM in Kandahar around December 2001, near the end of Ramadan. He also noted that al-Shibh speaks Arabic like a Yemeni and that he had seen al-Shibh in the media after the September 11, 2001, terrorist attacks.[149] On August 21, 2002, during his second period of enhanced interrogation, Abu Zubaydah "immediately recognized the photograph of Ramzi bin al Shibh."[150] Abu Zubaydah mentioned that he had heard "that al-Shibh had stayed at the secret guest house in Qandahar that Mukhtar had established for the pilots and others destined to be involved in the 9/11 attacks."[151]

(TS ███████████ NF) On May 19, 2002, and May 20, 2002, Abu Zubaydah identified a picture of bin al-Shibh as "al-Shiba" and "*noted that he is always with (KSM)*."[152] If

---

[144] *See supra*, pp. 33-36. The CIA began subjecting Abu Zubaydah to monitored sleep deprivation on April 15, 2002, the day he was discharged from the hospital. He was continued on a liquid diet and subjected to nudity. All three of these interrogation techniques were subsequently and formally categorized by the Department of Justice as "enhanced interrogation techniques." *See* CIA, ███ 10043, April 15, 2002, p. 2; CIA, ███ 10047, April 16, 2002, p. 2; Memorandum for John A. Rizzo, Senior Deputy General Counsel, Central Intelligence Agency, from Steven G. Bradbury, Principal Deputy Assistant Attorney General, Office of Legal Counsel, Department of Justice, May 30, 2005, *Re: Application of United States Obligations under Article 16 of the Convention Against Torture to Certain Techniques that May be Used in the Interrogation of High value Al Qaeda Detainees* (DTS 2009-1810, Tab-11).

[145] *See* CIA, ███ 10586, August 04, 2002, p. 4.

[146] SSCI Study, Executive Summary, December 3, 2014, p. 318.

[147] *See* CIA Study Response, *Case Studies (TAB C)*, June 27, 2013, p. 23 ("It is true that Abu [Zubaydah] provided no information *specifically* on Bin al-Shibh's whereabouts . . . .") (emphasis added).

[148] *See* FBI draft report of the interrogation of Abu Zubaydah, April 18, 2002, 6:10 a.m. to 10:40 a.m., p 1.

[149] *See* FBI draft report of the interrogation of Abu Zubaydah, June 3, 2002, 4:00 p.m. to 8:30 p.m., p 3; CIA, ███ 10428, June 7, 2002, p. 5.

[150] CIA, ███ 10656, August 21, 2002, p. 2. *See also* CIA, ███ 10654, August 21, 2002, p. 1-2.

[151] CIA, ███ 10656, August 21, 2002, p. 3.

[152] CIA, DIRECTOR ███████ May 27, 2002, p. 4.

that assertion was true, then Abu Zubaydah was essentially suggesting that bin al-Shibh was with KSM in or around Karachi, Pakistan, because he had also informed his interrogators that KSM was located in or around Karachi.[153] Abu Zubaydah confirmed this association while being subjected to enhanced interrogation on August 21, 2002, when he stated that bin al-Shibh was "one of the operatives working for Mukhtar aka Khalid Shaykh Mohammad,"[154] again suggesting that bin al-Shibh was likely in Karachi.

(TS███████████NF) The Study's claim that it found "no connection" between Abu Zubaydah's reporting and Ramzi bin al-Shibh's capture is the result of poor analysis. On August 20, 2002, during his second period of enhanced interrogation, when asked how he would find his former al-Qa'ida associates if he were set free, Abu Zubaydah told CIA interrogators that he would contact the well-known associate of Hassan Ghul, who could put him in touch with Hassan Ghul and other senior al-Qa'ida members.[155] The Study frames this interchange much more narrowly. It asserts that "Abu Zubaydah was asked specifically how he would find Hassan Ghul. In response, Abu Zubaydah provided corroborative reporting: that Hassan Ghul could possibly be located through a well-known associate."[156] This narrow framing of the question and response enables the Study to conclude incorrectly that the capture of bin al-Shibh was an "unexpected" result of the raids that failed to capture Hassan Ghul.[157] The Study's approach fails to understand the causal link between Abu Zubaydah's information and the successful Karachi safe house raids of September 11, 2002, which resulted in the collection of important intelligence information and the capture of 11 al-Qa'ida associates, including Ramzi bin al-Shibh.

(TS███████████NF) About six weeks before Abu Zubaydah identified the significance of the well-known associate of Hassan Ghul, Pakistani authorities ████████ ██████████ raided the well-known associate of Hassan Ghul's home ██████ in early July 2002. The well-known associate of Hassan Ghul was interviewed on the spot and cooperated with Pakistani authorities ████████████████████████████ The well-known associate of Hassan Ghul even sent ██████ with the Pakistani officers to identify a home where Hassan Ghul formerly resided.[158] The CIA officers observed that the location was "extremely close to (if not an exact match)" to a location where KSM once resided, according to a June 18, 2002, report from the FBI.[159]

---

[153] The draft report of this interview states: (1) "Abu Jafar told [Abu Zubaydah] that he and his friend had to get to Karachi because they had business with Muhktar"; (2) "This [group of 11 Filipinos or Malaysians] was on their way to Karachi to meet up with Muhktar"; (3) "the American and Kenyan [Zubaydah] sent to Muhktar in mid-March 2002 . . . [Zubaydah] actually sent them to Hassan Ghul and Amanullah (in Karachi) who would have then arranged for them to be taken to Muhktar"; and (4) "Subject advised that, prior to his arrest he was trying to coordinate a trip to Karachi to meet with Muhktar." FBI draft report of the interrogation of Abu Zubaydah, May 20, 5:25 p.m. to 8:40 p.m., pp. 3 and 5.

[154] CIA, DIRECTOR ████ August 26, 2002, p. 4.

[155] See Captures Resulting From Detainee Information: Four Case Studies, November 26, 2003, p. 2; CIA, ████ 10644, August 20, 2002, pp. 2-3; and CIA, ALEC ████ August 29, 2002, p. 2.

[156] SSCI Study, Executive Summary, December 3, 2014, p. 323.

[157] See SSCI Study, Executive Summary, December 3, 2014, pp. 75, 318, and 320.

[158] See CIA, CIA CABLE 11755████████

[159] See CIA, CIA CABLE 11755████████

(TS███████████NF) The Study dismisses Abu Zubaydah's identification of the well-known associate of Hassan Ghul as mere "corroborative reporting," and does not attach the appropriate significance to this information because of its rigid adherence to its flawed analytical methodology, which presumes that anything corroborative cannot be considered as "otherwise unavailable actionable intelligence."[160] The facts tell a different story. Abu Zubaydah was a recognized senior member of al-Qa'ida who had direct ties to multiple high-ranking terrorists, including Usama Bin Ladin. The CIA was focused on Hassan Ghul, another well-connected senior member of al-Qa'ida, and "other" al-Qa'ida associates of Abu Zubaydah. Therefore, Abu Zubaydah's disclosures were deemed by the CIA as significant and actionable intelligence. When Abu Zubaydah identified the well-known associate of Hassan Ghul as the first person he would contact to reconnect with Hassan Ghul and other al-Qa'ida associates, it is very likely that collecting additional intelligence from the well-known associate of Hassan Ghul became a top operational priority for U.S. and Pakistani officials.

(TS███████████NF) It is not surprising that CIA Headquarters ████████████ ████ on August 29, 2002, to request that Pakistani officials "reinterview the well-known associate of Hassan Ghul for additional intelligence on Hassan Ghul."[161] On September 3, 2002, ████████ reported that Pakistani officials had re-interviewed the well-known associate of Hassan Ghul an unknown number of times and that these officials noted that at times the well-known associate of Hassan Ghul contradicted himself.[162] On September 9, 2002, Pakistani officials returned to the well-known associate of Hassan Ghul's home and interviewed another well-known associate of Hassan Ghul who had recently returned to ████████. The other well-known associate of Hassan Ghul cooperated and disclosed the location of Hassan Ghul's apartment, which was promptly raided but found to be empty.[163] Pakistani authorities interviewed ████████████████████████and learned that while Hassan Ghul had vacated the apartment, he was scheduled to return to the complex ████ ████████████████████ The Pakistani authorities subsequently placed the complex under surveillance in an effort to capture Hassan Ghul.[164]

(TS███████████NF) On September 10, 2002, Pakistani authorities arrested two individuals believed to be Hassan Ghul and his driver outside of the apartment complex.[165] These individuals turned out to be Muhammad Ahmad Ghulam Rabbani, a.k.a. Abu Badr and Muhammad Madni, Abu Badr's driver.[166] Information obtained from Madni led to a series of raids on September 11, 2002, by Pakistani authorities of the identified safe houses, resulting in the arrest of 11 individuals, including Ramzi bin al-Shibh, Abdul Rahim Gulam Rabbani, Hassan

---

[160] See SSCI Study, Executive Summary, December 3, 2014, p. 323.
[161] CIA, ALEC ████ August 29, 2002, p. 3.
[162] See CIA, CIA CABLE 12207, September 5, 2002, p. 2.
[163] See CIA, CIA CABLE 12249, September 9, 2002, p. 2.
[164] See CIA, CIA CABLE 12249, September 9, 2002, pp. 2-3.
[165] See CIA, CIA CABLE 12251, September █ 2002, p. 2; CIA, CIA ████████████ September █ 2002, p. 2.
[166] See CIA, CIA CABLE 33363, September 11, 2002, p. 2. Abu Badr is the brother of Abdul Rahim Gulam Rabbani, aka Abu Rahama, who ran the KSM safe house used by the 9/11 al-Qa'ida terrorists. Abu Zubaydah made a photographic identification of Abu Badr and called him KSM's man in Karachi. See CIA, ALEC ████ ████████CIA, CIA CABLE 12267, September 11, 2002, p. 2.

Muhammad Ali bin Attash, and other al-Qa'ida members.[167] These raids also resulted in the collection of important al-Qa'ida operational documents, including financial records and the coded "perfume letter."[168]

(TS   NF) The Study's claims with respect to the capture of Ramzi bin al-Shibh do not hold up under a close examination of the CIA documentary record. There was a direct causal connection between the information provided by Abu Zubaydah during his second period of enhanced interrogation and bin al-Shibh's capture. Abu Zubaydah had informed his interrogators that bin al-Shibh was one of KSM's operatives in Karachi. Zubaydah confirmed the importance the well-known associate of Hassan Ghul to locate Hassan Ghul and other al-Qa'ida associates operating in Karachi, including bin al-Shibh.

(U) Since the Study's claims on this topic do not hold up to factual scrutiny, its criticisms of the CIA representations with respect to Ramzi bin al-Shibh and President Bush's references to bin al-Shibh in his September 6, 2006, speech on the CIA's Detention and Interrogation Program are not valid. The CIA said Abu Zubaydah's "knowledge of al-Qa'ida lower-level facilitators, modus operandi and safehouses . . . played a key role in the ultimate capture of Ramzi bin al-Shibh."[169] Far from a "misrepresentation," that statement was completely accurate and consistent with the circumstances that led to bin al-Shibh's ultimate capture. Similarly, the text in President Bush's September 6, 2006, speech on the CIA's Detention and Interrogation Program noting that "the information Zubaydah provided helped lead to the capture of Binalshibh" was also accurate.[170]

(U) The capture of Ramzi bin al-Shibh and the other al-Qa'ida terrorists during ▮▮▮▮ ▮▮▮▮ raids of September 10-11, 2002, were stunning operational successes, made possible, in part, by the CIA's Detention and Interrogation Program.

(U) *The Capture of Khalid Shaykh Mohammad*

Study Claim: (TS   NF) **"[T]here are no CIA records to support the assertion that Abu Zubaydah, Ramzi bin al-Shibh, or any other CIA detainee played any role in the 'the planning and execution of the operation that captured Khalid Sheikh Mohammed.'"[171]**

Fact: (TS   NF) **Information obtained from CIA detainee Abu Zubaydah was essential to furthering the CIA's understanding of KSM's role in the September 11, 2001, terrorist attacks and helped lead to the**

---

[167] *See* CIA, ALEC ▮▮▮ September 11, 2002, pp. 2-3. Madni informed the arresting officers that Abu Badr was a "major al-Qa'ida [facilitator]." *See also* CIA, CIA CABLE 12267, September 11, 2002, pp. 2-4. He also gave ▮▮▮ ▮▮▮▮▮▮▮▮ information about the locations of al-Qa'ida-affiliated residences and safe houses in Karachi. CIA, CIA CABLE 12251, September ▮ 2002, p. 2; CIA, ▮▮▮▮▮▮▮▮▮▮ September ▮ 2002, pp. 3-4.
[168] *See* CIA, ALEC ▮▮▮ October 3, 2002, p. 2.
[169] CIA, Memorandum to the Inspector General from James Pavitt, CIA Deputy Director for Operations, Comments to Draft IG Special Review, *Counterterrorism Detention and Interrogation Activities*, February 27, 2004.
[170] President George W. Bush, *Trying Detainees; Address on the Creation of Military Commissions*, Washington, D.C., September 6, 2006.
[171] SSCI Study, Executive Summary, December 3, 2014, p. 327.

capture of Ramzi bin al-Shibh. The ███████████████████
interrogations of bin al-Shibh and DETAINEE R provided key insights
about KSM███████████████ Information produced through detainee
interrogation was pivotal to the retention of a key CIA asset whose
cooperation led directly to the capture of KSM.

(TS███████████████NF) The Study almost exclusively attributes the capture of KSM
to a "unilateral CIA asset."[172] We agree with the Study that this asset provided information that
was crucial to KSM's capture in Rawalpindi, Pakistan, on March 1, 2003.[173] We also
acknowledge that the CIA had met with the asset as early as fall 2001 and that the asset had
provided good intelligence information related to KSM. However, the Study fails to
acknowledge the cascading sequence of revelations that began with Abu Zubaydah's
identification of the importance of the well-known associate of Hassan Ghul and culminated in
the information provided by the asset which led directly to the capture of KSM. Moreover, the
Study does not recognize that, but for the fortuitous intervention of a CIA officer—who was
aware of recently obtained detainee information which corroborated the asset's claims
concerning KSM—the asset would have been terminated as a CIA source prior to providing the
crucial pre-capture information about KSM.[174]

(TS███████████████NF) As stated previously, information obtained from Abu
Zubaydah about KSM prior to the use of enhanced interrogation techniques was key to the CIA's
realization of KSM's operational significance. The CIA disseminated an intelligence report,
███ within the Intelligence Community ███████████████ detailing KSM's identification as
"Mukhtar" and his role as the mastermind of 9/11.[175] Responses ████████████████
indicated they followed up and requested more information ██████ on him.[176] Zubaydah's
FBI interrogator Ali Soufan also described the information from Zubaydah on KSM as
significant. In 2008, Soufan told Committee staff that when Zubaydah provided that
information, "we had no idea at the time that Mukhtar was the KSM from 9/11. . . . Because we
had been working so diligently on trying to figure out the puzzles of 9/11 and who is Mukhtar,
and when Abu Zubaydah said that, I think the picture was complete."[177] Also, on May 13, 2009,
Soufan told the Senate Judiciary Committee that prior to Zubaydah providing information on
KSM's role as the mastermind of the 9/11 attacks, "we had no idea of KSM's role in 9/11 or of
his importance in the al Qaeda leadership structure."[178]

---

[172] SSCI Study, Executive Summary, December 3, 2014. p. 327.
[173] ███████████████████████████████████████
███████████████████████████████████████
███████████████████████████████████████
███████████████████████████████████████
[174] See CIA Oral History Program. *Interview of [REDACTED] by [REDACTED]*. October 14, 2004, pp. 5-7.
[175] See CIA. ███████████████████████
[176] See CIA, ███
[177] SSCI Transcript, *Staff Interview of FBI Special Agent. Ali Soufan*. April 28, 2008 (DTS 2008-2411).
[178] Ali Soufan, Statement for the Record, before the United States Senate Committee on the Judiciary, May 13, 2009.

42

(TS█████████████NF) The chain of events leading to KSM's capture begins in earnest with Zubaydah's interrogation on August 20, 2002, when, during his second period of being subjected to enhanced interrogation techniques, he was asked how he would go about locating Hassan Ghul and other al-Qa'ida associates if he were to be released.[179] Zubaydah responded to this question by stating that he would reach out to [the well-known associate of Hassan Ghul] █████████████████████████ to reconnect with Ghul and others.[180] As explained in greater detail in our discussion about the capture of Ramzi bin al-Shibh, this information from Zubaydah caused ████████ Pakistani authorities to intensify their investigative efforts [the well-known associate of Hassan Ghul] ███████████████ who had been previously located, interviewed, and surveilled.[181] These investigative efforts resulted in ████████ Pakistani raids of safe houses in Karachi on September 10-11, 2002.[182] Ramzi bin al-Shibh was among those captured during these raids.

(TS█████████████NF) Ramzi bin al-Shibh becomes one of the next links in the effort to track down and capture KSM. Shortly after his capture in Karachi, bin al-Shibh was transferred ████████████ In late 2002; ███████████████████████████ Ramzi indicated ████ that the best way to find KSM is to find███████████████ 'Ammar' who is also in Karachi."[183] A few days later, in a photographic identification, bin al-Shibh confirmed that 9/11 financier, Ali Abdul Aziz Ali, was Ammar al-Baluchi, ████████████████████████████ [184] The Study asserts that "Ammar al-Baluchi played no role in the operation that captured KSM, which centered around████ █████████████"[185] While Ammar might not have played a direct role in the "operation" that captured KSM, bin al-Shibh's key insights about Ammar clarified his importance such that Alec Station highlighted bin al-Shibh's photo-identification of Ammar al-Baluchi as a breakthrough.[186]

(TS█████████████NF) Moreover, according to the CIA, bin al-Shibh's information about Ammar al Baluchi was used to interrogate DETAINEE R.[187] This claim is supported by a CIA requirements cable which contained numerous questions concerning KSM ████ █████[188] In late 2002, DETAINEE R provided background and physical details on KSM ████ █████████[189]███████████████████the next day, DETAINEE R ████████████ █████

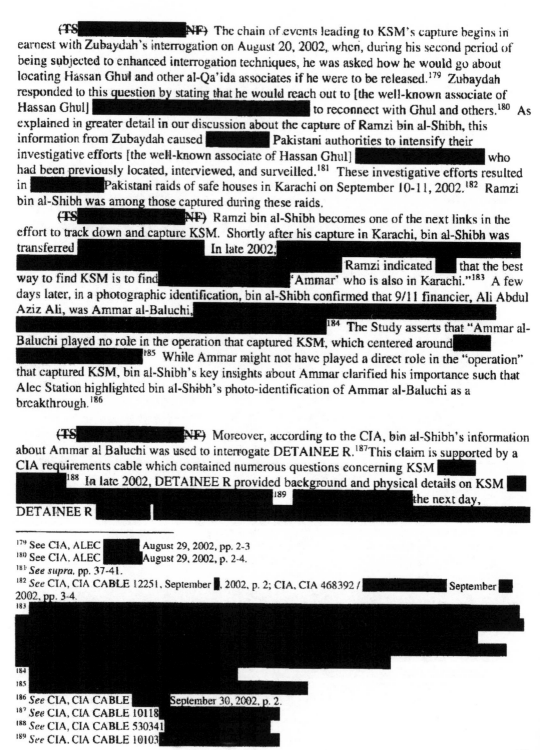

[179] See CIA, ALEC ████ August 29, 2002, pp. 2-3
[180] See CIA. ALEC ████ August 29, 2002, p. 2-4.
[181] See supra, pp. 37-41.
[182] See CIA, CIA CABLE 12251, September █, 2002, p. 2; CIA, CIA 468392 / █████████ September █ 2002, pp. 3-4.
[183] ████████████████████████████████████
[184] ████
[185] ████
[186] See CIA, CIA CABLE ████ September 30, 2002, p. 2.
[187] See CIA, CIA CABLE 10118
[188] See CIA, CIA CABLE 530341
[189] See CIA. CIA CABLE 10103

██████████████████████████ [190] The next day ████████████ the CIA interrogators continuing their questioning of DETAINEE R on the topic of KSM ████████████ DETAINEE R provided ████████████ [191] In late 2002 ███████████████ DETAINEE R was rendered into CIA custody and subjected to enhanced interrogation techniques. ████████████ ██████ CIA ████████ reported that ████████████ "said in no uncertain terms that none of the information provided by DETAINEE R has been of any use and ████████ ██████ wasted time here chasing people and places that are probably bogus." CIA urged interrogators to readdress the issues with DETAINEE R and acquire more—and more accurate—information. [192] ████████████████████ DETAINEE R was asked to provide as much locational information as possible on ████████████████████████████ ███ ███

(TS██████████████████NF) This brings us to ASSET X, who was initially undervalued by the CIA, despite his repeated claims that he could help locate KSM in Pakistan. In ████ 2001 the asset declined to work with the CIA because his proposed financial compensation package had been rejected. In ████ 2002, the Counterterrorism Center directed recruiters to reconnect with ASSET X. [194] By ████ of that same year, he was assigned to a new case officer. The case officer was unfamiliar with ASSET X's potential to provide information that might lead to the location of KSM, and the cables he sent to CIA Headquarters in pursuit of guidance in handling the asset went unread and unanswered when they were re-routed to a compartmented team which had been disbanded. [195]

(TS██████████████████NF) Having heard nothing back from CIA Headquarters, the case officer was on the verge of terminating the CIA's relationship with the asset in ████████ 2002. When the case officer met with his Chief of Base to discuss the termination, by chance, another CIA officer with prior operational contact with the asset [196] overheard their conversation as he was waiting to meet with the Chief of Base. This other CIA officer ████████ ████████ having come from ████████████ that reported information from DETAINEE R ███████████████████████ The officer's current mission included trying to track down KSM. He recognized ASSET X's information ████████ ███ He advised ASSET X's current case officer and the Chief of Base against proceeding with the termination, and joined in a meeting between the current case officer and ASSET X]. ASSET X was subsequently able to provide information that resulted in KSM's capture on March 1, 2003.

---

[190] *See* CIA, CIA CABLE 10120█████████
[191] *See* CIA, CIA CABLE 10140█████████
[192] *See* CIA. CIA CABLE 10250█████████
[193] *See* CIA████CIA CABLE] 30266.███████
[194] *See* CIA Oral History Program, *Interview of [REDACTED] by [REDACTED],* October 14, 2004, p. 3.
[195] *See* CIA Oral History Program, *Interview of [REDACTED] by [REDACTED],* October 14, 2004, p. 4.
[196] ███████████████████████████████████████
[197] ███████████████████████████████████████

(TS ███████████ NF) Although ASSET X's contributions were clearly important to KSM's capture, the true linchpin in the operation was the visiting officer's familiarity with the crucial information that the detainees had provided about KSM. Information from DETAINEE R background and ███████████ information on KSM ████████ lies at the end of a causal chain that traces back through Ramzi bin al-Shibh and Abu Zubaydah. Absent this collective body of information, the requisite understanding of KSM's activities, organizational stature, ███████████ would have eluded analysts, to make nothing of the fact ASSET X's relationship with the CIA would have been terminated in ████ 2002; months in advance of KSM's March 2003 capture.

(U) *The Disruption of the Karachi Hotels Bombing Plot*

Study Claim: (TS ███████████ NF) "[T]he CIA's enhanced interrogation techniques—to include the waterboard—played no role in the disruption of the Karachi Plot(s)."[198]

Fact: (U) CIA documents show that key intelligence collected through the CIA's Detention and Interrogation Program, including information obtained after the use of enhanced interrogation techniques, played a major role in disrupting the Karachi hotels bombing plot.

(TS ███████████ NF) As the Study notes, the reference to the "Karachi Plot(s)" refers to:

> terrorist plotting that targeted a variety of U.S. and western interests in the Karachi area, to include the U.S. Consulate, named hotels near the airport and beach, U.S. vehicles traveling between the Consulate and the airport, U.S. diplomatic housing, potential sniper attacks against U.S. personnel, as well as Pakistan's Faisal Army Base.[199]

(S//NF) The CIA has acknowledged that on several occasions, including in prominent representations such as President's Bush's 2006 speech, it mischaracterized the impact of the reporting acquired from detainees on the Karachi plots. Instead of claiming that the information "helped stop a planned attack on the U.S. Consulate in Karachi," the CIA should have stated that it "revealed ongoing attack plotting against the U.S. official presence in Karachi that prompted the Consulate to take further steps to protect its officers."[200]

(TS ███████████ NF) Our analysis will demonstrate that the intelligence collected through the CIA's Detention and Interrogation Program, including information obtained after the use of enhanced interrogation techniques, played a key role in the disruption of the Karachi hotels bombing plot. The Study notes that the CIA had information regarding the Karachi

---

[198] SSCI Study, Executive Summary, December 3, 2014, p. 242.
[199] SSCI Study, Executive Summary, December 3, 2014, p. 239; *see also* CIA, ████ 11454, April 30, 2003, pp. 1-4.
[200] CIA Study Response, *Case Studies (TAB C)*, June 27, 2013, p. 6.

terrorist plotting as early as September 11, 2002, in the form of the "perfume letter," which was obtained during a ▮▮▮ raid ▮▮▮▮▮▮▮▮▮▮▮▮▮▮▮▮ of a safe house in Karachi, Pakistan.[201] What the Study fails to point out, however, is that Abu Zubaydah provided crucial information which played a big role in leading to the ▮▮▮ raids of the al-Qa'ida safe houses on September 11, 2002—the same raids that yielded the "perfume letter" and disrupted the Karachi hotels plot. Specifically, ▮▮▮▮▮▮ Pakistani raids were the direct result of information provided by Abu Zubaydah on August 20, 2002, during his second period of enhanced interrogation.[202]

(TS▮▮▮▮▮▮▮▮▮▮▮▮NF) When asked how he would go about finding his former al-Qa'ida associates if he were set free, Abu Zubaydah told CIA interrogators that he would contact a well-known associate of Hassan Ghul who could put him in touch with Ghul and other senior al-Qa'ida members.[203] CIA officers then asked Pakistani officials to question the well-known associate of Hassan Ghul, who on September 7, 2002, provided vague information the Pakistanis assessed was untruthful.[204] The Pakistanis continued to watch the residence and, when another well-known associate of Hassan Ghul returned to the residence, questioned the other well-known associate of Hassan Ghul as well. The other well-known associate of Hassan Ghul cooperated and provided the location of Ghul's last apartment.[205] This information led to the arrest, on September 9, 2002, of an individual thought to be Ghul[206], but who turned out to be another al-Qa'ida terrorist.[207] Abu Zubaydah then positively identified this terrorist as Abu Badr, "KSM's driver and KSM's man in Karachi," facilitating the movement of al-Qa'ida operatives.[208] Badr's driver, who was also arrested, identified information about several al-Qa'ida safehouses and residences in Karachi.[209]

(TS▮▮▮▮▮▮▮▮▮▮▮▮NF) Based on this information, on September 11, 2002, ▮▮▮▮▮▮ ▮▮▮▮▮▮▮▮▮▮ conducted ▮▮▮ raids, which resulted in the arrests of several terrorists and key documents, including one dubbed the "perfume letter" because the word "perfumes" was used as a codeword.[210] In this May 2002 letter, KSM told Hamza Zubayr, a terrorist killed in the same raids, he would provide him with $30,000, with another $20,000 available upon request, and that "we have acquired the green light that is strong for the [hotels]" clearly indicating a plot of some kind.[211] More troubling, the letter suggested "[increasing] the number to make it three instead of one."[212] Were it not for Abu Zubaydah's original information about the significance

---

[201] See SSCI Study, Executive Summary, December 3, 2014, p. 242; CIA, ALEC ▮▮▮▮▮October 03, 2002, p. 2; and CIA, ALEC ▮▮▮▮October 3, 2002, pp. 2-4.
[202] See CIA, *Captures Resulting From Detainee Information: Four Case Studies*, November 26, 2003, p.2.
[203] See CIA, *Captures Resulting From Detainee Information: Four Case Studies*, November 26, 2003. p.2; CIA, ▮▮▮ 10644. August 29, 2002, pp. 1-2; CIA, ALEC ▮▮▮▮August 29, 2002, pp. 2-3.
[204] See CIA, ALEC ▮▮▮▮▮▮▮▮▮▮ CIA, CIA CABLE 12207, September 05, 2002, pp. 2-3.
[205] See CIA, CIA CABLE 12249, September 09, 2002, p. 2.
[206] See CIA, CIA CABLE 12251, September ▮, 2002, p. 2.
[207] See CIA, CIA CABLE 12254, September 10, 2002, p. 4; CIA, ALEC ▮▮▮▮▮▮▮▮▮▮▮▮▮
[208] CIA, ALEC ▮▮▮▮▮▮▮▮▮▮▮
[209] See CIA, CIA CABLE 12251, September ▮, 2002, p. 2.
[210] See CIA, CIA CABLE 12267, September 11, 2002, p. 2; CIA, CIA CABLE ▮▮▮▮October 03, 2002, p. 2.
[211] CIA, CIA CABLE 33804, September 19, 2002, p. 4; After his capture on April 1, 2003, KSM would confirm that the Karachi plot referenced in the "perfume letter" was the plot directed at three named hotels, chosen because they were frequented by American and German guests. See SSCI Study, Volume II, April 1, 2014, pp. 592-593
[212] CIA, CIA CABLE 33804, September 19, 2002, p. 4.

46

of the well-known associate of Hassan Ghul, which led to the Karachi safe house raids, it is unclear if the "perfume letter" would ever have been found.

(TS███████████NF) Abu Zubaydah's value, however, did not end with providing the true significance of the well-known associate of Hassan Ghul. Zubaydah subsequently translated the "perfume letter" for the CIA, identified the key word in the letter—"hotels"—that had not been previously translated, and told the CIA that the reference to "Khallad" in the letter may be the "one legged Yemeni." A CIA analyst noted that the one-legged Yemeni was terrorist Khallad bin Attash, who was later arrested and admitted to his involvement in the plot.[213]

(TS███████████NF) By early October 2002, the CIA had completed a search of the individuals identified in the "perfume letter" and concluded that most of those who had been assigned roles in support of the hotels operation had been arrested or killed by the Pakistani authorities during the September 11, 2002 raids.[214] Although the Karachi hotels plot had been thwarted by these raids, at least one of the individuals identified by Abu Zubaydah in the letter, Khallad bin Attash, a known al-Qa'ida operative, remained at large.[215] Eventually, on April 28, 2003, █████████████████████████ was able to capture several al-Qa'ida operatives, including Ammar al-Baluchi and bin Attash. █████ also successfully confiscated explosives, detonators, and ammunition as part of the capture operation.[216]

(TS███████████NF) On May 17, 2003, Khallad bin Attash confirmed that Ammar al-Baluchi had intended to use the explosives stashed for that operation to target the U.S. Consulate.[217] The next day, ████████████ indicated its clear understanding of how these interrelated Karachi plot events had improved the U.S. security posture in the area when it noted that although its options to enhance security:

> may appear limited . . . ████████████████████████ and what we have seen over past months as an increased aggressiveness of local authorities have provided some protection from these threats. We point specifically to the 11 September 2002 raids in Karachi, the 1 March 2003 take-down of KSM, and to the recent arrests of al-Baluchi and ba Attash as examples of how █████ have thwarted attacks.[218]

(U) *The Heathrow and Canary Wharf Plots*

Study Claim: (TS███████████NF) **"[C]ontrary to CIA representations, information acquired during or after the use of the CIA's enhanced interrogation techniques played no role in 'alert[ing]' the CIA to the threat to—or the**

---

[213] See E-mail from. CIA analyst; to: ████████; subject: *Re: AZ on the perfume letter;* date: October 10, 2002, at 9:50 AM, p. 6.
[214] *See CIA,* ALEC █████ October 3, 2002, pp. 2-12.
[215] *See CIA,* ALEC █████ October 3, 2002, pp. 2-12.
[216] *See* CIA, CIA CABLE 45028, ████████
[217] *See* CIA, [CIA CABLE] 38405, May 17, 2003, p. 4.
[218] CIA, CIA CABLE 14510████████████

'disrupt[ing]' the plotting against—Heathrow Airport and Canary Wharf."[219]

Fact: (TS███████████████ NF) The CIA interrogation program played a key role in disrupting the Heathrow and Canary Wharf plotting.

(TS███████████ NF) Despite its claim that information acquired during or after the use of enhanced interrogation techniques played "no role" in the disruption of the Heathrow Airport and Canary Wharf plots, the Study twice concedes these plots were "fully disrupted" with the detentions of Ramzi bin al-Shibh, KSM, Ammar al-Baluchi, and Khallad bin Attash.[220] The Study then incorrectly asserts that "[t]here are no CIA records to indicate that any of the detainees was captured as a result of CIA detainee reporting."[221] As we have previously demonstrated, information obtained from the CIA interrogation program played a key role in the capture of al-Shibh and KSM.[222] Also, Ramzi bin al-Shibh provided information about Ammar al-Baluchi and Abu Zubaydah provided information about Khallad bin Attash prior to their arrests.[223] The same detainee information that helped lead to the capture of these terrorists also played a key role in fully disrupting the Heathrow Airport and Canary Wharf plots.

(TS███████████ NF) Thus far, the following analytical dominoes have fallen in relation to the Heathrow and Canary Wharf plots: (1) "There is considerable evidence that the information Abu Zubaydah provided identifying KSM as "Mukhtar" and the mastermind of 9/11 was significant to CIA analysts, operators, and FBI interrogators";[224] (2) "Abu Zubaydah provided information about how he would go about locating Hassan Ghul and other al-Qa'ida associates in Karachi. This information caused ████████ Pakistani authorities to intensify their efforts and helped lead them to capture Ramzi bin al-Shibh and other al-Qa'ida associates during the Karachi safe house raids conducted on September 10-11, 2002";[225] (3) "Information produced through detainee interrogation was pivotal to the retention of a key CIA asset whose cooperation led directly to the capture of KSM";[226] (4) Zubaydah told the CIA that the reference to "Khallad" in the letter may be the "one legged Yemeni";[227] and (5) Pakistan's arrest of al-Qa'ida terrorists Ammar al-Baluchi and Khallad Bin Attash disrupted the al-Qa'ida plot to attack the U.S. Consulate in Karachi.[228] Taken together, these significant operational accomplishments, most of them resulting from information obtained from CIA detainees, also had the added bonus of disrupting the Heathrow and Canary Wharf plots.

(TS███████████ NF) The Study undercuts its own argument that the CIA interrogation program played no role in the disruption of the Heathrow and Canary Wharf

---

[219] SSCI Study, Executive Summary, December 3, 2014, pp. 297-298.

[220] See SSCI Study, Executive Summary, December 3, 2014, pp. 295 and 299.

[221] SSCI Study, Executive Summary, December 3, 2014, p. 299.

[222] See supra, pp. 37-45.

[223] See supra, pp. 43 and 47.

[224] See supra, pp. 29-33.

[225] See supra, pp. 37-41.

[226] See supra, pp. 41-45.

[227] E-mail from: CIA analyst; to: ████████ ; subject: Re: AZ on the perfume letter; date: October 10, 2002, at 9:50 AM, p. 6.

[228] See CIA Study Response, Case Studies (Tab C), p. 6.

plotting almost immediately after its narrative on the plots begins. The Study says "records indicate the Heathrow Airport plotting had not progressed beyond the initial planning stages when the operation was fully disrupted with the detention of Ramzi bin al-Shibh (detained on September 11, 2002), KSM (detained on March 1, 2003), Ammar al-Baluchi (detained on April 29, 2003), and Khallad bin Attash (detained on April 29, 2003)."[229] As we explained previously, Ramzi bin al-Shibh was detained as a result of information provided by Abu Zubaydah during a period of enhanced interrogation.[230] By asserting that the detention of Ramzi bin al-Shibh played a role in the disruption of the plot, certainly the detainee information that led to his detention also played a role in the plot's disruption.

(TS███████████NF) Additionally, while the Study claims that the CIA already had information in its possession prior to the detention and interrogation of those detainees the CIA credits with providing information on the plot (KSM, Ammar al-Baluchi, and Khallad bin Attash), much of that reporting, including identification of Heathrow airport as the target, came from interrogations of Ramzi bin al-Shibh occurring prior to CIA custody. Again, ███████████ were only able to detain and question Ramzi bin al-Shibh because information provided by Abu Zubaydah in CIA detention led to bin al-Shibh's arrest.

(TS███████████NF) While the Study cites a CIA document to support its claim that the plot "was fully disrupted" with the arrests of the four previously mentioned terrorists, the CIA document says that the plot was "disrupted," not "fully disrupted."[231] Perhaps for that reason, the CIA continued to interrogate detainees about the plot, long after the arrests of both Ramzi bin al-Shibh and KSM, to uncover more details about the plot and any operatives. For example, the CIA confronted Ramzi bin al-Shibh and KSM about e-mail addresses found in KSM's computer that belonged to the two Saudi-based operatives who could have been used in the plot, Ayyub and Azmari.[232] Although the Study notes that these two operatives were "unwitting" of the Heathrow plot, they appear to have been willing terrorist operatives, as the CIA learned that Ayyub participated in a suicide attack in Riyadh, Saudi Arabia on May 12, 2003, that killed 36 individuals and injured more than 160 others. Azmari was arrested on July 1, 2003 for his connections to the attack.[233]

(TS███████████NF) Additionally, as noted in several papers and briefings by the CIA, in mid-March 2003, the CIA questioned KSM about a hand-drawn illustration in his notebook of what appeared to be an I-beam with the term "Wharf" written in English, and "Cannery Wharf" in Arabic.[234] KSM told interrogators it was part of the "Heathrow program" to target Canary Wharf in London as well, a target that had not been previously discussed by other detainees.[235]

---

[229] SSCI Study, Volume II, April 1, 2014, pp. 1000-1062.
[230] See supra pp. 37-41.
[231] SSCI Study, Volume II, April 1, 2014, pp. 976-78.
[232] See SSCI Study, Volume II, April 1, 2014, p. 983.
[233] SSCI Study, Volume II, p. 983 n.4387.
[234] CIA, WASHINGTON DC ███████████ CIA, ███ 10787, March 13, 2003, p. 3.
[235] See CIA, ███ 10787, March 13, 2003, p. 3.

(TS███████████████NF) After the detention in April 29, 2003, of Khallad bin Attash and Ammar al-Baluchi, debriefers used the reporting from KSM and bin al-Shibh to confront them. In a document explaining the value of detainee reporting provided to the Department of Justice, CIA explained:

> Khallad admitted to having been involved in the plot and revealed that he directed group leader Hazim al-Sha'ir to begin locating pilots who could hijack planes and crash them into the airport. Khallad said he and operative Abu Talha al-Pakistani considered █████ countries as possible launch sites for the hijacking attempts and that they narrowed the options to the █████████████████████████ Khallad's statements provided leverage in debriefings of KSM. KSM fleshed out the status of the operation, including identifying an additional target in the United Kingdom, Canary Wharf.[236]

(U) In the years that followed the initial arrest of Ramzi bin al-Shibh, CIA officers continued to unravel the details of this plotting and provided information that helped lead to the detention and questioning of several other individuals involved in the plot.[237] In light of the information cited above, the Study's assertion that the CIA interrogation program played "no role" in the disruption of this plotting makes little sense, especially when the Study's own 62-page chart identifying the intelligence on the Heathrow plot devotes most of the pages to information from detainees in CIA's program or to Ramzi bin al-Shibh, who was captured because of CIA detainee information.[238]

(U) *The Capture of Hambali*

Study Claim: (TS████████████NF) "A review of CIA operational cables and other records found that information obtained from KSM during or after the use of the CIA's enhanced interrogation techniques played no role in the capture of Hambali."[239]

Fact: (TS████████████NF) CIA documents show that the interrogation of KSM and al-Qa'ida operative Zubair, during and after the use of enhanced interrogation techniques on both individuals, played a key role in the capture of Hambali.

(TS████████████NF) The Study's claim that the enhanced interrogation of KSM played "no role" in the capture of Hambali is not accurate, because two detainees subjected to enhanced interrogation techniques, KSM and Mohd Farik bin Amin, a senior member of Jemaah Islamiya (JI) and more commonly known as "Zubair,[240] provided significant information that helped lead to the capture of Hambali.

---

[236] CIA, *Briefing Notes on the Value of Detainee Reporting*, April 8, 2005, 10:47am, p. 4.

[237] *See* SSCI Study, Volume II, April 1, 2014, pp. 1000-1062.

[238] *See* SSCI Study, Volume II, April 1, 2014, pp. 1000-1062.

[239] SSCI Study, Executive Summary, December 3, 2014, p. 305.

[240] The Study acknowledges that Zubair was immediately subjected to CIA enhanced interrogation techniques upon being transferred into CIA custody on June██2003. *See* SSCI Study, Executive Summary, December 3, 2014, p. 309. It attempts to downplay this fact by noting that: (1) "CIA records indicate that Thai authorities were unilaterally following investigative leads related to Hambali and Zubair" and that "[i]t is unknown what specific investigative steps were taken by Thai authorities (or the CIA) between early June 2003 and July 16, 2003, to

(TS███████████NF) The claim that the enhanced interrogation of KSM played "no role" in the capture of Hambali ignores the fact that KSM provided the crucial piece of information permitting the CIA to recognize the significance of. and act upon, previously known connections that would ultimately lead to Hambali's capture. The Study correctly points out that on March 6, 2003, Majid Khan told foreign government ████████ interrogators about his travel to Bangkok in December 2002 and provision of $50,000 to an individual named "Zubair" at the behest of al-Qa'ida.[241] While the Study would like the reader to infer that Majid Khan provided a sufficient connection to Hambali, the Study ignores the fact that Khan never mentioned that the money was destined for Hambali. Moreover, the Study excludes the CIA's answer to the following question for the record: "Was there enough other information linking Zubair and Hambali?" The CIA's answer states:

> No. We assess, and believe the documentary record indicates that otherwise available intelligence was not sufficient to enable officers at the time to conclude Zubair was a targeting inroad to Hambali. A targeting study on Hambali in the late December timeframe, for example, lists a number of potential inroads but not Zubair. A look at the contemporaneous records as well as a plot summary from years later provide no evidence that Zubair played a role in the Bali Bombings.[242]

While Majid Khan's information was still an important piece of the puzzle, it is clear that something more was needed to help locate Hambali. That "something more" would come from KSM several days later.

(TS███████████NF) KSM had been rendered into CIA custody on March █ 2003, and immediately subjected to enhanced interrogation.[243] On March 11, 2003, KSM admitted to providing Hambali with $50,000 to conduct a terrorist attack in "approximately November 2002." KSM reported, however, that the money was "necessary materials" for a Hambali operation that was approaching "zero hour," information that created a sense of urgency for the CIA to uncover more about Hambali's location.[244] During this interrogation, KSM made no reference to Majid Khan or Zubair.[245] On March 13, 2003, CIA███████████ sent a

---

investigate [BUSINESS Q] ████ ████████████ and (2) the CIA has never represented "to policymakers that the information obtained from Zubair after the use of the CIA's enhanced interrogation techniques led to Hambali's capture." See SSCI Study, Executive Summary, December 3, 2014, pp. 309, n.1737. Although we might not know what specific "unilateral" steps were taken by the Thai authorities related to ████████, if any, CIA records provide a good description of the information provided by Zubair after the use of enhanced interrogation techniques and the subsequent steps taken by the CIA, including ████████████, to track down and capture Hambali. The absence of a CIA representation about Zubair does not invalidate the assertion that the information he provided after being subjected to enhanced interrogation techniques may have helped lead to the capture of Hambali, especially since this assertion is supported by the CIA documentary record.

[241] SSCI Study, Executive Summary, December 3, 2014, pp. 307-308.

[242] CIA Response to SSCI Request for Information, October 25, 2013, p. 4 (DTS 2013-3152). This answer contradicts the assertion by the Study that "[b]y this time, the CIA had significant information—prior to KSM's capture—indicating that a 'Zubair' played a central supporting role in the JI, was affiliated with al-Qa'ida figures like KSM, had expertise in ████████ in Southeast Asia, and was suspected of playing a role in Hambali's October 12, 2002, Bali bombings." SSCI Study, Executive Summary, December 3, 2014, p. 306-307.

[243] See CIA. [CIA CABLE] 34491, March 5, 2003, pp. 1-3.

[244] CIA, ███ 10755, March 11, 2003.

[245] See CIA, ███ 10755, March 11, 2003, pp. 1-3.

cable saying that in light of KSM's information that he arranged to send $50,000 to Hambali in November 2002 to procure materials for an operation that was approaching "zero hour," "we view [the information] from Majid Khan on his trip to Bangkok for an alleged money transfer between 26-29 December with ever greater concern."[246] Moreover, the same cable makes clear that at the time of KSM's reporting, the CIA did not know whether the information from KSM and Majid Khan were about the same transaction. The cable says, "KSM's information and Majid's 'story' may be unrelated, but it appears too premature to judge at this juncture, and we must assume they possibly are until additional facts are learned."[247]

(TS███████████NF) On March 17, 2003, KSM was questioned about the Majid Khan network. KSM positively identified a picture of Majid Khan as "Majid aka Yusif, the al-Qa'ida courier" KSM used to deliver the $50,000 for the next big Hambali operation, through "Hambali representatives in Thailand."[248] Significantly, KSM said that Khan had not been informed that the money was ultimately for Hambali and that KSM did not know who Hambali's intermediary was.[249] Days later, CIA officers still seemed to be trying to understand the connection between the KSM and the Majid Khan reporting. According to a March 20, 2003, cable, KSM's reporting that he used Majid Khan as a courier to transport al-Qa'ida funds to Hambali, "appears to confirm station [sic] earlier concerns that the $50,000 transfer involving KSM and Hambali may be one in the same with the $50,000 al-Qa'ida transfer facilitated by Khan.[250] Questioned again on March 22, 2003, Khan acknowledged that his trip to Thailand to deliver the $50,000 was at KSM's request.[251]

(U) While it would be difficult to know conclusively without talking to the analysts involved, CIA documents indicate it was the combination of reporting from KSM and Majid Khan that led to the efforts to find Hambali through Zubair. A CIA summary of Hambali's capture timeline states, while "numerous sources had placed Hambali in various Southeast Asian countries, it was captured al-Qa'ida leader KSM who put ███████████████ on Hambali's trail"—contradicting the Study's claim that the KSM interrogation played "no role."[252]

(TS███████████NF) On June 8, 2003, Zubair was detained by the Government of Thailand. ███████████, Zubair reported on ███████████ ███████and corroborated reporting on Business Q.[253] On June ██ 2003, Zubair was transferred into CIA custody and was immediately subjected to enhanced interrogation techniques.[254] Zubair told his interrogators about ██████████████████████████ ██████████████████████████████████████.[255] Zubair

---

[246] CIA, CIA CABLE, 81697, ██████████
[247] See CIA, CIA CABLE, 81697, ██████
[248] CIA, ██████ 10865, March 17, 2003, p. 3.
[249] See CIA, ██████ 10865, March 17, 2003, p. 3.
[250] CIA, CIA CABLE 81990, March 20, 2003, p. 2.
[251] See CIA, CIA CABLE 13890, ██████
[252] CIA, *Hambali Capture/Detention Timeline*, no date, p. 6.
[253] See CIA Study Response, *Case Studies (TAB C)*, June 27, 2013, p. 19.
[254] See CIA [CIA CABLE] 40568, ██████
[255] See CIA, *Hambali Capture/Detention Timeline*, no date, p. 7; CIA, [CIA CABLE] 40915 ██████ ██████ CIA, [CIA CABLE] 41017, ██████

also explained how he ██

.[256] This information was consistent with the information he had provided ████████

(TS█████████████NF)

████████the CIA planned an operation to find Hambali by watching██████████and waiting for Hambali's facilitators████████████████████ It appears that Zubair provided key information about these Hambali facilitators after being subjected to the CIA's enhanced interrogation techniques. Specifically, CIA documents show that analysts assessed that it would be "Zubair cohort and former roommate Lilie"███████████████████████ because "per the Zubair debriefings, Lilie is now████████████████████████████ and "finding Lilie, therefore, may be tantamount to finding Hambali."[258] ████████ Hambali associate Amer, who actually███████████████was tracked and Zubair identified a picture of him and speculated that "Lilie likely tasked [Amer] to handle██████ thus following Amer would likely lead to finding Lilie."[259] Amer was arrested on August 11, 2003, and cooperated in locating Lilie hours later.[260] Lilie was found to have a key fob in his possession imprinted with an address, which Lilie said was the address of two apartments he used for Hambali's activities, one of which was Hambali's residence.[261] Hambali was captured at the address found on the key fob several hours later.[262] It appears that Zubair's cooperation after being subjected to enhanced interrogation techniques played a significant role in the capture of Hambali through Amer and Lilie.

(U) *The Thwarting of the Second Wave Plots and Discovery of the Al-Ghuraba Group*

Study Claim: (TS███████████████NF) **"A review of CIA operational cables and other documents found that the CIA's enhanced interrogation techniques played no role in the 'discovery' or thwarting of either 'Second Wave' plot. Likewise, records indicate that the CIA's enhanced interrogation techniques played no role in the 'discovery' of a 17-member 'cell tasked with executing the 'Second Wave.'"[263]**

---

[256] See CIA. *Hambali Capture/Detention Timeline*. no date. p. 7; CIA, [CIA CABLE] 40915 ████████
[257] *See* CIA, *Hambali Capture/Detention Timeline*. no date, p. 7-8; CIA, ALEC ██████████
[258] CIA, *Hambali Capture/Detention Timeline*, no date, p. 2.
[259] CIA, *Hambali Capture/Detention Timeline*, no date, p. 5.
[260] CIA, *Hambali Capture/Detention Timeline*, no date, p. 5.
[261] CIA. *Hambali Capture/Detention Timeline*, no date, p. 6.
[262] CIA, *Hambali Capture/Detention Timeline*, no date, p. 5.
[263] SSCI Study, Executive Summary, December 3, 2014, p. 251. This claim has been modified from the version that appeared in the report that was approved by the Committee at the end of the 112th Congress. For example, it no longer claims that the CIA's interrogation program, excluding the use of enhanced interrogation techniques, did not play a role in the thwarting of the al-Ghuraba Group. It also substitutes the words "discovery *or* thwarting" in place of the original "identification *and* disruption." (emphasis added).

Fact: (TS███████████NF) **The CIA interrogation program played a key role in disrupting the "Second Wave" plot and led to the capture of the 17-member al-Ghuraba group.**

(TS███████████NF) The Study asserts that because Hambali's brother, Gun Gun Ruswan Gunawan, first identified a group of 17 Malaysian and Indonesian Jemaah Islamiya (JI) affiliated students in Karachi, "the use of the CIA's enhanced interrogation techniques against Hambali did not result in the 'discovery' of 'the Ghuraba Cell' that was 'tasked with executing the 'Second Wave' plotting.'"[264] While Gunawan did identify the group of JI students in Karachi, the Study ignores that KSM, who had also been subjected to the CIA's enhanced interrogation techniques, provided information months earlier on this same group of JI students and their location in Karachi—information that had helped lead to the capture of Gunawan himself. The Study also ignores information provided by other detainees in CIA's interrogation program.

(TS███████████NF) In April 2003, KSM provided information about Gunawan's role in Karachi as a communications conduit between Hambali and al-Qa'ida and reported that he was living in the dormitory where he was enrolled at Abu Bakr-Sadeeq University.[265] KSM also drew a map with the location of a house he called "Colony Gate" where he met Gunawan, where he said a group of JI students would meet.[266] According to CIA information, while the CIA was already aware of Gunawan, "KSM's identification of his role as Hambali's potential successor prioritized his capture. Information from multiple detainees, including KSM, narrowed down [Gunawan's] location and enabled his capture in September 2003."[267] This information was excluded from the Study. Hambali provided very similar information after his capture in August 2003 ███████████.[268]

(TS███████████NF) On August 20, 2003, CIA headquarters provided information on Gunawan ███████████ "which solidly ties Rusman Gunawan to al-Qa'ida and al-Qa'ida's terrorist attacks" ███████████[269] The information provided was largely from interrogations of KSM, including information about Gunawan working as a communications conduit for Hambali and al-Qa'ida, his location in Karachi, a description of Gunawan, but also provided information from another detainee in CIA custody, Ammar al-Baluchi.[270] Gunawan was arrested on ███████████, at the Abu Bakr Madrassa, locational information first provided by KSM, along with most of JI student group.[271]

(TS███████████NF) After Gunawan's arrest he was caught trying to send a coded message which he admitted was intended to warn the group of JI-affiliated students about

---

[264] SSCI Study, Executive Summary, December 3, 2014, pp. 255-256.
[265] See CIA, ███ 11192, April 8, 2003, p. 3.
[266] See CIA, ███ 11212, April 11, 2003, p. 2.
[267] CIA, Detainee Reporting Pivotal for the War Against Al-Qa'ida, June 1, 2005, p. 2 (DTS 2009-1387).
[268] See CIA, CIA CABLE 87551, August 15, 2003, pp. 4-5.
[269] CIA, ALEC ███████████
[270] CIA, ALEC ███████████
[271] See CIA, CIA CABLE 15252, ███████████

his arrest.[272] ████████ participating in the interrogation recognized Gunawan's information about this group of mostly Malaysian students as similar to intelligence reporting provided previously by KSM that he was planning to recruit Malaysians in a "next wave of attacks."[273] The officers asked that Hambali be questioned about the reporting.[274]

(TS████████NF) During a CIA interrogation of Hambali days later. Hambali, now in CIA custody and undergoing enhanced interrogation, provided more information about the group, identifying them as the "al-Ghuraba" group and describing how they were set up by Hambali and sent to Karachi because of its "proximity to Afghanistan and the availability of military-style training facilities there."[275] He said the Program was designed to "give a select few the opportunity for military-style training to prepare them for jihad" and identified two who were ready for operations.[276] Hambali provided information about the identities and backgrounds of several of the al-Ghuraba group members and described conversations he had with KSM about possible future attacks on the United States.[277] In a subsequent interrogation, Hambali said the group was not yet ready for operations, but may be in 2003-2004 (it was already late 2003 when he provided this information) and he named individuals who were being groomed as suicide and other operatives.[278]

(TS████████NF) ████████ arrested the members of the al-Ghuraba group during raids on ████████. A cable describing the arrests said, "[W]e captured this cell based on the debriefings of captured senior al-Qa'ida operatives, who stated that some members of this cell were to be part of senior al-Qa['ida leader Khalid Shaykh Muhammad (KSM)['s] [']second wave['] operation to attack the United States using the same modus operandi as was used in the September 11, 2001 attacks."[279]

(TS████████NF) In a seeming effort to suggest CIA's assessment of the threat posed by the al-Ghuraba group had diminished over time, the Study identified an October 27, 2006, CIA cable that stated, "[A]ll of the members of the former al-Ghuraba cell have now been released."[280] It also cited an April 18, 2008, CIA intelligence report focusing on the Jemaah Islamiya and referencing the al-Ghuraba group that makes no reference to the group serving as potential operatives for KSM's 'Second Wave' plotting."[281]

(TS/████████NF) These statements are misleading in several ways. The April 18, 2008 intelligence report was about Jemaah Islamiya in Pakistan, not the al-Ghuraba group, and provided only a minor description of the "al-Ghuraba cell in Karachi," but did mention that its leader was in direct contact with Hambali and "al-Qa'ida external operations chief Khalid

---

[272] See CIA, CIA CABLE 15359, ████████
[273] CIA, CIA CABLE 15359, ████████
[274] See CIA, CIA CABLE 15359, ████████
[275] CIA, [CIA CABLE] 45915, September 14, 2003, p. 2.
[276] CIA, [CIA CABLE] 45915, September 14, 2003, p. 2.
[277] See CIA. [CIA CABLE] 45915, September 14, 2003, p. 2.
[278] CIA, [CIA CABLE] 45953, September 15, 2003, p. 3.
[279] CIA, CIA CABLE 52981, ████████
[280] CIA, CIA CABLE 131396, October 27, 2006, p. 2.
[281] See CIA, Jemaah Islamiya: Counterterrorism Scrutiny Limiting Extremist Agenda in Pakistan, April 18, 2008.

Shaykh Muhammad."[282] The Study omitted a report focused on Jemaah Islamiya's al-Ghuraba group published five months later that said "members of the cell had also been identified by Khalid Shaykh Muhammad, the mastermind of the attacks of 11 September 2001, and senior al-Qa'ida and JI operative Hambali as candidates for post-11 September attacks against the U.S. Homeland," including for "second wave suicide hijacking operations in the Unites States and Europe."[283] Far from suggesting the CIA was unconcerned about the al-Ghuraba group, this report devoted 20 pages to describing the threat from its members including their "jihad activities" and the caution that "as this group of radicalized militants reconnects and mingles with other young Southeast Asian Muslims, it poses a revived threat to US and Western interests."[284]

(U) *Critical Intelligence Alerting the CIA to Jaffar al-Tayyar*

Study Claim: (TS███████████NF) "CIA representations [about detainee reporting on Jaffar al-Tayyar] also omitted key contextual facts, including that . . . (2) CIA detainee Abu Zubaydah provided a description and information on a KSM associate named Jaffar al-Tayyar to FBI Special Agents in May 2002, prior to being subjected to the CIA's enhanced interrogation techniques . . . and (5) CIA records indicate that KSM did not know al-Tayyar's true name and that it was Jose Padilla—in military custody and being questioned by the FBI—who provided al-Tayyar's true name as Adnan el-Shukrijumah."[286]

Fact: (TS███████████NF) Abu Zubaydah provided a description of and information about Jaffar al-Tayyar to FBI special agents in May 2002 *after* being subjected to enhanced interrogation between April 15, 2002 and April 21, 2002. Although KSM did not know al-Tayyar's true name, he did report that Padilla might know al-Tayyar's true name. Padilla subsequently confirmed Jaffar's true name as Adnan El Shukrijumah.

(TS███████████NF) On May 20, 2002, while in CIA custody, Abu Zubaydah provided information on an associate of KSM by the name of Abu Jaffar al-Thayer. Abu Zubaydah provided a detailed description of Abu Jaffar al-Thayer, including that he spoke English well and may have studied in the United States.[287] The Study incorrectly claims that this May 20, 2002, interrogation took place prior to the initiation of the CIA's enhanced interrogation techniques.[288] Abu Zubaydah had already been subjected to an extended period of sleep deprivation and other enhanced interrogation techniques during his interrogation between April 15, 2002 and April 21, 2002, about one month *prior* to his May 20 interrogation.[289]

---

[282] CIA, *Jemaah Islamiya: Counterterrorism Scrutiny Limiting Extremist Agenda in Pakistan*, April 18, 2008, p. 1.

[283] CIA, Southeast Asia: Jemaah Islamiya's Al-Ghuraba Cell Coalescing, September 17, 2008, pp. 1 and 2.

[284] CIA, Southeast Asia: Jemaah Islamiya's Al-Ghuraba Cell Coalescing, September 17, 2008, pp. 1-2.

[285] CIA, Southeast Asia: Jemaah Islamiya's Al-Ghuraba Cell Coalescing, September 17, 2008, p. 2.

[286] SSCI Study, Executive Summary, December 3, 2014, pp. 358-359.

[287] *See* FBI draft report of the interrogation of Abu Zubaydah, May 20, 2002, 5:25 p.m. to 8:40 p.m., p 3.

[288] *See* SSCI Study, Executive Summary, December 3, 2014, p. 362.

[289] *See supra*, pp. 33-36.

(TS███████████NF) The Study also cites as a key contextual fact omitted from CIA representations that KSM did not know al-Tayyar's true name, and it was Jose Padilla, in military custody and being questioned by the FBI, who provided al-Tayyar's true name as Adnan el-Shukrijumah.[290] However, this omission was rendered moot because, as the Study itself notes a few pages later,[291] the "FBI began participating in the military debriefings [of Padilla] in March 2003, *after KSM reported Padilla might know the true name of a US-bound al-Qa'ida operative known at the time only as Jaffar al-Tayyar*. Padilla subsequently confirmed Jaffar's true name as Adnan El Shukrijumah."[292]

(U) *The Identification and Arrest of Saleh al-Marri*

Study Claim: (TS███████████NF) **The Study correctly asserts, "[t]he CIA represented to the CIA Office of Inspector General that 'as a result of the lawful use of EITs,' KSM 'provided information that helped lead t the arrests of terrorists including . . . Saleh Almari, a sleeper operative in New York.'"** [293]

Fact: (TS███████████NF) **KSM provided valuable intelligence that helped to clarify Saleh al-Marri's role in al-Qa'ida operations and played a significant role in al-Marri's prosecution.**

(TS███████████NF) The Study cites an interview between the OIG and the Deputy Chief of the Counterterrorist Center, in which the deputy chief claims that information from KSM helped lead to the arrest of al-Marri.[294] As the Study makes clear, al-Marri was not arrested based on information from KSM, and could not have been, because al-Marri was arrested in December 2001, before the detention of KSM in March 2003. Two days after the interview with the IG, the deputy chief wrote in an email that al-Marri "had been detained on a material witness warrant based on information linking him to the 9/11 financier Hasawi."[295] The Study correctly notes that this inaccuracy appears in the final version of the OIG's May 2004 Special Review[296], as referenced in an Office of Legal Counsel memorandum analyzing the legality of the CIA's enhanced interrogation techniques.[297] In its response to the Study, the CIA

---

[290] *See* SSCI Study, Executive Summary, December 3, 2014, pp. 359.

[291] *See* SSCI Study, Executive Summary, December 3, 2014, p. 365.

[292] *See* CIA, *Briefing Notes on the Value of Detainee Reporting*, April 15, 2005, p. 3 (emphasis added); *See also* CIA, ALEC ████ March 21, 2003, p. 6 ("Our service has developed new information, based on leads from detained al-Qa'ida operations chief Khalid Shaykh Muhammad (KSM), that al-Qa'ida operative Jafar al-Tayyar's true name is Adnan Shukri Jumah and he could be involved in an imminent suicide attack in the United States").

[293] SSCI Study, Executive Summary, December 3, 2014, p. 366.

[294] SSCI Study, Executive Summary, December 3, 2014, p. 366 n.2064.

[295] Email from: ████████████; to: ████████ et al.; subject: value of detainees; date: July 18, 2003, at 2:30 PM.

[296] *See* CIA Office of Inspector General, *Special Review: Counterterrorism Detention and Interrogation Activities (September 2001 – October 2003)*, May 7, 2004, p. 87 (DTS 2004-2710).

[297] *See* Memorandum for John A. Rizzo, Senior Deputy General Counsel, Central Intelligence Agency, from Steven G. Bradbury, Principal Deputy Assistant Attorney General, Office of Legal Counsel, May 30, 2005, Re: Application of United States Obligations Under Article 16 of the Convention Against Torture to Certain Techniques that May be Used in the Interrogation of high Value Al Qaeda Detainees, p.9 (DTS 2009-1810, Tab 11).

concedes that the agency erred in describing detainee reporting as contributing to al-Marri's arrest. However, the agency stresses that KSM did provide valuable intelligence on al-Marri—intelligence that played a significant role in al-Marri's prosecution.[298]

(TS█████████████NF) The Study's focus on this factual error is out of proportion with its significance. The IG's Special Review section on effectiveness contains approximately six pages of discussion, including numerous success stories attributed to intelligence collected from detainees.[299] Incorrectly characterizing the manner in which detainee intelligence was valuable—arrest versus prosecution—for one item in a list of terrorists identified, captured, and prosecuted does not diminish the overall value that detainee intelligence provided in helping to identify, capture, and prosecute terrorists.

(TS█████████████NF) The Study also notes that the CIA and the FBI had information about al-Marri prior to KSM's interrogation, in an apparent attempt to downplay the importance of the information obtained from KSM.[300] It was KSM who identified a photograph of al-Marri and described him as an al-Qa'ida sleeper operative sent to the United States shortly before 9/11. KSM said his plan was for al-Marri, who "had the perfect built-in cover for travel to the United States as a student pursuing his advanced degree in computer studies at a university near New York," was to serve as al-Qa'ida's point of contact to settle other operatives in the United States for follow-on attacks after 9/11.[301] KSM also said that al-Marri trained at the al-Faruq camp and had poisons training and said al-Marri offered himself as a martyr to Bin Ladin.[302] Prior to the information from KSM, al-Marri was charged with credit card fraud and false statements. After the information from KSM, al-Marri was designated as an enemy combatant. In 2009, after being transferred to federal court, al-Marri pled guilty to one count of conspiracy to provide material support to al-Qa'ida. In his plea, he admitted that he attended terrorist training camps and met with KSM to offer his services to al-Qa'ida, who told him to travel to the United States before 9/11 and await instructs—*all information initially provided by KSM.*

(U) *The Arrest and Prosecution of Iyman Faris*

Study Claim: (U) "Over a period of years, the CIA provided the 'identification,' 'arrest,' 'capture,' 'investigation,' and 'prosecution' of Iyman Faris as evidence for the effectiveness of the CIA's enhanced interrogation techniques. These representations were inaccurate."[303]

Fact: (U) CIA, FBI, and Department of Justice documents show that information obtained from KSM after he was waterboarded led directly to Faris's arrest and was key in his prosecution.

---

[298] See CIA Study Response, *Case Studies (TAB C)*, June 27, 2013, p. 35.
[299] *See* CIA Office of Inspector General, *Special Review: Counterterrorism Detention and Interrogation Activities (September 2001 – October 2003)*, May 7, 2004, pp. 85-91 (DTS 2004-2710).
[300] See SSCI Study, Executive Summary, December 3, 2014, pp. 367-368.
[301] CIA, WASHINGTON DC ████████████████
[302] *See* CIA, CIA WASHINGTON DC ████████████
[303] SSCI Study, Executive Summary, December 3, 2014, p. 276.

(U) The Study correctly points out that CIA statements implying that detainee information had led to the "identification" or "investigation" of Iyman Faris were inaccurate. However, contrary to the Study's claims, the CIA representations that information obtained from KSM after he was subjected to enhanced interrogation techniques directly led to the arrest and prosecution of Iyman Faris were accurate.

(S//OC/NF) The CIA has admitted that, in a few cases, it incorrectly stated or implied that KSM's information led to the investigation of Iyman Faris when it should have stated that KSM's reporting informed and focused the investigation.[304] The CIA's mistake is somewhat understandable, given that the CIA only began to focus on Iyman Faris in March 2003 and was not aware that the FBI had opened and closed a preliminary investigation on Faris back in 2001. In essence, Faris was a new investigative target to the CIA in March 2003.[305] Regardless, the CIA's representation concerning the identification and initial investigation of Faris is much less important than the details that led to his arrest and prosecution.

(TS███████████FISA/NF) On March 5, 2003, Majid Khan, an al-Qa'ida operative directly subordinate to KSM, was taken into custody by Pakistani authorities.[306] That same day, the FBI's authorized electronic surveillance of Majid Khan's residence in Maryland indicated ████████, Majid Kahn's ███, made a suspicious call to an individual, later confirmed to be Iyman Faris. They spoke about the possible arrest of Majid Khan and █████ 's suspicions that he was under FBI surveillance. ████████ asked Faris whether he had been approached or questioned and warned Faris not to contact anyone using his phone.[307] The FBI reopened its international terrorism investigation on Iyman Faris soon thereafter.[308]

(TS███████████NF) On March 10, 2003, in response to a requirements cable from CIA Headquarters reporting that al-Qa'ida was targeting U.S. suspension bridges,[309] KSM stated that any such plans were "theoretical" and only "on paper." He also stated that no one was currently pursuing such a plot.[310]

(TS███████████NF) On March 11, 2003, Majid Khan identified a photograph of Iyman Faris before he was in CIA custody. Among other details, Khan said that Faris was a 35-year old truck driver of Pakistani origin who was a "business partner of his ████," █████ ███.[311] The next day, Majid Khan described Faris as "an Islamic extremist."[312] On March 14, 2003, Majid Khan provided the following additional details on Faris: (1) Faris was a mujahedeen "during the Afghan/Soviet period"; (2) Faris was a close associate of Maqsood

---

[304] CIA Study Response, *Case Studies (TAB C)*, June 27, 2013, p. 13.
[305] *See* CIA Study Response, *Case Studies (TAB C)*, June 27, 2013, p. 14.
[306] *See* CIA, CIA CABLE 13658, March 5, 2003, pp. 1-2.
[307] CIA, CIA CABLE ████, March 6, 2003, p. 4.
[308] SSCI Study, Executive Summary, December 3, 2014, p. 280; FBI information confirmed by the FBI on November 30, 2010, SSCI Study, Executive Summary, December 3, 2014, p. 280, n.1581.
[309] CIA, ALEC ████ March 7, 2003, p. 1.
[310] CIA, ████ 10752, March 10, 2003, p. 2; CIA, DIRECTOR ████ March 12, 2003, p. 5. *See also* ████
[311] CIA, CIA CABLE 13758, ███████████
[312] CIA, CIA CABLE 13765, ████

Khan, a known al-Qa'ida associate in contact with senior al-Qa'ida members and Majid's uncle; and (3) Faris had contacted Majid Khan's family after the capture of KSM became public and requested that the family pass a message to Maqsood Khan regarding the status of KSM.[313]

(TS███████████NF) On March 16, 2003, when asked again about the targeting of U.S. suspension bridges, KSM repeated his earlier assertions, noting that, while Usama Bin Ladin officially endorsed attacks against suspension bridges in the United States, he "had no planned targets in the [United States] which were pending attack and that after 9/11 the [United States] had become too hard a target."[314] KSM never referenced Iyman Faris during his March 10 and March 16 interrogations. Thus far, none of the information collected by the U.S. Intelligence Community would have been sufficient to prosecute Iyman Faris on charges of material support to terrorism.

(TS███████████NF) On March 17 and 18, 2003, the CIA questioned KSM about Majid Khan's family and KSM stated that another Khan relative, whom he identified from a picture of Faris, was a "truck driver in Ohio."[315] On March 18, 2003, KSM told interrogators he tasked the truck driver to procure specialized machine tools that would be useful to al-Qaida in loosening the nuts and bolts of suspension bridges in the United States. KSM said he was informed by an intermediary that Faris could not find the tools.[316] This revelation would turn out to be a key piece of incriminating evidence against Iyman Faris.

(TS███████████NF) The Study excluded information found in CIA documents which shows that, immediately after obtaining information from KSM and Majid Khan regarding Faris, the CIA queried the FBI for "additional details" on Faris, "including a readout on his current activities and plans for FBI continued investigation."[317] The cable specifically noted that "KSM seems to have accurately identified" Faris from a photograph as the "truck driver in Ohio." On March 20, 2003, the FBI picked Faris up for questioning and conducted a consent search of his apartment, seizing his laptop. When our staff asked the FBI why Faris was picked up, they cited the cables from CIA.[318] The FBI investigators went into this interview armed with the information revealed by KSM and Majid Khan, which enabled them to explore Faris's ties with KSM and al-Qa'ida plotting in the United States.[319] The Study notes that when approached by law enforcement, Iyman Faris voluntarily provided information and self-incriminating statements.[320] This gives a false impression that the information provided by KSM was unnecessary to securing the arrest and prosecution of Faris by omitting the important context that the FBI questioned Faris armed with incriminating information obtained from KSM on March 17 and 18, 2003.[321]

---

[313] CIA, CIA CABLE 13785, ████████

[314] CIA, ███ 10858, March 9, 2003, p. 2.

[315] CIA, ███ 10886, March 18, 2003, pp 5-6.

[316] CIA, ███ 10886, March 18, 2003, pp 5-6.

[317] CIA, ████████████████████████████████, *Information from KSM on Majid Khan.*

[318] Phone call from the FBI responding to Staff questions from a document review, January 25, 2013.

[319] *See* CIA Study Response, *Case Studies (TAB C)*, June 27, 2013, p. 13; FBI WASH 040537Z, April 4, 2003, p. 2.

[320] SSCI Study, Executive Summary, December 3, 2014, pp. 283-284.

[321] SSCI Study, Executive Summary, December 3, 2014, pp. 281-282.

(U) There is further proof that the incriminating revelations obtained from KSM after he was subjected to enhanced interrogation techniques led directly to the successful arrest and prosecution of Iyman Faris—On May 1, 2003, Faris pled guilty to "casing a New York City bridge for al Qaeda, and researching and providing information to al Qaeda regarding the tools necessary for possible attacks on U.S. targets," *the exact terrorist activities described by KSM.*

(U) *The Arrest and Prosecution of Uzhair Paracha and the Arrest of Saifullah Paracha*

Study Claim: (TS███████████NF) "The CIA represented that information obtained through the use of the CIA's enhanced interrogation techniques produced otherwise unavailable intelligence that led to the identification and/or arrest of Uzhair Paracha and his father Saifullah Paracha (aka, Sayf al-Rahman Paracha). These CIA representations included inaccurate information and omitted significant material information, specifically a body [of] intelligence reporting—acquired prior to CIA detainee reporting—that linked the Parachas to al-Qa'ida-related terrorist activities."[322]

Fact: (TS███████████NF) Information obtained from KSM during his enhanced interrogation on March 25, 2003, about alleged explosives smuggling into the United States, attacks on U.S. gas stations, and related material support to al-Qa'ida, motivated the FBI to track down and arrest Uzhair Paracha in New York a few days later on March 31, 2003. The Intelligence Community continued its pursuit of Saifullah, who was later arrested ███████████ on July 6, 2003. Among other charges, Uzhair was successfully convicted on November 23, 2005, of providing material support to al-Qa'ida and sentenced to 30 years in prison. KSM's description of Uzhair's involvement in the gas station plots and his claim that Uzhair may have provided other logistical support for Majid's entry into the United States was consistent with the press release's description of some of the evidence used during Uzhair's trial.

(TS███████████NF) On March 25, 2003, while being subjected to enhanced interrogation techniques, KSM provided U.S. domestic threat information concerning Saifullah Paracha and his son, Uzhair Paracha. KSM stated that Saifullah Paracha was a Pakistani businessman in Karachi, who owned a textile business with a branch in New York City. KSM alleged that his nephew, Ammar al-Baluchi, and Majid Khan had discussed a plan with Saifullah to use his textile business to smuggle explosives into the United States. According to this plan, the explosives would be shipped in containers that Saifullah used to ship the clothes that he sold in the United States. KSM stated that Saifullah agreed to the plan, but he was unclear how much Uzhair Paracha knew about it.[323] KSM added that Majid Khan planned to rent a storage space in whatever area of United States he chose, not necessarily close to New York City, and that the

---

[322] SSCI Study, Executive Summary, December 3, 2014, p. 352.
[323] CIA, DIRECTOR ███████████

explosives would be used in al-Qa'ida's campaign against economic targets in the United States.[324]

(TS███████████████NF) KSM was also aware that Ammar al-Baluchi and Majid Khan had approached Saifullah and Uzhair to help resettle Majid Khan in the United States, where Majid had plans *to blow up several gas stations.* KSM stated that Ammar was hoping that Paracha could sponsor Majid's entry into the United States, if necessary. KSM also told his interrogators that *"Uzhair may have provided other logistical support for Majid's entry into the United States."*[325] Finally, KSM noted that Saifullah owned a media company in Pakistan and had traveled to Kandahar, Afghanistan, in 1999 to meet with Usama Bin Ladin for the purpose of offering al-Qa'ida the services of his media company.[326]

(TS███████████████NF) Threat information related to the allegation of explosives smuggling motivated the FBI to begin searching in earnest for Saifullah and Uzhair Paracha. The next day, on March 26, 2003, the FBI's field division in Washington, DC requested the CIA to approve the following tearline based upon KSM's reporting:

> Subject: Sayf Al-Rahman Paracha's Possible Involvement in Plot to Smuggle Explosives to the United States. It has come to our attention that one Sayf al-Rahman Paracha, a Pakistani businessman and owner of an import-export textile business in Karachi, Pakistan, may be involved in a plan to smuggle explosives to the United States for al-Qa'ida terrorist related activities. There is a possibility that Mr. Paracha's son Uzhair may be involved as well. Our information indicates that Uzhair traveled from Pakistan to the U.S. circa 17 February 2003. We seek your assistance in providing any information you may have regarding these individuals, their activities, and personalities. Your cooperation and assistance in this matter is greatly appreciated.[327]

In the same cable request, the FBI noted that it had conducted routine records checks and that both Parachas ████████████████████████████████████.[328]

(TS███████████████NF) The FBI arrested Uzhair in New York on March 31, 2003. The CIA was able to develop an operation that lured Saifullah Paracha out of Pakistan, which resulted in his arrest ████████████████████████████ on July 6, 2003.[329] On November 23, 2005—after a two-week jury trial—Uzhair was convicted on all charges in the

---

[324] CIA, DIRECTOR ████████████████
[325] CIA, DIRECTOR ████████████████
[326] CIA, DIRECTOR ████████████████ During a subsequent interrogation, KSM provided additional incriminating information about Saifullah Paracha. The cable reports that "[i]n light of Paracha's past history of handling money for al-Qa'ida, [KSM] approached Paracha with approximately U.S. $260,000-275,000 in cash and asked him to hold it for al-Qa'ida. [KSM] told Paracha not to invest the money in any business ventures and instructed him to keep the money in a safe at his office." KSM had received these funds from Usama Bin Ladin. CIA, ████ 11123, April 3, 2003, p. 3.
[327] FBI, WASH 261909Z, March 26, 2003, pp. 2-3.
[328] FBI, WASH 261909Z, March 26, 2003, p. 2.
[329] CIA Study Response, *Case Studies (TAB C),* June 27, 2013, p. 31.

five-count indictment of providing material support to al-Qa'ida and sentenced to 30 years in prison.[330] The press release announcing the trial results stated,

> The evidence at trial proved that PARACHA, 26, agreed with his father, Saifullah Paracha, and two al Qaeda members, Majid Khan and Ammar Al-Baluchi, to provide support to al Qaeda by, among other things, *trying to help Khan obtain a travel document that would have allowed Khan to re-enter the United States to commit a terrorist act.* Statements from Khan admitted at trial revealed that, once inside the United States, *Khan intended to carry out an attack on gasoline stations.[331]*

The decision to conduct the "late night" interrogation session with KSM on March 25, 2003, was made after reviewing recent intelligence obtained from Majid Khan and Iyman Faris.[332] The March 22, 2003, interview of Majid Khan was conducted by ████████████████████ ██.[333] The resulting cable from that interview explained the relationship between the Parachas and al-Qa'ida, specifically Majid Khan and Ammar al-Baluchi.[334] It also provided details explaining how Uzhair impersonated Majid Khan by using Majid's debit card and a phone conversation between Uzhair and Majid Khan related to Majid's bank account and "calls to the INS."[335] This information from the March 22, 2003, interrogation of Majid Khan was consistent with the charges described in Uzhair Paracha's indictment, although it did not include any reference to the gas station attacks mentioned by KSM.[336]

(TS██████████NF) Based on these facts, we conclude that KSM's allegations of Saifullah Paracha's involvement in a plan to smuggle explosives into the United States motivated the FBI to track down and arrest Uzhair Paracha in New York just a few days later, on March 31, 2003. The CIA was able to develop an operation that lured Saifullah Paracha out of Pakistan, which resulted in his arrest in ████████████, on July 6, 2003. There appears to be a direct causal link between the information provided by KSM and the subsequent actions by the Intelligence Community that led to the arrests of Saifullah and Uzhair Paracha. Moreover, KSM's description of Uzhair's involvement in the gas station plots and his claim that Uzhair

---

[330] DOJ, United States Attorney, Southern District of New York, *Pakistani Man Convicted of Providing Material Support to Al Qaeda Sentenced to 30 Years in Federal Prison.* July 20, 2006, p.1.

[331] DOJ, United States Attorney, Southern District of New York, *Pakistani Man Convicted of Providing Material Support to Al Qaeda Sentenced to 30 Years in Federal Prison.* July 20, 2006, p. 2.

[332] CIA, ████ 10984, March 24, 2003, p. 2 ("Base decided to hold a late night session with KSM upon reviewing latest Karachi readout on [Majid Khan] debriefs [CIA CABLE 13890] and FBI intel report . . . from debriefings of . . . [Iyman Faris]").

[333] CIA, CIA CABLE 13890, ████████

[334] CIA, CIA CABLE 13890, ████████████████

[335] CIA, CIA CABLE 13890, ████████████████

[336] *Compare* CIA, CIA CABLE 13890, ████████████, *with* Indictment, *United States v. Uzair Paracha,* United States District Court, Southern District of New York. Our review of the initial cables related to the plan to attack gas stations in the United States revealed that on March 18, 2003, Majid Khan was the first to disclose KSM's interest in "operational procedures of U.S. gas stations and the tanker trucks that service them," but provided no real details about specific plans other than being later tasked by KSM to investigate the procedures for purchasing gas stations in Pakistan. CIA CIA CABLE 13816, March 18, 2003, p. 3. On March 18, 2003, KSM provided incriminating details about his conspiracy with Majid Khan to attack gas stations in the United States. *See* CIA, ████ 10886, March 18, 2003, pp. 2-4.

may have provided other logistical support for Majid's entry into the United States was consistent with the description of evidence used during Uzhair's trial that was included in the press release announcing the trial results.[337]

(TS███████████NF) The Study asserts that KSM's allegations of explosives smuggling were inaccurate because Saifullah Paracha and others denied being involved in such a plot and at least one senior CIA counterterrorism official questioned the validity of the smuggling plot.[338] The fact that Saifullah Paracha and his alleged co-conspirators denied their involvement in an explosives smuggling plot is not persuasive. Also, we have no intention of countering the CIA official's speculative judgment about the alleged plot with further speculation of our own. Regardless of whether the allegations of explosives smuggling were true, the allegations alone were sufficient to trigger the immediate responsive actions by the FBI and CIA that helped lead to the capture of these two terrorists.

(TS███████████NF) The Study also attempts to lessen the significance of the information provided by KSM by suggesting that the Intelligence Community had sufficient information prior to KSM's reporting to identify and arrest Saifullah and Uzhair Paracha. In support of this assertion, the Study identifies what it considers to be "significant material information" acquired by the Intelligence Community prior to any reporting from CIA detainees.[339] Quibbling about the omission of "significant material information,"—including previously obtained information about an individual named Paracha other than Uzhair and Saifullah or contained in un-disseminated FBI case files[340]—seems largely tangential to the fact that detainee information, including some information obtained after using enhanced interrogation techniques, helped lead to the successful arrests of both men and was consistent with evidence used in the successful prosecution of Uzhair Paracha.

(U) *Tactical Intelligence on Shkai, Pakistan*

(TS███████████NF) The Study asserts that the "CIA representation that the use of the CIA's enhanced interrogation techniques produced *otherwise unavailable* tactical intelligence related to Shkai, Pakistan, was provided to senior policymakers and the Department of Justice between 2004 and 2009."[341] Here is the actual text of the CIA representation at issue:

> *Shkai, Pakistan:* The interrogation of Hassan Ghul provided *detailed* tactical intelligence showing that Shkai, Pakistan was a major Al-Qa'ida hub in the tribal areas. Through [the] use of ███████████ during the Ghul interrogation, we mapped out and pinpointed the residences of key AQ leaders in

---

[337] *Compare* DOJ, United States Attorney, Southern District of New York, *Pakistani Man Convicted of Providing Material Support to Al Qaeda Sentenced to 30 Years in Federal Prison,* July 20, 2006, p.1 *with* CIA, DIRECTOR ███████

[338] SSCI Study, Executive Summary, December 3, 2014, p. 352.

[339] SSCI Study, Executive Summary, December 3, 2014, pp. 352-355.

[340] *See* SSCI Study, Executive Summary, December 3, 2014, pp. 354-355; *see also,* CIA Study Response, *Case Studies,* June 27, 2013, pp. 31-32.

[341] SSCI Study, Executive Summary, December 3, 2014, p. 370 (emphasis added).

Shkai. This intelligence was provided ██████████████████████████████
████████████████████████████████████ [342]

This representation does not assert that the intelligence was "otherwise unavailable" tactical intelligence, but rather, "detailed" tactical intelligence. More important, while the Study's paraphrase of the representation is not accurate, the CIA's representation itself was factually accurate.

(TS ██████████ OC/NF) The CIA Response to the Study makes it clear that Ghul provided detailed tactical intelligence on Shkai, Pakistan, after he was subjected to enhanced interrogation techniques. Specifically, he sat down with ██████ experts and pointed to specific locations where he had met some of the senior al-Qa'ida members who the CIA was trying to find.[343] Ghul also revealed his understanding about how Hamza Rabia, a then little-known al-Qa'ida operative, had taken over as the group's lead attack coordinator after the capture of KSM in 2003.[344] He used ██████ to give more details about the "Bachelor House," the "Ida Khan Complex" and a separate compound used by a group of al-Qa'ida-aligned Uzbeks. He even described the group's evacuation plans in the event of an attack on Shkai.[345] During an interrogation on January 28, 2004, Hassan Ghul drew a detailed map of the locations of a training camp/safehouse near Shkai, provided route information to the site, provided a detailed sketch of the compound and specified the rooms where explosives were stored. Ghul was shown ██████ the area and located the route ██████████.[346] He also identified nine al-Qa'ida members—including Hamza Rabia, Abu Faraj al-Libia, and Spin Ghul—who were located at the safehouse as of June 2003.[347]

(TS ██████████ NF) Senior U.S. officials presented the CIA's analysis of Ghul's debriefings and other intelligence about Shkai ████████████████████████████████
██
████████████ [348] As the Study notes, a July 2004 CIA report says that t███████
██
██████ "[a]l-Qaida's senior operatives who were in Shkai ██████████████
remained in South Waziristan as of mid-June [2004]."[349] However, the CIA report also notes that ██
██

---

[342] CIA Memorandum for Steve Bradbury at Office of Legal Counsel, Department of Justice, dated March 2, 2005, from CIA attorney, ██████ Legal Group, DCI Counterterrorist Center, subject "Effectiveness of the CIA Counterterrorist Interrogation Techniques" (emphasis added).

[343] CIA Study Response, *Case Studies (TAB C)*, June 27, 2013, p. 36; ALEC ██████ February ██ 2004, pp. 5 and 11.

[344] CIA, CIA CABLE 20397, February ██ 2004, p. 5.

[345] CIA, CIA CABLE ██████, February ██, 2004, pp. 10 and 12; CIA, CIA CABLE 1299, January ██, 2004, pp. 2-3.

[346] CIA, CIA CABLE ██████, February ██, 2004, pp. 10 and 12; CIA, CIA CABLE 1299, January ██, 2004, pp. 2-3.

[347] CIA, CIA CABLE ██████, February ██ 2004, pp. 10 and 12; CIA, CIA CABLE 1299, January ██ 2004, pp. 2-3.

[348] CIA, ALEC ██████ February ██ 2004, pp. 1-2; CIA, CIA CABLE 67575, May 6, 2004, p. 1-2; CIA, CIA CABLE 66803, April 26, 2004, pp. 1-11.

[349] SSCI Study Response, Executive Summary, December 3, 2004, p. 378; CIA, DIRECTOR ████████████ ██████ CIA, *Al-Qaida's Waziristan Sanctuary Disrupted but Still Viable*, July 21, 2004, p. 1, (DTS 2004-3240).

███

(TS███████████████NF) This particular case study has been a bit of a "moving target" since it first appeared in the original Study approved by the Committee during the 112th Congress.[351] Its revised claims seek to undermine the significance of the information provided by Ghul after the use of the enhanced interrogation techniques. These revised claims basically assert that: (1) the "vast majority" of Ghul's information was provided prior to his being subjected to enhanced interrogation techniques; (2) the CIA's ████████████ assessed that this prior information was sufficient to press the Pakistani ██████████████ and (3) Ghul's information confirmed earlier reporting that the Shkai Valley of Pakistan served as al-Qa'ida's command and control center after its exodus from Afghanistan in 2001.[352] These claims are little more than an effort to distract the reader from the previously referenced, significant tactical intelligence provided by Ghul after the use of enhanced interrogation techniques. Again, one of the problems with the Study's flawed analytical methodology is that it often turns a blind eye to information obtained after the use of enhanced interrogation techniques if it cannot readily undermine its significance, because such "inconvenient" facts disprove the Study's main conclusion that the CIA's use of enhanced interrogation techniques was not an effective means of acquiring intelligence or gaining cooperation from detainees.

(TS███████████████NF) In a similar vein, the Study asserts that "CIA records do not indicate that information provided by Ghul during this period, or after, resulted in the identification or capture of any al-Qa'ida leaders."[353] In fact, prior to the use of enhanced interrogation techniques, Hassan Ghul speculated that Abu Ahmad al-Kuwaiti: (1) could be one of three people with Usama Bin Ladin; and (2) may have handled Bin Ladin's needs, including sending messages to his gatekeeper, Abu Faraj al-Libi. After the use of enhanced interrogation techniques, Hassan Ghul cooperated by telling his interrogators that Abu Ahmad specifically passed a letter from Bin Ladin to Abu Faraj in late 2003 and that Abu Ahmad had "disappeared" from Karachi, Pakistan, in 2002. This information was not only more concrete than Ghul's earlier speculations, but it corroborated information from another detainee, Ammar al Baluchi, that Abu Ahmad served as a courier for Bin Ladin.[354] While this information technically didn't result in the "identification" or "capture" of Bin Ladin, it most certainly played a crucial role in the U.S. Government's successful efforts to locate and neutralize Bin Ladin in his Abbottabad compound in Pakistan on May 2, 2011.

---

[350] CIA, *Al-Qaida's Waziristan Sanctuary Disrupted but Still Viable*. July 21, 2004, p. 1, (DTS 2004-3240).
[351] *Compare* CIA Study Response, *Case Studies (TAB C)*, June 27, 2013, p. 36 (citing the original Study claims concerning the CIA's representation about Ghul's tactical intelligence on Shkai in the appendix to the Study's original findings and conclusions) *with* SSCI Study, Executive Summary, December 3, 2014, p. 368.
[352] SSCI Study, Executive Summary, December 3, 2014, p. 369.
[353] SSCI Study, Executive Summary, December 3, 2014, p. 376.
[354] CIA, DIRECTOR ████████████████

(U) *The Thwarting of the Camp Lemonier Plotting*

(TS███████████NF) In a September 6, 2006 speech, President Bush highlighted the thwarting of a planned strike against Camp Lemonier in Djibouti as an example of the value of information obtained as a part of CIA's Detention and Interrogation Program. The core claim in this section of the Study is not only inaccurate; it was never made.

Study Claim: (TS███████████NF) **"The CIA represented that intelligence derived from the use of CIA's enhanced interrogation techniques thwarted plotting against the U.S. military base, Camp Lemonier, in Djibouti. These representations are inaccurate."[355]**

Fact: (TS███████████NF) **Representations about the thwarting of an attack against Camp Lemonier in Djibouti, specifically President Bush's 2006 comments that "Terrorists held in CIA custody have also provided information that helped stop a planned strike on U.S. Marines at Camp Lemonier in Djibouti," were accurate and have been mischaracterized by the Study.[356]**

(TS███████████NF) In this section of the Executive Summary, the Study fundamentally mischaracterizes two representations attributed to President Bush and the CIA. The first representation, which comes from the President's September 6, 2006, speech, is attributed to the CIA by the Study because of the CIA's vetting of the speech. In his speech, the President stated, *"[t]errorists held in CIA custody* have also provided information that *helped stop a planned strike* on U.S. Marines at Camp Lemonier in Djibouti . . . ."[357] Contrary to the Study's assertions, the President did not attribute the thwarting of this plot exclusively to the use of enhanced interrogation techniques, but information from "[t]errorists held in CIA custody." In addition, the President never stated that the plot was disrupted exclusively because of information from detainees in CIA custody. The President was clear that information from detainees "helped" to stop the planned strike. This idea that detainee reporting builds on and contextualizes previous and subsequent reporting is repeated a few lines later in the speech, when the President makes clear, "[t]he information we get from these detainees is corroborated by intelligence . . . that we've received from other sources, and together this intelligence has helped us connect the dots and stop attacks before they occur."[358] This is another example of where the President and the CIA are pilloried by the Study for representations they actually never made.

(TS███████████NF) The second example cited in the Study is pulled from a set of talking points drafted for use in an October 30, 2007, briefing to then-Chairman of the House

---

[355] SSCI Study, Executive Summary, December 3, 2014, p. 336.

[356] President George W. Bush, *Trying Detainees; Address on the Creation of Military Commissions*, Washington, D.C., September 6, 2006.

[357] President George W. Bush, *Trying Detainees; Address on the Creation of Military Commissions*, Washington, D.C., September 6, 2006 (emphasis added).

[358] President George W. Bush, *Trying Detainees; Address on the Creation of Military Commissions*, Washington, D.C., September 6, 2006.

Defense Appropriations Subcommittee, former Congressman John Murtha. In the written talking points, the CIA states, "[A CIA detainee] informed us of an operation underway to attack the U.S. military at Camp Lemonier in Djibouti. We believe our understanding of this plot helped us prevent the attack."[359] Setting aside the question of whether these talking points were ever actually employed (which is virtually unanswerable, given the passing of Congressman Murtha in 1010 and the Study's failure to interview the relevant intelligence officers), this representation, like the President's 2006 speech, does not include a reference to enhanced interrogation techniques. Moreover, as was previously the case, the CIA does not claim that the attacks were thwarted solely because of detainee information. They clearly point to their "understanding of this plot," which was a mosaic based on many different sources of intelligence.

(TS███████████NF) The President's claim that "[t]errorists held in CIA custody have also provided information that helped stop a planned strike on U.S. Marines at Camp Lemonier in Djibouti" was accurate.[360] The detention of two terrorists by the CIA, KSM and Guleed Hassan Ahmed, affected al-Qa'ida's ongoing plotting against Camp Lemonier. The March 3, 2003, arrest of KSM came days after a late-February meeting with Abu Yasir, al-Qa'ida's link to affiliated terrorist cells in Somalia and Kenya, and prevented KSM from attending a follow-on meeting, at which he was to discuss the provision of operational funds with al-Qa'ida leaders in East Africa, some of whom were plotting an attack against Camp Lemonier.[361] Guleed Hassan Ahmed, who conducted reconnaissance of Camp Lemonier for al-Qa'ida, provided information about the Camp Lemonier plot and al-Qa'ida's Somali support network.[362] The information Guleed provided, both prior to and after being transferred into CIA custody, combined with intelligence derived from other sources and methods, was central in driving CIA's targeting of al-Qa'ida proxies based in East Africa.[363] Although these events are not independently responsible for thwarting the plot against Camp Lemonier, they undoubtedly "helped" or contributed to the disruption of the plot.

(TS███████████NF) Finally, the Study claims that plotting against Camp Lemonier "did not 'stop' because of information acquired from CIA detainee Guleed in 2004, but rather, continued well into 2007," implying that continued terrorist targeting of Camp Lemonier excludes the possibility a planned strike was thwarted.[364] This assertion undervalues Camp Lemonier's appeal as a terrorist target, and is willfully blind to the victory even a single obstructed terrorist plot represents. Camp Lemonier is the only major U.S. military base in sub-Saharan Africa, hosting approximately 1,600 military personnel.[365] It is also located within striking distance of, and an active threat to, al-Qa'ida operatives throughout the Horn of Africa. It stands to reason that Camp Lemonier exists as a target of sustained terrorist focus.

---

[359] SSCI Study, Executive Summary, December 3, 2014, p. 338; *DCIA Meeting with Chairman Murtha re Rendition and Detention Programs*, October 30, 2007, p. 1.
[360] President George W. Bush, *Trying Detainees; Address on the Creation of Military Commissions*, Washington, D.C., September 6, 2006.
[361] CIA, DIRECTOR,███████████; CIA, HEADQUARTERS███████████
[362] CIA, CIA ██████
[363] CIA, HEADQUARTERS███████
[364] SSCI Study, Executive Summary, December 3, 2014, p. 338.
[365] CIA, CIA CABLE 207044, May 22, 2003, p. 9.

(U) *CIA Detainees Subjected to EITs Validated CIA Sources*

Study Claim: (TS███████████████NF) "[T]he CIA also represented that its enhanced interrogation techniques were necessary to validate CIA sources. The claim was based on one CIA detainee—Janat Gul—contradicting the reporting of one CIA asset."[366]

Fact: (TS███████████████NF) Contrary to the Study's claim, the CIA representations cited by the Study do not assert that enhanced interrogation techniques helped to validate sources. Rather, the representations only make reference to "detainee information" or detainee "reporting." Also contrary to the Study's claim, we found evidence in the documentary record where the CIA representations about Janat Gul also contained additional examples of source validation. Moreover, the three items of information that the Study asserts should have been included in the Janat Gul asset validation representations were not "critical" and their inclusion does not alter the fact that Gul's persistent contradiction of the asset's claims did help the CIA "validate" that particular asset.

(TS███████████████NF) The Study complains that the CIA justified the use of enhanced interrogation techniques by repeatedly using the same Janat Gul example of detainee reporting to determine that one of its assets had fabricated information. The Study first provides the following representation made by CIA Director Hayden during one of our Committee hearings:

> Detainee information is a key tool for validating clandestine sources. In fact, in one case, the detainee's information proved to be the accurate story, and the clandestine source was confronted and subsequently admitted to embellishing or fabricating some or all of the details in his report.[367]

The Study also provides one other example of an asset validation justification:

> Pakistan-based facilitator *Janat Gul's most significant reporting* helped us validate a CIA asset who was providing information about the 2004 pre-election threat. The asset claimed that Gul had arranged a meeting between himself and al-Qa'ida's chief of finance, Shaykh Sa'id, a claim that Gul vehemently denied. Gul's reporting was later matched with information obtained from Sharif al-Masri and Abu Talha al-Pakistani, captured after Gul. With this reporting in hand, CIA

---

[366] *See* SSCI Study, Executive Summary, December 3, 2014, p. 342.
[367] SSCI Study, Executive Summary, December 3, 2014, p. 342 (citing General Michal Hayden, Director, Central Intelligence Agency, *Classified Statement for the Record*, Senate Select Committee on Intelligence, April 12, 2007, p. 8 (DTS 2007-1563)).

69

███████████ the asset, who subsequently admitted to fabricating his reporting about the meeting.[368]

Contrary to the Study's claim here, the first observation that should be made about these representations is that they do not contain any reference to the use of "enhanced interrogation techniques." In the first representation, Director Hayden uses the words "detainee information." In the second, the briefing notes simply use the term "reporting."

(TS██████████████NF) Another part of the Study's claim is also factually inaccurate. The Study asserts that the CIA's representation "was based on *one* CIA detainee—Janat Gul . . . ."[369] During our review of the documentary record we found numerous copies of the "Briefing Notes on the Value of Detainee Reporting," that contained the exact representation cited by the Study above, although the version we selected did not place special emphasis on "Janat Gul's most significant reporting."[370] More important, the representations in the August 2005 version contain the following additional examples under the same heading of "Helping to Validate Other Sources":

> In other instances, detainee information has been useful in identifying clandestine assets who are providing good reporting. *For example*, Hassan Ghul's reporting on Shkai *helped us validate several assets* in the field who also told us that al-Qa'ida members had found safehaven at this location. . . .
>
> Sometimes *one detainee validates reporting from others.* ███████ corroborated information from key ██████████ who were involved in facilitating the movement of al-Qa'ida personnel, money, and messages into and out of ██████. *For example*, ██████ indicated that ██████████████████████████ was the link between al-Qa'ida and ████████████, and ██████ *corroborated that fact* when he noted that ████████████ was the "go-between" for al-Qa'ida and ██████.[371]

Ironically, the Study's omission of these additional examples of source validation from its own analysis deprives the reader of "significant context."

(TS██████████████NF) The Study seems to imply that the omission of certain "critical" contextual information from the CIA's representations about source validation somehow nullifies the Janat Gul example.[372] Our examination of the three items of contextual information cited by the Study leads us to conclude that the Janat Gul case remains illustrative of

---

[368] SSCI Study, Executive Summary, December 3, 2014, p. 343 (citing CIA, Briefing for Obama National Security Team - "Renditions, Detentions, and Interrogations (RDI)" including "Tab 7," named "RDG Copy- Briefing on RDI Program 09 Jan. 2009." (emphasis in original).

[369] SSCI Study, Executive Summary, December 4, 2014, p. 342 (emphasis added).

[370] CIA, *Briefing Notes on the Value of Detainee Reporting*, August 2005, p. 8. This document is attached as Appendix II, *see infra*, p. II-1.

[371] CIA, *Briefing Notes on the Value of Detainee Reporting*, August 2005, pp. 8-9 (emphasis added).

[372] SSCI Study, Executive Summary, December 4, 2014, p. 343.

detainee information helping to determine that a CIA source had fabricated certain aspects of his reporting.

(TS███████████████NF) First, the Study faults the CIA for failing to include in its representations that the asset's reporting about the 2004 pre-election threat was doubted by CIA officers prior to the use of enhanced interrogation techniques against Janat Gul.[373] This concern is easily dismissed because a review of the e-mail reveals that the concerns raised by the CIA officers were not about the credibility of the sources, but more about the possibility that al-Qa'ida might be using this threat information to test the sources who had provided the pre-election threat information. The email raising the concern specifically states, "this is not to say that either ASSET Y or [source name REDACTED] are wrong or that the AQ statement below[374] is anything more than disinformation."[375] The reply email stated that it was possible the sources were just hearing the same rumors, but recollected that when al-Qa'ida put out similar rumors in the summer of 2001, those turned out to be true.[376] These emails do not support any inference about early suspicions of the source's credibility nor do they dismiss the legitimacy of the threat information provided by the sources.

(TS███████████████NF) The Study criticizes the asset validation representations by the CIA because they did not acknowledge that the source's fabricated reporting was the reason that Janat Gul was subjected to the enhanced interrogation techniques.[377] There are two problems with this criticism. First, the CIA believed that the source's allegations about Janat Gul meeting with Shayk Sa'id, al-Qa'ida's chief of finance, were true when they began to use enhanced interrogation techniques against Gul between August 3, 2004, and August 10, 2004, and then again from August 21, 2004, to August 25, 2004.[378] The CIA source did not recant some of the underlying threat information pertaining to Gul until October █ and █, 2004, *more than two months after Gul's enhanced interrogation began and 15 days after his enhanced interrogation ended.* It is also important to understand that the source's information was not the only

---

[373] *See* SSCI Study, Executive Summary, December 4, 2014, pp. 343.

[374] The referenced statement was issued by al-Qa'ida on March 17, 2004, and asserted that al-Qa'ida would not operate any large-scale operation prior to the election.

[375] Email from: ███████; to: ███████, ███████, [REDACTED], ███████, ███████; subject: could AQ be testing [ASSET Y] and [source name REDACTED]?; date: March █, 2004, at 06:55 AM; Email from: ███████; to ███████; cc: ███████, ███████, [REDACTED], ███████; subject: Re: could AQ be testing [ASSET Y] and [source name REDACTED]?: date: March █, 2004, at 7:52:32 AM. p. 1 (footnote added). This document is attached as Appendix III, *see infra*, p. III-1.

[376] Email from: ███████; to: ███████, ███████, [REDACTED], ███████, ███████; subject: could AQ be testing [ASSET Y] and [source name REDACTED]?; date: March █, 2004, at 06:55 AM; Email from: ███████; to ███████; cc: ███████, [REDACTED], ███████; subject: Re: could AQ be testing [ASSET Y] and [source name REDACTED]?: date: March █, 2004, at 7:52:32 AM. p. 1 (footnote added). This email confirms that the sensitive source who subsequently admitted to fabricating information was not the only source providing information related to a possible pre-election terrorist threat. ███████

[377] SSCI Study, Executive Summary, December 4, 2014, p. 343.

[378] CIA, ███ 1512, ███ 2004, p. 2; CIA, ███ 1545, ███, 2004, p. 1; CIA, ███ 1603, ███ 2004, p. 3; and CIA, ███ 1632, ███ 2004, p. 2.

information that caused the CIA to believe that Gul was an al-Qa'ida facilitator with connections to multiple high value targets. The source's information was also not solely responsible for the request and authorization to subject Gul to enhanced interrogation techniques.[379] The CIA cable requesting interrogation authorities makes clear those authorities were being pursued to "collect critical threat, locational, and other high priority information."[380] This same communication cited a previous cable detailing CIA approval to detain Gul, in which Gul's apprehension was justified on grounds that he was "one of the highest level extremist facilitators remaining in Pakistan, and multiple source reporting indicates that he has connections to various HVTS."[381]

(TS█████████NF) Second, the Study does not fully support its claim that the CIA source's representations about the pre-election threat were inaccurate.[382] Specifically, the cable reporting the fabrication by one of these sources in October 2004 clearly indicates that some of the source's pre-election threat information was considered to be "generally truthful." The Study states that the source "was deceptive in response to questions regarding . . . the pre-election threat."[383] This assertion is not entirely accurate. In fact, the cited cable indicated that the source █████████████ on the issue of the pre-election threat ████████████████████████[384] Moreover, the assessment paragraph in the cited cable states: "Based on [the source's] seemingly genuine concern and constant return to the issue, COB believes that [the source] is being generally truthful about his discussions . . . on the pre-election threat."[385]

(TS█████████NF) The Study's final piece of "critical" contextual information that was missing from the CIA representations on this issue was the failure of the CIA to disclose that it eventually concluded that Janat Gul was not a high-level al-Qa'ida figure and never had threat information.[386] This seems to miscast Janat Gul as a hapless victim of circumstance, when in fact he was a known terrorist facilitator. Beyond that, the question of whether every accusation made against Gul was proven or not, is fundamentally immaterial to the matter of his detainee reporting being used to validate—or, in this instance, invalidate—an intelligence source.

(TS█████████NF) Our analysis has demonstrated that this claim suffers from multiple fatal defects: (1) the representations do not reference enhanced interrogation techniques; (2) representations in the documentary record were found to have additional examples of asset validation beyond the Janat Gul example; and (3) including any of the three problematic contextual items raised by the Study would not alter the fact that Janat Gul's persistent contradiction of the asset's claims did help the CIA "validate" that particular asset.

---

[379] CIA, ALEC ██████ ██████
[380] CIA, ██████ 1484, ██████ 2004, p. 2.
[381] CIA, ALEC ██████
[382] See SSCI Study, Executive Summary, December 3, 2014, p. 417.
[383] SSCI Study, Executive Summary, December 3, 2014, p. 348.
[384] CIA, CIA CABLE 1411, ██████ 2004, p. 4.
[385] CIA, CIA CABLE 1411, ██████ 2004, p. 5.
[386] SSCI Study, Executive Summary, December 3, p. 343.

(U) *The Identification of Bin Ladin's Courier*

(TS███████████NF) Shortly after the May 2011 raid on the Usama Bin Ladin compound, current and former CIA employees highlighted the role of reporting from the CIA Detention and Interrogation Program in the operation. These officials represented that CIA detainees provided the "tip-off" information on Abu Ahmad al-Kuwaiti (variant Abu Ahmed al-Kuwaiti), the Bin Ladin courier who ultimately led to finding Bin Ladin.[387] As we show below, these representations were accurate.

Study Claim: (TS███████████NF) **"[T]he 'tipoff' on Abu Ahmad al-Kuwaiti in 2002 did not come from the interrogation of CIA detainees and was obtained prior to any CIA detainee reporting."[388]**

Fact: (TS███████████NF) **CIA documents show that detainee information served as the "tip-off" and played a significant role in leading CIA analysts to the courier Abu Ahmad al-Kuwaiti. While there was other information in CIA databases about al-Kuwaiti, this information was not recognized as important by analysts until after detainees provided information on him.**

(TS███████████NF) In the days immediately after the Bin Ladin raid, CIA analysts and operators testified before the Committee about how they tracked down Bin Ladin. The CIA described the lead information as being provided by detainees in U.S. custody at CIA secret sites and the detention facility at Guantanamo Bay, Cuba, and from detainees in the custody of foreign governments that helped the CIA recognize the importance of Bin Ladin's courier, Abu Ahmad al-Kuwaiti.[389] CIA officers were clear that the information was from detainees, but never portrayed the information as originating solely from detainees held by the CIA.

(TS███████████NF) CIA documents show that even before the raid took place, CIA analysts prepared briefings and papers on their analysis of what led them to the courier. These briefings and papers clearly described the key role that detainee reporting played in this analytical and operational process. A CIA paper in November 2007 noted that "over twenty mid to high-value detainees have discussed Abu Ahmad's ties to senior al-Qa'ida leaders, including his role in delivering messages from Bin Ladin and his close association with former al-Qa'ida third-in-command Abu Faraj al-Libi."[390] The report highlighted specific reporting from two detainees, Hassan Ghul and Ammar al-Baluchi, who both identified Abu Faraj al-Libi's role in

---

[387] SSCI and SASC Transcript, *Briefing on Operation Neptune's Spear*, May 4, 2011, pp. 53-54 (DTS 2011-2049) (CIA Director Panetta stated, "I want to be able to get back to you with specifics . . . But clearly the tipoff on the couriers came from those [detainee] interviews."); Scott Hennen radio interview of former CIA Director Michael Hayden, May 3, 2011 (Former Director Hayden stated, "What we got, the original lead information—and frankly it was incomplete identity information on the couriers—began with information from CIA detainees at the black sites").

[388] SSCI Study, Executive Summary, December 3, 2014, p. 389.

[389] SSCI Transcript, *Briefing on the Operation That Killed Usama Bin Ladin*, May 2, 2011, pp. 7 and 39 (DTS 2011-1941).

[390] CIA Intelligence Assessment, *Al-Qa'ida Watch, Probable Identification of Suspected Bin Ladin Facilitator Abu Ahmad al-Kuwaiti*, November 23, 2007, p. 2.

communicating to Bin Ladin through Abu Ahmad. It was this and similar reporting from other detainees that helped analysts realize Abu Faraj's categorical denials that he even knew anyone named Abu Ahmad al-Kuwaiti, "almost certainly were an attempt to protect Abu Ahmed," thus showing his importance.[391]

(<del>TS</del> ███████████ <del>NF</del>) Additionally, a retrospective prepared by the CIA's Study for the Center of Intelligence after the raid also made clear in its report that detainee information was significant in the identification of the courier. The report noted that High-Value Terrorist analysts, targeters, and their managers told the Center that:

> debriefing al-Qa'ida detainees provided them with unparalleled expertise and knowledge of the organization. The ability to cross-check detainee statements against one another—specifically Abu Faraj's with that of numerous other detainees—ultimately led to the assessment that Abu Ahmad was directly serving as Bin Ladin's facilitator and possibly harboring him. In sum, 25 detainees provided information on Abu Ahmad al-Kuwaiti, his al-Qa'ida membership, and his historic role as a courier for Bin Ladin. Nine of the 25 were held in non-CIA custody. Of the 16 held in CIA custody, all but three had given information after being subjected to enhanced interrogation techniques (EITs), although of the 13 only two (KSM and Abu Zubaydah) had been waterboarded. Even so, KSM gave false information about Abu Ahmad, as did Abu Faraj, who received lesser EITs. Ironically, the falsity of the information was itself important in establishing Abu Ahmad's significance.[392]

(<del>TS</del> ████████████ <del>NF</del>) The Study asserts that information acquired in 2002 ████ ██████████████ was the "tip-off" to Abu Ahmad al-Kuwaiti, but this information sat unnoticed in a CIA database for five years.[393] It was multiple detainee reports about a Bin Ladin courier with the alias Abu Ahmad al-Kuwaiti that triggered a search that uncovered the old information.[394] This is another example of the Study's use of hindsight to criticize the CIA for not recognizing the significance of previously collected, but not fully-understood, intelligence information. It is also an attempt to use this ████████████████ information to categorize the subsequently collected detainee information as being "otherwise obtainable." Under the Study's flawed analytical methodology, information in that category cannot be used as evidence of the effectiveness of the CIA's Detention and Interrogation Program. We are not similarly constrained.

(<del>TS</del> ████████████ <del>NF</del>) The Study—benefiting from the ability to search a database compiled of only information relevant to its specific task (something intelligence analysts are not

---

[391] CIA Intelligence Assessment, *Al-Qa'ida Watch, Probable Identification of Suspected Bin Ladin Facilitator Abu Ahmad al-Kuwaiti*, November 23, 2007, p. 2.

[392] CIA Center for the Study of Intelligence, *Lessons from the Hunt for Usama Bin Ladin*, September 2012, p. 14 (DTS 2012-3826).

[393] CIA Center for the Study of Intelligence, *Lessons from the Hunt for Usama Bin Ladin*, September 2012, p. 9 (DTS 2012-3826).

[394] SSCI Transcript, *Briefing on Operation Neptune's Spear Targeting Usama Bin Ladin, May 4, 2011*, pp 13-14, 47-49, and 53-54 (DTS 2011-2049).

able to do) with the advantage of hindsight to understand which names are now important—asserts that prior to receiving information from CIA detainees, the CIA had other critical reporting on the courier. The Study cites Abu Ahmad's phone number and e-mail address, a body of intelligence reporting linking him to KSM's operational planning, and reporting on Abu Ahmad's age, physical appearance, and family—including information the CIA would later cite as pivotal in identifying his true name.[395]

(TS⬛⬛⬛⬛⬛NF) While it is true that the CIA was conducting technical intelligence collection linked to Abu Ahmad al-Kuwaiti in 2002, CIA fact-checking confirmed that this information was meaningless because: (1) it did not link Abu Ahmad to Bin Ladin; (2) Abu Ahmad had stopped using the phone number and e-mail address in 2002; and (3) Abu Ahmad was not linked to that email address in any of his subsequent correspondence.[396] According to the CIA,

> [t]hat intelligence was insufficient to distinguish Abu Ahmad from many other Bin Ladin associates until additional information from detainees put it into context and allowed us to better understand his true role and potential in the hunt for Bin Ladin.[397]

Further review of CIA records confirmed that the phone number at issue was an Inmarsat number associated with "Mukhtar" and "Ahmad 'al-Kuwahadi."[398] According to Adam Robinson, the author of *Bin Laden Behind the Mask of the Terrorist*, "[a]fter a long period of use of the Inmarsat system, Osama learned that this system is open to interception, both for covert observation and possibly for homing in on the signal . . . After he became aware of this, he used the system only periodically for calling his mother."[399] If this claim about Bin Ladin's belief is accurate and al-Qa'ida leadership believed that phones were vulnerable, it may explain why this particular phone number was abandoned by KSM and Abu Ahmad.

(TS⬛⬛⬛⬛⬛NF) The information providing Kuwaiti's physical description and family details was critical to ultimately identifying al-Kuwaiti's true name, but not until years later—2007 to be exact—after detainee reporting provided enough information about the courier that a search of old records illuminated key information in that reporting. The CIA Center for the Study of Intelligence said such information was "an unnoticed needle in the haystack on an unending plain of haystacks" until that time.[400] One of the lead CIA analysts called similar information that later turned out to be important "meaningless" until years later when detainee reporting illuminated its importance.[401] Thus, this information really only became

---

[395] SSCI Study, Executive Summary. December 3, 2014, p. 385.

[396] CIA Study Response, *Case Studies (TAB C)*, June 27, 2013, p. 40.

[397] CIA Study Response, *Case Studies (TAB C)*, June 27, 2013, p. 38; CIA Study Response, *Comments (TAB A)*, June 27, 2013, p. 14.

[398] CIA, ALEC ⬛⬛⬛⬛⬛

[399] Adam Robinson, *Bin Laden Behind the Mask of the Terrorist*, Arcade Publishing, Inc., New York, 2002. p. 247.

[400] CIA Center for the Study of Intelligence, *Lessons from the Hunt for Usama Bin Ladin*, September 2012, p. 9 (DTS 2012-3826).

[401] CIA Center for the Study of Intelligence, *Lessons from the Hunt for Usama Bin Ladin*, September 2012, p. 9 (DTS 2012-3826).

critical to the CIA after detainee reporting provided enough information about the courier that a search of old records illuminated key information in that reporting.

Study Claim: (TS███████████NF) "[T]he most accurate information on Abu Ahmad al-Kuwaiti obtained from a CIA detainee [Hassan Ghul] was provided by a CIA detainee who had not yet been subjected to the CIA's enhanced interrogation techniques."[402]

Fact: (TS███████████NF) Detainees who provided useful and accurate information on Abu Ahmad al-Kuwaiti and Bin Ladin had undergone enhanced interrogation prior to providing the information. For example, Hassan Ghul provided more specificity about Abu Ahmad after being transferred from COBALT and receiving enhanced interrogation techniques.

(U) The Study disputes statements from current and former CIA officials that information from detainees in CIA's enhanced interrogation program provided valuable information on Abu Ahmad al-Kuwaiti. For example, then-CIA Director Leon Panetta told ABC News in May 2011, soon after the Bin Ladin raid, that enhanced interrogation techniques were used to extract information that led to the mission's success.[403] Former Director Hayden said in an interview that "the original lead information—and frankly it was incomplete identity information on the couriers—began with information from CIA detainees at the black sites."[404] Both of these statements are accurate.

(TS███████████NF) While numerous detainees at CIA black sites provided information on Abu Ahmad al-Kuwaiti, as noted above, two detainees, Hassan Ghul and Ammar al-Baluchi, in particular were cited by the lead CIA analyst as leading her to search old intelligence files.[405] Ammar al-Baluchi, who appears to be the first detainee to mention Abu Ahmad al-Kuwaiti's role as a Bin Ladin courier and a possible connection with Abu Faraj al-Libi, provided this information at a CIA black site during a period of enhanced interrogation.[406]

(TS███████████NF) The second detainee, Hassan Ghul, is described in the Study as providing the "best" and "most accurate" information on the courier. While we are not sure it was the "best" or "most accurate" information, a CIA report on the Bin Ladin raid described Ghul's information as a "milestone in the long analytic targeting trek that led to Bin Ladin."[407] Clearly it was important. According the CIA,

Gul, while in CIA custody–before undergoing enhanced techniques–speculated that Abu Ahmad could be one of three people with Bin Ladin and speculated that

---

[402] SSCI Study, Executive Summary, December 3, 2014, p. 379.
[403] Interview with CIA Director Leon Panetta, Brian Williams, ABC News, May 3, 2011.
[404] Interview with former CIA Director Michael Hayden, Scott Hennen Show, May 3, 2011.
[405] CIA Intelligence Assessment, *Al-Qa'ida Watch, Probable Identification of Suspected Bin Ladin Facilitator Abu Ahmad al-Kuwaiti*, November 23, 2007, p. 2.
[406] CIA, WASHINGTON DC ███████████████ Ammar al-Baluchi attempted to recant his earlier description of Abu Ahmad as a Bin Ladin courier. CIA, DIRECTOR ████████
[407] CIA Center for the Study of Intelligence, *Lessons from the Hunt for Usama Bin Ladin*, dated September 2012, p. 9 (DTS 2012-3826).

Abu Ahmad may have handled Bin Ladin's needs, including sending messages to his gatekeeper, Abu Faraj al-Libi.[408]

Additional CIA fact-checking explained that Ghul offered more details about Abu Ahmad's role after being transferred from COBALT and receiving enhanced interrogation. Specifically, the CIA stated:

> After undergoing enhanced techniques, Gul stated that Abu Ahmad specifically passed a letter from Bin Ladin to Abu Faraj in late 2003 and that Abu Ahmad had "disappeared" from Karachi, Pakistan, in 2002. This information was not only more concrete and less speculative, it also corroborated information from Ammar that Khalid Shaykh Muhammad (KSM) was lying when he claimed Abu Ahmad left al-Qa'ida in 2002.[409]

Ghul stated that while he had "no proof," he believed that Abu Faraj was in contact with Abu Ahmad and that Abu Ahmad might act as an intermediary contact between Abu Faraj and Bin Ladin. Ghul said that this belief "made sense" since Abu Ahmad had disappeared and Ghul had heard that Abu Ahmad was in contact with Abu Faraj.[410] Months later, Ghul also told his interrogators that he knew Abu Ahmad was close to Bin Ladin, which was another reason he suggested that Abu Ahmad had direct contact with Bin Ladin as one of his couriers.[411]

(TS███████████NF) CIA documents make clear that when detainees like Abu Zubaydah, KSM, and Abu Faraj al-Libi—who had undergone enhanced interrogation and were otherwise cooperative—denied knowing Abu Ahmad al-Kuwaiti or suggested that he had "retired," it was a clear sign to CIA analysts that these detainees had something to hide, and it further confirmed other detainee information that had tipped them off about the true importance of Abu Ahmad al-Kuwaiti.[412]

(U) Conclusion 6 (CIA Impeded Congressional Oversight)

(TS███████████NF) Conclusion 6 states: "[t]he CIA has actively avoided or impeded congressional oversight of the program."[413] In reality, the overall pattern of engagement with the Congress on this issue shows that the CIA attempted to keep the Congress informed of its activities. From 2002 to 2008, the CIA claims to have provided more than 35 briefings to SSCI members and staff, more than 30 similar briefings to HPSCI members and staff, and more than 20 congressional notifications.[414] For some of these briefings, there are no

---

[408] CIA Study Response, *Case Studies (TAB C)*, June 27, 2013, p. 38 (citing CIA, DIRECTOR ███████).

[409] CIA Study Response, *Case Studies (TAB C)*, June 27, 2013, p. 38 (citing CIA, ███████████).

[410] CIA, ███████████████████████.

[411] CIA, DIRECTOR ███████████████.

[412] CIA, DIRECTOR ███████████████ CIA Center for the Study of Intelligence, *Lessons from the Hunt for Usama Bin Ladin*, dated September 2012, pp. 9-10 (DTS 2012-3826); CIA Intelligence Assessment, *Al-Qa'ida Watch, Probable Identification of Suspected Bin Ladin Facilitator Abu Ahmad al-Kuwaiti*, November 23, 2007, p. 2.

[413] SSCI Study, Findings and Conclusions, December 3, 2014, p. 5.

[414] CIA Study Response, *Conclusions (TAB B)*, June 27, 2013, p. 35.

transcripts[415], likely because they were limited to the Chairman and Vice Chairman/Ranking Member of the congressional intelligence committees. Because the Study did not interview the participants in these restricted briefings, it is impossible to document how much information the CIA provided to Committee leadership during those briefings. Often, the Study's own examples contradict the assertion that the CIA tried to avoid its overseers' scrutiny. For example, the Study notes that the CIA reacted to Vice Chairman Rockefeller's suspicion about the agency's honesty by planning a detailed briefing on the Program for him.[416]

(U) *Timing of the CIA's Briefings on Enhanced Interrogation Techniques*

Study Claim: (TS███████████████NF) "The CIA did not brief the Senate Intelligence Committee leadership on the CIA's enhanced interrogation techniques until September 2002, after the techniques had been approved and used."[417]

Fact: (TS███████████████NF) The CIA provided information to the Committee in hearings, briefings, and notifications beginning shortly after the signing of the Memorandum of Notification (MON) on September 17, 2001.

(TS███████████NF) Conclusion 6 opens with the statement that the CIA did not brief the Senate Intelligence Committee leadership on the CIA's enhanced interrogation techniques until after the techniques had been approved and used, setting the tone for a narrative that the CIA actively and systematically concealed information from the Congress. In reality, the CIA began discussing concerns about interrogation with the Committee even prior to the creation of the Program. The Study's review of the CIA's representations to Congress cites CIA hearing testimony from November 7, 2001, discussing the uncertainty in the boundaries on interrogation techniques.[418] The Study also cites additional discussions between staff and CIA lawyers in February 2002.[419]

(TS███████████NF) The Study seems to fault the CIA for not briefing the Committee leadership until after the enhanced interrogation techniques had been approved and used. The CIA briefed HPSCI leadership on September 4, 2002. SSCI leadership received the same briefing on September 27, 2002.[420] The Study does not include information on when the CIA offered briefings to Congress or how long it took to schedule them. Briefing Committee leadership in the month after beginning a new activity does not constitute actively avoiding or impeding congressional oversight.

---

[415] SSCI Study, Executive Summary, December 3, 2014, p. 441.

[416] SSCI Study, Executive Summary, December 3, 2014, p. 441.

[417] SSCI Study, Findings and Conclusions, December 3, 2014, p. 5.

[418] SSCI Study, Executive Summary, December 3, 2014, p. 437 n.2447. *See also* SSCI Transcript, *Briefing on Covert Action*, November 7, 2001, p. 56 (DTS 2002-0611).

[419] SSCI Study, Executive Summary, December 3, 2014, p. 437. *See also* Email from: Christopher Ford, SSCI Staff, to: ███ Cleared SSCI staff; subject: Meeting yesterday with CIA lawyers on ███████; date: February 26, 2002 (DTS 2002-0925).

[420] CIA Study Response, *Conclusions (TAB B)*, June 27, 2013, p. 36.

(U) *Access to Documents*

Study Claim: (TS ███████████ NF) "The CIA subsequently resisted efforts by then-Vice Chairman John D. Rockefeller, IV, to investigate the program, including by refusing in 2006 to provide requested documents."[421]

Fact: (TS ███████ NF) The CIA provided access to the documents requested.

(TS ███████████ NF) The Study asserts that the CIA refused to provide requested documents. However, this misrepresents both the Vice Chairman's document request and the Intelligence Community's response. As noted in the Study, on January 5, 2006, the Director of National Intelligence's Chief of Staff wrote a letter to Vice Chairman Rockefeller which denied an earlier request for full Committee access to over 100 documents related to the Inspector General's May 2004 Special Review.[422] However, this denial of "full Committee access," did not mean that the documents were not made available to the CIA's congressional overseers. In fact, the Chief of Staff's letter stated, "Consistent with the provisions of the National Security Act of 1947, the White House has directed that specific information related to aspects of the detention and interrogation program be provided only to the SSCI leadership and staff directors."[423] The letter concluded by advising Vice Chairman Rockefeller that the documents "remain available for review by SSCI leadership and staff directors at any time through arrangements with CIA's Office of Congressional Affairs."[424]

(U) *Breadth of Congressional Access*

Study Claim: (TS ███████ NF) The CIA impeded congressional oversight by restricting access to information about the Program from members of the Committee beyond the Chairman and Vice Chairman.[425]

Fact: (TS ███████ NF) The CIA's limitation of access to sensitive covert action information is a long-standing practice codified in Section 503 of the National Security Act of 1947, as amended.

(TS ███████ NF) The Study notes numerous times that the CIA refused to provide information on its Detention and Interrogation Program to Committee members and staff.[426] The underlying assertion is that the CIA's restriction of access to the Chairman and Vice Chairman somehow constituted an attempt to avoid or impede congressional oversight of the Program. This is simply untrue. According to section 503(c)(2) of the National Security Act of 1947, as amended:

---

[421] SSCI Study, Findings and Conclusions. December 3, 2014, pp 5-6.
[422] SSCI Study, Executive Summary, December 3, 2014, p. 442.
[423] Letter from David Shedd to Andy Johnson, January 5, 2006 (DTS 2006-0373).
[424] Letter from David Shedd to Andy Johnson, January 5, 2006 (DTS 2006-0373).
[425] SSCI Study, Findings and Conclusions, December 3, 2014, p. 6.
[426] SSCI Study, Executive Summary, December 3, 2014, pp. 439-441.

If the president determines that it is essential to limit access to the finding to meet extraordinary circumstances affecting vital interests of the United States, the finding may be reported to the chairmen and ranking minority members of the congressional intelligence committees, the Speaker and minority leader of the House of Representatives, the majority and minority leaders of the Senate, and such other member or members of the congressional leadership as may be included by the President.

The CIA's decision to limit the briefing of this particularly sensitive covert action program to the Chairman and Vice Chairman was in keeping with customary practice and complied with the law. The Committee has conducted oversight of other sensitive covert action programs under similar access limitations and continues to do so at this time.

(TS██████████NF) The Study notes that the CIA briefed a number of additional senators who were not on the Select Committee on Intelligence.[427] As cited above, the law allows the President discretion to provide senators with information about covert action programs at his discretion, without regard to Committee membership. Moreover, providing a briefing to inform key senators working on legislation relevant to the CIA's program is inconsistent with the narrative that the CIA sought to avoid congressional scrutiny.

(U) Conclusion 7 (CIA Impeded White House Oversight)

(U) Conclusion 7 states, "[t]he CIA impeded effective White House oversight and decision-making."[428] It is important to place this serious allegation within its proper context— the CIA's Detention and Interrogation Program was conducted as a covert action.[429] Covert action is the sole responsibility of the White House, a principle enshrined in law since the National Security Act of 1947.[430] The President, working with his National Security Staff, approves and oversees all covert action programs. The congressional intelligence committees also conduct ongoing oversight of all covert actions and receive quarterly covert action briefings. Given this extensive covert action oversight regime, this conclusion seems to imply falsely that the CIA was operating a rogue intelligence operation designed to "impede" the White House. We reject this unfounded implication and it appears the CIA has rejected it as well:

---

[427] SSCI Study, Executive Summary, December 3, 2014, p. 443.

[428] SSCI Study, Findings and Conclusions, December 3, 2014, p. 6.

[429] See SSCI Study, Executive Summary, December 3, 2014, p. 11. "On September 17, 2001, six days after the terrorist attacks of September 11, 2001, President George W. Bush signed a covert action MON to authorize the Director of Central Intelligence (DCI) to 'undertake operations designed to capture and detain persons who pose a continuing, serious threat of violence or death to U.S. persons and interests or who are planning terrorist activities.'" (emphasis added).

[430] In 1974, the Hughes-Ryan amendment to the Foreign Assistance Act of 1961 created the requirement for presidential "Findings" for covert action. The Intelligence Oversight Acts of 1980 and 1988 amended the Finding process, and the Intelligence Oversight Act of 1991 replaced Hughes-Ryan with the current Finding process. See William Daugherty, Executive Secrets, Covert Action and the Presidency, The University Press of Kentucky, 2004, pp. 92-98.

While we were able to find points in the preceding themes with which to both agree and disagree, the *Study* seems to most seriously diverge from the facts and, indeed, from simple plausibility in its characterizations of the manner in which CIA dealt with others with regard to the RDI program. The *Study* would have the reader believe that CIA 'actively' avoided and interfered with oversight by the Executive Branch and Congress . . . [and] withheld information from the President . . . .

We would observe that, to accomplish this, there would have had to have been a years-long conspiracy among CIA leaders at all levels, supported by a large number of analysts and other line officers. This conspiracy would have had to include three former CIA Directors . . . .

We cannot vouch for every individual statement that was made over the years of the program, and we acknowledge that some of those statements were wrong. But the image portrayed in the *Study* of an organization that–on an institutional scale–intentionally misled and routinely resisted oversight from the White House, the Congress, the Department of Justice, and its own OIG simply does not comport with the record. . . .

[The] CIA did not, as the *Study* alleges, intentionally misrepresent to anyone the overall value of the intelligence acquired, the number of detainees, the propensity of detainees to withhold and fabricate, or other aspects of the program.[431]

Our analysis of the documentary record demonstrates that most of the CIA's representations about the Detention and Interrogation Program were accurate.

(U) *Executive Branch Oversight*

Study Claim: (TS███████████NF) "According to CIA records, no CIA officer, up to and including CIA Directors George Tenet and Porter Goss, briefed the President on the specific CIA enhanced interrogation techniques before April 2006. By that time, 38 of the 39 detainees identified as having been subjected to the CIA's enhanced interrogation techniques had already been subjected to the techniques."[432]

Fact: (U) CIA records are contradictory and incomplete regarding when the President was briefed, but President Bush himself says he was briefed in 2002, before any techniques were used.[433]

(TS███████████NF) The Study finds that the CIA "impeded" executive branch oversight, not just by withholding information about the Program, but by providing inaccurate

---

[431] CIA Study Response, *Comments (TAB A)*, June 27, 2013, pp. 15-16 (emphasis in original).
[432] SSCI Study, Findings and Conclusions, December 3, 2014, p. 6.
[433] George W. Bush, *Decision Points*, Broadway Paperbacks, New York, 2010, p. 169.

information about its operation and effectiveness. Beginning with the premise that the CIA did not obtain approval from the President or the National Security Council prior to using enhanced interrogation techniques on Abu Zubaydah, the Study identifies records that cast some doubt on whether the President was briefed before April 2006.[434] However, CIA records are inconsistent on this point.

(TS███████████████NF) One chronology of the approvals obtained for the CIA program, dated April 2008, lists a meeting held on August 1, 2002, between the President and the Deputy Director of the CIA concerning the "Next Phase of the Abu Zubaydah Interrogation," which strongly suggests that the President had been briefed on the interrogation. Another undated chronology, however, notes that, according to a July 31, 2002, memorandum, the National Security Council communicated to the CIA that the President would not be briefed.[435] An Inspector General interview with former DCI Tenet also suggests that he did not brief the President on enhanced interrogation techniques (EITs). Tenet said "he had never spoken to the President regarding EITs, nor was he aware of whether the President had been briefed by his staff."[436] An interview of the former Director or his staff, or a review of Director Tenet's e-mail communications and those of his staff, might also have helped clarify this point.

(U) Since no interviews were conducted and since—as we learned during the course of our review of the Study material—the majority never requested e-mail communications from Director Tenet or other senior CIA leaders, such a clarification was impossible. In fact, as noted earlier, we learned that the majority did not request the e-mail communications of *any* senior CIA leaders who likely would have discussed the Program with the President—not Director Tenet, Director Goss, Deputy Director McLaughlin, Director of Operations Pavitt, Director of Operations Kappes, Director of the Counterterrorism Center Bob Grenier, and many others. Because of this gap in emails from critical participants, the majority's document review is incomplete. In the absence of interviews and with the gap in documents, the Study's reliance on the CIA records it did review, therefore, is simply not definitive on whether the President was briefed on the use of interrogation techniques on Zubaydah. Yet the Study interprets the absence of clarity on this point as confirmation that the CIA must have withheld information from the President.

(U) There is at least one person, however, who disputes this narrative and says that the President was briefed and approved the use of enhanced techniques on Zubaydah—President George W. Bush. In his book, *Decision Points*, the President has a different recollection than Director Tenet. The President recalls being told that Abu Zubaydah was withholding information; that "CIA experts drew up a list of interrogation techniques that differed from those Zubaydah had successfully resisted;" and that "Department of Justice and CIA lawyers conducted a careful legal review."[437] He describes looking at the list of techniques, including

---

[434] *See, e.g.*, SSCI Study, Findings and Conclusions, December 3, 2014, p.18 n.17. SSCI Study, Executive Summary, December 3, 2014, pp. 38-40.

[435] Chronology of Renditions, *Detainees and Interrogations Program and Interrogation Approvals: 2001-2008*, undated; *see also April 3, 2014*, SSCI Study, Executive Summary, December 3, 2014, p. 40 n.179.

[436] Office of the General Counsel, Comments on the Inspector General, Special Review, Counterterrorism Detention and Interrogation Activities (September 2001 – October 2003), May 7, 2004 (DTS 2004-2710).

[437] Bush, p 169.

waterboarding, and approving their use, while directing the CIA not to use two of them that he "felt went too far, even if they were legal."[438] President Bush also confirms that he approved the use of enhanced interrogation techniques, including the waterboard, on KSM.[439] So while the Study assumes the President did not give his approval prior to the use of enhanced techniques on Abu Zubaydah because the majority cannot find CIA records that unequivocally say when and how it happened, the President's own words set the record straight.[440]

(TS██████████NF) Regardless, even if it were true that the President had not been briefed by the CIA, we find it odd that the Study would assign blame for "withholding information" to the CIA, when the Study itself acknowledges the role of officials outside the CIA in making determinations about what should be briefed to policymakers. For example, the Study correctly notes that the description of the waterboard was removed from the 2002 Deputy DCI (DDCI) talking points for the meeting with the President, but its account of why this change was made is misleading.[441] In describing an e-mail regarding the planned briefing, the Study states that "per an agreement between DCI Tenet and White House Counsel Gonzales, the briefing would include no 'further details about the interrogation techniques than those in the (revised) talking points.'"[442] In reality, the e-mail says that the "WH asks that DDCI brief POTUS tomorrow at 0800 meeting without any further details about the interrogation techniques than those in the talking points."[443] Thus, it was at the request of the White House—not the CIA, that only a broad description of the nature of the techniques would be provided; specifically, that the "techniques incorporate mild physical pressure, while others may place Abu Zubaydah in fear for his life" and they "include an intense physical and psychological stressor used by the U.S. Navy in its interrogation resistance training for the Navy SEALS."[444]

(U) *Accuracy of Information Provided*

Study Claim: (TS██████████NF) **"The information provided connecting the CIA's detention and interrogation program directly to [the "Dirty Bomb" Plot/Tall Buildings Plot, the Karachi Plots, Heathrow and Canary Wharf**

---

[438] Bush, p. 169.

[439] Bush, p. 170, ("George Tenet asked if he had permission to use enhanced interrogation techniques, including waterboarding, on Khalid Sheikh Mohammed. I thought about my meeting with Danny Pearl's widow, who was pregnant with his son when he was murdered. I thought about the 2,973 people stolen from their families by al Qaeda on 9/11. And I thought about my duty to protect the country from another act of terror. 'Damn right,' I said").

[440] The CIA Study response also made reference to President Bush's autobiography, noting that "he discussed the program, including the use of enhanced techniques, with then [DCI] Tenet in 2002, prior to the application of the techniques on Abu Zubaydah, and personally approved the techniques." CIA Study Response, *Conclusions*, p. 6. The Study chooses to rebut President Bush's recollections of these events by stating, "A memoir by former Acting CIA General Counsel John Rizzo disputes the President's autobiographical account." SSCI Study, Findings and Conclusions, December 3, 2014, p.18 n17. Again, further clarification of these events was hampered by the lack of witness interviews.

[441] SSCI Study, Executive Summary, December 3, 2014, p. 38.

[442] SSCI Study, Volume I, March 31, 2014, p. 135.

[443] CIA, E-mail to DDCI, dated July 31, 2002, *Briefing of POTUS tomorrow (1 Aug) re AZ interrogation.*

[444] DDCI Talking Points for Meeting with the President. 31 July 2001 (sic).

Plot, and the Identification/Capture of Iyman Faris] was, to a great extent, inaccurate."[445]

Fact: (U) **The information provided to the White House attributing the arrests of these terrorists and the thwarting of these plots to the CIA's Detention and Interrogation Program was accurate.**

(S//NF) The Study accuses the CIA of providing inaccurate information to the White House and the National Security Council Principals about the Program and its effectiveness. Pivotal to this allegation is a July 29, 2003, briefing that the CIA Director and General Counsel had with executive branch officials, including the Vice President, the National Security Advisor, the White House Counsel, and the Attorney General. According to the six-page memorandum for the record prepared by the CIA General Counsel on August 5, 2003, the purpose of the meeting was to "discuss current, past and future CIA policies and practices concerning the interrogation of certain detainees held by CIA."[446]

(TS███████████NF) The Study notes that the memorandum provided four of the eight "most frequently cited examples from 2002-2009" as evidence of the effectiveness of CIA's interrogation program, including: "the 'dirty bomb' plot/tall buildings plot (also referenced as the Capture of Jose Padilla), the Karachi Plots, the Heathrow and Canary Wharf Plot, and the Identification/Capture of Iyman Faris."[447] While the Study asserts, "the information provided connecting the CIA's detention and interrogation program directly to the above disruptions and captures was, to a great extent, inaccurate," we found that the examples provided were, in fact, accurate.[448]

(U) Conclusion 8 (CIA Impeded National Security Missions of Executive Branch Agencies)

(U) Conclusion 8 states, "[t]he CIA's operation and management of the program complicated, and in some cases impeded, the national security missions of other Executive Branch agencies."[449]

(TS███████████NF) The standard by which the Study claims the CIA "impeded" national security missions of other executive branch agencies is based entirely on subjective standards that are never defined in the text. Equally problematic are statements that the CIA blocked or denied requests for information from other executive branch agencies. By inference this implies the President and the National Security Council did not control access to the covert action program. However, the September 17, 2001, Memorandum of Notification authorizing the detainee program, states: "Approval of the Principals shall be sought in advance

---

[445] SSCI Study, April 1, 2014, Volume II, p. 446.
[446] CIA General Counsel Memorandum for the Record, August 5, 2003, *Review of Interrogation Program on 29 July 2003.*
[447] SSCI Study, Volume II, April 1, 2014, p. 446.
[448] *See supra, The Thwarting of the Dirty Bomb/Tall Buildings Plot and the Capture of Jose Padilla,* pp. 33-36; *The Thwarting of the Karachi Plots,* pp. 45-47; *The Heathrow and Canary Wharf Plots,* pp. 47-50; and *The Arrest and Prosecution of Iyman Faris,* pp. 58-61.
[449] SSCI Study, Findings and Conclusions, December 3, 2014, p. 7.

whenever feasible with respect to such operations . . . ."[450] As noted in the CIA response to the Study, "the National Security Council established the parameters for when and how CIA could engage on the program with other executive branch agencies."[451] The CIA was not responsible nor did it have control over the sharing or dissemination of information to other executive branch agencies or members of the Principals Committee itself. That responsibility rested solely with the White House.

(U) *Access to the Covert Action Program*

Study Claim: (TS ██████████ NF) "The CIA blocked State Department leadership from access to information crucial to foreign policy decision-making and diplomatic activities."[452]

Fact: (TS ██████████ NF) The National Security Staff controlled access to the covert action program and there is no evidence that the CIA refused to brief State Department leadership when directed.

(TS ██████████ NF) The Study does not provide any evidence that the CIA deliberately impeded, obstructed or blocked the State Department from obtaining information about the Program inconsistent with directions from the White House or the National Security Council. In fact, the Study acknowledges that CIA officers were in close and constant contact with their State Department counterparts where detention facilities were located and among senior leadership to include the Secretary of State and the U.S. Deputy Secretary of State. For example, leading to the establishment of a facility in Country █, the Study notes that the chief of station (COS) was coordinating activities with the ambassador. Because the Program was highly compartmented, the ambassador was directed by the National Security Council not to discuss with his immediate superior at headquarters due to the highly compartmented nature of the covert action. Instead, the COS, sent feedback from the ambassador through CIA channels, to the NSC, whereby the Deputy Secretary of State with the knowledge of the Secretary, would discuss any issues or concerns with the ambassador in country.[453] While the process was less direct, the security precautions to protect sensitive information did not impede the national security mission of the State Department.

(U) *CIA Denied FBI Requests*

Study Claim: (TS ██████████ NF) "The CIA denied specific requests from FBI Director Robert Mueller, III, for FBI access to CIA detainees that the FBI believed was necessary to understand CIA detainee reporting on threats to the U.S. Homeland."[454]

---

[450] DTS 2002-0371, p. 3.
[451] CIA Study Response, *Comments (TAB A)*, June 27, 2013, p. 11.
[452] SSCI Study, Findings and Conclusions, December 3, 2014, p. 7.
[453] ██████ CIA CABLE ████████████████ CIA CABLE ██████████ CIA CABLE ████████████
[454] SSCI Study, Findings and Conclusions, December 3, 2014, p. 7.

Fact: (TS███████████NF) While the FBI's participation in the interrogation of detainees was self-proscribed, the Bureau was still able to submit requirements to the CIA and received reports on interrogations.

(TS███████████NF) This Study claim appears to focus on FBI access to KSM in 2003 after FBI Director Mueller read an interrogation report that vaguely referenced possible threats to New York, Washington, DC, Chicago, Dallas, and San Francisco.[455] However, the Study acknowledges the FBI's fear that the use of enhanced techniques activity would place FBI agents at future legal risk if they participated in interrogations.[456] Recognizing the need for FBI access to detainees, both agencies finalized a memorandum of understanding in the fall of 2003 that detailed how FBI ███████████████████████████████ agents would be provided access to detainees ███████████████████.[457]

(U) *The ODNI was Provided with Inaccurate and Incomplete Information*

Study Claim: (TS███████████NF) "The ODNI was provided with inaccurate and incomplete information about the program, preventing the ODNI from effectively carrying out its statutory responsibility to serve as the principal advisor to the President on intelligence matters."[458]

Fact: (TS███████████NF) The Study incorrectly claims that inaccurate information was provided to the Office of the Director of National Intelligence.

(U) The updated Study treats this claim differently than it did in the version that was adopted by the Committee during the 112th Congress. The original Study sought to dispute claims regarding the use of enhanced interrogation techniques and disruption of several plots. However, the updated Study drops the direct reference to coercive measures and instead focuses on the Detention and Interrogation Program in general.[459] The 2006 press release from the Office of Director of National Intelligence[460] does not reference the use of enhanced interrogation techniques, but states unequivocally: "The detention of terrorists disrupts—at least temporarily—the plots they were involved in." To claim that the detention and interrogation of terrorists did not yield intelligence of value is simply not credible.

(U) Conclusion 5 (CIA Provided Inaccurate Information to the Department of Justice)

(U) Conclusion 5 states, "[t]he CIA repeatedly provided inaccurate information to the Department of Justice, impeding a proper legal analysis of the CIA's detention and Interrogation

---

[455] SSCI Study, Volume I, March 31, 2014, p. 414.
[456] Email from: James Pavitt; to: ███████████; subject: Re: Mueller's Interest in FBI Access to KSM; Date: April 24, 2003, 2:35 PM.
[457] SSCI Study, Volume I, March 31, 2014, p. 413.
[458] SSCI Study, Findings and Conclusions, December 3, 2014, p. 8.
[459] SSCI Study, Findings and Conclusions, December 3, 2014, p. 8.
[460] ODNI Press Release, September 6, 2006, "Information on the High Value Terrorist Detainee Program."

Program."[461] Our analysis of the claims used in support of this conclusion revealed that many of the Study's claims were themselves inaccurate or otherwise without merit.

(U) *"Novel" Use of the Necessity Defense*

Study Claim: (TS█████████NF) "CIA attorneys stated that 'a novel application of using the necessity defense' could be used 'to avoid prosecution of U.S. officials who tortured to obtain information that saved many lives.'"[462]

Fact: (TS█████████NF) The draft CIA Office of General Counsel (OGC) legal appendix cited by the report contained a cursory discussion of the necessity defense that *did not* support the use of such defense in the context of the CIA's Detention and Interrogation Program.[463]

(U) This particular claim appears to be a remnant from what had been "Conclusion 2" in the original version of the Study approved by the SSCI during the 112th Congress. Our original minority views were very critical of the claims made in support of the "necessity defense" conclusion. We were pleased to see that the original "Conclusion 2" was dropped from the conclusions in the updated version of the Study; however, we are disappointed to see this factually and legally incorrect claim repeated here in support of a conclusion alleging that the CIA provided inaccurate information to the Department of Justice.

(U) This claim advances the faulty proposition that a "novel application" of the necessity defense could be used by participants in the CIA's Detention and Interrogation Program to avoid criminal liability. On its face, this claim leaves the reader with the false impression that CIA attorneys endorsed the possible use of the "necessity" defense in the context of the CIA's Detention and Interrogation Program, when, in fact, the draft legal appendix cited by the Study[464] actually reached the *opposite* conclusion.[465]

(TS█████████NF) Contrary to the Study's claim, the legal analysis provided in the cited draft legal appendix *did not* support the use of the necessity defense in the context of the CIA's program. The Study achieved this erroneous result by modifying the following original quote that it cherry picked from the legal analysis: "It would, therefore, be a novel application of the necessity defense to avoid prosecution of U.S. officials who tortured to obtain information that saved many lives . . . ."[466] Specifically, the Study modified this quote by separating portions of the text and inserting its own factually misleading text, which was not supported by the legal analysis, to achieve the following result: "*CIA attorneys stated that a*

---

[461] SSCI Study, Findings and Conclusions, December 3, 2014, p. 4.

[462] SSCI Study, Findings and Conclusions, December 3, 2014, p. 5.

[463] *See* CIA Office of General Counsel draft *Legal Appendix: Paragraph 5--Hostile Interrogations: Legal Considerations for CIA Officers*, November 26, 2001, pp. 5-6 (CIA, Draft Appendix on Necessity Defense). This document is attached as Appendix IV, *see infra*, p. IV-1.

[464] SSCI Study, Findings and Conclusions, December 3, 2014, p. 5 n.13.

[465] *See* CIA, CIA Draft Appendix on Necessity Defense.

[466] CIA, CIA Draft Appendix on Necessity Defense, p. 6. *See also* SSCI Study, Executive Summary, December 3, 2014, p. 179 (the Study provides an accurate quotation of this text).

novel application of the necessity defense *could be used* to avoid prosecution of U.S. officials who tortured to obtain information that saved lives."[467] Fortunately, this erroneously doctored quotation only appears once in the Study—in this Conclusion.

(TS███████████NF) The Study does, however, cite the original "novel application" quotation in at least 12 different places in its updated report to support its incorrect assertion that CIA attorneys viewed necessity "as a defense" or as a "potential legal defense."[468] While this quotation is technically accurate, it is consistently removed from its context within the legal analysis to create the false impression that the defense of necessity might have been available to CIA employees engaged in interrogation activities. The legal appendix clearly conceded that since "U.S. courts have not yet considered the necessity defense in the context of torture/murder/assault cases . . . [i]t would, therefore, be a novel application of the necessity defense to avoid prosecution . . . ."[469] When the "novel application" quote is placed back into its proper original context, it becomes clear that the legal analysis *did not* conclude that the necessity defense could be used to avoid prosecution. The use of the word "novel" in this context clearly suggests the drafting attorney viewed the approach as problematic.[470]

(TS███████████NF) The Study's Executive Summary contains a section entitled, "The Origins of CIA Representations Regarding the Effectiveness of the CIA's Enhanced Interrogation Techniques As Having "Saved Lives," "Thwarted Plots" and "Captured Terrorists."[471] In that section, the Study cites to the "novel application" of the necessity defense contained in the draft legal appendix. This "Origins" section, when combined with the erroneous necessity defense claim made here, appears to have been designed to guide the reader into falsely inferring that the CIA represented that the enhanced interrogation techniques were necessary to acquire "otherwise unavailable" intelligence that "saved lives" because of the draft legal appendix's discussion of the necessity defense.

(U) There are a number of problems with this false inference. If this inference is based simply on the fact that the CIA's representations were made *after* the circulation of the draft legal appendix's discussion of the necessity defense, then the claim is little more than a classic example of *"post hoc"* erroneous reasoning. Simply put, just because the CIA represented that the Program saved lives does not mean that such representations were caused by the draft legal appendix.

(TS███████████NF) It seems unlikely that the single appearance of the phrase "saved many lives" in the context of the draft legal appendix's discussion of the necessity defense was the reason behind the use of similar terminology in subsequent accounts of the

---

[467] SSCI Study, Findings and Conclusions, December 3, 2014, p. 5 (Erroneous text indicated by italics).
[468] *See* SSCI Study, Executive Summary, December 3, 2014, pp. 19 and 179; SSCI Study, Volume I, March 31, 2014, pp 55, 220, 255, 262 n.1700, and 283 n.1854; SSCI Study, Volume II, April 1, 2014, pp. 28, 316, and 1753; and SSCI Study, Volume III, March 31, 2014,, pp. 1179 and 1723 n.10679.
[469] CIA, Draft Appendix on Necessity Defense. p. 6.
[470] The CIA confirmed that the use of "novel" in the context of this document meant "tenuous" or "untested," because U.S. courts had not accepted such an argument. *See* CIA Study Response, *Comments*, p. 7 and CIA Study Response, *Conclusions*, pp. 4-5.
[471] SSCI Study, Executive Summary, December 3, 2014, p. 179.

Program. Aside from the false inference made in the "Origins" section, there is no evidence to support this leap of logic.

(TS█████████NF) Moreover, the draft legal appendix concluded that the necessity defense did not apply in the context of the CIA's Detention and Interrogation Program. Therefore, this false inference—that the CIA's representations regarding the "otherwise unavailable intelligence" that "saved lives" were the result of efforts to preserve the necessity defense—does not make sense because the draft legal appendix had already concluded that the necessity defense raised in the context of a torture prosecution was unlikely to succeed in a U.S. court.

(U) In this conclusion, the Study appears to buttress its argument about the applicability of the necessity defense in the context of the CIA's Detention and Interrogation Program by noting that OLC included a discussion of the "necessity defense" in its August 1, 2002, memorandum to the White House.[472] That memorandum opinion stated: *"under the current circumstances, necessity or self-defense* **may** *justify* interrogation methods that *might* violate" the criminal prohibition against torture.[473] Not surprisingly, this August 1, 2002, memorandum opinion was withdrawn in June 2004 and formally superseded in its entirety on December 30, 2004. Specifically, the superseding memorandum stated, "Because the discussion in that memorandum concerning the President's Commander-in-Chief power and *the potential defenses to liability was—and remains—unnecessary, it has been eliminated from the analysis that follows.*"[474] Although the Study acknowledges this subsequent withdrawal of the necessity defense analysis in a footnote,[475] it suggests that OLC included its discussion of the necessity defense at the request of the CIA.[476]

(U) The August 1, 2002, memorandum opinion, however, did finally conclude with the somewhat more definitive statement: "even if an interrogation method might violate [the criminal prohibition against torture], necessity or self-defense could provide justifications that would eliminate any criminal liability."[477] Regardless, the Study's apparent reliance upon this *withdrawn* OLC opinion is misplaced, because it actually seems to undermine its conclusion that the CIA provided inaccurate information to the Department of Justice. Assuming for the sake of argument that the CIA provided OLC with a copy of its legal analysis on the necessity defense— which seems highly unlikely—the CIA legal opinion was correct about necessity being a "novel"

---

[472] SSCI Study, Findings and Conclusions, December 3, 2014, p. 5 (citing DOJ, Memorandum from Jay S. Bybee, Assistant Attorney General, Office of Legal Counsel, DOJ, to Alberto R. Gonzales, Counsel to the President, *re: Standards of Conduct for Interrogation,* August 1, 2002).

[473] DOJ, Memorandum from Jay S. Bybee, Assistant Attorney General, Office of Legal Counsel, DOJ, to Alberto R. Gonzales, Counsel to the President, *re: Standards of Conduct for Interrogation,* August 1, 2002, p. 46 (emphasis added).

[474] DOJ, Memorandum from Daniel Levin, Acting Assistant Attorney General, Office of Legal Counsel, to James B. Comey, Deputy Attorney General, *Re: Legal Standards Applicable under 18 U.S.C. §§ 2340-2340A,* December 30, 2004, p. 2.

[475] SSCI Study, Executive Summary, December 3, 2014, p. 181 n.1069.

[476] *See* SSCI Study, Executive Summary, December 3, 2014, p. 181.

[477] SSCI Study, Executive Summary, December 3, 2014, p. 180 n.1065 (citing DOJ, Memorandum from Jay S. Bybee, Assistant Attorney General, Office of Legal Counsel, DOJ, to Alberto R. Gonzales, Counsel to the President, *re: Standards of Conduct for Interrogation,* August 1, 2002, p. 46).

application, while the OLC opinion reached a different result by concluding incorrectly that the defense of necessity would eliminate criminal liability.

(U) *Accuracy of Claims about Abu Zubaydah*

Study Claim: (TS█████████NF) The OLC "relied on inaccurate CIA representations about Abu Zubaydah's status in al-Qa'ida and the interrogation team's 'certain[ty]' that Abu Zubaydah was withholding information about planned terrorist attacks."[478]

(TS█████████NF) The CIA assessment that Abu Zubaydah was the "third or fourth man" in al-Qa'ida was "based on single-source reporting that was recanted prior to the August 1, 2002, OLC memorandum."[479]

(TS█████████NF) "The CIA later concluded that Abu Zubaydah was not a member of al-Qa'ida."[480]

Fact: (TS█████████NF) The information relied upon by the Study to criticize the CIA's representations about Abu Zubaydah withholding of information about planned terrorists attacks neglected to include important statements from within that same intelligence cable, which supported those representations by the CIA.

(TS█████████NF) The CIA was in possession of multiple threads of intelligence supporting Abu Zubaydah's prominent role in al-Qa'ida. The 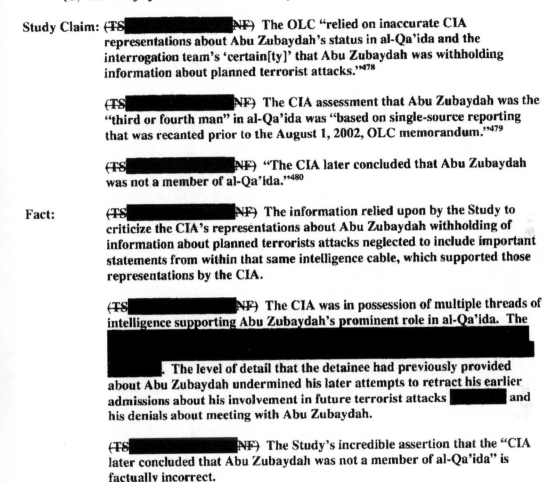. The level of detail that the detainee had previously provided about Abu Zubaydah undermined his later attempts to retract his earlier admissions about his involvement in future terrorist attacks ██████ and his denials about meeting with Abu Zubaydah.

(TS█████████NF) The Study's incredible assertion that the "CIA later concluded that Abu Zubaydah was not a member of al-Qa'ida" is factually incorrect.

(TS█████████NF) On August 1, 2002, the OLC provided the CIA with a memorandum on its legal analysis of the application of enhanced interrogation techniques to Abu Zubaydah. The Study asserts that "[m]uch of the information provided by the CIA to the OLC, however, was unsupported by CIA records."[481] While the CIA acknowledges that it should have

---

[478] SSCI Study, Findings and Conclusions, December 3, 2014, p. 5.
[479] SSCI Study, Executive Summary, December 3, 2014, p. 410.
[480] SSCI Study, Executive Summary, December 3, 2014, p. 410.
[481] SSCI Study, Executive Summary, December 3, 2014, p. 410.

kept OLC better informed and up-to-date, the Agency found no evidence that any information was known to be false when it was provided to OLC.[482]

(TS███████████NF) The Study claims that the CIA's unsupported representations to OLC included the characterization of Abu Zubaydah as withholding critical threat information.[483] The Study cites an email from the CIA's interrogation team that included the sentence: "[o]ur assumption is the objective of this operation [the interrogation of Abu Zubaydah] is to achieve a high degree of confidence that [Abu Zubaydah] is not holding back actionable information concerning threats to the United States beyond that which [Abu Zubaydah] has already provided."[484] However, this carefully chosen text omits critical statements from later in the same cable: "[t]here is information and analysis to indicate that subject has information on terrorist threats to the United States" and "[h]e is an incredibly strong willed individual which is why he has resisted this long."[485]

(TS███████████NF) The Study argues that the CIA provided inaccurate information to OLC which was subsequently included in the OLC legal guidance contained in its August 1, 2002, memorandum.[486] Specifically, the Study argues that the CIA information about Abu Zubaydah's status in al-Qa'ida was inaccurate because the representation that Abu Zubaydah was the "third or fourth man" in al-Qa'ida was based on single source reporting of a ███████████ who had recanted prior to the issuance of the memorandum, and unbelievably, *"[t]he CIA later concluded that Abu Zubaydah was not a member of al-Qa'ida."*[487] Our review of the underlying documents revealed that both of these Study assertions were wrong.

(TS███████████NF) The Study criticizes the CIA representation that Abu Zubaydah was the "third or fourth man" in al-Qa'ida was based on a single source who had recanted prior to the drafting of the August 1, 2002, OLC memorandum.[488] The CIA counters this criticism by stating that the Agency had:

> multiple threads of reporting indicating that Zubaydah was a dangerous terrorist, close associate of senior al Qa'ida leaders, and was aware of critical logistical and operational details of the organization, whether or not he held formal rank in al-Qa'ida. Analysts did not alter their fundamental assessment of Zubaydah's

---

[482] CIA Study Response, *Conclusions (TAB B)*, June 27, 2013, p. 32.

[483] SSCI Study, Executive Summary, December 3, 2014, p. 411.

[484] CIA, [REDACTED] 73208, July 23, 2003, p. 3; Email from: CIA staff officer; to: [REDACTED], [REDACTED], ███████; subject: Addendum from ██████, [REDACTED] 73208 (231043Z JUL 02); date: July 23, 2004, at 07:56:49 PM. *See also* email from: [REDACTED]; to: [REDACTED]; subject: Re: Grayson SWIGERT and Hammond DUNBAR; date: August 8, 21, 2002, at 10:21 PM.

[485] CIA, [REDACTED] 73208, July 23, 2003, p. 3; email from: CIA staff officer; to: [REDACTED], [REDACTED], ███████; subject: Addendum from ██████, [REDACTED] 73208 (231043Z JUL 02); date: July 23, 2004, at 07:56 PM. *See also* Email from: [REDACTED]; to: [REDACTED]; subject: Re: Grayson SWIGERT and Hammond DUNBAR; date: August 8, 21, 2002, at 10:21 PM.

[486] SSCI Study, Executive Summary, December 3, 2014, p. 410.

[487] SSCI Study, Executive Summary, December 3, 2014, p. 410 (emphasis added).

[488] SSCI Study, Executive Summary, December 3, 2014, p. 410.

intelligence value as a result of anything said or later recanted by the single source.[489]

███████ ██████████ who had admitted that he was sent by Abu Zubaydah to conduct terrorist operations ███████, including an attack on a U.S. embassy.[490] ███████ had also reported to interrogators that Abu Zubaydah was considered the "third or fourth ranking individual after Bin Ladin."[491] He provided the following additional information that Abu Zubaydah: (1) was considered the financial officer; (2) handled the "fraudulent" operations; (3) was considered to be responsible for the Gulf networks; and (4) was considered to be experienced in military affairs.[492] ███████ also admitted to meeting with Abu Zubaydah at least twice.[493] An intelligence cable indicates that "as of 2 October 2001, [███████] had retracted his previous admissions . . . to carry out a terrorist attack against the U.S. embassy . . . "[494] ███████ were certain, however, that despite ███████ retraction of his admissions concerning a plot against a U.S. embassy, he was involved in terrorist planning activity against unknown targets. They also assessed that ███████ had not been previously aware of the September 11, 2001, terrorist attacks by al-Qa'ida when he made his earlier admissions related to Abu Zubaydah.[495]

(TS██████████NF) ███████ further "denied that he ever met [Abu Zubaydah]" and "also denied any affiliation" with al-Qa'ida.[496] Given the level of detail ███████ provided about Abu Zubaydah, including Abu Zubaydah's rank within al-Qa'ida, his denials of meeting with Abu Zubaydah do not ring true. Moreover, Abu Zubaydah himself admitted to at least one meeting with ███████, which undermines the ███████ denials about such meetings.[497] Based on this information, we are not so quick to dismiss the validity of ███████ original assessments of Abu Zubaydah's stature within al-Qa'ida, especially since the timing of his recantation ████████████████████

(TS██████████NF) The Study cites to a finished intelligence product entitled, *Countering Misconceptions About Training Camps in Afghanistan, 1990-2001*, as support for its stunning claim that Abu Zubaydah was not a member of al-Qa'ida. In a text box, this intelligence product makes the following assertions:

> A common misperception in outside articles is that Khaldan camp was run by al-Qa'ida. Pre-911 September 2001 reporting miscast Abu Zubaydah as a "senior al-Qa'ida lieutenant," which led to the inference that the Khaldan camp he was administering was tied to Usama Bin Ladin . . . .

---

[489] *See* CIA Study Response, *Conclusions (TAB B)*, June 27, 2013, p. 32.
[490] CIA, ALEC ███████
[491] CIA, CIA ███████
[492] CIA, CIA ███████
[493] CIA, CIA ███████
[494] CIA, CIA ███████ *See also* CIA, ALEC ███████
[495] *See* CIA, CIA ███████
[496] *See* CIA, CIA ███████
[497] CIA, ALEC ███████ CIA, ALEC ███████ Abu Zubaydah and ███████ accounts differ as to the location of this meeting(s).

Al-Qa'ida rejected Abu Zubaydah's request *in 1993* to join the group and that Khaldan was not overseen by Bin Ladin's organization.[498]

At best, this text supports the rather useless assertion that in August 2006, a CIA intelligence product stated that *Abu Zubaydah was not a member of al-Qa'ida in 1993*—not the Study's erroneous claim that the CIA later concluded in 2006 that "Abu Zubaydah was not a member of al-Qa'ida." This misrepresentation of the actual text is another example of poor analytical tradecraft by the Study. As previously noted, there were multiple threads of intelligence demonstrating Abu Zubaydah's leadership role in al-Qa'ida prior to September 11, 2001.[499] Moreover, by the Study's own count, the interrogations of Abu Zubaydah resulted in 766 sole-source disseminated intelligence reports.[500] There should be absolutely no doubt in the Study that Abu Zubaydah was a senior and very-well informed member of al-Qa'ida.

(U) *Breadth of Application of Enhanced Interrogation Techniques*

Study Claim: (TS███████████NF) "[T]he CIA applied its enhanced interrogation techniques to numerous other CIA detainees without seeking additional formal legal advice from the OLC."[501]

Fact: (TS███████████NF) The CIA appropriately applied the legal principles of the August 1, 2002, OLC memorandum to other CIA detainees.

(TS███████████NF) The Study authors appear to misunderstand the role of the OLC. The OLC does not exercise line management responsibility for CIA organizations, nor is it responsible for day-to-day legal advice to the agency. The OLC does provide legal analysis on specific questions of law applicable to a defined set of facts. The CIA then applies the OLC's guidance to similar scenarios under the guidance of its own legal counsel. The fact that the CIA felt comfortable enough with OLC's August 1, 2002, legal opinion to apply the same legal principles to other detainees does not constitute an impediment to DOJ's legal analysis of the Program. In fact, the Attorney General later expressed the view that "the legal principles reflected in DOJ's specific original advice could appropriately be extended to allow use of the same approved techniques (under the same conditions and subject to the same safeguards) to other individuals besides the subject of DOJ's specific original advice."[502]

---

[498] CIA, *Countering Misconceptions About Training Camps in Afghanistan, 1990-2001*, August 16, 2006, p. 2 (emphasis added).

[499] *See* CIA Study Response, *Conclusions (TAB B)*, June 27, 2013, p. 32.

[500] SSCI Study, Volume III, March 31, 2014, pp. 282-283.

[501] SSCI Study, Executive Summary, December 3, 2014, p. 411.

[502] *See* Memorandum from Jack Goldsmith III, Assistant Attorney General, Office of Legal Counsel, Department of Justice, to John Helgerson, Inspector General, Central Intelligence Agency, June 18, 2004, Addendum, p. 2 (DTS 2004-2730).

(U) *Detainees' Importance Overstated*

Study Claim: (TS █████████████ NF) The CIA made inaccurate representations to DOJ that Janat Gul and Ahmed Khalfan Ghailani were high-value al Qaeda operatives with knowledge of a pre-election plot against the United States when seeking legal guidance on whether the use of four additional interrogation techniques might violate U.S. law or treaty obligations.[503]

(TS █████████████ NF) "[T]he threat of a terrorist attack to precede the November 2004 U.S. election was found to be based on a CIA source whose information was questioned by senior CTC officials at the time and who admitted to fabricating the information after a ████████ in ████October 2004."[504]

Fact: (TS █████████████ NF) Contrary to the Study's claim, the CIA believed the representations to be true at the time it made them to the OLC. The CIA did not learn that some of these representations had been fabricated by a sensitive CIA source until months *after* OLC had approved the use of enhanced interrogation techniques against Janat Gul and Ahmed Khalfan Ghailani.

(TS █████████████ NF) The email relied upon by the Study does not support the proposition that senior CTC officials questioned the veracity of the sensitive CIA source. Also, while the source did admit to fabricating information about a meeting that never occurred, the Study does not acknowledge that the Chief of Base believed that the source was "generally truthful" about his discussions on the pre-election threat, despite ████████████████████████████ result on that issue.

(TS █████████████ NF) The Study notes that the August 26, 2004, OLC letter advising that the use of four particular interrogation techniques on Janat Gul outside of the United States would not violate U.S. law or treaty obligations was based on the understanding that Janat Gul is a "high-value al Qaeda operative who is believed to possess information concerning an imminent terrorist threat to the United States."[505] The Study also notes that the September 6, 2004, OLC letter advising that the use of twelve particular interrogation techniques outside of the United States on Ahmed Khalfan Ghailani would not violate U.S. law or treaty obligations was based on the understanding that "Ghailani is an al-Qa'ida operative who 'is believed to be involved in the operational planning of an al-Qa'ida attack or attacks to take place

---

[503] *See* SSCI Study, Executive Summary, December 3, 2014, pp. 417-418.

[504] SSCI Study, Executive Summary, December 3, 2014, p. 417.

[505] DOJ, Letter from Dan Levin, Acting Assistant Attorney General, to John A. Rizzo, Acting General Counsel, August 26, 2004, p. 1; SSCI Study, Executive Summary, December 3, 2014, p. 417.

in the United states prior to the November elections.'"[506] With the benefit of faulty hindsight, the Study claims that these representations were inaccurate.[507]

(TS████████████NF) This claim gives the false impression that the CIA intentionally withheld information from OLC about known fabrications from a questionable source. The truth is that the sensitive CIA source did not recant some of the underlying threat information that was contained in the CIA representations until October █ and █ 2004, *40 days after the issuance of the OLC letter for Gul and 29 days after the issuance of OLC letter for Ghailani.* Thus, the CIA made its August and September representations to OLC in good faith, believing them to be accurate.

(TS████████████NF) Moreover, the authorities cited by the Study do not fully support its claim that the CIA source's representations about the pre-election threat were inaccurate.[508] Specifically, the cited email does not question the credibility of the sources who provided the threat information in March 2004; and the cable reporting the fabrication by one of these sources in October 2004 clearly indicates that some of the source's pre-election threat information was considered to be "generally truthful."

(TS████████████NF) As the subject of the email implies—"Re: could AQ be testing ASSET Y and [source name REDACTED]?"—the concerns raised were not about the credibility of the sources, but more about the possibility that al-Qa'ida might be using this threat information to test the sources who had provided the pre-election threat information. The email raising the concern specifically states, "this is not to say that either ASSET Y or [source name REDACTED] are wrong or that the AQ statement below[509] is anything more than disinformation."[510] The reply email stated that it was possible the sources were just hearing the same rumors, but recollected that when al-Qa'ida put out similar rumors in the summer of 2001, those turned out to be true.[511] These emails do not support any inference about early suspicions of the source's credibility nor do they dismiss the legitimacy of the threat information provided by the sources.

---

[506] DOJ, Letter from Dan Levin, Acting Assistant Attorney General, to John A. Rizzo, Acting General Counsel, September 6, 2004, p. 1; SSCI Study, Executive Summary, December 3, 2014, p. 417-418.
[507] SSCI Study, Executive Summary, December 3, 2014, p. 417.
[508] *See* SSCI Study, Executive Summary, December 3, 2014, p. 417.
[509] The referenced statement was issued by al-Qa'ida on March 17, 2004, and asserted that al-Qa'ida would not operate any large-scale operation prior to the election.
[510] Email from: ████████; to: ████████, ████████, [REDACTED], ████████, ████████; subject: could AQ be testing [ASSET Y] and [source name REDACTED]?; date: March █ 2004, at 06:55 AM; Email from: ████████; to ████████; cc: ████████, ████████, [REDACTED], ████████; subject: Re: could AQ be testing [the source] and ████?; date: March █, 2004, at 7:52:32 AM, p. 1 (footnote added).
[511] Email from ████████ to ████████ REDACTED ████████ subject: could AQ be testing [ASSET Y] and [source name REDACTED]?; date: March █ 2004, at 06:55 AM; Email from ████████ [REDACTED], ████████ subject: Re: could AQ be testing [the source] and ████; date: March █ 2004, at 7:52:32 AM, p. 1 (footnote added). This email confirms that the sensitive source who subsequently admitted to fabricating information was not the only source providing information related to a possible pre-election terrorist threat. ████████████████

(TS ████████████ NF) The Study states that ████████████████ indicated that ASSET Y was "deceptive in response to questions regarding . . . the pre-election threat."[512] This assertion is not entirely accurate. In fact, the cited cable indicated that the source ████ ████████████ on the issue of the pre-election threat ████████████ ████████████████."[513] Moreover, the assessment paragraph in the cited cable states: "Based on ASSET Y's seemingly genuine concern and constant return to the issue, COB believes that ASSET Y is being generally truthful about his discussions . . . on the pre-election threat."[514]

(U) *Effectiveness of the Program*

Study Claim: (TS ████████████ NF) The CIA's "representations of 'effectiveness' were almost entirely inaccurate and mirrored other inaccurate information provided to the White House, Congress, and the CIA inspector general."[515]

Fact: (TS ████████████ NF) The CIA's Detention and Interrogation Program, to include the use of enhanced interrogation techniques, was effective and yielded valuable intelligence. The Study's exaggerated and absolute claims about inaccurate "effectiveness" representations by the CIA have been largely discredited by these minority views and the CIA's June 27, 2013, response to the Study.

(TS ████████████ NF) In our view, the CIA's June 27, 2013, response to the Study identified significant problems with the original Study approved by the SSCI during the 112th Congress. Their response also fairly addressed the Study's many allegations of inaccurate representations in the context of the effectiveness of the Detention and Interrogation Program. For the most part, we found that the CIA acknowledged those representations that were made in error or could have benefited from the inclusion of additional clarification.

(TS ████████████ NF) As previously discussed, our own review of the documentary record in response to these serious allegations against the CIA found that many of the Study's claims of alleged misrepresentations were themselves inaccurate. As a reminder of these inaccurate Study claims, we provide the following sampling of our findings related to the CIA's effectiveness representations: (1) "There is considerable evidence that the information Abu Zubaydah provided identifying KSM as 'Mukhtar' and the mastermind of 9/11 was significant to CIA analysts, operators, and FBI interrogators";[516] (2) "CIA records clearly indicate that sleep deprivation played a significant role in Abu Zubaydah's identification of Jose Padilla as an al-Qa'ida operative tasked to carry out an attack against the United States";[517] (3) "Abu Zubaydah provided information about how he would go about locating Hassan Ghul and

---

[512] SSCI Study, Executive Summary, December 3, 2014, p. 348.
[513] CIA, CIA CABLE 1411, ████████ 2004, p. 4.
[514] CIA, CIA CABLE 1411, ████████ 2004, p. 5.
[515] SSCI Study, Executive Summary, December 3, 2014, p. 426.
[516] *See supra.* pp. 29-31.
[517] *See supra.* pp. 33-36.

other al-Qa'ida associates in Karachi. This information caused ███████ Pakistani authorities to intensify their efforts and helped lead them to capture Ramzi bin al-Shibh and other al-Qa'ida associates during the Karachi safe house raids conducted on September 10-11, 2002";[518] (4) "Information produced through detainee interrogation was pivotal to the retention of a key CIA asset whose cooperation led directly to the capture of KSM";[519] (5) "CIA documents show that key intelligence collected through the CIA's Detention and Interrogation Program, including information obtained after the use of enhanced interrogation techniques, played a major role in disrupting the Karachi hotels bombing plot";[520] (6) "The CIA interrogation program played a key role in disrupting the Heathrow and Canary Wharf plotting";[521] (7) "CIA documents show that the interrogation of KSM and al-Qa'ida operative Zubair, during and after the use of enhanced interrogation techniques on both individuals, played a key role in the capture of Hambali";[522] (8) "The CIA interrogation program played a key role in disrupting the "Second Wave" plot and led to the capture of the 17-member al-Ghuraba group";[523] (9) "CIA, FBI, and Department of Justice documents show that information obtained from detainees in CIA custody was important to identifying Ja'far al-Tayyar";[524] (10) "KSM provided valuable intelligence that helped to clarify Saleh al-Marri's role in al Qa'ida operations";[525] (11) "CIA, FBI, and Department of Justice documents show that information obtained from KSM after he was waterboarded led directly to Faris's arrest and was key in his prosecution"[526] (12) "Information obtained from detainee reporting, particularly KSM, provided otherwise unavailable intelligence that led to the identification of Saifullah Paracha as an al-Qa'ida operative involved in a potential plot, which spurred FBI action against him and his son, Uzhair";[527] (13) "Representations about the thwarting of an attack against Camp Lemonier in Djibouti, specifically President Bush's 2006 comments that 'Terrorists held in CIA custody have also provided information that helped stop a planned strike on U.S. Marines at Camp Lemonier in Djibouti,' were accurate and have been mischaracterized by the Study";[528] and (14) "CIA documents show that detainee information served as the "tip-off" and played a significant role in leading CIA analysts to the courier Abu Ahmad al-Kuwaiti. While there was other information in CIA databases about al-Kuwaiti, this information was not recognized as important by analysts until after detainees provided information on him."[529]

---

[518] *See supra,* pp. 37-41.
[519] *See supra,* pp. 41-45.
[520] *See supra,* pp. 45-47.
[521] *See supra,* pp. 47-50.
[522] *See supra,* pp. 50-53.
[523] *See supra,* pp. 53-56.
[524] *See supra,* pp. 56-57.
[525] *See supra,* pp. 57-58.
[526] *See supra,* pp. 58-61.
[527] *See supra,* pp. 61-64.
[528] *See supra,* pp. 67-68.
[529] *See supra,* pp. 73-75.

(U) Use of Constant Light, White Noise, and Shaving of Detainees

Study Claim: **(TS** ███████████ **NF)** **CIA assertions to the OLC that loud music and white noise, constant light, and 24-hour shackling were all for security purposes were inaccurate.**[530]

Fact: **(TS** ███████████ **NF)** **The CIA disclosed to OLC that these confinement conditions were both for security and for other purposes.**

(TS ███████████ **NF)** The Study asserts that the CIA inaccurately represented its purpose for confining detainees in conditions including loud music, white noise, constant light, 24-hour shackling, and shaving of the head and face.[531] The CIA's response asserts that this characterization takes the CIA's representations out of context. The Agency claimed that such conditions were necessary for security, not that the mechanisms served no other purpose. The Agency noted that in responding to a draft OLC opinion, the CIA tried to correct the misunderstanding, noting that "these conditions are also used for other valid reasons, such as to create an environment conducive to transitioning captured and resistant terrorist to detainees participating in debriefings."[532]

(U) Conclusion 9 (CIA Impeded Oversight by CIA Office of Inspector General)

(U) Conclusion 9 states, "[t]he CIA impeded oversight by the CIA's Office of Inspector General."[533] This allegation is among the most serious charges the Study levels against the CIA. As such, the Study should back up this charge with clear and convincing evidence. In our opinion it not only fails in that effort, but the Study itself is replete with examples that lead to the opposite conclusion——that the CIA did not significantly impede oversight by the CIA Office of the Inspector General (OIG).

(U) The law requires the CIA Inspector General to certify that "the Inspector General has had full and direct access to all information relevant to the performance of his function."[534] If the CIA OIG had been impeded in its oversight related to the CIA's Detention and Interrogation Program, it would have had to report that it was unable to make the required certification with respect to its oversight of this program. Yet, during the timeframe of the Program, the Inspector General certified in every one of its semiannual reports that it had "full and direct access to all CIA information relevant to the performance of its oversight duties."[535] The law also requires

---

[530] SSCI Study, Executive Summary, December 3, 2014, pp. 428-429.

[531] SSCI Study, Executive Summary, December 3, 2014, pp. 428-429.

[532] CIA Study Response, *Conclusions (TAB B)*, June 27, 2013, p. 34.

[533] SSCI Study, Findings and Conclusions, December 3, 2014, p. 8.

[534] 50 U.S.C. 3517(d)(1)(D).

[535] *See* CIA OIG, *Semi-Annual Report to the Director, Central Intelligence Agency*. July-December 2006, p. 5 (DTS 2007-0669); CIA OIG, *Semi-Annual Report to the Director, Central Intelligence Agency*, January-June 2006, p. 5 (DTS 2006-3195); CIA OIG, *Semi-Annual Report to the Director, Central Intelligence Agency*, July-December 2005, p. 5 (DTS 2006-0678); CIA OIG, *Semi-Annual Report to the Director, Central Intelligence Agency*, January-June 2005, p. 5 (DTS 2005-3140); CIA OIG, *Semi-Annual Report to the Director of Central Intelligence*, January-June 2004, p. 5 (DTS 2004-3307); and CIA OIG, *Semi-Annual Report to the Director of Central Intelligence*.

the Inspector General to *immediately* report to the congressional intelligence committees if the Inspector General is "unable to obtain significant documentary information in the course of an investigation, inspection or audit . . . ."[536] Again, we are not aware of any such report being made to the SSCI during the relevant time period. We do know, however, that John Helgerson, the CIA Inspector General, testified before SSCI prior to the commencement of the SSCI's review of the CIA Detention and Interrogation Program in February 2007 and did not complain of access to Agency information.[537] Instead, he said that, during 2006, the IG took a comprehensive look at the operations of the CIA's Counterterrorism Center and conducted a separate, comprehensive audit of detention facilities. General Helgerson also testified,

> [W]e look carefully at *all* cases of alleged abuse of detainees. The first paper of this kind that came to the Committee was in October 2003, not long after these programs had begun, when we looked at allegations of unauthorized interrogation techniques used at one of our facilities. It proved that indeed unauthorized techniques had been used. I'm happy to say that the processes worked properly. An Accountability Board was held. The individuals were in fact disciplined. The system worked as it should.

> On this subject, Mr. Chairman, I cannot but underscore that we also look at a fair number of cases where, at the end of the day, we find that we cannot find that there was substance to the allegation that came to our attention. We, of course, make careful record of these investigations because we think it important that you and others know that we investigate all allegations, some of which are borne out, some of which are not.[538]

Thus, the allegation made by this conclusion is attacking the credibility and integrity of both the CIA OIG and the CIA. Issues of credibility and integrity can rarely be resolved by resorting to a documentary record alone. They are best resolved by personally interviewing and assessing the performance of relevant witnesses, which, with some limited exceptions, was not done during the course of this Study. The absence of evidence relating to these statutory reporting requirements is a strong indicator the CIA OIG was not impeded in its oversight of the CIA's Detention and Interrogation Program.

(U) Another possible indicator of impeded oversight would be evidence that the CIA OIG was blocked from conducting or completing its desired reviews of the program. If such oversight had been impeded, we would expect to see few, if any, completed investigations, reviews, or audits of the Program. Instead, it appears that the opposite took place. The Study itself acknowledges the existence of at least 29 OIG investigations on detainee-related issues,

---

January-June 2003, p. 5 (DTS 2003-3327); CIA Study Response, *Comments (TAB A)*, June 27, 2013, pp. 4-6; and 10; and CIA Study Response, *Conclusions (TAB B)*, June 27, 2013, pp. 7-9.

[536] 50 U.S.C. 3517(d)(3)(E).

[537] *See* SSCI Transcript, *Hearing on the Central Intelligence Agency Rendition Program*, February 14, 2007, p. 24 (DTS 2007-1337).

[538] SSCI Transcript, *Hearing on the Central Intelligence Agency Rendition Program*, February 14, 2007, p. 25 (DTS 2007-1337) (emphasis added).

including 23 that were open or had been completed in 2005.[539] We would also expect to see indications in completed OIG reports that the investigation was hampered by limited access to documents, personnel, or site locations necessary for completing such investigations. Again, according to the OIG's own reports, we found evidence that the OIG had extensive access to documents, personnel, and locations. For example, in its May 2004 Special Review of the RDI program, the CIA OIG reported that it was provided more than 38,000 pages of documents and conducted more than 100 interviews, including with the DCI, the Deputy Director of the CIA, the Executive Director, the General Counsel, and the Deputy Director of Operations. The OIG made site visits to two interrogation facilities ████████████████ and reviewed 92 videotapes of the interrogation of Abu Zubaydah. The CIA IG's 2006 Audit is another good example of extensive access to documents, personnel, and locations. During this audit, the OIG not only conducted interviews of current and former officials responsible for CIA-controlled detention facilities, but it also reviewed operational cable traffic in extremely restricted access databases, reports, other Agency documents, policies, standard operating procedures, and guidelines pertaining to the detention program. The OIG also had access to the facilities and officials responsible for managing and operating three detention sites. The OIG was able to review documentation on site, observe detainees through closed-circuit television or one-way mirrors, and the IG even observed the transfer of a detainee aboard a transport aircraft. They even reviewed the medical and operational files maintained on each detainee in those locations.[540]

(U) The Study's case in support of this conclusion seems to rest mainly upon the following four observations: (1) the CIA did not inform the CIA OIG of the existence of the Program until November 2002; (2) some CIA employees provided the OIG with some inaccurate information about the Program; (3) CIA Director Goss directed the Inspector General in 2005 not to initiate planned review of the Program until the reviews already underway were completed; and (4) Director Hayden ordered a review of the OIG itself in 2007.[541] Our examination of these observations supports our conclusion that the CIA OIG was not impeded in its oversight of the CIA's Detention and Interrogation Program.

(U) The Study seems to fault the CIA for not briefing the CIA Inspector General on the existence of the Detention and Interrogation Program until November 2002, but does not really pursue why this fact alone was a problem or how it actually "impeded" the CIA OIG. Acting

---

[539] SSCI Study, Volume I, March 31, 2014, p. 899 n.6257. The CIA asserts that the "OIG conducted nearly 60 investigations" related to the CIA's Detention and Interrogation Program and that the OIG found the initial allegations in 50 of these investigations to be unsubstantiated or did not make findings warranting an accountability review. Of the remaining 10 investigations, one resulted in a felony conviction, one resulted in the termination of a contractor and the revocation of his security clearances, and six led to Agency accountability reviews. CIA Study Response, *Conclusions (TAB B)*, June 27, 2013, p. 7.

[540] CIA OIG, *CIA-controlled Detention Facilities Operated Under the 17 September 2001 Memorandum of Notification*, July 14, 2006, APPENDIX A, pp. 1-2 (DTS 2006-2793).

[541] SSCI Study, Findings and Conclusions, April 3, 2014, p. 8. [[This factual error and misrepresentation of events was corrected in the December 3, 2014, version of the Findings and Conclusions by editing the text to read, "In 2005, CIA Director Goss *requested* in writing that the inspector general not initiate further reviews of the CIA's Detention and Interrogation Program until review already underway were completed." (emphasis added). *Compare* SSCI Study, Findings and Conclusions, April 3, 2014, p. 8 *with* SSCI Study, Findings and Conclusions, December 3, 2014, p. 8.]]

under the authority of the President's September 17, 2001, Memorandum of Notification, the CIA initiated the Program in late-March, 2002, when the first detainee was taken into its custody.[542] The CIA's Detention and Interrogation Program was part of a highly classified and compartmented covert action program. As the Program was being implemented, the CIA sought legal guidance from the Department of Justice and began briefing the White House.[543] Congressional access to details about the Program was restricted to leadership of the congressional intelligence committees during that same timeframe.[544] The CIA Inspector General was notified in November about the Program's existence in November 2002, because of the need for an OIG investigation into the death of a detainee who had been in the custody of the CIA.[545] At that point, the OIG had a clear "need to know" about the Program. We see nothing sinister in these events.

(U) The second "impeding" observation concerned the fact that CIA personnel provided the OIG with inaccurate information on the operation and management of the Detention and Interrogation Program, which was subsequently not corrected by the CIA and was included in the OIG's final report. The CIA has acknowledged in two cases that it made "mistakes that caused the IG to incorrectly describe in its 2004 *Special Review* the precise role that information acquired from KSM played in the detention of two terrorists involved in plots against targets in the [United States]."[546] The inclusion of erroneous information in an oversight report is disappointing, but absolute precision in matters such as these is rarely obtainable. Overall, these errors did not fundamentally alter the overall representations the CIA made about the RDI program to the OIG and policy makers.

(U) The Study's third observation about CIA Director Goss contains an error. It states that in 2005, "CIA Director Goss *directed* the Inspector General not to initiate planned reviews of the CIA Detention and Interrogation Program until reviews already underway were completed."[547] In fact, Director Goss did not "direct," but rather asked that a newly proposed review by the OIG be rescheduled until a mutually agreed-upon date. We find that the actual text from Director Goss's request provides sufficient justification against any allegation of "impeding" OIG oversight with the respect to the timing of the proposed OIG review. The memorandum states:

---

[542] *See* CIA, ALEC ███████████████

[543] *See* CIA OIG, *Special Review: Counterterrorism Detention and Interrogation Activities, (September 2001 – October 2003)*, May 7, 2004, p. 4 (DTS 2004-2710).

[544] The CIA briefed HPSCI leadership on September 4, 2002, shortly after the August recess. SSCI leadership was briefed on the Program on September 27, 2002. *See* CIA Study Response, *Conclusions*, June 27, 2013, p. 36.

[545] CIA OIG, *Special Review: Counterterrorism Detention and Interrogation Activities, (September 2001 – October 2003)*, May 7, 2004, p. 52 (DTS 2004-2710).

[546] CIA Study Response, *Conclusions (TAB B)*, June 27, 2013, p. 22 (emphasis in original).

[547] SSCI Study, Findings and Conclusions, April 3, 2014, p. 8 (emphasis added). [[This factual error and misrepresentation of events was corrected in the December 3, 2014, version of the Findings and Conclusions by editing the text to read, "In 2005, CIA Director Goss *requested* in writing that the inspector general not initiate further reviews of the CIA's Detention and Interrogation Program until review already underway were completed." (emphasis added). *Compare* SSCI Study, Findings and Conclusions, April 3, 2014, p. 8 *with* SSCI Study, Findings and Conclusions, December 3, 2014, p. 8.]]

101

Given its mission, CTC unquestionably must be subjected to rigorous independent oversight. This, in fact, has been the case, as evidenced by the 20 or so ongoing, incomplete OIG reviews directed at the Center. I am increasingly concerned about the cumulative impact of the OIG's work on CTC's performance. As I have said in previous correspondence to you, I believe it makes sense to complete existing reviews, particularly resource-intensive investigations such as those now impacting CTC, before opening new ones. As CIA continues to wage battle in the Global War on Terrorism, I *ask* that you reschedule these aspects of the new CTC review until a mutually agreeable time in the future.[548]

(U) The final observation in support of this "impeding" conclusion was that CIA Director Michael Hayden ordered a review of the OIG itself in 2007. The law governing the CIA OIG states, "The Inspector General shall report directly to and be under the general supervision of the Director."[549] Director Hayden's request for this review stemmed from a disagreement between the Office of the General Counsel (OGC) and the OIG over a legal interpretation related to the CIA's Detention and Interrogation Program. Director Hayden tasked Special Counselor Robert Dietz to assess how OGC and OIG interacted on legal issues. He also subsequently tasked Dietz with reviewing complaints of alleged OIG bias and unfair treatment of CIA officers as part of this review. On October 24, 2007, Deitz and his review team made an oral presentation to the Inspector General and his senior staff. They presented a number of recommendations regarding modifications to the OIG's procedures and practices, a number of which were adopted by the Inspector General. Director Hayden subsequently sent a message to the CIA workforce, stating that the Inspector General had "chosen to take a number of steps to heighten the efficiency, assure the quality, and increase the transparency of the investigative process." Director Hayden's message listed the agreed-upon recommendations.[550] Rather than impeding the CIA OIG's oversight, it appears that Director Hayden's order resulted in agreed-upon improvements to that office.

(U) We find that these observations, whether considered individually or in combination, do not support the conclusion that the CIA improperly impeded oversight of the CIA's Detention and Interrogation Program by the CIA OIG.

---

[548] CIA, Memorandum from Porter J. Goss, Director, Central Intelligence Agency to CIA Inspector General, re: *New IG Work Impacting the CounterTerrorism Center*. July 21, 2005 (emphasis added). In this same memorandum, Director Goss did exercise his statutory authority to direct the Inspector General to stand down from talking directly with high-value detainees until he received a compelling explanation. Ibid., p. 1. *See* 50 U.S.C. 403q. A few days later, a compromise was reached that permitted the audit of the CIA black sites with the agreement that no high value detainees would be interviewed by the OIG during the audit. *See* July 28, 2005, 08:54 AM, email from [REDACTED], DCI/OIG/Audit Staff/Operations Division to: [REDACTED] cc: ███████ [REDACTED], [REDACTED], [REDACTED], [REDACTED], Robert Grenier, ███████, [REDACTED], John P. Mudd, [REDACTED], [REDACTED], CIA attorney, CIA attorney, [REDACTED], [REDACTED]Re: Request for TDY Support: CIA OIG, *CIA-controlled Detention Facilities Operated Under the 17 September 2001 Memorandum of Notification*, July 14, 2006, Appendix A, p. 3 (DTS 2006-2793). Director Goss's lawful exercise of his statutory authority cannot be labeled as "impeding" oversight, especially here, where a reasonable accommodation was reached within a matter of days.

[549] 50 U.S.C. 403q.

[550] *See* Letter from DCIA Michael Hayden to Senator John D. Rockefeller, January 29, 2008 (DTS 2012-0606).

(U) Conclusion 10 (The CIA Released Classified Information on EITs to the Media)

(U) Conclusion 10 asserts, "[t]he CIA coordinated the release of classified information to the media, including inaccurate information concerning the effectiveness of the CIA's enhanced interrogation techniques."[551] This conclusion insinuates that there was something improper about the manner in which the CIA managed the process by which information about the Detention and Interrogation Program was disclosed to the media. It also repeats one of its main faulty claims—that the CIA released inaccurate information about the Program's effectiveness. Our examination of the record revealed that the CIA's disclosures were authorized and that the CIA's representations about the Program were largely accurate.

Study Claim: (TS   NF) **"The CIA's Office of Public Affairs and senior CIA officials coordinated to share classified information on the CIA's Detention and Interrogation Program to select members of the media to counter public criticism, shape public opinion, and avoid potential congressional action to restrict the CIA's detention and interrogation authorities and budget. These disclosures occurred when the program was a classified covert action program and before the CIA had briefed the full Committee membership on the program."[552]**

Fact: **(U) The National Security Council Policy Coordinating Committee designated the CIA as "the lead" on the "Public Diplomacy issue regarding detainees."**

(U) The Study seems to confuse the difference between an authorized disclosure of classified information and the unauthorized "leak" of that same information. Despite acknowledging that the "National Security Council Principals Committee discussed a public campaign for the CIA's Detention and Interrogation Program,[553] the Study tries to cast the authorized disclosures as a "media campaign" that must be "done cleverly,"[554] and dwells on CIA officers providing information on the Program to journalists.[555] Specifically, on April 15, 2005, the National Security Council (NSC) Policy Coordinating Committee (PCC) determined that the CIA would have "the lead" on the "Public Diplomacy issue regarding detainees."[556] Once the PCC designated CIA as "the lead" on this matter, the CIA was authorized to make determinations on what information related to this highly classified covert action could be disclosed to the public on a case-by-case basis, without having to return to the White House for subsequent approvals.

(U) The White House did, however, retain its authority with respect to protecting sources and methods in the context of keeping the congressional intelligence fully and currently

---

[551] SSCI Study, Findings and Conclusions, December 3, 2014, p. 8.
[552] SSCI Study, Findings and Conclusions, December 3, 2014, p. 8.
[553] SSCI Study, Executive Summary, December 3, 2014, p. 403.
[554] SSCI Study, Volume II, April 1, 2014, pp. 1521-1522.
[555] SSCI Study, Executive Summary, December 3, 2014, pp. 403-404.
[556] Email from: ; to: CIA attorney; subject: Brokaw interview: Take one; date: April 15, 2005, at 1:00 PM.

informed of this particular covert action. It is within the President's discretion to determine which members of Congress beyond the "gang of eight," are briefed on sensitive covert action programs. There is no requirement for the White House to brief the full Committee as a prerequisite to the declassification or disclosure of information to the media.

(U) The Study acknowledges the White House's guiding influence on opening aspects of the Program to public scrutiny[557] in a section entitled, "NSC Principals Agree to Public Campaign Defending the CIA Detention and Interrogation Program."[558] In a subsequent section, referring to another "media plan," the Study states, "In the fall of 2005, the CIA expanded on its draft public briefing document. One draft, dated November 8, 2005, was specifically intended for National Security Advisor Stephen Hadley, who had requested it."[559] Later, "[t]hroughout the summer of 2006, the CIA assisted the White House in preparing the public roll-out of the program, culminating in President Bush's September 6, 2006 speech describing specific intelligence obtained from CIA detainees."[560] The Study cites no examples of the White House objecting to CIA activities that followed from these discussions.

(U) The Study is correct that, "The CIA's Office of Public Affairs and senior CIA officials coordinated to share classified information on the CIA's Detention and Interrogation Program to select members of the media."[561] That is the function of the Office of Public Affairs (OPA), which is the CIA office primarily responsible for dealing with the routine daily inquiries from the media. The CIA response to the Study indicates that the "vast majority of CIA's engagement with the media on the program was the result of queries from reporters seeking Agency comment on information they had obtained *elsewhere.*[562] The Study made no effort to review established procedures at OPA. The OPA's guidelines and practices include coordinating any information with "senior CIA officials," in order to mitigate or limit the disclosure of classified information. The OPA responds to media requests in a variety of ways that range from "no comment," to, in some cases, working with the media to provide context and improve the accuracy of stories that do not damage the CIA's equities.

(U) The Study cites a few select examples of media inquiries that resulted in stories about the Detention and Interrogation Program. The Study does not make clear, in most cases, who initiated these requests, nor does the Study make clear in what way their selected examples represent the body of media exchanges that OPA had with the media during the period of the Program. Interviews with OPA personnel would have rendered some clarity on these questions.

---

[557] DECISION PAPER: Background for 10 March Principals Committee Meeting on Long-Term Disposition of · Selected High Value Detainees, March 4, 2005. *See also* email from: ███████ to Robert L. Grenier; cc: John P. Mudd, ███████████, [REDACTED], ██████████; subject: DCI Briefing Material/Talking points for upcoming PC; date: 3/01/05 11:33 AM. SSCI Study, Volume II, April 1, 2004, pp. 1508-54.
[558] SSCI Study, Volume II, April 1, 2014, p. 1521.
[559] SSCI Study, Volume II, April 1, 2014, p. 1528.
[560] SSCI Study, Volume II, April 1, 2014, p. 1535.
[561] SSCI Study, Findings and Conclusions, December 3, 2014, p. 8.
[562] CIA Study Response, *Conclusions (TAB B)*, June 27, 2013, p. 39 (emphasis in original).

(U) The Study quotes, inconclusively, emails with various CIA counsels on how to handle the protection of covert action equities against public revelations[563] and chat sessions between officers in CTC who were tasked to prepare and review talking points for an appearance by senior CIA officials on NBC Dateline with Tom Brokaw. Their exchanges include comments on the rhetorical context of the possible media discussion, ("we either get out and sell, or we get hammered . . . we either put out our story or get eaten. there is no middle ground").[564] As noted in the CIA response to the Study, "the informal comments of any one CIA officer do not constitute Agency policy with regard to media interactions."[565] One officer's speculation in a chat session about the risks of the Congress' reaction to unfavorable media coverage does not support the conclusion that the CIA shaped its public affairs strategy as a means to avoid congressional action. Moreover, the CIA refuted the suggestion that this chat session exchange related to the disclosure of classified information by stating that the NBC Dateline broadcast for which the officers were preparing, "contained no public disclosures of classified CIA information; indeed, *the RDI program was not discussed.*"[566]

Study Claim: (TS███████████NF) "Much of the information the CIA provided to the media on the operation of the CIA's Detention and Interrogation Program and the effectiveness of its enhanced interrogation techniques was inaccurate and was similar to the inaccurate information provided by the CIA to the Congress, the Department of Justice, and the White House."[567]

Fact: (TS███████████NF) The CIA's Detention and Interrogation Program, to include the use of enhanced interrogation techniques, was effective and yielded valuable intelligence. The Study's exaggerated and absolute claims about inaccurate "effectiveness" representations by the CIA have been largely discredited by these minority views and the CIA's June 27, 2013, response to the Study.

(TS███████████NF) As previously discussed, our own review of the documentary record in response to the Study's serious allegations against the CIA found that many of these claims of alleged misrepresentations were themselves inaccurate. The Study's flawed analytical methodology cannot suppress the reality that the CIA's Detention and Interrogation Program set up an effective cycle of events whereby al-Qa'ida terrorists were removed from the battlefield, which had a disruptive effect on their current terrorist activities and often permitted the Intelligence Community to collect additional intelligence, which, in turn, often led back to the capture of more terrorists. We found, with a few limited exceptions, that the CIA generally did a good job in explaining the Program's accomplishments to policymakers. We will not repeat the listing of our specific effectiveness findings here.[568]

---

[563] SSCI Study, Executive Summary, December 3, 2014, p. 403-405.

[564] CIA, Sametime communication, between John P. Mudd and ███████████ dated April 13, 2005, from 19:23:50 to 19:56:05.

[565] CIA Study Response, *Conclusions (TAB B)*, June 27, 2013, p. 40.

[566] CIA Study Response, *Conclusions (TAB B)*, June 27, 2013, p. 40 (emphasis in original).

[567] CIA Study Response, *Conclusions (TAB B)*, June 27, 2013, p. 9.

[568] That list may be found in the discussion of Conclusion 5 under the *Effectiveness of the Program* heading, *supra*, pp. 96-97.

(U) CONCLUSION

(U) The Study concludes that the CIA was unprepared to initiate a program of indefinite, clandestine detention using coercive interrogation techniques, something we found obvious, as no element of our government was immediately prepared to deal with the aftermath of what had happened on September 11, 2001. In reviewing the information the CIA provided for the Study, however, we were in awe of what the men and women of the CIA accomplished in their efforts to prevent another attack. The rendition, detention, and interrogation program they created, of which enhanced interrogation was only a small part, enabled a stream of collection and intelligence validation that was unprecedented. The most important capability this program provided had nothing to do with enhanced interrogation—it was the ability to hold and question terrorists, who, if released, would certainly return to the fight, but whose guilt would be difficult to establish in a criminal proceeding without compromising sensitive sources and methods. The CIA called the detention program a "crucial pillar of US counterterrorism efforts, aiding intelligence and law enforcement operations to capture additional terrorists, helping to thwart terrorist plots, and advancing our analysis of the al-Qa'ida target."[569] We agree. We have no doubt that the CIA's detention program saved lives and played a vital role in weakening al-Qa'ida while the Program was in operation. When asked about the value of detainee information and whether he missed the intelligence from it, one senior CIA operator ▮▮▮▮▮ told members, "I miss it every day."[570] We understand why.

---

[569] Detainee Reporting Pivotal for the War Against al-Qa'ida, June 1, 2005, p. i.
[570] ▮▮▮ Chambliss, ▮▮▮▮, conversation between SSCI members and CIA officers, ▮▮▮▮

(U) APPENDIX I: CIA, *Countering Misconceptions About Training Camps in Afghanistan, 1990-2001, August 16, 2006*

16 August 2006

Countering Misconceptions About Training Camps in Afghanistan, 1990-2001 ████

- Arab mujahidin took courses in explosives, electronics, and document falsification in private residences in Kabul where instructors charged fees of between $50 and $100 per month.

- A Moroccan guesthouse in Kabul provided target reconnaissance training primarily to Moroccans.

- One trainee received informal training on the placement, extraction, and camouflage of antitank and antipersonnel mines while on the frontlines in Bagram. ▮▮▮▮▮

The degree of al-Qa'ida involvement in the Afghanistan training scene during the 1990s is often overstated. Al-Qa'ida had only a peripheral role in training during the middle part of the decade when Bin Ladin and most of his group were located in Sudan. From 1993 to 1997, al-Faruq was used to train Tajiks with only a few al-Qa'ida members assisting. Al-Qa'ida reportedly was "in control of al-Faruq" again in 1997.

- Some of the camps have been misidentified as being run by al-Qa'ida, including Khaldan and Abu Khabab al-Masri's poisons-related facilities at Derunta and Kargha.

- Recent reporting suggests that the degree to which al-Qa'ida financed non-al-Qa'ida camps may have been exaggerated. For example, a senior al-Qa'ida leader reportedly said that he did not know of al-Qa'ida providing any money, material, or trainers to non-al-Qa'ida camps. ▮▮▮▮▮

By the late 1990s, al-Qa'ida—with the assistance of the Taliban—sought to gain hegemony over training in Afghanistan, but the group never controlled all the camps.

Khaldan Not Affiliated With Al-Qa'ida ▮▮▮▮

A common misperception in outside articles is that Khaldan camp was run by al-Qa'ida. Pre–11 September 2001 reporting miscast Abu Zubaydah as a "senior al-Qa'ida lieutenant," which led to the inference that the Khaldan camp he was administering was tied to Usama Bin Ladin.

- The group's flagship camp, al-Faruq, reportedly was created in the late 1980s so that Bin Ladin's new organization could have a training infrastructure independent of 'Abdullah Azzam's Maktab al-Khidamat, the nongovernmental organization that supported Khaldan.

- Al-Qa'ida rejected Abu Zubaydah's request in 1993 to join the group and that Khaldan was not overseen by Bin Ladin's organization.

- There were relations between the al-Qa'ida camps and Khaldan. Trainees, particularly Saudis, who had finished basic training at Khaldan were referred to al-Qa'ida camps for advanced courses, and Khaldan staff observed al-Qa'ida training. The two groups, however, did not exchange trainers. ▮▮▮▮▮

- An al-Qa'ida facilitator reportedly said that in 1998 Bin Ladin began to pressure other Arabs to close their facilities because he wanted all the recruits sent to al-Qa'ida.

- Ibn al-Shaykh al-Libi initially foiled attempts to shut down Khaldan, but by April 2000 the camp had closed.

- The Libyan Islamic Fighting Group and Abu Mus'ab al-Suri were able to bribe or convince Taliban officials to allow them to continue operating their camps despite al-Qa'ida's pressure on the Taliban to close them. ▮▮▮▮▮

(U) APPENDIX II: CIA, *Briefing Notes on the Value of Detainee Reporting*, August 2005

Briefing Notes on the Value of Detainee Reporting

August 2005

I'm glad to speak to you today about the results we have seen from high and mid value detainee reporting, which since 9/11 has become a crucial pillar of US counterterrorism efforts. To get a sense for the importance of this reporting to CIA's overall collection effort, let me share some statistics with you:

- **Since we began the program in March 2002, detainees have produced over 6,000 disseminated intelligence reports.**

- **Approximately half of CTC's disseminated intelligence reporting in 2004 on al-Qa'ida came from CIA-held detainees.**

- For both warning and operational purposes, detainee reporting is disseminated broadly among US intelligence and law enforcement entities ███████ **(S//NF)**

For today's briefing, I'm going to highlight five key areas in which detainee reporting has played a critical role: **aiding intelligence and law enforcement operations to capture additional terrorists, helping to thwart terrorist plots, advancing our analysis of the al-Qa'ida target, illuminating other collection, and validating sources. (S//NF)**

Capturing Other Terrorists

Detainees have given us a wealth of useful targeting information on al-Qa'ida members and associates. **Detainees have played some role—from identification of photos to providing initial lead and in depth targeting information—in nearly every capture of al-Qa'ida members and associates since 2002, including ███████████ detentions we assess as "key" because the individuals captured represented a significant threat to the United States or were playing leading roles in assisting al-Qa'ida.**

I have handed you graphics that tell the story of two such cases:

Unraveling Hambali's network. In March 2003, al-Qa'ida operations chief Khalid Shaykh Muhammad (KSM) provided information about an al-Qa'ida operative, Majid Khan, whom he was aware had recently been captured. KSM—possibly believing the detained operative was "talking"—admitted to having tasked Majid with delivering a large sum of money to individuals working for another senior al-Qa'ida associate.

- In an example of how information from one detainee can be used in debriefing another detainee in a "building block" process, Khan—confronted with KSM's information about the money—acknowledged that he delivered the money to an operative named "Zubair" and provided Zubair's physical description and contact number. Based on that information, Zubair was captured in June 2003.

- During debriefings, Zubair revealed that he worked directly for Jemaah Islamiyah (JI) leader and al-Qa'ida's South Asia representative Hambali. Zubair provided information ███████████████████████████████████████ ███████████████████████████████████████ ███████████████████████████████████ and arrest Hambali.

- Next, KSM—when explicitly queried on the issue—identified Hambali's brother, 'Abd al-Hadi, as a prospective successor to Hambali. Information from multiple detainees, including KSM, narrowed down 'Abd al-Hadi's location and enabled his capture ███████████████████████

- Bringing the story full circle, 'Abd al-Hadi identified a cell of JI operatives— some of them pilots—whom Hambali had sent to Karachi for possible al-Qa'ida operations. When confronted with his brother's revelations, Hambali admitted that he was grooming members of the cell for US operations—at the behest of KSM—probably as part of KSM's plot to fly hijacked planes into the tallest building on the US West Coast. (S/███████████NF)

The Arrest of Dhiren Barot (aka Issa al-Hindi). KSM also provided the first lead to an operative known as "Issa al-Hindi," while other detainees gave additional identifying information. KSM also provided the first lead to an operative known as "Issa al-Hindi," while other detainees gave additional identifying information. Issa was well known in jihadi circles because he penned a book about his time fighting in Kashmir under his "al-Hindi" *nom de guerre*; however, no one seemed to know his true name. In March 2004, our hunt for Issa intensified when we receive reporting about a possible attack against the US Homeland.

██ ██████████████████ KSM positively identifies the photo as Issa al-Hindi, and we are able to identified through a new search mechanism a separate individual who had traveled to the United States with Issa prior to 9/11.

- Issa and his former traveling companion —who were arrested in 2004—appear to have been involved in plots in the UK. Moreover, in early 2004, Issa had briefed US targeting packages to al-Qa'ida senior leadership in Pakistan. Issa was well known in jihadi circles because he penned a book about his time fighting in Kashmir under his "al-Hindi" *nom de guerre*; it was only through police work coupled with detainee confirmation on his identity, that ████████████ were able to find him. (S/███NF██

2

In addition to these two prominent cases, a number of other significant captures have resulted thanks to detainee reporting. It is important to highlight that a number of these cases involve law enforcement's use of our detainee reporting:

- **_Arrest of key al-Qa`ida facilitator_** ███████████████ In debriefings, KSM in March 2003 noted that he had created and used a specified e-mail account to communicate with senior ████████████████████ CIA then determined that KSM had been using this account actively in ongoing operational planning for an ████threat, which KSM confirmed. Analysis of ████████ e-mails after KSM's detention led to his being located and arrested on ████████ 2003.

- **_Identifying the "other" shoe bomber._** Leads provided by KSM in November 2003 led directly to the arrest of shoe bomber Richard Reid's one-time partner Sajid Badat in the UK. KSM had volunteered the existence of Badat—whom he knew as "Issa al-Pakistani"—as the operative who was slated to launch a simultaneous shoe bomb attack with Richard Reid in December 2001.

- **_Jose Padilla._** After his capture in March 2002, Abu Zubaydah provided information leading to the identification of alleged al-Qa'ida operative Jose Padilla. Arrested by the FBI in 2002 as he arrived at O'Hare Airport in Chicago, he was transferred to military custody in Charleston, South Carolina, where he is currently being held. The FBI began participating in the military debriefings in March 2003, after KSM reported Padilla might know the true name of a US-bound al-Qa'ida operative known at the time only as Jafar al-Tayyar. Padilla confirmed Jafar's true name as Adnan El Shukrijumah.

- **_Iyman Faris._** Soon after his arrest, KSM described an Ohio-based truck driver whom the FBI identified as Iyman Faris, already under suspicion for his contacts with al-Qa'ida operative Majid Khan. FBI and CIA shared intelligence from interviews of KSM, Khan, and Faris on a near real-time basis and quickly ascertained that Faris had met and accepted operational taskings from KSM on several occasions. Faris is currently serving a 20-year sentence for conspiracy and material support to a terrorist organization. (TS/████████████/NF████—

Bringing new targets to light. A variety of detainee reporting has provided our initial information about individuals having links to al-Qa'ida and has given us insight into individuals about whom we had reporting but whose al-Qa'ida involvement was unclear. For example, detainees in mid-2003 helped us build a list of ████████████████individuals—many of whom we had never heard of before—that al-Qa'ida deemed suitable for Western operations. We have shared this list broadly within the US intelligence and law enforcement communities, ████████████████████████

3

- **Jafar al-Tayyar first came to FBI's attention when Abu Zubaydah named him as one of the most likely individuals to be used by al-Qa'ida for operations in the United States or Europe.** Jafar was further described by detainees, whose description of Jafar's family in the United States was key to uncovering Jafar's true name. An FBI investigation identified Gulshair El Shukrijumah, leader of a mosque in Hollywood, Florida, as having a son named Adnan who matched the biographical and physical descriptions given by the detainees. A "Be On The Lookout" notice has been issued for Adnan El Shukrijumah.

- **Most recently, for example, Abu Faraj al-Libi has revealed that an operative we were only vaguely aware of was actually sent to ▮▮▮▮ in 2004 to lay the groundwork for al-Qa'ida attacks there:** ▮▮▮▮▮▮▮▮▮▮▮
  ▮▮▮▮▮▮▮▮ (S/ ▮▮▮▮ NF)

Revealing Plots, Potential Targets (S//NF)

One of the fall-outs of detaining these additional terrorists has been the unearthing and at least temporary thwarting of a number of al-Qa'ida operations in the United States and overseas.

Possible Nuclear Threat to the United States. In some of the most groundbreaking information on al-Qa'ida collected in 2004, detainee Sharif al-Masri provided at least 11 intelligence reports on nuclear and biological issues related to al-Qa'ida and may have revealed a new nuclear threat to the US Homeland associated with al-Qa'ida's key explosives expert Abu 'Abd al-Rahman al-Muhajir.

- Sharif's debriefings indicated that he was aware of recent and possibly ongoing efforts to move an unspecified nuclear "bomb" into the United States, possibly via Mexico, through his discussion in February 2004 with Muhajir. This reporting confirmed and fleshed out ▮▮▮▮▮▮▮▮ reporting from 2004 about a plan to move people into the US through Mexico. The nuclear aspects to the threat, however, were new and confirmed al-Qa'ida's continuing interest in WMD. (TS ▮▮▮▮ NF)

Heathrow Airport plot. Shortly after his capture in March 2003, KSM divulged limited information about his plot to use commercial airliners to attack Heathrow Airport and other targets in the United Kingdom; he discussed this plot probably because he believed that key Heathrow plotter Ramzi bin al-Shibh, who had been detained six months previously, had already revealed the information.

4

- Debriefers used KSM's and Bin al-Shibh's reporting to confront Khallad and Ammar al-Baluchi, who were caught two months after KSM. Khallad admitted to having been involved in the plot and revealed that he directed group leader Hazim al-Sha'ir to begin locating pilots who could hijack planes and crash them into the airport. Khallad said he and operative Abu Talha al-Pakistani considered ▮▮▮▮▮ countries as possible launch sites for the hijacking attempts and that they narrowed the options to ▮▮▮▮▮▮▮▮▮▮▮ ▮▮▮▮▮▮▮▮▮▮

- Khallad's statements provided leverage in debriefings of KSM. KSM fleshed out the status of the operation, including identifying an additional target in the United Kingdom, Canary Wharf. (S//NF)

Revealing the Karachi plots. When confronted with information provided by al-Qa'ida senior facilitator Ammar al-Baluchi, Khallad admitted during debriefings that al-Qa'ida was planning to attack the US Consulate in Karachi, Westerners at the Karachi Airport, and Western housing areas. (S//NF)

Aiding Our Understanding Of Al-Qa'ida (S//NF)

The capture and debriefing of detainees has transformed our understanding of al-Qa'ida and affiliated terrorist groups, providing increased avenues for sophisticated analysis. Prior to the capture of Abu Zubaydah in March 2002, we had large gaps in knowledge of al-Qa'ida's organizational structure, key members and associates, intentions and capabilities, possible targets for the next attack, and its presence around the globe.

- **Within months of his arrest, Abu Zubaydah provided details about al-Qa'ida's organizational structure, key operatives, and modus operandi. It also was Abu Zubaydah, early in his detention, who identified KSM as the mastermind of 9/11.** (S/▮▮▮/NF)

In the years since 9/11, successive detainees have helped us gauge our progress in the fight against al-Qa'ida by providing updated information on the changing structure and health of the organization.

Hassan Ghul. After his early 2004 capture, Hassan Ghul provided considerable intelligence on al-Qa'ida's senior operatives in Waziristan and elsewhere in the tribal regions of Pakistan. **We had fragmentary information ▮▮▮▮▮▮▮▮ ▮▮▮▮▮▮▮▮▮▮▮▮▮▮▮▮▮▮▮▮dentifying the Shkai valley as a safehaven for al-Qa'ida and associated mujahidin before Ghul's capture; however, Ghul's reporting brought instant credibility to all this disparate reporting and added minute details to what had previously been a murky, nascent picture.** Ghul helped us assess that this valley, as of December 2003, was not just one haven for al-Qa'ida in Waziristan, but the home base for al-Qa'ida in the area and one that al-Qa'ida was reluctant to abandon.

- ██████████████, Ghul—a key al-Qa'ida facilitator—pointed out the location in the Shkai valley, Waziristan, Pakistan of safehouses of specific al-Qa'ida senior leaders. ███ ██████████████████████████ Although we had a body of reporting from clandestine and other sources indicating that senior al-Qa'ida targets were congregating in the Shkai valley in 2004, Ghul's confirmation and critical narrative helped counterterrorism officers ████████████████████████████████ ███████████████████████████

- Ghul also provided our first knowledge of Pakistani operatives trained██ ██ Ghul then supplied detailed insight into the nature of their training, the al-Qa'ida operatives involved in their grooming, and the location of ██ facilities in Shkai where the operatives trained. ████ learned later through debriefings of Abu Talha al-Pakistani—who helped recruit the Pakistanis—that one of the operatives, ████████████ was attempting to apply for a US student visa██ ████ (S████████NF)

Sharif al-Masri. Sharif al-Masri also provided invaluable insights in over 150 disseminated reports that have aided our analysis of al-Qa'ida's current organization, the personalities of its key members, and al-Qa'ida's decisionmaking process. (TS//████████████NF)

Various operatives discuss capabilities, including CBRN. Detained al-Qa'ida technical experts—some of whom had very focused roles in the organization—have provided unique insight into the origins of the group's efforts to develop weapons and the technical limitations of key al-Qa'ida personnel—in particular, detainees have helped to clarify al-Qa'ida's CBRN program.

- Abu Zubaydah and senior al-Qa'ida military trainer Ibn al-Shaykh identified ████████████—who had been associated with poison training—as the individual who conducted experiments with mustard on rabbits and dogs.

- KSM's reporting advanced our understanding of al-Qa'ida's interest in developing a nuclear weapons program, and also revealed important information about al-Qa'ida's program to produce anthrax. He apparently calculated incorrectly that we had this information already, given that one of the three—Yazid Sufaat—had been in foreign custody ████████████ ████████████

- After being confronted with KSM's reporting, Yazid eventually admitted his principal role in the anthrax program and provided fragmentary information on ███ (S/ NF)

Illuminating Other Collection (S//NF)

Detainee reporting has allowed us to confirm reporting from clandestine and other sources, and makes sense of fragmentary information. ███████

- As noted earlier, Abu Faraj—along with other detainees—has begun to flesh out threat reporting received ████████████████ during 2004, including tasking to send operatives to the US via Mexico and hopes to mount an attack prior to the 2004 US Presidential elections. While we are still in the early stages of exploiting the full extent of Abu Faraj's knowledge on Homeland threats, information he and others have provided has confirmed that efforts were underway to mount an attack in the US Homeland beginning in late 2003.

- Hassan Ghul's disc containing a message from Zarqawi for Bin Ladin about Zarqawi's plan in Iraq coupled with Ghul's own reporting brought the burgeoning relationship between Zarqawi and al-Qa'ida into clear focus for the first time since the US entry into Iraq. (S ███████ NF)

7

Detainees have been particularly useful in sorting out the large volumes of documents and computer data seized in raids. Such information potentially can be used in legal proceedings, as physical evidence, ██████████ ████████████████████████████████ It also can be used in confronting detainees to get them to talk about topics they would otherwise not reveal.

- For example, lists of names found on Mustafa al-Hawsawi's computer seized in March 2003 represented al-Qa'ida members who were to receive money. Debriefers questioned detainees extensively on these names to determine who they were and how important they were to the organization. This information helped us to better understand al-Qa'ida's revenues and expenditures, particularly in Pakistan, and money that was available to families.

- The same computer had a list of e-mail addresses for individuals KSM helped deploy abroad that he hoped would execute operations; most of these names were unknown to us, and we used this information in debriefings of KSM and other detainees to unravel KSM's plots. (S/██████████NF)

Helping To Validate Other Sources (S//NF)

Detainee information is a key tool for validating clandestine sources who may have reported false information. In one case, the detainee's information proved to be the accurate story, and the clandestine source was confronted and subsequently admitted to embellishing or fabricating some or all the details in his report.

- Pakistan-based facilitator Janat Gul's most significant reporting helped us validate a CIA asset who was providing information about the 2004 pre-election threat. The asset claimed that Gul had arranged a meeting between himself and al-Qa'ida's chief of finance, Shaykh Sa'id, a claim that Gul vehemently denied.

- Gul's reporting was later matched with information obtained from Sharif al-Masri and Abu Talha, captured after Gul. With this reporting in hand, CIA ██████████ the asset, who subsequently admitted to fabricating his reporting about the meeting. (S/██████████NF)

In other instances, detainee information has been useful in identifying clandestine assets who are providing good reporting. For example, Hassan Ghul's reporting on Shkai helped us validate several assets ██████████ who also told us that al-Qa'ida members had found safehaven at this location.

8

- Sometimes one detainee validates reporting from others. Sharif corroborated information from ████████████who were involved in facilitating the movement of al-Qa'ida personnel, money, and messages into and out of ████ For example, ████████████ indicated that ██████████████████████████ ████████████████-was the link between al-Qa'ida and ██████████ and Sharif corroborated that fact when he noted that████████ was the "go-between" for al-Qa'ida and ████████ (S/██████████NF)

Challenges of Detainee Reporting (S//NF)

I don't want to leave you with the impression that we do not assess detainee reporting with the same critical eye that we would other sources of intelligence. Detainees' information must be corroborated using multiple sources of intelligence; uncorroborated information from detainees must be regarded with some degree of suspicion. A detainee is more likely to budge if the debriefer, using information from another source, can demonstrate that the detainee possesses knowledge of the particular subject.

- This tendency to reveal information when cornered with facts is one of the reasons we view unilateral custody as so critical. Not only are we certain of the exact questions being asked and answers being given, ████████████ ██ ██ ██████████████████████(S/██████████NF)

9

(U) APPENDIX III: Email from: ███████████ ; to: ███████████
███████ [REDACTED]. ███████████████████ subject: could AQ be
testing [the source] and ████████ date: March ███ 2004, at 06:55 AM; Email from:
███████████ to ███████ cc: ███████
[REDACTED]. ███████████ subject: Re: could AQ be testing [the source] and
███████ ; date: March ███ 2004, at 7:52:32 AM

1

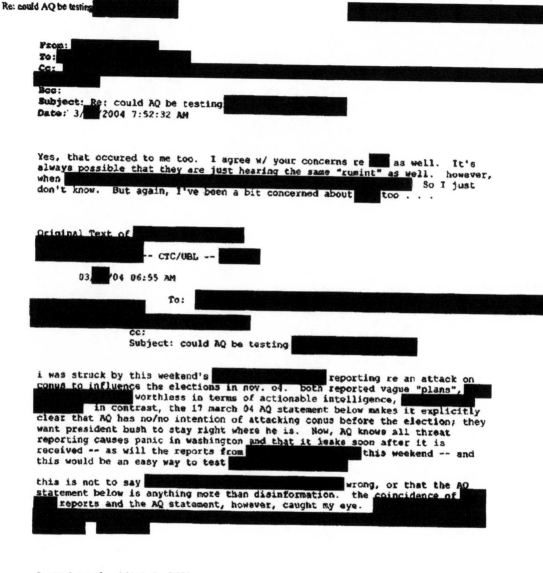

Re: could AQ be testing ▮▮▮▮▮▮▮▮▮▮   ▮▮▮▮▮▮▮▮▮▮▮▮▮▮

From: ▮▮▮▮▮▮▮▮▮▮▮▮▮▮▮▮▮▮▮▮▮▮▮▮▮▮▮▮▮▮▮▮▮▮
To: ▮▮▮▮▮▮▮▮▮▮▮▮▮▮▮▮▮▮▮▮▮▮▮▮▮▮▮▮▮▮▮▮
Cc: ▮▮▮▮▮▮▮▮▮▮▮▮▮▮▮▮▮▮▮▮▮▮▮▮▮▮▮▮▮▮▮▮▮▮
Bcc:
Subject: Re: could AQ be testing ▮▮▮▮▮▮▮▮▮▮▮▮
Date: 3/▮▮/2004 7:52:32 AM

Yes, that occured to me too. I agree w/ your concerns re ▮▮▮ as well. It's
always possible that they are just hearing the same "rumint" as well. however,
when ▮▮   So I just
don't know. But again, I've been a bit concerned about ▮▮▮ too . . .

Original Text of ▮▮▮▮▮▮▮▮▮▮▮▮▮▮▮▮▮▮

                    -- CTC/UBL -- ▮▮▮▮▮▮▮▮▮

    03.▮▮/04 06:55 AM

                To: ▮▮▮▮▮▮▮▮▮▮▮▮▮▮▮▮▮▮▮▮▮▮▮▮▮▮▮▮▮▮▮▮▮▮▮▮▮▮

                Cc: ▮▮▮▮▮▮
                Subject: could AQ be testing ▮▮▮▮▮▮▮▮▮▮▮▮

i was struck by this weekend's ▮▮▮▮▮▮▮▮▮▮▮▮▮▮▮▮ reporting re an attack on
conus to influence the elections in nov. 04. both reported vague "plans",
▮▮▮▮▮▮▮▮▮▮ worthless in terms of actionable intelligence, ▮▮▮▮▮▮▮▮
▮▮▮▮▮▮▮▮ in contrast, the 17 march 04 AQ statement below makes it explicitly
clear that AQ has no/no intention of attacking conus before the election; they
want president bush to stay right where he is. Now, AQ knows all threat
reporting causes panic in washington and that it leaks soon after it is
received -- as will the reports from ▮▮▮▮▮▮▮▮▮▮▮ this weekend -- and
this would be an easy way to test ▮▮▮▮▮▮▮▮▮▮

this is not to say ▮▮▮▮▮▮▮▮▮▮▮▮▮▮▮▮▮▮▮▮▮▮▮ wrong, or that the AQ
statement below is anything more than disinformation. the coincidence of ▮▮▮
▮ reports and the AQ statement, however, caught my eye.
▮▮

A word to the idiot Bush[0]

    We know you live the worst days of your life in fear of the brigades of
death that ruined
your life.   We tell you we are all keen that you do not lose the forthcoming
elections.
We are aware that any large-scale operation will destroy your government but we
do not
want this to happen.   We will not find a person dumber[0] than you.   You
adopt force
rather than wisdom and shrewdness.   Yes, your stupidity and religious
fanaticism is what
we want because our nation will not wake up from its sleep unless an enemy
emerges
that lies in wait for the nation.   Actually, there is no difference between

ould AQ be testing

you and
[Democratic presidential candidate John] Kerry.   Kerry will take our nation unawares and
kill it.   Kerry and the Democrats possess enough deception to give a face-lift to atheism
and convince the Arab and Islamic nation to support it in the name of modernization.
Therefore, we are very keen that you, criminal Bush(0), will win the upcoming elections.

(U) APPENDIX IV: CIA, Office of General Counsel draft *Legal Appendix: Paragraph 5—* *Hostile Interrogations: Legal Considerations for CIA Officers*, November 26, 2002

D – R – A – F – T
26 November 2001 @ 1600

I.   U.S. federal law makes it a crime for a U.S. citizen to torture someone both at home and abroad, even when directed to do so by superiors.

A.   18 U.S.C. §§ 2340 - 2340B implements the United Nations Convention Against Torture and Other Cruel, Inhumane, or Degrading Treatment or Punishment, and incorporates verbatim the definition of "torture" from that treaty; namely, the Convention defines torture as "an act committed by a person acting under color of law specifically intended to inflict severe physical or mental pain or suffering," where "severe mental suffering" is further defined as "the prolonged mental harm resulting from" either causing or threatening infliction of severe physical pain; the administration or threat of administration of mind-altering drugs; the threat of imminent death; or threatening to do the above to someone else.

B.   Use of necessity as a defense to prosecution in a U.S. court.

1.   Israel's Supreme Court has recognized that government officials who are prosecuted for torture may use the affirmative defense of necessity—i.e., "for the purpose of saving the life, liberty, body or property, of either himself or his fellow person, from substantial danger of serious harm, imminent from the particular state of things (circumstances), at the requisite timing, and absent alternative means for avoiding the harm."[3] That is, a government officer can avoid criminal prosecution if the torture was necessary to prevent a danger "certain to materialize" and when no other means of preventing the harm are available.

2.   The ruling, however, specifically notes that although necessity can be used as a *post factum* defense, it cannot serve as a source of positive, *ab initio* authority for the systemic (even if rare) use of torture as a valid interrogation tool.

3.   The U.S. Code does not contain a statutory necessity defense provision, but U.S. common law has recognized an analogous doctrine:

   • State v. Marley, 509 P.2d 1095, 1097(1973): Defendants were charged with criminal trespass on the property of Honeywell Corporation in Honolulu. They argued that they were seeking to stop the Vietnam War and raised as one of their defenses the "necessity defense." The court stated:

      The "necessity defense" exonerates persons who commit a crime under the pressure of circumstances if the harm that would have

---

[3] H.C. 5100/94, 4054/95, 6536/95, 5188/96, 7563/97, 7628/97, 1043/99.

5

resulted from compliance with the law would have significantly exceeded the harm actually resulting from the defendant's breach of the law. Successful use of the "necessity defense" requires (a) that there is no third and legal alternative available, (b) that the harm to be prevented be imminent, and (c) that a direct, causal relationship be reasonable anticipated to exist between defendant's action and the avoidance of harm.

Although the Marley court decided the necessity defense was not available to these particular defendants, the standard they set out is the norm.

- In United States v. Seward, 687 F.2d 1270, 1275 (10th Cir. 1982) (en banc), cert. denied, 459 U.S. 1147 (1983), the court held that a defendant may successfully use a defense of necessity to excuse otherwise illegal acts if (1) there is no legal alternative to violating the law, (2) the harm to be prevented is imminent, and (3) a direct, causal relationship is reasonable anticipated to exist between defendant's action and the avoidance of harm. Under the defense of necessity, "one principle remains constant: if there was a reasonable, legal alternative to violating the law, 'a chance both to refuse to do the criminal act and also to avoid the threatened harm,' the defense[] will fail," Id. at 1276, quoting United States v. Bailey, 444 U.S. 394 (1980). In proving that there were no legal alternatives available to assist him, a defendant must show he was "confronted with ... a crisis which did not permit a selection from among several solutions, some of which did not involve criminal acts." Id.

- See also United States v. Contento-Pachon, 723 F.2d 691, 695 n.2 (9th Cir. 1984) (defense of necessity available when person faced with a choice of two evils and must decide whether to commit a crime or an alternative act that constitutes a greater evil); United States v. Nolan, 700 F.2d 479, 484 (9th Cir.) (the necessity defense requires a showing that the defendant acted to prevent an imminent harm which no available options could similarly prevent).

- In sum: U.S. courts have not yet considered the necessity defense in the context of torture/murder/assault cases, primarily because in cases where one or two individuals were hurt out of necessity, this was treated as a self-defense analysis. See Tab 2, supra. It would, therefore, be a novel application of the necessity defense to avoid prosecution of U.S. officials who tortured to obtain information that saved many lives; however, if we follow the Israeli example, CIA could argue that the torture was necessary to prevent imminent, significant, physical harm to persons, where there is no other available means to prevent the harm.

6

Minority Views by Senator Coburn,
Vice Chairman Saxby Chambliss, Senators Burr, Risch, Coats and Rubio

(U) As parts of the Senate Select Committee on Intelligence (SSCI) "Committee Study of the Interrogation and Detention Program" (hereafter, the "Study") become declassified, it is our hope that, in addition to these and the other Minority views, the Central Intelligence Agency (CIA) response of June, 2013 also be declassified. Interested and objective readers will be able to balance these various views as they make their own assessments of the flaws, errors, initiatives and value of the CIA's detention and interrogation program conducted and terminated in the previous decade.

(S//NF) For those who hold already set views, they may or may not be surprised that the CIA agreed with a number of the Study's findings, at least in part, although the CIA disagreed, in substance, with the core assertions of the Study: that the interrogation program provided little valuable intelligence and that the CIA misrepresented the program to the White House, other executive agencies, the Congress and the public (through the media).

(U) As stated in the Minority views and the CIA response, so only briefly reiterated here, the methodology for the Study was inherently flawed. A SSCI investigation of this depth and importance requires that, in addition to a document review, interviews with participants and managers be conducted. This standard approach was included in the terms of reference that established the Study in March, 2009. For a recent and relevant example, the SSCI's investigation into the intelligence failures regarding weapons of mass destruction in Iraq, "U.S. Intelligence Community's Prewar Intelligence Assessments on Iraq," (July, 2004), was based on Committee interviews with more than 200 intelligence community (IC) officers, including analysts and senior officials, in addition to a review of tens of thousands of documents. Some of those individuals were interviewed up to 4 times, as Committee staff worked to reconcile the complex documentary record with the perspectives of those involved in the analytic production. (That report, when published, was supported unanimously by the Committee, 15-0. This is significant in that properly performed reviews tend to gain bipartisan approval.)

(COMMITTEE SENSITIVE) In addition, no Committee hearings were conducted with members of the IC once the Study was initiated in 2009 until it was first voted out of Committee in 2012. In sum, a massive (but still incomplete) outlay of documents was reviewed in isolation (outside of Committee spaces), without the benefit of interpretation or perspective provided by the actual participants in the program.

(**COMMITTEE SENSITIVE**) Perhaps if such interviews had occurred, the authors of the Study would have had better exposure to the analytic processes that underpin a global collection program that sought, in response to the attacks of 9/11, to assemble an analytic picture of a poorly understood global terrorism network, al-Qa'ida. Thousands of analysts worked with the reports that were derived from the interrogations (most of which were conducted without the use of enhanced interrogation procedures) and thousands of analytic products were generated to build an understanding of the terror organization that attacked us on September 11, 2001. To read the Committee Study, the reader could conclude that majority of those analysts did not properly understand their profession and their products were flawed. That conclusion would be false.

(U) A fundamental fact is missing from the point of departure for the Study: For any nation to respond to an attack by an insurgency, terrorist organization or armed group, the primary source of human intelligence will be detainee reporting. The CIA's program, improvised in its early stages because the CIA had no established protocols to draw on, sought to build the capacity to gather this intelligence by creating a global information network where the intelligence gained from interrogations around the world could be assessed, corroborated and challenged by analysts working in real-time to better develop an intelligence picture of a very real threat whose dimensions and direction were unknown to us.

(U) How detainee reporting is collected – through what protocols of interrogation -- is the challenge that every nation, and, in particular, nations bound by the rule of law, must answer. This fundamental question is not addressed in the Study.

(U) Instead, the most adamant supporters of the Study have declared that the effect of this Study will be that the abuses they assess occurred will never happen again. This is an odd conclusion, in that the CIA's interrogation program was ended in the last decade, and President Obama's Executive Orders put in place measures and procedures that clearly indicate the program would not be reconstituted. If the point of the Study was to end something the supporters of the Study wanted to terminate, the objective was achieved before the Study began.

(U) But if the point of the Study is to ensure that abuses assessed by the supporters of the Study never occur again, the Study made no contribution to ensuring this because it failed to offer recommendations for lawful interrogation protocols for the collection of detainee intelligence in the future. Even more striking than the fact that the Study was completed without conducting interviews is the complete absence of any recommendations, recommendations that could provide meaningful guideposts for the future.

(U) There is a cycle that can be observed in democracies fighting armed groups and relying upon detainee intelligence gained from interrogation. It is a cycle that has occurred in democracies throughout the last century and, in fact, throughout American history.[1] An episode of national security crisis is responded to with urgency and frenzy, and the detention cycle begins. The early stage of the cycle is usually when the instances of brutality may occur. Over time, interrogation protocols are reconciled with the rule of law (and practicality, as brutality does not guarantee good intelligence). A consideration of American, British and Israeli history – to cite three examples of democratic societies – provides examples of this cycle in each country.

(S//NF) That this cycle can repeat reflects an apparent weakness in democracies, including our own, in their inability to process and retain "lessons learned." We have certainly seen this elsewhere in the national security sphere – how our various national security institutions have "forgotten," for example, counterinsurgency theory, public diplomacy, and covert influence practices.

(U) This Study has many flaws, articulated in the other Minority views and the CIA response. To that we would add is the failure to extract "lessons learned," in the form of recommendations that provide insights into which interrogation techniques work in gathering foreign intelligence and are consistent with rule-of-law principles. This knowledge, were it to be captured and held in doctrine, would provide the tools for this nation as it continues to face threats from terrorist organization or other armed group overseas. Only in this way could the intent of "never again" be in fact ensured.

(U) The Study provided no such recommendations for the future. Instead it is a partisan prosecutor's brief against history. It is a 6,000 page exercise in the rhetorical trope of synecdoche, where a part -- in this case, the most egregious abuses, such as waterboarding – is substituted for the whole – in this case, the entire CIA detention and interrogation program, most of which did not rely on

---

[1]. Dr. Coburn is grateful to have had access to *United States Detention Policy in Counterterrorism and Counterinsurgency Operations: 2001 to 2011*, particularly chapter 1, "Detention in US History from 1775 to 2000," Dr. Ahmed Qureshi, unpublished thesis submitted for the Degree of Philosophy (PhD), Kings College, University of London, 2013.

enhanced interrogation techniques and most of which provided the intelligence picture of al-Qai'da in the first decade of the 21st century. We caution any reader of the Study against ever concluding that the threats of today and tomorrow can be addressed without the value of detainee intelligence that provided this picture of al-Qa'ida that allows us to prevail against it in the second decade of the 21st century.

MINORITY VIEWS OF SENATORS RISCH, COATS, AND RUBIO

(U) As the only two members of both the Senate Foreign Relations Committee and the Senate Select Committee on Intelligence (SSCI), and as a former U.S. Ambassador to Germany, we maintain a unique perspective on declassification of the Study as it pertains to U.S. foreign policy and the security of U.S. embassies and consulates overseas. That perspective was further informed by the Department of State's intelligence chief, who warned the SSCI in 2013 that declassification could endanger U.S. personnel and jeopardize U.S. relations with other countries. This warning was particularly significant following the Benghazi terrorist attacks, which serve as a fresh reminder of the enormous risk facing U.S. embassies and consulates overseas. As a result, we voted against declassification of the Study.

U.S. Foreign Policy Considerations

(TS/███████████████/NF) On June 10, 2013, the SSCI received a classified letter from Assistant Secretary of State Philip Goldberg regarding the potential declassification of the Study. The letter raised two "significant State Department equities" pertaining to foreign policy concerns and the security of diplomatic facilities. With respect to foreign policy concerns, the letter states:

> If the report is declassified or disclosed without appropriate preparation or precautions, it could negatively impact foreign relations with multiple U.S. allies and partners who have participated in or have had nationals involved in the detention and interrogation program. Even with some country names redacted, context and publicly available information make it possible to identify some specific countries and facilities. Many of these countries cooperated with the United States on this program based on the understanding that their involvement would not be publicly disclosed. Publicly acknowledging their roles at this stage would have significant implications for our bilateral relationships and future cooperation on a variety of national security priorities, and could impact our relationships with countries even beyond those involved in the program. Should the report be declassified or released in any form, the Department would request notice well in advance to allow for coordination with our embassies and foreign counterparts. ██

These concerns were not limited to the U.S. Department of State. Multiple diplomatic envoys posted in Washington raised similar concerns with us individually.

Diplomatic Security

(TS/███████████████/NF) With respect to the security of diplomatic facilities, the letter states: "With heightened threats and ongoing instability in the Middle East, North Africa, and elsewhere, the release of this report has the potential to provoke additional demonstrations against U.S. interests and to increase targeting of U.S. missions and U.S. citizens around the globe." In the days leading up to the SSCI vote to declassify the Study, the Minority also contacted the White House to obtain their views on this issue. The Minority learned that at the time of the vote to declassify the Study, the Executive Branch was already developing security upgrades at various diplomatic facilities to coincide with the expected release of the Study. This fact was confirmed in a letter the SSCI received on April 18, 2014, from White House Counsel Kathryn Ruemmler. This letter stated: "Prior to the release of any information related to the former RDI program, the Administration will also need to take a series of security steps to prepare our personnel and facilities overseas."

Conclusion

(U) While we generally support efforts to provide the American public with as much information as possible, our experiences and the stark warnings provided by the Department of State, the White House, and foreign diplomats serving in Washington made a compelling case to keep this material classified. We hope and pray the declassification process does not jeopardize the safety and security of the men and women who serve our country overseas or U.S. foreign policy. Ultimately, we could not take the risk to vote to declassify the Study, especially given our shared concerns for the utility of the underlying process and report.

The Naval Institute Press is the book-publishing arm of the U.S. Naval Institute, a private, nonprofit, membership society for sea service professionals and others who share an interest in naval and maritime affairs. Established in 1873 at the U.S. Naval Academy in Annapolis, Maryland, where its offices remain today, the Naval Institute has members worldwide.

Members of the Naval Institute support the education programs of the society and receive the influential monthly magazine *Proceedings* or the colorful bimonthly magazine *Naval History* and discounts on fine nautical prints and on ship and aircraft photos. They also have access to the transcripts of the Institute's Oral History Program and get discounted admission to any of the Institute-sponsored seminars offered around the country.

The Naval Institute's book-publishing program, begun in 1898 with basic guides to naval practices, has broadened its scope to include books of more general interest. Now the Naval Institute Press publishes about seventy titles each year, ranging from how-to books on boating and navigation to battle histories, biographies, ship and aircraft guides, and novels. Institute members receive significant discounts on the Press's more than eight hundred books in print.

Full-time students are eligible for special half-price membership rates. Life memberships are also available.

For a free catalog describing Naval Institute Press books currently available, and for further information about joining the U.S. Naval Institute, please write to:

Member Services
U.S. NAVAL INSTITUTE
291 Wood Road
Annapolis, MD 21402-5034
Telephone: (800) 233-8764
Fax: (410) 571-1703
Web address: www.usni.org